# JENNIE GERHARDT

# JENNIE GERHARDT

## A NOVEL

BY

THEODORE DREISER

Introduction by
Helen Yglesias

SCHOCKEN BOOKS • NEW YORK

First published by Schocken Books 1982
10 9 8 7 6 5 4 3 2 1      82 83 84 85
Copyright © 1911 by Harper & Brothers
Copyright © 1938 by Theodore Dreiser
Introduction copyright © 1982 by Helen Yglesias
Published by arrangement with The Dreiser Trust

Library of Congress Cataloging in Publication Data
Dreiser, Theodore, 1871–1945.
Jennie Gerhardt.
Reprint. Originally published: New York:
Harper & Bros., 1911.
I. Title.
PS3507.R55J4   1982      813'.52      81–84117      AACR2

Manufactured in the United States of America
ISBN 0-8052-0692-2

# INTRODUCTION
## Helen Yglesias

S O MUCH drama surrounded the publication of *Sister Carrie*, Theodore Dreiser's first novel, that the intrinsic value of his second, *Jennie Gerhardt*, has been unjustifiably diminished in the light of the inevitable comparisons made between the two books. Like all of Dreiser's work, *Jennie Gerhardt* bears the clumsy weight of his stylistic faults and the heavy hand of his philosophy, while the special quality of his genius prevails to produce an original, moving, and lasting masterpiece that stands entirely on its own. Why then in an introduction to *Jennie*, an immediate reference to *Carrie?* Because our present feminist sensibilities create a need to so arrange these sisterly books in our minds that they reflect new views of one another.

Dreiser completed *Sister Carrie* at the beginning of the twentieth century. The book was submitted to Frank Norris at Doubleday who recommended publication. Two additional Doubleday editors agreed but their decision was vetoed by the publisher because of the book's "immorality." Though there was no formal contract, only letters of agreement, Dreiser insisted on holding Doubleday to its written promises. As a result only one thousand copies of *Sister Carrie* were printed; there was no fanfare; reviews were generally negative; and about five hundred copies in all sold—for the author a bitter (if not unusual in those days or these) publishing history for his first novel—which happened to be one of the lasting novels of our time.

The legend had it that the killing of the book went far beyond the account I have given. Doubleday was said to have buried the entire printing of *Sister Carrie* in the cellar of the publishing house. And among other reports, it was widely believed that the prime instigator of all the blind literary damage directed at *Carrie* was not Frank Doubleday himself, but his wife, who found the story distasteful to her ladylike delicacy of feeling. It is clearer now from carefully documented research into the event that the embellishments provided by Dreiser and his supporters are difficult to prove. (The facts, of course, are quite bad enough without embellishment.) Yet if Mrs. Doubleday's outraged sensibilities were not at play, her role clearly needed to be invented. *Sister Carrie* was a brilliant assault on the genteel tradition in American writing, American culture, and American society. In the controversy it created, the good guys were the bold, male writers who were telling the truth; the bad guys were the hypocritical, feminine, false moralists of the drawing room—ladies wielding their power from behind the backs of their weakened men. In the plot against *Sister Carrie,* Mrs. Doubleday was cast as the villainous embodiment of the genteel or feminine influence in our culture.

From our present vantage point, what interests us in all this is the male ambiguity at the heart of the matter. Witches, saints, bad girls, good girls, whores, or heroines: what is Dreiser's definition of *feminine,* of *woman,* or of feminine values? Does he indeed propose any? In this search, *Jennie Gerhardt* is more instructive than *Sister Carrie.*

Carrie is a "bad" girl whom Dreiser refused to punish in the sense that Tolstoy punished Anna, say. There is some evidence that he flirted with the idea of correcting this lapse in *Jennie Gerhardt,* perhaps for no better reason than his lust for fame and fortune. He wanted very much to be a successful novelist and he became one with the publication of *Jennie Gerhardt,* perhaps just because she was perceived as having been punished for her sins. But was she? Dreiser began writing *Jennie Gerhardt* immediately after finishing *Sister Carrie* in 1901. (Interestingly enough, its working title was then *The Transgressor.)* He was going through a bad time. There was the pain of *Sister Carrie's* reception. His marriage was disintegrating. He suffered acute nervous disorders and severe depression. He was having trouble writing, and trouble publishing, even in journals. *Jennie Gerhardt* proceeded in fits and starts until it bogged down completely.

Almost accidentally, and much like the story of a Dreiserian hero, the young writer's career took a spectacular turn. Through journalism, he entered the magazine world and within a few years achieved the commercial success he coveted. When he was forced to resign as the head of a magazine publishing group, characteristically it was because of his other powerful lust—for women. He returned to the writing of *Jennie Gerhardt* then and, completing it within the year, published it ten years after his first novel, establishing himself as an important American writer and following it with three more novels, all within a five year period.

The author of *Jennie Gerhardt* was a different man from the younger Dreiser who had begun it ten years earlier. He knew worldliness from the inside now, and he had exercised his obsession with women. Dreiser was captivated by women, beginning with the mother he revered and the sisters he surely identified with in his own helplessness and vague longings for a bright life beyond the poor, striving, uneducated, religious, immigrant background of his own large family. Carrie was a likeness of one of his sisters and Jennie was drawn from another—or from a mix of two others—in the loose fashion that fiction reflects autobiography and biography.

In her virtues, Jennie is an absolute Dickens heroine, but Dreiser's observations of real life are too acute for him to idealize her. If she is innocent, generous, loving, and faithful, she is also a woman of open sexuality, realistic sense, and a considerable susceptibility to worldly position and luxury. In short, like Flaubert and Emma Bovary, Jennie Gerhardt contains a big chunk of Theodore Dreiser himself. Her qualities, however charming and virtuous, are of no consequence to society since they operate within the marginal boundaries of her helplessness as a female without a shred of economic power. She is left with her basic gift—the sexual charm she exerts over men—to further herself and to help her family. But without society's imprimatur, Jennie's gifts are full of sin. Instinctively she pulls against this view, trying to burrow out to a new morality.

Dreiser doesn't quite know where he stands here. From the first scene of the book, where Jennie and her mother are polishing the brass in the lobby of a downtown Cincinnati hotel and she notices the senator who will later become her lover and the father of her child, there is a strong element of choice and self-determination in Jennie. But Dreiser hesitates to grant her the license to control her own life. His philosophy demands that the inexorable march of destiny heavily circumscribe Jennie's end, even without the ambivalent attitude revealed by an excerpt from Dreiser's autobiography:

> Moral problems such as the lives of my several sisters presented to me had no great weight. . . . It is the way of life, however much socially it may be denied, concealed or disguised. At times, assuming I heard someone else discussing them moralistically—my father, say—I was inclined to experience a depression or reduction in pride. . . . And yet, at times . . . I had the notion that they were not doing right;

> that men were using them as mere playthings; but most of the time I had a feeling that they were their own masters or might be if they would. . . . And through it all ran the feeling that good, bad or indifferent as individuals or things might be, life was a splendid surge, a rich sensation, and that it was fine to be alive. You may measure the thinness of literature and of moral dogma and religious control by your observations and experiences. Look back over your own life and see!

Caught in the complexities of cruelly warring concepts, Jennie strives toward good, as she understands it, but everything turns out bad. She *chooses* to turn to the senator for help. The senator means right by her, but he dies suddenly, leaving her pregnant. Though Lester Kane presses his need upon her, it is she who *chooses* to meet him at the hotel. Lester Kane delights in Jennie and craves her for his happiness, but he makes the inevitable decision to sacrifice feelings for social and financial position. In a speech that gives the full measure of the autonomy of her character, she tells her lover:

> If you married me you would only get ten thousand a year. . . . if you didn't and still lived with me you would get nothing at all. If you would leave me, or I would leave you, you would get all of a million and a half. Don't you think you had better leave me now?

"He cared but he didn't care *enough*," Jennie tells herself in a clear-eyed recognition of the limitations of love, when Kane does leave her. She is echoing almost word for word the ache Dreiser records about himself in the manuscript of his autobiography, *Dawn:* "No one ever wanted me *enough* . . . "

Jennie exemplifies feminine values—of course, not genteel ones. Jennie suffers not because she does wrong but because the world wastefully tosses aside what is most valuable in her—her womanliness, her sexuality, the exquisitely nurturing response to the birth of her daughter, the protective loyalties she maintains toward her family, her mother and father, and Lester Kane, the man she loves and lives with. Jennie is the moral center of Dreiser's book in a way that Carrie is not. It is against Jennie's values that the male characters are measured. Contact with her makes them better people, if not good enough. The senator responds to her natural affection with generosity; Lester reacts to her passionately feeling nature with as much love as he can muster for anybody; her father, before he dies, calls her "a good woman" though his religious tenets declare her nothing but bad. Dogma, rigid principle, coarse materialism, class position, and plain old Dreiserian fate smash her life finally, but none of these diminishes her moral stature. In the final scene, shut out of the public mourning for the death of her lover, she is woman as outsider, a symbol of what society has shunned, thus leaving itself harder, meaner, and narrower.

# JENNIE GERHARDT

# CHAPTER I

ONE morning, in the fall of 1880, a middle-aged woman, accompanied by a young girl of eighteen, presented herself at the clerk's desk of the principal hotel in Columbus, Ohio, and made inquiry as to whether there was anything about the place that she could do. She was of a helpless, fleshy build, with a frank, open countenance and an innocent, diffident manner. Her eyes were large and patient, and in them dwelt such a shadow of distress as only those who have looked sympathetically into the countenances of the distraught and helpless poor know anything about. Any one could see where the daughter behind her got the timidity and shame-facedness which now caused her to stand back and look indifferently away. She was a product of the fancy, the feeling, the innate affection of the untutored but poetic mind of her mother combined with the gravity and poise which were characteristic of her father. Poverty was driving them. Together they presented so appealing a picture of honest necessity that even the clerk was affected.

" What is it you would like to do ? " he said.

" Maybe you have some cleaning or scrubbing," she replied, timidly. " I could wash the floors."

The daughter, hearing the statement, turned uneasily, not because it irritated her to work, but because she hated people to guess at the poverty that made it necessary. The clerk, manlike, was affected by the evidence of beauty in distress. The innocent helplessness of the daughter made their lot seem hard indeed.

" Wait a moment," he said ; and, stepping into a back office, he called the head housekeeper.

There was work to be done. The main staircase and parlour hall were unswept because of the absence of the regular scrub-woman.

" Is that her daughter with her ? " asked the housekeeper, who could see them from where she was standing.

" Yes, I believe so."

" She might come this afternoon if she wants to. The girl helps her, I suppose ? "

" You go see the housekeeper," said the clerk, pleasantly, as he came back to the desk. " Right through there "— pointing to a near-by door. " She'll arrange with you about it."

A succession of misfortunes, of which this little scene might have been called the tragic culmination, had taken place in the life and family of William Gerhardt, a glass-blower by trade. Having suffered the reverses so common in the lower walks of life, this man was forced to see his wife, his six children, and himself dependent for the necessaries of life upon whatever windfall of fortune the morning of each recurring day might bring. He himself was sick in bed. His oldest boy, Sebastian, or " Bass," as his associates transformed it, worked as an apprentice to a local freight-car builder, but received only four dollars a week. Genevieve, the oldest of the girls, was past eighteen, but had not as yet been trained to any special work. The other children, George, aged fourteen ; Martha, twelve ; William, ten, and Veronica, eight, were too young to do anything, and only made the problem of existence the more complicated. Their one mainstay was the home, which, barring a six-hundred-dollar mortgage, the father owned. He had borrowed this money at a time when, having saved enough to buy the house, he desired to add three rooms and a porch, and so make it large enough for them to live in. A few years were still to run on the mortgage, but times had been so bad that he had been forced to use up not only the little he had saved to pay off the principal, but the annual interest also. Gerhardt was helpless, and the consciousness of his precarious situation—the doctor's bill, the interest due upon the mortgage, together with the sums owed butcher and baker, who, through knowing him to be absolutely honest, had trusted him until they could trust no longer—all these perplexities weighed upon his mind and racked him so nervously as to delay his recovery.

Mrs. Gerhardt was no weakling. For a time she took in washing, what little she could get, devoting the intermediate hours to dressing the children, cooking, seeing that they got off to school, mending their clothes, waiting on her husband, and occasionally weeping. Not infrequently she went personally to some new grocer, each time farther and farther away, and, starting an account with a little cash, would receive credit until other grocers warned the philanthropist of his folly. Corn was cheap. Sometimes she would make a kettle of lye hominy, and this would last, with scarcely anything else, for an entire week. Corn-meal also, when made into mush, was better than nothing, and this, with a little milk, made almost a feast. Potatoes fried was the nearest they ever came to luxurious food, and coffee was an infrequent treat. Coal was got by picking it up in buckets and baskets along the maze of tracks in the near-by railroad yard. Wood, by similar journeys to surrounding lumber-yards. Thus they lived from day to day, each hour hoping that the father would get well and that the glass-works would soon start up. But as the winter approached Gerhardt began to feel desperate.

" I must get out of this now pretty soon," was the sturdy German's regular comment, and his anxiety found but weak expression in the modest quality of his voice.

To add to all this trouble little Veronica took the measles, and, for a few days, it was thought that she would die. The mother neglected everything else to hover over her and pray for the best. Doctor Ellwanger came every day, out of purely human sympathy, and gravely examined the child. The Lutheran minister, Pastor Wundt, called to offer the consolation of the Church. Both of these men brought an atmosphere of grim ecclesiasticism into the house. They were the black-garbed, sanctimonious emissaries of superior forces. Mrs. Gerhardt felt as if she were going to lose her child, and watched sorrowfully by the cot-side. After three days the worst was over, but there was no bread in the house. Sebastian's wages had been spent for medicine. Only coal was free for the picking, and several times the children had been scared from the railroad yards. Mrs. Gerhardt thought of all the places to which she might apply, and despairingly hit upon the hotel. Now, by a miracle, she had her chance.

" How much do you charge ? " the housekeeper asked her.

Mrs. Gerhardt had not thought this would be left to her, but need emboldened her.

" Would a dollar a day be too much ? "

" No," said the housekeeper ; " there is only about three

days work to do every week. If you would come every afternoon you could do it."

" Very well," said the applicant.   " Shall we start to-day ? "

" Yes ; if you'll come with me now I'll show you where the cleaning things are."

The hotel, into which they were thus summarily introduced, was a rather remarkable specimen for the time and place. Columbus, being the State capital, and having a population of fifty thousand and a fair passenger traffic, was a good field for the hotel business, and the opportunity had been improved ; so at least the Columbus people proudly thought. The structure, five stories in height, and of imposing proportions, stood at one corner of the central public square, where were the Capitol building and principal stores. The lobby was large and had been recently redecorated. Both floor and wainscot were of white marble, kept shiny by frequent polishing. There was an imposing staircase with hand-rails of walnut and toe-strips of brass. An inviting corner was devoted to a news and cigar-stand. Where the staircase curved upward the clerk's desk and offices had been located, all done in hardwood and ornamented by novel gas-fixtures. One could see through a door at one end of the lobby to the barber-shop, with its chairs and array of shaving-mugs. Out-side were usually two or three buses, arriving or departing, in accordance with the movement of the trains.

To this caravanserai came the best of the political and social patronage of the State.   Several Governors had made it their permanent abiding place during their terms of office.   The two United States Senators, whenever business called them to Columbus, invariably maintained parlour chambers at the hotel.   One of them, Senator Brander, was looked upon by the proprietor as more or less of a permanent guest, because he was not only a resident of the city, but an otherwise home-less bachelor.   Other and more transient guests included Congressmen, State legislators and lobbyists, merchants, professional men, and, after them, the whole raft of indescrib-ables who, coming and going, make up the glow and stir of this kaleidoscopic world.

Mother and daughter, suddenly flung into this realm of superior brightness, felt immeasurably overawed. They went about too timid to touch anything for fear of giving offence.

The great red-carpeted hallway, which they were set to sweep, had for them all the magnificence of a palace ; they kept their eyes down and spoke in their lowest tones. When it came to scrubbing the steps and polishing the brass-work of the splendid stairs both needed to steel themselves, the mother against her timidity, the daughter against the shame at so public an exposure. Wide beneath lay the imposing lobby, and men, lounging, smoking, passing constantly in and out, could see them both.

" Isn't it fine ? " whispered Genevieve, and started nervously at the sound of her own voice.

" Yes," returned her mother, who, upon her knees, was wringing out her cloth with earnest but clumsy hands.

" It must cost a good deal to live here, don't you think ? "

" Yes," said her mother. " Don't forget to rub into these little corners. Look here what you've left."

Jennie, mortified by this correction, fell earnestly to her task, and polished vigorously, without again daring to lift her eyes.

With painstaking diligence they worked downward until about five o'clock ; it was dark outside, and all the lobby was brightly lighted. Now they were very near the bottom of the stairway.

Through the big swinging doors there entered from the chilly world without a tall, distinguished, middle-aged gentleman, whose silk hat and loose military cape-coat marked him at once, among the crowd of general idlers, as some one of importance. His face was of a dark and solemn cast, but broad and sympathetic in its lines, and his bright eyes were heavily shaded with thick, bushy, black eyebrows. Passing to the desk he picked up the key that had already been laid out for him, and coming to the staircase, started up.

The middle-aged woman, scrubbing at his feet, he acknowledged not only by walking around her, but by graciously waving his hand, as much as to say, " Don't move for me."

The daughter, however, caught his eye by standing up, her troubled glance showing that she feared she was in his way.

He bowed and smiled pleasantly.

" You shouldn't have troubled yourself," he said.

Jennie only smiled.

When he had reached the upper landing an impulsive sidewise glance assured him, more clearly than before, of her uncommonly prepossessing appearance. He noted the high, white forehead, with its smoothly parted and plaited hair. The eyes he saw were blue and the complexion fair. He had even time to admire the mouth and the full cheeks—above all, the well-rounded, graceful form, full of youth, health, and that hopeful expectancy which to the middle-aged is so suggestive of all that is worth begging of Providence. Without another look he went dignifiedly upon his way, but the impression of her charming personality went with him. This was the Hon. George Sylvester Brander, junior Senator.

"Wasn't that a fine-looking man who went up just now ?" observed Jennie a few moments later.

"Yes, he was," said her mother.

"He had a gold-headed cane."

"You mustn't stare at people when they pass," cautioned her mother, wisely. "It isn't nice."

"I didn't stare at him," returned Jennie, innocently. "He bowed to me."

"Well, don't you pay any attention to anybody," said her mother. "They may not like it."

Jennie fell to her task in silence, but the glamour of the great world was having its effect upon her senses. She could not help giving ear to the sounds, the brightness, the buzz of conversation and laughter surrounding her. In one section of the parlour floor was the dining-room, and from the clink of dishes one could tell that supper was being prepared. In another was the parlour proper, and there some one came to play on the piano. That feeling of rest and relaxation which comes before the evening meal pervaded the place. It touched the heart of the innocent working-girl with hope, for hers were the years, and poverty could not as yet fill her young mind with cares. She rubbed diligently always, and sometimes forgot the troubled mother at her side, whose kindly eyes were becoming invested with crows' feet, and whose lips half repeated the hundred cares of the day. She could only think that all of this was very fascinating, and wish that a portion of it might come to her.

At half-past five, the housekeeper, remembering them, came and told them that they might go. The fully finished stairway was relinquished by both with a sigh of relief, and, after putting their implements away, they hastened homeward, the mother, at least, pleased to think that at last she had something to do.

As they passed several fine houses Jennie was again touched by that half-defined emotion which the unwonted novelty of the hotel life had engendered in her consciousness.

" Isn't it fine to be rich ? " she said.

" Yes," answered her mother, who was thinking of the suffering Veronica.

" Did you see what a big dining-room they had there ? "

" Yes."

They went on past the low cottages and among the dead leaves of the year.

" I wish we were rich," murmured Jennie, half to herself.

" I don't know just what to do," confided her mother with a long-drawn sigh. " I don't believe there's a thing to eat in the house."

" Let's stop and see Mr. Bauman again," exclaimed Jennie, her natural sympathies restored by the hopeless note in her mother's voice.

" Do you think he would trust us any more ? "

" Let's tell him where we're working. I will."

" Well," said her mother, wearily.

Into the small, dimly lighted grocery store, which was two blocks from their house, they ventured nervously. Mrs. Gerhardt was about to begin, but Jennie spoke first.

" Will you let us have some bread to-night, and a little bacon ? We're working now at the Columbus House, and we'll be sure to pay you Saturday."

" Yes," added Mrs. Gerhardt, " I have something to do."

Bauman, who had long supplied them before illness and trouble began, knew that they told the truth.

" How long have you been working there ? " he asked.

" Just this afternoon."

" You know, Mrs. Gerhardt," he said, " how it is with me. I don't want to refuse you. Mr. Gerhardt is good for it, but I am poor, too. Times are hard," he explained further, " I have my family to keep."

" Yes, I know," said Mrs. Gerhardt, weakly.

Her old shoddy shawl hid her rough hands, red from the

day's work, but they were working nervously.  Jennie stood by in strained silence.

" Well," concluded Mr. Bauman, " I guess it's all right this time.  Do what you can for me Saturday."

He wrapped up the bread and bacon, and, handing Jennie the parcel, he added, with a touch of cynicism :

" When you get money again I guess you'll go and trade somewhere else."

" No," returned Mrs. Gerhardt ; " you know better than that."  But she was too nervous to parley long.

They went out into the shadowy street, and on past the low cottages to their own home.

" I wonder," said the mother, wearily, when they neared the door, " if they've got any coal ? "

" Don't worry," said Jennie.  " If they haven't I'll go."

" A man run us away," was almost the first greeting that the perturbed George offered when the mother made her inquiry about the coal.  " I got a little, though," he added.  " I threw it off a car."

Mrs. Gerhardt only smiled, but Jennie laughed.

" How is Veronica ? " she inquired.

" She seems to be sleeping," said the father.  " I gave her medicine again at five."

While the scanty meal was being prepared the mother went to the sick child's bedside, taking up another long night's vigil quite as a matter of course.

While the supper was being eaten Sebastian offered a suggestion, and his larger experience in social and commercial matters made his proposition worth considering.  Though only a car-builder's apprentice, without any education except such as pertained to Lutheran doctrine, to which he objected very strongly, he was imbued with American colour and energy.  His transformed name of Bass suited him exactly. Tall, athletic, and well-featured for his age, he was a typical stripling of the town.  Already he had formulated a philosophy of life.  To succeed one must do something—one must associate, or at least seem to associate, with those who were foremost in the world of appearances.

For this reason the young boy loved to hang about the Columbus House.  It seemed to him that this hotel was the centre and circumference of all that was worth while in the social sense. He would go downtown evenings, when he first secured money enough to buy a decent suit of clothes, and stand around the hotel entrance with his friends, kicking his heels, smoking a two-for-five-cent cigar, preening himself on his stylish appearance, and looking after the girls. Others were there with him—town dandies and nobodies, young men who came there to get shaved or to drink a glass of whisky. And all of these he admired and sought to emulate. Clothes were the main touchstone. If men wore nice clothes and had rings and pins, whatever they did seemed appropriate. He wanted to be like them and to act like them, and so his experience of the more pointless forms of life rapidly broadened.

" Why don't you get some of those hotel fellows to give you their laundry ? " he asked of Jennie after she had related the afternoon's experiences. " It would be better than scrubbing the stairs."

" How do you get it ? " she replied.

" Why, ask the clerk, of course."

This plan struck Jennie as very much worth while.

" Don't you ever speak to me if you meet me around there," he cautioned her a little later, privately. " Don't you let on that you know me."

" Why ? " she asked, innocently.

" Well, you know why," he answered, having indicated before that when they looked so poor he did not want to be disgraced by having to own them as relatives. " Just you go on by. Do you hear ? "

" All right," she returned, meekly, for although this youth was not much over a year her senior, his superior will dominated.

The next day on their way to the hotel she spoke of it to her mother.

" Bass said we might get some of the laundry of the men at the hotel to do."

Mrs. Gerhardt, whose mind had been straining all night at the problem of adding something to the three dollars which her six afternoons would bring her, approved of the idea.

" So we might," she said. " I'll ask that clerk."

When they reached the hotel, however, no immediate opportunity presented itself. They worked on until late in the afternoon. Then, as fortune would have it, the housekeeper sent them in to scrub up the floor behind the clerk's desk. That important individual felt very kindly toward mother and daughter. He liked the former's sweetly troubled countenance and the latter's pretty face. So he listened graciously when Mrs. Gerhardt ventured meekly to put the question which she had been revolving in her mind all the afternoon.

" Is there any gentleman here," she said, " who would give me his washing to do ?  I'd be so very much obliged for it."

The clerk looked at her, and again recognised that absolute want was written all over her anxious face.

" Let's see," he answered, thinking of Senator Brander and Marshall Hopkins. Both were charitable men, who would be more than glad to aid a poor woman. " You go up and see Senator Brander," he continued. " He's in twenty-two. Here," he added, writing out the number, " you go up and tell him I sent you."

Mrs. Gerhardt took the card with a tremour of gratefulness. Her eyes looked the words she could not say.

" That's all right," said the clerk, observing her emotion. " You go right up.  You'll find him in his room now."

With the greatest diffidence Mrs. Gerhardt knocked at number twenty-two. Jennie stood silently at her side.

After a moment the door was opened, and in the full radiance of the bright room stood the Senator. Attired in a handsome smoking-coat, he looked younger than at their first meeting.

" Well, madam," he said, recognising the couple, and particularly the daughter, " what can I do for you ? "

Very much abashed, the mother hesitated in her reply.

" We would like to know if you have any washing you could let us have to do ? "

" Washing ? " he repeated after her, in a voice which had a peculiarly resonant quality. " Washing ?  Come right in. Let me see."

He stepped aside with much grace, waved them in and closed the door. " Let me see," he repeated, opening and closing drawer after drawer of the massive black-walnut bureau. Jennie studied the room with interest. Such an array of nicknacks and pretty things on mantel and dressing-table she had never seen before. The Senator's easy-chair.

with a green-shaded lamp beside it, the rich heavy carpet and the fine rugs upon the floor—what comfort, what luxury !

" Sit down ; take those two chairs there," said the Senator graciously, disappearing into a closet.

Still overawed, mother and daughter thought it more polite to decline, but now the Senator had completed his researches and he reiterated his invitation. Very uncomfortably they yielded and took chairs.

" Is this your daughter ? " he continued, with a smile at Jennie.

" Yes, sir," said the mother ; " she's my oldest girl."

" Is your husband alive ? "

" What is his name ? "

" Where does he live ? "

To all of these questions Mrs. Gerhardt very humbly answered.

" How many children have you ? " he went on.

" Six," said Mrs. Gerhardt.

" Well," he returned, " that's quite a family. You've certainly done your duty to the nation."

" Yes, sir," returned Mrs. Gerhardt, who was touched by his genial and interesting manner.

" And you say this is your oldest daughter ? "

" Yes, sir."

" What does your husband do ? "

" He's a glass-blower. But he's sick now."

During the colloquy Jennie's large blue eyes were wide with interest. Whenever he looked at her she turned upon him such a frank, unsophisticated gaze, and smiled in such a vague, sweet way, that he could not keep his eyes off of her for more than a minute of the time.

" Well," he continued, sympathetically, " that is too bad ! I have some washing here—not very much—but you are welcome to it. Next week there may be more."

He went about now, stuffing articles of apparel into a blue cotton bag with a pretty design on the side.

" Do you want these any certain day ? " questioned Mrs. Gerhardt.

" No," he said, reflectively, " any day next week will do."

She thanked him with a simple phrase, and started to go.

" Let me see," he said, stepping ahead of them and opening the door, " you may bring them back Monday ! "

" Yes, sir," said Mrs. Gerhardt.   " Thank you."

They went out and the Senator returned to his reading, but it was with a peculiarly disturbed mind.

" Too bad," he said, closing his volume.   " There's something very pathetic about those people."   Jennie's spirit of wonder and appreciation was abroad in the room.

Mrs. Gerhardt and Jennie made their way anew through the shadowy streets.   They felt immeasurably encouraged by this fortunate venture.

" Didn't he have a fine room ? " whispered Jennie.

" Yes," answered the mother ; " he's a great man."

" He's a senator, isn't he ? " continued the daughter.

" Yes."

" It must be nice to be famous," said the girl, softly.

## CHAPTER II

THE spirit of Jennie—who shall express it? This daughter of poverty, who was now to fetch and carry the laundry of this distinguished citizen of Columbus, was a creature of a mellowness of temperament which words can but vaguely suggest. There are natures born to the inheritance of flesh that come without understanding, and that go again without seeming to have wondered why. Life, so long as they endure it, is a true wonderland, a thing of infinite beauty, which could they but wander into it wonderingly, would be heaven enough. Opening their eyes, they see a comfortable and perfect world. Trees, flowers, the world of sound and the world of colour. These are the valued inheritance of their state. If no one said to them " Mine " they would wander radiantly forth, singing the song which all the earth may some day hope to hear. It is the song of goodness.

Caged in the world of the material, however, such a nature is almost invariably an anomaly. That other world of flesh into which has been woven pride and greed looks askance at the idealist, the dreamer. If one says it is sweet to look at the clouds, the answer is a warning against idleness. If one seeks to give ear to the winds, it shall be well with his soul, but they will seize upon his possessions. If all the world of the so-called inanimate delay one, calling with tenderness in sounds that seem to be too perfect to be less than understanding, it shall be ill with the body. The hands of the actual are forever reaching toward such as these—forever seizing greedily upon them. It is of such that the bond servants are made.

In the world of the actual, Jennie was such a spirit. From her earliest youth goodness and mercy had moulded her every impulse. Did Sebastian fall and injure himself, it was she who struggled with straining anxiety, carried him safely to his mother. Did George complain that he was hungry, she gave him all of her bread. Many were the hours in which she had rocked her younger brothers and sisters to sleep, singing whole-heartedly betimes and dreaming far dreams. Since her

earliest walking period she had been as the right hand of her
mother.  What scrubbing, baking, errand-running, and nursing
there had been to do she did.  No one had ever heard her
rudely complain, though she often thought of the hardness
of her lot.  She knew that there were other girls whose lives
were infinitely freer and fuller, but, it never occurred to her
to be meanly envious ; her heart might be lonely, but her lips
continued to sing.  When the days were fair she looked out
of her kitchen window and longed to go where the meadows
were.  Nature's fine curves and shadows touched her as a
song itself.  There were times when she had gone with George
and the others, leading them away to where a patch of hickory-
trees flourished, because there were open fields, with shade
for comfort and a brook of living water.  No artist in the
formulating of conceptions, her soul still responded to these
things, and every sound and every sigh were welcome to her
because of their beauty.

When the soft, low call of the wood-doves, those spirits
of the summer, came out of the distance, she would incline
her head and listen, the whole spiritual quality of it dropping
like silver bubbles into her own great heart.

Where the sunlight was warm and the shadows flecked with
its splendid radiance she delighted to wonder at the pattern
of it, to walk where it was most golden, and follow with
instinctive appreciation the holy corridors of the trees.

Colour was not lost upon her.  That wonderful radiance
which fills the western sky at evening touched and unburdened
her heart.

" I wonder," she said once with girlish simplicity, " how
it would feel to float away off there among those clouds."

She had discovered a natural swing of a wild grape-vine,
and was sitting in it with Martha and George.

" Oh, wouldn't it be nice if you had a boat up there," said
George.

She was looking with uplifted face at a far-off cloud, a red
island in a sea of silver.

" Just supposing," she said, " people could live on an island
like that."

Her soul was already up there, and its elysian paths knew
the lightness of her feet.

" There goes a bee," said George, noting a bumbler winging by.

" Yes," she said, dreamily, " it's going home."

" Does everything have a home ? " asked Martha.

" Nearly everything," she answered.

" Do the birds go home ? " questioned George.

" Yes," she said, deeply feeling the poetry of it herself, " the birds go home."

" Do the bees go home ? " urged Martha.

" Yes, the bees go home."

" Do the dogs go home ? " said George, who saw one travelling lonesomely along the nearby road.

" Why, of course," she said, " you know that dogs go home."

" Do the gnats ? " he persisted, seeing one of those curious spirals of minute insects turning energetically in the waning light.

" Yes," she said, half believing her remark. " Listen ! "

" Oho," exclaimed George, incredulously, " I wonder what kind of houses they live in."

" Listen ! " she persisted, putting out her hand to still him.

It was that halcyon hour when the Angelus falls like a benediction upon the waning day. Far off the notes were sounding gently, and nature, now that she listened, seemed to have paused also. A scarlet-breasted robin was hopping in short spaces upon the grass before her. A humming bee hummed, a cow-bell tinkled, while some suspicious cracklings told of a secretly reconnoitering squirrel. Keeping her pretty hand weighed in the air, she listened until the long, soft notes spread and faded and her heart could hold no more. Then she arose.

" Oh," she said, clenching her fingers in an agony of poetic feeling. There were crystal tears overflowing in her eyes. The wondrous sea of feeling in her had stormed its banks. Of such was the spirit of Jennie.

# CHAPTER III

THE junior Senator, George Sylvester Brander, was a man of peculiar mould. In him there were joined, to a remarkable degree, the wisdom of the opportunist and the sympathetic nature of the true representative of the people. Born a native of southern Ohio, he had been raised and educated there, if one might except the two years in which he had studied law at Columbia University. He knew common and criminal law, perhaps, as well as any citizen of his State, but he had never practised with that assiduity which makes for pre-eminent success at the bar. He had made money, and had had splendid opportunities to make a great deal more if he had been willing to stultify his conscience, but that he had never been able to do. And yet his integrity had not been at all times proof against the claims of friendship. Only in the last presidential election he had thrown his support to a man for Governor who, he well knew, had no claim which strictly honourable conscience could have recognised.

In the same way, he had been guilty of some very questionable, and one or two actually unsavory, appointments. Whenever his conscience pricked him too keenly he would endeavour to hearten himself with his pet phrase, " All in a lifetime." Thinking over things quite alone in his easy-chair, he would sometimes rise up with these words on his lips, and smile sheepishly as he did so. Conscience was not by any means dead in him. His sympathies, if anything, were keener than ever.

This man, three times Congressman from the district of which Columbus was a part, and twice United States Senator, had never married. In his youth he had had a serious love affair, but there was nothing discreditable to him in the fact that it came to nothing. The lady found it inconvenient to wait for him. He was too long in earning a competence upon which they might subsist.

Tall, straight-shouldered, neither lean nor stout, he was to-day an imposing figure. Having received his hard knocks and endured his losses, there was that about him which touched and awakened the sympathies of the imaginative. People thought him naturally agreeable, and his senatorial peers looked upon him as not any too heavy mentally, but personally a fine man.

His presence in Columbus at this particular time was due to the fact that his political fences needed careful repairing. The general election had weakened his party in the State Legislature. There were enough votes to re-elect him, but it would require the most careful political manipulation to hold them together. Other men were ambitious. There were a half-dozen available candidates, any one of whom would have rejoiced to step into his shoes. He realised the exigencies of the occasion. They could not well beat him, he thought; but even if this should happen, surely the President could be induced to give him a ministry abroad.

Yes, he might be called a successful man, but for all that Senator Brander felt that he had missed something. He had wanted to do so many things. Here he was, fifty-two years of age, clean, honourable, highly distinguished, as the world takes it, but single. He could not help looking about him now and then and speculating upon the fact that he had no one to care for him. His chamber seemed strangely hollow at times—his own personality exceedingly disagreeable.

" Fifty ! " he often thought to himself. " Alone—absolutely alone."

Sitting in his chamber that Saturday afternoon, a rap at his door aroused him. He had been speculating upon the futility of his political energy in the light of the impermanence of life and fame.

" What a great fight we make to sustain ourselves ? " he thought. " How little difference it will make to me a few years hence ? "

He arose, and opening wide his door, perceived Jennie. She had come, as she had suggested to her mother, at this time, instead of on Monday, in order to give a more favourable impression of promptness.

" Come right in," said the Senator ; and, as on the first occasion, he graciously made way for her.

Jennie passed in, momentarily expecting some compliment upon the promptitude with which the washing had been done. The Senator never noticed it at all.

"Well, my young lady," he said when she had put the bundle down, "how do you find yourself this evening?"

"Very well," replied Jennie. "We thought we'd better bring your clothes to-day instead of Monday."

"Oh, that would not have made any difference," replied Brander lightly. "Just leave them on the chair."

Jennie, without considering the fact that she had been offered no payment for the service rendered, was about to retire, had not the Senator detained her.

"How is your mother?" he asked pleasantly.

"She's very well," said Jennie simply.

"And your little sister? Is she any better?"

"The doctor thinks so," she replied.

"Sit down," he continued graciously. "I want to talk to you."

Moving to a near-by chair, the young girl seated herself.

"Hem!" he went on, clearing his throat lightly. "What seems to be the matter with her?"

"She has the measles," returned Jennie. "We thought once that she was going to die."

Brander studied her face as she said this, and he thought he saw something exceedingly pathetic there. The girl's poor clothes and her wondering admiration for his exalted station in life affected him. It made him feel almost ashamed of the comfort and luxury that surrounded him. How high up he was in the world, indeed!

"I am glad she is better now," he said kindly. "How old is your father?"

"Fifty-seven."

"And is he any better?"

"Oh yes, sir; he's around now, although he can't go out just yet."

"I believe your mother said he was a glass-blower by trade?"

"Yes, sir."

Brander well knew the depressed local conditions in this branch of manufacture. It had been part of the political issue in the last campaign. They must be in a bad way truly.

"Do all of the children go to school?" he inquired.

"Why, yes, sir," returned Jennie, stammering. She was too shamefaced to own that one of the children had been obliged to leave school for the lack of shoes. The utterance of the falsehood troubled her.

He reflected awhile ; then realising that he had no good excuse for further detaining her, he arose and came over to her. From his pocket he took a thin layer of bills, and removing one, handed it to her.

" You take that," he said, " and tell your mother that I said she should use it for whatever she wants."

Jennie accepted the money with mingled feelings ; it did not occur to her to look and see how much it was. The great man was so near her, the wonderful chamber in which he dwelt so impressive, that she scarcely realised what she was doing.

" Thank you," she said. " Is there any day you want your washing called for ? " she added.

" Oh yes," he answered ; " Monday—Monday evenings."

She went away, and in a half reverie he closed the door behind her. The interest that he felt in these people was unusual. Poverty and beauty certainly made up an affecting combination. He sat down in his chair and gave himself over to the pleasant speculations which her coming had aroused. Why should he not help them ?

" I'll find out where they live," he finally resolved.

In the days that followed Jennie regularly came for the clothes. Senator Brander found himself more and more interested in her, and in time he managed to remove from her mind that timidity and fear which had made her feel uncomfortable in his presence. One thing which helped toward this was his calling her by her first name. This began with her third visit, and thereafter he used it with almost unconscious frequency.

It could scarcely be said that he did this in a fatherly spirit, for he had little of that attitude toward any one. He felt exceedingly young as he talked to this girl, and he often wondered whether it were not possible for her to perceive and appreciate him on his youthful side.

As for Jennie, she was immensely taken with the comfort and luxury surrounding this man, and subconsciously with the man himself, the most attractive she had ever known. Everything he had was fine, everything he did was gentle, distinguished, and considerate. From some far source, perhaps some old German ancestors, she had inherited an understanding and appreciation of all this. Life ought to be lived as he lived it; the privilege of being generous particularly appealed to her.

Part of her attitude was due to that of her mother, in whose mind sympathy was always a more potent factor than reason. For instance, when she brought to her the ten dollars Mrs. Gerhardt was transported with joy.

" Oh," said Jennie, " I didn't know until I got outside that it was so much. He said I should give it to you."

Mrs. Gerhardt took it, and holding it loosely in her folded hands, saw distinctly before her the tall Senator with his fine manners.

" What a fine man he is ! " she said. " He has a good heart."

Frequently throughout the evening and the next day Mrs. Gerhardt commented upon this wonderful treasure-trove, repeating again and again how good he must be or how large must be his heart. When it came to washing his clothes she almost rubbed them to pieces, feeling that whatever she did she could scarcely do enough. Gerhardt was not to know. He had such stern views about accepting money without earning it that even in their distress, she would have experienced some difficulty in getting him to take it. Consequently she said nothing, but used it to buy bread and meat, and going as it did such a little way, the sudden windfall was never noticed.

Jennie from now on, reflected this attitude toward the Senator, and, feeling so grateful toward him, she began to talk more freely. They came to be on such good terms that he gave her a little leather picture-case from his dresser which he had observed her admiring. Every time she came he found excuse to detain her, and soon discovered that, for all her soft girlishness, there lay deep-seated in her a conscious deprecation of poverty and a shame of having to own any need. He honestly admired her for this, and, seeing that her clothes were poor and her shoes worn, he began to wonder how he could help her without offending.

Not infrequently he thought to follow her some evening, and see for himself what the condition of the family might be. He was a United States Senator, however. The neighbourhood they lived in must be very poor. He stopped to consider, and for the time the counsels of prudence prevailed. Consequently the contemplated visit was put off.

Early in December, Senator Brander returned to Washington for three weeks, and both Mrs. Gerhardt and Jennie were surprised to learn one day that he had gone. Never had he given them less than two dollars a week for his washing, and several times it had been five. He had not realised, perhaps, what a breach his absence would make in their finances. But there was nothing to do about it ; they managed to pinch along. Gerhardt, now better, searched for work at the various mills, and finding nothing, procured a saw-buck and saw, and going from door to door, sought for the privilege of sawing wood. There was not a great deal of this to do, but he managed by the most earnest labour to earn two, and sometimes three, dollars a week. This added to what his wife earned and what Sebastian gave was enough to keep bread in their mouths, but scarcely more.

It was at the opening of the joyous Christmas-time that the bitterness of their poverty affected them most. The Germans love to make a great display at Christmas. It is the one season of the year when the fullness of their large family affection manifests itself. Warm in the appreciation of the joys of childhood, they love to see the little ones enjoy their toys and games. Father Gerhardt at his saw-buck during the weeks before Christmas thought of this very often. What would little Veronica not deserve after her long illness ! How he would have liked to give each of the children a stout pair of shoes, the boys a warm cap, the girls a pretty hood. Toys and games and candy they always had had before. He hated to think of the snow-covered Christmas morning and no table richly piled with what their young hearts would most desire.

As for Mrs. Gerhardt, one could better imagine than describe her feelings. She felt so keenly about it that she could hardly bring herself to speak of the dreaded hour to her husband. She had managed to lay aside three dollars in the hope of getting enough to buy a ton of coal, and so put an end to poor George's daily pilgrimage to the coalyard, but now as the Christmas week drew near she decided to use it for gifts. Father Gerhardt was also secreting two dollars without the knowledge of his wife, thinking that on Christmas Eve he could produce it at a critical moment, and so relieve her maternal anxiety.

When the actual time arrived, however, there was very little to be said for the comfort that they got out of the occasion.

The whole city was rife with Christmas atmosphere. Grocery stores and meat markets were strung with holly. The toy shops and candy stores were radiant with fine displays of everything that a self-respecting Santa Claus should have about him. Both parents and children observed it all—the former with serious thoughts of need and anxiety, the latter with wild fancy and only partially suppressed longings.

Frequently had Gerhardt said in their presence.

" Kriss Kringle is very poor this year. He hasn't so very much to give."

But no child, however poverty-stricken, could be made to believe this. Every time after so saying he looked into their eyes, but in spite of the warning, expectation flamed in them undiminished.

Christmas coming on Tuesday, the Monday before there was no school. Before going to the hotel Mrs. Gerhardt had cautioned George that he must bring enough coal from the yards to last over Christmas day. The latter went at once with his two younger sisters, but there being a dearth of good picking, it took them a long time to fill their baskets, and by night they had gathered only a scanty supply.

" Did you go for the coal ? " asked Mrs. Gerhardt the first thing when she returned from the hotel that evening.

" Yes," said George.

" Did you get enough for to-morrow ? "

" Yes," he replied, " I guess so."

" Well, now, I'll go and look," she replied. Taking the lamp, they went out into the woodshed where the coal was deposited.

" Oh, my ! " she exclaimed when she saw it ; " why, that isn't near enough. You must go right off and get some more.

" Oh," said George, pouting his lips, " I don't want to go. Let Bass go."

Bass, who had returned promptly at a quarter-past six, was already busy in the back bedroom washing and dressing preparatory to going downtown.

" No," said Mrs. Gerhardt. " Bass has worked hard all day. You must go."

" I don't want to," pouted George.

" All right," said Mrs. Gerhardt, " maybe to-morrow you'll be without a fire, and then what ? "

They went back to the house, but George's conscience was too troubled to allow him to consider the case as closed.

"Bass, you come too," he called to his elder brother when he was inside.

"Go where?" said Bass.

"To get some coal."

"No," said the former, "I guess not. What do you take me for?"

"Well, then, I'll not," said George, with an obstinate jerk of his head.

"Why didn't you get it up this afternoon?" questioned his brother sharply; "you've had all day to do it."

"Aw, I did try," said George. "We couldn't find enough. I can't get any when there ain't any, can I?"

"I guess you didn't try very hard," said the dandy.

"What's the matter now?" asked Jennie, who, coming in after having stopped at the grocer's for her mother, saw George with a solemn pout on his face.

"Oh, Bass won't go with me to get any coal?"

"Didn't you get any this afternoon?"

"Yes," said George, "but ma says I didn't get enough."

"I'll go with you," said his sister. "Bass will you come along?"

"No," said the young man, indifferently, "I won't." He was adjusting his necktie and felt irritated.

"There ain't any," said George, "unless we get it off the cars. There wasn't any cars where I was."

"There are, too," exclaimed Bass.

"There ain't," said George.

"Oh don't quarrel," said Jennie. "Get the baskets and let's go right now before it gets too late."

The other children, who had a fondness for their big sister got out the implements of supply—Veronica a basket, Martha and William buckets, and George a big clothes-basket, which he and Jennie were to fill and carry between them. Bass, moved by his sister's willingness and the little regard he still maintained for her, now made a suggestion.

"I'll tell you what you do, Jen," he said. "You go over there with the kids to Eighth Street and wait around those cars. I'll be along in a minute. When I come by don't any of you pretend to know me. Just you say, 'Mister won't

you please throw us some coal down ? ' and then I'll get up
on the cars and pitch off enough to fill the baskets. D'ye
understand ? "

" All right," said Jennie, very much pleased.

Out into the snowy night they went, and made their way
to the railroad tracks. At the intersection of the street and
the broad railroad yard were many heavily laden cars of
bituminous coal newly backed in. All of the children gathered
within the shadow of one. While they were standing there,
waiting the arrival of their brother, the Washington Special
arrived, a long, fine train with several of the new style drawing-
room cars, the big plate-glass windows shining and the
passengers looking out from the depths of their comfortable
chairs. The children instinctively drew back as it thundered
past.

" Oh, wasn't it long ? " said George.

" Wouldn't I like to be a brakeman, though," sighed William.

Jennie, alone, kept silent, but to her particularly the suggestion of travel and comfort had appealed. How beautiful life
must be for the rich !

Sebastian now appeared in the distance, a mannish spring
in his stride, and with every evidence that he took himself
seriously. He was of that peculiar stubbornness and determination that had the children failed to carry out his plan of
procedure he would have gone deliberately by and refused
to help them at all.

Martha, however, took the situation as it needed to be taken,
and piped out childishly, " Mister, won't you please throw
us down some coal ? "

Sebastian stopped abruptly, and looked sharply at them
as though he were really a stranger, exclaimed " Why, certainly,"
and proceeded to climb up on the car, from whence he cast
down with remarkable celerity more than enough chunks to
fill their baskets. Then as though not caring to linger any
longer amid such plebeian company, he hastened across the
network of tracks and was lost to view.

On their way home they encountered another gentleman,
this time a real one, with high hat and distinguished cape coat,
whom Jennie immediately recognised. This was the honourable
Senator himself, newly returned from Washington, and
anticipating a very unprofitable Christmas. He had arrived

upon the express which had enlisted the attention of the children, and was carrying his light grip for the pleasure of it to the hotel. As he passed he thought that he recognised Jennie.

"Is that you, Jennie?" he said, and paused to be more certain.

The latter, who had discovered him even more quickly than he had her, exclaimed, "Oh, there is Mr. Brander!" Then, dropping her end of the basket, with a caution to the children to take it right home, she hurried away in the opposite direction

The Senator followed, vainly calling three or four times "Jennie! Jennie!" Losing hope of overtaking her, and suddenly recognising, and thereupon respecting, her simple, girlish shame, he stopped, and turning back, decided to follow the children. Again he felt that same sensation which he seemed always to get from this girl—the far cry between her estate and his. It was something to be a Senator to-night, here where these children were picking coal. What could the joyous holiday of the morrow hold for them? He tramped along sympathetically, an honest lightness coming into his step, and soon he saw them enter the gateway of the low cottage. Crossing the street, he stood in the weak shade of the snow-laden trees. The light was burning with a yellow glow in a rear window. All about was the white snow. In the woodshed he could hear the voices of the children, and once he thought he detected the form of Mrs. Gerhardt. After a time another form came shadowlike through the side gate. He knew who it was. It touched him to the quick, and he bit his lip sharply to suppress any further show of emotion. Then he turned vigorously on his heel and walked away.

The chief grocery of the city was conducted by one Manning, a stanch adherent of Brander, and one who felt honoured by the Senator's acquaintance. To him at his busy desk came the Senator this same night.

"Manning," he said, "could I get you to undertake a little work for me this evening?"

"Why, certainly, Senator, certainly," said the grocery-man. "When did you get back? Glad to see you. Certainly."

"I want you to get everything together that would make a nice Christmas for a family of eight—father and mother and six children—Christmas tree, groceries, toys—you know what I mean."

"Certainly, certainly, Senator."

"Never mind the cost now. Send plenty of everything. I'll give you the address," and he picked up a note-book to write it.

"Why, I'll be delighted, Senator," went on Mr. Manning, rather affected himself. "I'll be delighted. You always were generous."

"Here you are, Manning," said the Senator, grimly, from the mere necessity of preserving his senatorial dignity. "Send everything at once, and the bill to me."

"I'll be delighted," was all the astonished and approving grocery-man could say.

The Senator passed out, but remembering the old people, visited a clothier and shoe man, and, finding that he could only guess at what sizes might be required, ordered the several articles with the privilege of exchange. When his labours were over, he returned to his room.

"Carrying coal," he thought, over and over. "Really, it was very thoughtless in me. I mustn't forget them any more."

# CHAPTER IV

THE desire to flee which Jennie experienced upon seeing the Senator again was attributable to what she considered the disgrace of her position. She was ashamed to think that he, who thought so well of her, should discover her doing so common a thing. Girl-like, she was inclined to imagine that his interest in her depended upon something else than her mere personality.

When she reached home Mrs. Gerhardt had heard of her flight from the other children.

"What was the matter with you, anyway?" asked George, when she came in.

"Oh, nothing," she answered, but immediately turned to her mother and said, "Mr. Brander came by and saw us."

"Oh, did he?" softly exclaimed her mother. "He's back then. What made you run, though, you foolish girl?"

"Well, I didn't want him to see me."

"Well, maybe he didn't know you, anyhow," she said, with a certain sympathy for her daughter's predicament.

"Oh yes, he did, too," whispered Jennie. "He called after me three or four times."

Mrs. Gerhardt shook her head.

"What is it?" said Gerhardt, who had been hearing the conversation from the adjoining room, and now came out.

"Oh, nothing," said the mother, who hated to explain the significance which the Senator's personality had come to have in their lives. "A man frightened them when they were bringing the coal."

The arrival of the Christmas presents later in the evening threw the household into an uproar of excitement. Neither Gerhardt nor the mother could believe their eyes when a grocery wagon halted in front of their cottage and a lusty clerk began to carry in the gifts. After failing to persuade the clerk that he had made a mistake, the large assortment of good things was looked over with very human glee.

"Just you never mind," was the clerk's authoritative words.

"I know what I'm about. Gerhardt, isn't it? Well, you're the people."

Mrs. Gerhardt moved about, rubbing her hands in her excitement, and giving vent to an occasional "Well, isn't that nice now!"

Gerhardt himself was melted at the thought of the generosity of the unknown benefactor, and was inclined to lay it all to the goodness of a great local mill owner, who knew him and wished him well. Mrs. Gerhardt tearfully suspected the source, but said nothing. Jennie knew, by instinct, the author of it all.

The afternoon of the day after Christmas Brander encountered the mother in the hotel, Jennie having been left at home to look after the house.

"How do you do, Mrs. Gerhardt," he exclaimed genially extending his hand. "How did you enjoy your Christmas?"

Poor Mrs. Gerhardt took it nervously; her eyes filled rapidly with tears.

"There, there," he said, patting her on the shoulder. "Don't cry. You mustn't forget to get my laundry to-day."

"Oh no, sir," she returned, and would have said more had he not walked away.

From this on, Gerhardt heard continually of the fine Senator at the hotel, how pleasant he was, and how much he paid for his washing. With the simplicity of a German working man, he was easily persuaded that Mr. Brander must be a very great and a very good man.

Jennie, whose feelings needed no encouragement in this direction, was more than ever prejudiced in his favour.

There was developing in her that perfection of womanhood, the full mould of form, which could not help but attract any man. Already she was well built, and tall for a girl. Had she been dressing in the trailing skirts of a woman of fashion she would have made a fitting companion for a man the height of the Senator. Her eyes were wondrously clear and bright, her skin fair, and her teeth white and even. She was clever, too, in a sensible way, and by no means deficient in observation. All that she lacked was training and the assurance of which the knowledge of utter dependency despoils one. But the carrying of washing and the compulsion to acknowledge almost anything as a favour put her at a disadvantage.

Nowadays when she came to the hotel upon her semi-weekly errand Senator Brander took her presence with easy grace, and to this she responded. He often gave her little presents for herself, or for her brothers and sisters, and he talked to her so unaffectedly that finally the overawing sense of the great difference between them was brushed away, and she looked upon him more as a generous friend than as a distinguished Senator. He asked her once how she would like to go to a seminary, thinking all the while how attractive she would be when she came out. Finally, one evening, he called her to his side.

"Come over here, Jennie," he said, "and stand by me."

She came, and, moved by a sudden impulse, he took her hand.

"Well, Jennie," he said, studying her face in a quizzical, interrogative way, "what do you think of me, anyhow?"

"Oh," she answered, looking consciously away, "I don't know. What makes you ask me that?"

"Oh yes, you do," he returned. "You have some opinion of me. Tell me now, what is it?"

"No, I haven't," she said, innocently.

"Oh yes, you have," he went on, pleasantly, interested by her transparent evasiveness. "You must think something of me. Now, what is it?"

"Do you mean do I like you?" she asked, frankly, looking down at the big mop of black hair well streaked with grey, which hung about his forehead, and gave an almost leonine cast to his fine face.

"Well, yes," he said, with a sense of disappointment. She was barren of the art of the coquette.

"Why, of course I like you," she replied, prettily.

"Haven't you ever thought anything else about me?" he went on.

"I think you're very kind," she went on, even more bashfully; she realised now that he was still holding her hand.

"Is that all?" he asked.

"Well," she said, with fluttering eyelids, "isn't that enough?"

He looked at her, and the playful, companionable directness of her answering gaze thrilled him through and through. He studied her face in silence while she turned and twisted, feeling, but scarcely understanding, the deep import of his scrutiny.

"Well," he said at last, "I think you're a fine girl.  Don't you think I'm a pretty nice man ? "

"Yes," said Jennie, promptly.

He leaned back in his chair and laughed at the unconscious drollery of her reply.  She looked at him curiously and smiled.

"What made you laugh ? " she inquired.

"Oh, your answer," he returned.  "I really ought not to laugh, though.  You don't appreciate me in the least. I don't believe you like me at all."

"But I do, though," she replied, earnestly.  "I think you're so good."  Her eyes showed very plainly that she felt what she was saying.

"Well," he said, drawing her gently down to him ; then, at the same instant he pressed his lips to her cheek.

"Oh ! " she cried, straightening up, at once startled and frightened.

It was a new note in their relationship.  The senatorial quality vanished in an instant.  She recognised in him something that she had not felt before.  He seemed younger, too. She was a woman to him, and he was playing the part of a lover.  She hesitated, but not knowing just what to do, did nothing at all.

"Well," he said, "did I frighten you ? "

She looked at him, but moved by her underlying respect for this great man, she said, with a smile, "Yes, you did."

"I did it because I like you so much."

She meditated upon this a moment, and then said, "I think I'd better be going."

"Now then," he pleaded, "are you going to run away because of that ? "

"No," she said, moved by a curious feeling of ingratitude ; "but I ought to be going.  They'll be wondering where I am."

"You're sure you're not angry about it ? "

"No," she replied, and with more of a womanly air than she had ever shown before.  It was a novel experience to be in so authoritative a position.  It was so remarkable that it was somewhat confusing to both of them.

"You're my girl, anyhow," the Senator said, rising.  "I'm going to take care of you in the future."

Jennie heard this, and it pleased her.  He was so well

fitted, she thought, to do wondrous things; he was nothing less than a veritable magician. She looked about her, and the thought of coming into such a life and such an atmosphere was heavenly. Not that she fully understood his meaning, however. He meant to be good and generous, and to give her fine things. Naturally she was happy. She took up the package that she had come for, not seeing or feeling the incongruity of her position, while he felt it as a direct reproof.

"She ought not to carry that," he thought. A great wave of sympathy swept over him. He took her cheeks between his hands, this time in a superior and more generous way. "Never mind, little girl," he said. "You won't have to do this always. I'll see what I can do."

The outcome of this was simply a more sympathetic relationship between them. He did not hesitate to ask her to sit beside him on the arm of his chair the next time she came, and to question her intimately about the family's condition and her own desires. Several times he noticed that she was evading his questions, particularly in regard to what her father was doing. She was ashamed to own that he was sawing wood. Fearing lest something more serious was impending, he decided to go out some day and see for himself.

This he did when a convenient morning presented itself and his other duties did not press upon him. It was three days before the great fight in the Legislature began which ended in his defeat. Nothing could be done in these few remaining days. So he took his cane and strolled forth, coming to the cottage in the course of a half hour, and knocked boldly at the door.

Mrs. Gerhardt opened it.

"Good-morning," he said, cheerily; then, seeing her hesitate he added, "May I come in?"

The good mother, who was all but overcome by his astonishing presence, wiped her hands furtively upon her much-mended apron, and, seeing that he waited for a reply, said:

"Oh yes. Come right in."

She hurried forward, forgetting to close the door, and, offering him a chair, asked him to be seated.

Brander, feeling sorry that he was the occasion of so much confusion, said: "Don't trouble yourself, Mrs. Gerhardt. I was passing and thought I'd come in. How is your husband?"

"He's well, thank you," returned the mother. "He's out working to-day."

"Then he has found employment ? "

"Yes, sir," said Mrs. Gerhardt, who hesitated, like Jennie to say what it was.

"The children are all well now, and in school I hope ? "

"Yes," replied Mrs. Gerhardt. She had now unfastened her apron, and was nervously turning it in her lap.

"That's good, and where is Jennie ! "

The latter, who had been ironing, had abandoned the board and had concealed herself in the bedroom, where she was busy tidying herself in the fear that her mother would not have the forethought to say that she was out, and so let her have a chance for escape.

"She's here," returned the mother. "I'll call her."

"What did you tell him I was here for ? " said Jennie, weakly.

"What could I do ? " asked the mother.

Together they hesitated while the Senator surveyed the room. He felt sorry to think that such deserving people must suffer so ; he intended, in a vague way, to ameliorate their condition if possible.

"Good-morning," the Senator said to Jennie, when finally she came hesitatingly into the room. "How do you do to-day ? "

Jennie came forward, extending her hand and blushing. She found herself so much disturbed by this visit that she could hardly find tongue to answer his questions.

"I thought," he said, "I'd come out and find where you live. This is a quite comfortable house. How many rooms have you ? "

"Five," said Jennie. "You'll have to excuse the looks this morning. We've been ironing, and it's all upset."

"I know," said Brander, gently. "Don't you think I understand, Jennie ? You mustn't feel nervous about me."

She noticed the comforting, personal tone he always used with her when she was at his room, and it helped to subdue her flustered senses.

"You mustn't think it anything if I come here occasionally, I intend to come. I want to meet your father."

"Oh," said Jennie, "he's out to-day."

While they were talking however, the honest wood-cutter was coming in at the gate with his buck and saw. Brander saw him, and at once recognised him by a slight resemblance to his daughter.

" There he is now, I believe," he said.

" Oh, is he ? " said Jennie looking out.

Gerhardt, who was given to speculation these days, passed by the window without looking up. He put his wooden buck down, and, hanging his saw on a nail on the side of the house, came in.

" Mother," he called, in German, and, then not seeing her, he came to the door of the front room and looked in.

Brander arose and extended his hand. The knotted and weather-beaten German came forward, and took it with a very questioning expression of countenance.

" This is my father, Mr. Brander," said Jennie, all her diffidence dissolved by sympathy. " This is the gentleman from the hotel, papa, Mr. Brander."

" What's the name ? " said the German, turning his head.

" Brander," said the Senator.

" Oh yes," he said, with a considerable German accent. " Since I had the fever I don't hear good. My wife, she spoke to me of you."

" Yes," said the Senator, " I thought I'd come out and make your acquaintance. You have quite a family."

" Yes," said the father, who was conscious of his very poor garments and anxious to get away. " I have six children—all young. She's the oldest girl."

Mrs. Gerhardt now came back, and Gerhardt, seeing his chance, said hurriedly :

" Well, if you'll excuse me, I'll go. I broke my saw, and so I had to stop work."

" Certainly," said Brander, graciously, realising now why Jennie had never wanted to explain. He half wished that she were courageous enough not to conceal anything.

" Well, Mrs. Gerhardt," he said, when the mother was stiffly seated, " I want to tell you that you mustn't look on me as a stranger. Hereafter I want you to keep me informed of how things are going with you. Jennie won't always do it."

Jennie smiled quietly. Mrs. Gerhardt only rubbed her hands.

" Yes," she answered, humbly grateful.

They talked for a few minutes, and then the Senator rose.

" Tell your husband," he said, " to come and see me next Monday at my office in the hotel. I want to do something for him."

" Thank you," faltered Mrs. Gerhardt.

" I'll not stay any longer now," he added. " Don't forget to have him come."

" Oh, he'll come," she returned.

Adjusting a glove on one hand, he extended the other to Jennie.

" Here is your finest treasure, Mrs. Gerhardt," he said. " I think I'll take her."

" Well, I don't know," said the mother, " whether I could spare her or not."

" Well," said the Senator, going toward the door, and giving Mrs. Gerhardt his hand, " good-morning."

He nodded and walked out, while a half-dozen neighbours, who had observe his entrance, peeked from behind curtains and drawn blinds at the astonishing sight.

" Who can that be, anyhow ? " was the general query.

" See what he gave me," said the innocent mother to her daughter the moment he had closed the door.

It was a ten-dollar bill. He had placed it softly in her hand as he said good-bye.

# CHAPTER V

HAVING been led by circumstances into an attitude of obligation toward the Senator, it was not unnatural that Jennie should become imbued with a most generous spirit of appreciation for everything he had done and now continued to do. The Senator gave her father a letter to a local mill owner, who saw that he received something to do. It was not much, to be sure, a mere job as night-watchman, but it helped, and old Gerhardt's gratitude was extravagant. Never was there such a great, such a good man !

Nor was Mrs. Gerhardt overlooked. Once Brander sent her a dress, and at another time a shawl. All these benefactions were made in a spirit of mingled charity and self-gratification, but to Mrs. Gerhardt they glowed with but one motive. Senator Brander was good-hearted.

As for Jennie, he drew nearer to her in every possible way, so that at last she came to see him in a light which would require considerable analysis to make clear. This fresh, young soul, however, had too much innocence and buoyancy to consider for a moment the world's point of view. Since that one notable and halcyon visit upon which he had robbed her of her original shyness, and implanted a tender kiss upon her cheek, they had lived in a different atmosphere Jennie was his companion now, and as he more and more unbended, and even joyously flung aside the habiliments of his dignity, her perception of him grew clearer. They laughed and chatted in a natural way, and he keenly enjoyed this new entrance into the radiant world of youthful happiness.

One thing that disturbed him, however, was the occasional thought, which he could not repress, that he was not doing right. Other people must soon discover that he was not confining himself strictly to conventional relations, with this washer-woman's daughter. He suspected that the housekeeper was not without knowledge that Jennie almost invariably lingered from a quarter to three-quarters of an hour whenever she came for or returned his laundry. He knew that it might come to the ears of the hotel clerks, and so, in a general way, get about town and work serious injury, but the reflection did not cause him to modify his conduct. Sometimes he consoled himself with the thought that he was not doing her any actual harm, and at other times he would argue that he could not put this one delightful tenderness out of his life. Did he not wish honestly to do her much good?

He thought of these things occasionally, and decided that he could not stop. The self-approval which such a resolution might bring him was hardly worth the inevitable pain of the abnegation. He had not so very many more years to live. Why die unsatisfied.

One evening he put his arm around her and strained her to his breast. Another time he drew her to his knee, and told her of his life at Washington. Always now he had a caress and a kiss for her, but it was still in a tentative, uncertain way. He did not want to reach for her soul too deeply.

Jennie enjoyed it all innocently. Elements of fancy and novelty entered into her life. She was an unsophisticated creature, emotional, totally inexperienced in the matter of the affections, and yet mature enough mentally to enjoy the attentions of this great man who had thus bowed from his high position to make friends with her.

One evening she pushed his hair back from his forehead as she stood by his chair, and, finding nothing else to do, took out his watch. The great man thrilled as he looked at her pretty innocence.

"Would you like to have a watch, too?" he asked.

"Yes, indeed, I would," said Jennie with a deep breath.

The next day he stopped as he was passing a jewellery store and bought one. It was gold, and had pretty ornamented hands.

"Jennie," he said, when she came the next time, "I want to show you something. See what time it is by my watch."

Jennie drew out the watch from his waistcoat pocket and started in surprise.

"This isn't your watch!" she exclaimed, her face full of innocent wonder.

"No," he said, delighted with his little deception. "It's yours."

"Mine!" exclaimed Jennie. "Mine! Oh, isn't it lovely!"

" Do you think so ? " he said.

Her delight touched and pleased him immensely. Her face shone with light and her eyes fairly danced.

" That's yours," he said. " See that you wear it now, and don't lose it."

" You're so good ! " she exclaimed.

" No," he said, but he held her at arm's length by the waist to make up his mind what his reward should be. Slowly he drew her toward him until, when very close, she put her arms about his neck, and laid her cheek in gratitude against his own. This was the quintessence of pleasure for him. He felt as he had been longing to feel for years.

The progress of his idyl suffered a check when the great senatorial fight came on in the Legislature. Attacked by a combination of rivals, Brander was given the fight of his life. To his amazement he discovered that a great railroad corporation, which had always been friendly, was secretly throwing its strength in behalf of an already too powerful candidate. Shocked by this defection, he was thrown alternately into the deepest gloom and into paroxysms of wrath. These slings of fortune, however lightly he pretended to receive them, never failed to lacerate him. It had been long since he had suffered a defeat—too long.

During this period Jennie received her earliest lesson in the vagaries of man. For two weeks she did not even see him, and one evening, after an extremely comfortless conference with his leader, he met her with the most chilling formality. When she knocked at his door he only troubled to open it a foot, exclaiming almost harshly : " I can't bother about the clothes to-night. Come to-morrow."

Jennie retreated, shocked and surprised by this reception. She did not know what to think of it. He was restored on the instant to his far-off, mighty throne, and left to rule in peace. Why should he not withdraw the light of his countenance if it pleased him. But why——

A day or two later he repented mildly, but had no time to readjust matters. His washing was taken and delivered with considerable formality, and he went on toiling forgetfully, until at last he was miserably defeated by two votes. Astounded by this result, he lapsed into gloomy dejection of soul. What was he to do now.

Into this atmosphere came Jennie, bringing with her the lightness and comfort of her own hopeful disposition. Nagged to desperation by his thoughts, Brander first talked to her to amuse himself; but soon his distress imperceptibly took flight; he found himself actually smiling.

"Ah, Jennie," he said, speaking to her as he might have done to a child, "youth is on your side. You possess the most valuable thing in life."

"Do I?"

"Yes, but you don't realise it. You never will until it is too late."

"I love that girl," he thought to himself that night. "I wish I could have her with me always."

But fortune had another fling for him to endure. It got about the hotel that Jennie was, to use the mildest expression, conducting herself strangely. A girl who carries washing must expect criticism if anything not befitting her station is observed in her apparel. Jennie was seen wearing the gold watch. Her mother was informed by the housekeeper of the state of things.

"I thought I'd speak to you about it," she said. "People are talking. You'd better not let your daughter go to his room for the laundry."

Mrs. Gerhardt was too astonished and hurt for utterance. Jennie had told her nothing, but even now she did not believe there was anything to tell. The watch had been both approved of and admired by her. She had not thought that it was endangering her daughter's reputation.

Going home she worried almost incessantly, and talked with Jennie about it. The latter did not admit the implication that things had gone too far. In fact, she did not look at it in that light. She did not own, it is true, what really had happened while she was visiting the Senator.

"It's so terrible that people should begin to talk!" said her mother. "Did you really stay so long in the room?"

"I don't know," returned Jennie, compelled by her conscience to admit at least part of the truth. "Perhaps I did."

"He has never said anything out of the way to you, has he?"

"No," answered her daughter, who did not attach any suspicion of evil to what had passed between them.

If the mother had only gone a little bit further she might have learned more, but she was only too glad, for her own peace of mind, to hush the matter up. People were slandering a good man, that she knew. Jennie had been the least bit indiscreet. People were always so ready to talk. How could the poor girl, amid such unfortunate circumstances, do otherwise than she did. It made her cry to think of it.

The result of it all was that she decided to get the washing herself.

She came to his door the next Monday after this decision. Brander, who was expecting Jennie, was both surprised and disappointed.

"Why," he said to her, "what has become of Jennie ? "

Having hoped that he would not notice, or, at least, not comment upon the change, Mrs. Gerhardt did not know what to say. She looked up at him weakly in her innocent, motherly way, and said, " She couldn't come to-night."

" Not ill, is she ? " he inquired.

" No."

" I'm glad to hear that," he said resignedly. " How have you been ? "

Mrs. Gerhardt answered his kindly inquiries and departed. After she had gone he got to thinking the matter over, and wondered what could have happened. It seemed rather odd that he should be wondering over it.

On Saturday, however, when she returned the clothes he felt that there must be something wrong.

" What's the matter, Mrs. Gerhardt ? " he inquired. " Has anything happened to your daughter ? "

" No, sir," she returned, too troubled to wish to deceive him.

" Isn't she coming for the laundry any more ? "

" I—I——" ventured the mother, stammering in her perturbation ; " she—they have been talking about her," she at last forced herself to say.

" Who has been talking ? " he asked gravely.

" The people here in the hotel."

" Who, what people ? " he interrupted, a touch of annoyance showing in his voice.

" The housekeeper."

" The housekeeper, eh ! " he exclaimed. " What has she got to say ? "

The mother related to him her experience.

" And she told you that, did she ? " he remarked in wrath.

" She ventures to trouble herself about my affairs, does she ? I wonder people can't mind their own business without interfering with mine. Your daughter, Mrs. Gerhardt, is perfectly safe with me. I have no intention of doing her an injury. It's a shame," he added indignantly, " that a girl can't come to my room in this hotel without having her motive questioned. I'll look into this matter."

" I hope you don't think that I have anything to do with it," said the mother apologetically. " I know you like Jennie and wouldn't injure her. You've done so much for her and all of us, Mr. Brander, I feel ashamed to keep her away."

" That's all right, Mrs. Gerhardt," he said quietly. " You did perfectly right. I don't blame you in the least. It is the lying accusation passed about in this hotel that I object to. We'll see about that."

Mrs. Gerhardt stood there, pale with excitement. She was afraid she had deeply offended this man who had done so much for them. If she could only say something, she thought, that would clear this matter up and make him feel that she was no tattler. Scandal was distressing to her.

" I thought I was doing everything for the best," she said at last.

" So you were," he replied. " I like Jennie very much. I have always enjoyed her coming here. It is my intention to do well by her, but perhaps it will be better to keep her away, at least for the present."

Again that evening the Senator sat in his easy-chair and brooded over this new development. Jennie was really much more precious to him than he had thought. Now that he had no hope of seeing her there any more, he began to realise how much these little visits of hers had meant. He thought the matter over very carefully, realised instantly that there was nothing to be done so far as the hotel gossip was concerned, and concluded that he had really placed the girl in a very unsatisfactory position.

" Perhaps I had better end this little affair," he thought. " It isn't a wise thing to pursue."

On the strength of this conclusion he went to Washington and finished his term. Then he returned to Columbus to await the friendly recognition from the President which was to send him upon some ministry abroad. Jennie had not been forgotten in the least. The longer he stayed away the more eager he was to get back. When he was again permanently settled in his old quarters he took up his cane one morning, and strolled out in the direction of the cottage. Arriving there, he made up his mind to go in, and knocking at the door, he was greeted by Mrs. Gerhardt and her daughter with astonished and diffident smiles. He explained vaguely that he had been away, and mentioned his laundry as if that were the object of his visit. Then, when chance gave him a few moments with Jennie alone, he plunged in boldly.

" How would you like to take a drive with me to-morrow evening ? " he asked.

" I'd like it," said Jennie, to whom the proposition was a glorious novelty.

He smiled and patted her cheek, foolishly happy to see her again. Every day seemed to add to her beauty. Graced with her clean white apron, her shapely head crowned by the glory of her simply plaited hair, she was a pleasing sight for any man to look upon.

He waited until Mrs. Gerhardt returned, and then, having accomplished the purpose of his visit, he arose.

" I'm going to take your daughter out riding to-morrow evening," he explained. " I want to talk to her about her future."

" Won't that be nice ? " said the mother. She saw nothing incongruous in the proposal. They parted with smiles and much handshaking.

" That man has the best heart," commented Mrs. Gerhardt. " Doesn't he always speak so nicely of you ? He may help you to an education. You ought to be proud."

" I am," said Jennie frankly.

" I don't know whether we had better tell your father or not," concluded Mrs. Gerhardt. " He doesn't like for you to be out evenings."

Finally they decided not to tell him. He might not understand.

Jennie was ready when he called. He could see by the weak-flamed, unpretentious parlour-lamp that she was dressed for him, and that the occasion had called out the best she had. A pale lavender gingham, starched and ironed, until it was a model of laundering, set off her pretty figure to perfection.

There were little lace-edged cuffs and a rather high collar attached to it. She had no gloves nor any jewellery, nor yet a jacket good enough to wear, but her hair was done up in such a dainty way that it set off her well-shaped head better than any hat, and the few ringlets that could escape crowned her as with a halo. When Brander suggested that she should wear a jacket she hesitated a moment; then she went in and borrowed her mother's cape, a plain grey woollen one. Brander realised now that she had no jacket, and suffered keenly to think that she had contemplated going without one.

" She would have endured the raw night air," he thought, " and said nothing of it."

He looked at her and shook his head reflectively. Then they started, and he quickly forgot everything but the great fact that she was at his side. She talked with freedom and with a gentle girlish enthusiasm that he found irresistibly charming.

" Why, Jennie," he said, when she had called upon him to notice how soft the trees looked, where, outlined dimly against the new rising moon, they were touched with its yellow light, " you're a great one. I believe you would write poetry if you were schooled a little."

" Do you suppose I could ? " she asked innocently.

" Do I suppose, little girl ? " he said, taking her hand. " Do I suppose ? Why, I know. You're the dearest little day-dreamer in the world. Of course you could write poetry. You live it. You are poetry, my dear. Don't you worry about writing any."

This eulogy touched her as nothing else possibly could have done. He was always saying such nice things. No one ever seemed to like or to appreciate her half as much as he did. And how good he was ! Everybody said that. Her own father.

They rode still farther, until suddenly remembering, he said : " I wonder what time it is. Perhaps we had better be turning back. Have you your watch ? "

Jennie started, for this watch had been the one thing of which she had hoped he would not speak. Ever since he had returned it had been on her mind.

In his absence the family finances had become so strained that she had been compelled to pawn it. Martha had got to that place in the matter of apparel where she could no longer go to school unless something new were provided for her. And so, after much discussion, it was decided that the watch must go.

Bass took it, and after much argument with the local pawnbroker, he had been able to bring home ten dollars. Mrs. Gerhardt expended the money upon her children, and heaved a sigh of relief. Martha looked very much better. Naturally, Jennie was glad.

Now, however, when the Senator spoke of it, her hour of retribution seemed at hand. She actually trembled, and he noticed her discomfiture.

"Why, Jennie," he said gently, "what made you start like that?"

"Nothing," she answered.

"Haven't you your watch?"

She paused, for it seemed impossible to tell a deliberate falsehood. There was a strained silence; then she said, with a voice that had too much of a sob in it for him not to suspect the truth, "No, sir." He persisted, and she confessed everything.

"Well," he said, "dearest, don't feel badly about it. There never was such another girl. I'll get your watch for you. Hereafter when you need anything I want you to come to me. Do you hear? I want you to promise me that. If I'm not here, I want you to write me. I'll always be in touch with you from now on. You will have my address. Just let me know, and I'll help you. Do you understand?"

"Yes," said Jennie.

"You'll promise to do that now, will you?"

"Yes," she replied.

For a moment neither of them spoke.

"Jennie," he said at last, the spring-like quality of the night moving him to a burst of feeling, "I've about decided that I can't do without you. Do you think you could make up your mind to live with me from now on?"

Jennie looked away, not clearly understanding his words as he meant them.

"I don't know," she said vaguely.

"Well, you think about it," he said pleasantly. "I'm serious. Would you be willing to marry me, and let me put you away in a seminary for a few years?"

" Go away to school ? "

" Yes, after you marry me."

" I guess so," she replied.   Her mother came into her mind.
Maybe she could help the family.

He looked around at her, and tried to make out the expression
on her face.   It was not dark.   The moon was now above the
trees in the east, and already the vast host of stars were paling
before it.

" Don't you care for me at all, Jennie ? " he asked.

" Yes ! "

" You never come for my laundry any more, though," he
returned pathetically.   It touched her to hear him say this.

" I didn't do that," she answered.   " I couldn't help it ;
Mother thought it was best."

" So it was," he assented.   " Don't feel badly.   I was only
joking with you.   You'd be glad to come if you could, wouldn't
you ? "

" Yes, I would," she answered frankly.

He took her hand and pressed it so feelingly that all his
kindly words seemed doubly emphasised to her.   Reaching
up impulsively, she put her arms about him.   " You're so good
to me," she said with the loving tone of a daughter.

" You're my girl, Jennie," he said with deep feeling.   " I'd
do anything in the world for you."

# CHAPTER VI

THE father of this unfortunate family, William Gerhardt, was a man of considerable interest on his personal side. Born in the kingdom of Saxony, he had had character enough to oppose the army conscription iniquity, and to flee in his eighteenth year, to Paris. From there he had set forth for America, the land of promise.

Arrived in this country, he had made his way, by slow stages from New York to Philadelphia, and thence westward, working for a time in the various glass factories in Pennsylvania. In one romantic village of this new world he had found his heart's ideal. With her, a simple American girl of German extraction, he had removed to Youngstown, and thence to Columbus, each time following a glass manufacturer by the name of Hammond, whose business prospered and waned by turns.

Gerhardt was an honest man, and he liked to think that others appreciated his integrity. " William," his employer used to say to him, " I want you because I can trust you," and this, to him, was more than silver and gold.

This honesty, like his religious convictions, was wholly due to inheritance. He had never reasoned about it. Father and grandfather before him were sturdy German artisans, who had never cheated anybody out of a dollar, and this honesty of intention came into his veins undiminished.

His Lutheran proclivities had been strengthened by years of church-going and the religious observances of home life. In his father's cottage the influence of the Lutheran minister had been all-powerful ; he had inherited the feeling that the Lutheran Church was a perfect institution, and that its teachings were of all-importance when it came to the issue of the future life. His wife, nominally of the Mennonite faith, was quite willing to accept her husband's creed. And so his household became a God-fearing one ; wherever they went their first public step was to ally themselves with the local Lutheran church, and the minister was always a welcome guest in the Gerhardt home.

Pastor Wundt, the shepherd of the Columbus church, was a sincere and ardent Christian, but his bigotry and hard-and-fast orthodoxy made him intolerant. He considered that the members of his flock were jeopardising their eternal salvation if they danced, played cards, or went to theatres, and he did not hesitate to declare vociferously that hell was yawning for those who disobeyed his injunctions. Drinking, even temperately, was a sin. Smoking—well, he smoked himself. Right conduct in marriage, however, and innocence before that state were absolute essentials of Christian living. Let no one talk of salvation, he had said, for a daughter who had failed to keep her chastity unstained, or for the parents who, by negligence, had permitted her to fall. Hell was yawning for all such. You must walk the straight and narrow way if you would escape eternal punishment, and a just God was angry with sinners every day.

Gerhardt and his wife, and also Jennie, accepted the doctrines of their Church as expounded by Mr. Wundt without reserve. With Jennie, however, the assent was little more than nominal. Religion had as yet no striking hold upon her. It was a pleasant thing to know that there was a heaven, a fearsome one to realise that there was a hell. Young girls and boys ought to be good and obey their parents. Otherwise the whole religious problem was badly jumbled in her mind.

Gerhardt was convinced that everything spoken from the pulpit of his church was literally true. Death and the future life were realities to him.

Now that the years were slipping away and the problem of the world was becoming more and more inexplicable, he clung with pathetic anxiety to the doctrines which contained a solution. Oh, if he could only be so honest and upright that the Lord might have no excuse for ruling him out. He trembled not only for himself, but for his wife and children. Would he not some day be held responsible for them ? Would not his own laxity and lack of system in inculcating the laws of eternal life to them end in his and their damnation ? He pictured to himself the torments of hell, and wondered how it would be with him and his in the final hour.

Naturally, such a deep religious feeling made him stern with his children. He was prone to scan with a narrow eye the pleasures and foibles of youthful desire. Jennie was never to have a lover if her father had any voice in the matter. Any flirtation with the youths she might meet upon the streets of Columbus could have no continuation in her home. Gerhardt forgot that he was once young himself, and looked only to the welfare of her spirit. So the Senator was a novel factor in her life.

When he first began to be a part of their family affairs the conventional standards of Father Gerhardt proved untrustworthy. He had no means of judging such a character. This was no ordinary person coquetting with his pretty daughter. The manner in which the Senator entered the family life was so original and so plausible that he became an active part before any one thought anything about it. Gerhardt himself was deceived, and, expecting nothing but honour and profit to flow to the family from such a source, accepted the interest and the service, and plodded peacefully on. His wife did not tell him of the many presents which had come before and since the wonderful Christmas.

But one morning as Gerhardt was coming home from his night work a neighbour named Otto Weaver accosted him.

" Gerhardt," he said, " I want to speak a word with you. As a friend of yours, I want to tell you what I hear. The neighbours, you know, they talk now about the man who comes to see your daughter."

" My daughter ? " said Gerhardt, more puzzled and pained by this abrupt attack than mere words could indicate. " Whom do you mean ? I don't know of any one who comes to see my daughter."

" No ? " inquired Weaver, nearly as much astonished as the recipient of his confidences. " The middle-aged man, with grey hair. He carries a cane sometimes. You don't know him ? "

Gerhardt racked his memory with a puzzled face.

" They say he was a senator once," went on Weaver, doubtful of what he had got into ; " I don't know."

" Ah," returned Gerhardt, measurably relieved. " Senator Brander. Yes. He has come sometimes—so. Well, what of it ? "

" It is nothing," returned the neighbour, " only they talk. He is no longer a young man, you know. Your daughter, she goes out with him now a few times. These people, they see that, and now they talk about her. I thought you might want to know."

Gerhardt was shocked to the depths of his being by these terrible words. People must have a reason for saying such things. Jennie and her mother were seriously at fault. Still he did not hesitate to defend his daughter.

" He is a friend of the family," he said confusedly. " People should not talk until they know. My daughter has done nothing."

" That is so. It is nothing," continued Weaver. " People talk before they have any grounds. You and I are old friends. I thought you might want to know."

Gerhardt stood there motionless another minute or so, his jaw fallen and a strange helplessness upon him. The world was such a grim thing to have antagonistic to you. Its opinions and good favour were so essential. How hard he had tried to live up to its rules ! Why should it not be satisfied and let him alone ?

" I am glad you told me," he murmured as he started homeward. " I will see about it. Good-bye."

Gerhardt took the first opportunity to question his wife.

" What is this about Senator Brander coming out to call on Jennie ? " he asked in German. " The neighbours are talking about it."

" Why, nothing," answered Mrs. Gerhardt, in the same language. She was decidedly taken aback at his question. " He did call two or three times."

" You didn't tell me that," he returned, a sense of her frailty in tolerating and shielding such weakness in one of their children irritating him.

" No," she replied, absolutely nonplussed. " He has only been here two or three times."

" Two or three times," exclaimed Gerhardt, the German tendency to talk loud coming upon him. " Two or three times ! The whole neighbourhood talks about it. What is this, then ? "

" He only called two or three times," Mrs. Gerhardt repeated weakly.

" Weaver comes to me on the street," continued Gerhardt, " and tells me that my neighbours are talking of the man my daughter is going with. I didn't know anything about it.

There I stood. I didn't know what to say. What kind of a way is that ? What must the man think of me ? "

" There is nothing the matter," declared the mother, using an effective German idiom. " Jennie has gone walking with him once or twice. He has called here at the house. What is there now in that for the people to talk about ? Can't the girl have any pleasure at all ? "

" But he is an old man," returned Gerhardt, voicing the words of Weaver. " He is a public citizen. What should he want to call on a girl like Jennie for ? "

" I don't know," said Mrs. Gerhardt, defensively. " He comes here to the house. I don't know anything but good about the man. Can I tell him not to come ? "

Gerhardt paused at this. All that he knew of the Senator was excellent. What was there now that was so terrible about it ?

" The neighbours are so ready to talk. They haven't got anything else to talk about now, so they talk about Jennie. You know whether she is a good girl or not. Why should they say such things ? " and tears came into the soft little mother's eyes.

" That is all right," grumbled Gerhardt, " but he ought not to want to come around and take a girl of her age out walking. It looks bad, even if he don't mean any harm."

At this moment Jennie came in. She had heard the talking in the front bedroom, where she slept with one of the children, but had not suspected its import. Now her mother turned her back and bent over the table where she was making biscuit, in order that her daughter might not see her red eyes.

" What's the matter ? " she inquired, vaguely troubled by the tense stillness in the attitude of both her parents.

" Nothing," said Gerhardt firmly.

Mrs. Gerhardt made no sign, but her very immobility told something. Jennie went over to her and quickly discovered that she had been weeping.

" What's the matter ? " she repeated wonderingly, gazing at her father.

Gerhardt only stood there, his daughter's innocence dominating his terror of evil.

" What's the matter ? " she urged softly of her mother.

" Oh, it's the neighbours," returned the mother brokenly.

" They're always ready to talk about something they don't know anything about."

" Is it me again ? " inquired Jennie, her face flushing faintly.

" You see," observed Gerhardt, apparently addressing the world in general, " she knows. Now, why didn't you tell me that he was coming here ? The neighbours talk, and I hear nothing about it until to-day. What kind of a way is that, anyhow ? "

" Oh," exclaimed Jennie, out of the purest sympathy for her mother, " what difference does it make ? "

" What difference ? " cried Gerhardt, still talking in German, although Jennie answered in English. " Is it no difference that men stop me on the street and speak of it ? You should be ashamed of yourself to say that. I always thought well of this man, but now, since you don't tell me about him, and the neighbours talk, I don't know what to think. Must I get my knowledge of what is going on in my own home from my neighbours ? "

Mother and daughter paused. Jennie had already begun to think that their error was serious.

" I didn't keep anything from you because it was evil," she said. " Why, he only took me out riding once."

" Yes, but you didn't tell me that," answered her father.

" You know you don't like me to go out after dark," replied Jennie. " That's why I didn't. There wasn't anything else to hide about it."

" He shouldn't want you to go out after dark with him," observed Gerhardt, always mindful of the world outside. " What can he want with you. Why does he come here ? He is too old, anyhow. I don't think you ought to have anything to do with him—such a young girl as you are."

" He doesn't want to do anything except help me," murmured Jennie. " He wants to marry me."

" Marry you ? Ha ! Why doesn't he tell me that ! " exclaimed Gerhardt. " I shall look into this. I won't have him running around with my daughter, and the neighbours talking. Besides, he is too old. I shall tell him that. He ought to know better than to put a girl where she gets talked about. It is better he should stay away altogether."

This threat of Gerhardt's, that he would tell Brander to stay away, seemed simply terrible to Jennie and to her mother.

What good could come of any such attitude ? Why must they be degraded before him ? Of course Brander did call again, while Gerhardt was away at work, and they trembled lest the father should hear of it. A few days later the Senator came and took Jennie for a long walk. Neither she nor her mother said anything to Gerhardt. But he was not to be put off the scent for long.

"Has Jennie been out again with that man ? " he inquired of Mrs. Gerhardt the next evening.

"He was here last night," returned the mother, evasively.

"Did she tell him he shouldn't come any more ? "

"I don't know. I don't think so."

"Well, now, I will see for myself once whether this thing will be stopped or not," said the determined father. "I shall talk with him. Wait till he comes again."

In accordance with this, he took occasion to come up from his factory on three different evenings, each time carefully surveying the house, in order to discover whether any visitor was being entertained. On the fourth evening Brander came, and inquiring for Jennie, who was exceedingly nervous, he took her out for a walk. She was afraid of her father, lest some unseemly things should happen, but did not know exactly what to do.

Gerhardt, who was on his way to the house at the time, observed her departure. That was enough for him. Walking deliberately in upon his wife, he said :

"Where is Jennie ? "

"She is out somewhere," said her mother.

"Yes, I know where," said Gerhardt. "I saw her. Now wait till she comes home. I will tell him."

He sat down calmly, reading a German paper and keeping an eye upon his wife, until, at last, the gate clicked, and the front door opened. Then he got up.

"Where have you been ? " he exclaimed in German.

Brander, who had not suspected that any trouble of this character was pending, felt irritated and uncomfortable. Jennie was covered with confusion. Her mother was suffering an agony of torment in the kitchen.

"Why, I have been out for a walk," she answered confusedly.

"Didn't I tell you not to go out any more after dark ? " said Gerhardt, utterly ignoring Brander.

Jennie coloured furiously, unable to speak a word.

" What is the trouble ? " inquired Brander gravely. " Why should you talk to her like that ? "

" She should not go out after dark," returned the father rudely. " I have told her two or three times now. I don't think you ought to come here any more, either."

" And why ? " asked the Senator, pausing to consider and choose his words. " Isn't this rather peculiar ? What has your daughter done ? "

" What has she done ! " exclaimed Gerhardt, his excitement growing under the strain he was enduring, and speaking almost unaccented English in consequence. " She is running around the streets at night when she 'oughtn't to be. I don't want my daughter taken out after dark by a man of your age. What do you want with her anyway ? She is only a child yet."

" Want ? " said the Senator, straining to regain his ruffled dignity. " I want to talk with her, of course. She is old enough to be interesting to me. I want to marry her if she will have me."

" I want you to go out of here and stay out of here," returned the father losing all sense of logic, and descending to the ordinary level of parental compulsion. " I don't want you to come around my house any more. I have enough trouble without my daughter being taken out and given a bad name."

" I tell you frankly," said the Senator, drawing himself up to his full height, " that you will have to make clear your meaning. I have done nothing that I am ashamed of. Your daughter has not come to any harm through me. Now, I want to know what you mean by conducting yourself in this manner."

" I mean," said Gerhardt, excitedly repeating himself, " I mean, I mean that the whole neighbourhood talks about how you come around here, and have buggy-rides and walks with my daughter when I am not here—that's what I mean. I mean that you are no man of honourable intentions, or you would not come taking up with a little girl who is only old enough to be your daughter. People tell me well enough what you are. Just you go and leave my daughter alone."

" People ! " said the Senator. " Well, I care nothing for your people. I love your daughter, and I am here to see her because I do love her. It is my intention to marry her, and if your neighbours have anything to say to that, let them say it. There is no reason why you should conduct yourself in this manner before you know what my intentions are."

Unnerved by this unexpected and terrible altercation, Jennie had backed away to the door leading out into the dining-room, and her mother, seeing her, came forward.

"Oh," said the latter, breathing excitedly, "he came home when you were away. What shall we do?" They clung together, as women do, and wept silently. The dispute continued.

"Marry, eh," exclaimed the father. "Is that it?"

"Yes," said the Senator, "marry, that is exactly it. Your daughter is eighteen years of age and can decide for herself. You have insulted me and outraged your daughter's feelings. Now, I wish you to know that it cannot stop here. If you have any cause to say anything against me outside of mere hearsay I wish you to say it."

The Senator stood before him, a very citadel of righteousness. He was neither loud-voiced nor angry-mannered, but there was a tightness about his lips which bespoke the man of force and determination.

"I don't want to talk to you any more," returned Gerhardt, who was checked but not overawed. "My daughter is my daughter. I am the one who will say whether she shall go out at night, or whether she shall marry you, either. I know what you politicians are. When I first met you I thought you were a fine man, but now, since I see the way you conduct yourself with my daughter, I don't want anything more to do with you. Just you go and stay away from here. That's all I ask of you."

"I am sorry, Mrs. Gerhardt," said Brander, turning deliberately away from the angry father, "to have had such an argument in your home. I had no idea that your husband was opposed to my visits. However, I will leave the matter as it stands for the present. You must not take all this as badly as it seems."

Gerhardt looked on in astonishment at his coolness.

"I will go now," he said, again addressing Gerhardt, "but you mustn't think that I am leaving this matter for good. You have made a serious mistake this evening. I hope you

will realise that.   I bid you good-night."   He bowed slightly
and went out.

Gerhardt closed the door firmly.   " Now," he said, turning
to his daughter and wife, " we will see whether we are rid of
him or not.   I will show you how to go after night upon
the streets when everybody is talking already."

In so far as words were concerned, the argument ceased,
but looks and feelings ran strong and deep, and for days
thereafter scarcely a word was spoken in the little cottage.
Gerhardt began to brood over the fact that he had accepted
his place from the Senator and decided to give it up.   He made
it known that no more of the Senator's washing was to be done
in their house, and if he had not been sure that Mrs. Gerhardt's
hotel work was due to her own efforts in finding it he would have
stopped that.   No good would come out of it, anyway.   If
she had never gone to the hotel all this talk would never have
come upon them.

As for the Senator, he went away decidedly ruffled by this
crude occurrence.   Neighbourhood slanders are bad enough
on their own plane, but for a man of his standing to descend
and become involved in one struck him now as being a little
bit unworthy.   He did not know what to do about the situation, and while he was trying to come to some decision several
days went by.   Then he was called to Washington, and he
went away without having seen Jennie again.

In the meantime the Gerhardt family struggled along
as before.   They were poor, indeed, but Gerhardt was willing
to face poverty if only it could be endured with honour.
The grocery bills were of the same size, however.   The
children's clothing was steadily wearing out.   Economy had
to be practised, and payments stopped on old bills that
Gerhardt was trying to adjust.

Then came a day when the annual interest on the mortgage
was due, and yet another when two different grocery-men met
Gerhardt on the street and asked about their little bills.   He
did not hesitate to explain just what the situation was, and to
tell them with convincing honesty that he would try hard and
do the best he could.   But his spirit was unstrung by his
misfortunes.   He prayed for the favour of Heaven while at
his labour, and did not hesitate to use the daylight hours that
he should have had for sleeping to go about—either looking

for a more remunerative position or to obtain such little jobs as he could now and then pick up. One of them was that of cutting grass.

Mrs. Gerhardt protested that he was killing himself, but he explained his procedure by pointing to their necessity.

"When people stop me on the street and ask me for money I have no time to sleep."

It was a distressing situation for all of them.

To cap it all, Sebastian got in jail. It was that old coal-stealing ruse of his practised once too often. He got up on a car one evening while Jennie and the children waited for him, and a railroad detective arrested him. There had been a good deal of coal stealing during the past two years, but so long as it was confined to moderate quantities the railroad took no notice. When, however, customers of shippers complained that cars from the Pennsylvania fields lost thousands of pounds in transit to Cleveland, Cincinnati, Chicago, and other points, detectives were set to work. Gerhardt's children were not the only ones who preyed upon the railroad in this way. Other families in Columbus—many of them—were constantly doing the same thing, but Sebastian happened to be seized upon as the Columbus example.

"You come off that car now," said the detective, suddenly appearing out of the shadows. Jennie and the other children dropped their baskets and buckets and fled for their lives. Sebastian's first impulse was to jump and run, but when he tried it the detective grabbed him by the coat.

"Hold on here," he exclaimed. "I want you."

"Aw, let go," said Sebastian savagely, for he was no weakling. There was nerve and determination in him, as well as a keen sense of his awkward predicament.

"Let go, I tell you," he reiterated, and giving a jerk, he almost upset his captor.

"Come here now," said the detective, pulling him viciously in an effort to establish his authority.

Sebastian came, but it was with a blow which staggered his adversary.

There was more struggling, and then a passing railroad hand came to the detective's assistance. Together they hurried him toward the depôt, and there discovering the local officer, turned him over. It was with a torn coat, scarred hands and face, and a black eye that Sebastian was locked up for the night.

When the children came home they could not say what had happened to their brother, but as nine o'clock struck, and then ten and eleven, and Sebastian did not return, Mrs. Gerhardt was beside herself. He had stayed out many a night as late as twelve and one, but his mother had a foreboding of something terrible to-night. When half-past one arrived, and no Sebastian, she began to cry.

" Some one ought to go up and tell your father," she said. " He may be in jail."

Jennie volunteered, but George, who was soundly sleeping, was awakened to go along with her.

" What ! " said Gerhardt, astonished to see his two children.

" Bass hasn't come yet," said Jennie, and then told the story of the evening's adventure in explanation.

Gerhardt left his work at once, walking back with his two children to a point where he could turn off to go to the jail. He guessed what had happened, and his heart was troubled.

" Is that so, now ! " he repeated nervously, rubbing his clumsy hands across his wet forehead.

Arrived at the station-house, the sergeant in charge told him curtly that Bass was under arrest.

" Sebastian Gerhardt ? " he said, looking over his blotter ; " yes, here he is. Stealing coal and resisting an officer. Is he your boy ? "

" Oh, my ! " said Gerhardt, " *Ach Gott !* " He actually wrung his hands in distress.

" Want to see him ? " asked the sergeant.

" Yes, yes," said the father.

" Take him back, Fred," said the other to the old watchman in charge, " and let him see the boy."

When Gerhardt stood in the back room, and Sebastian was brought out all marked and tousled, he broke down and began to cry. No word could cross his lips because of his emotion.

" Don't cry, pop," said Sebastian bravely. " I couldn't help it. It's all right. I'll be out in the morning."

Gerhardt only shook with his grief.

" Don't cry," continued Sebastian, doing his very best to

restrain his own tears. " I'll be all right. What's the use of crying ? "

" I know, I know," said the grey-headed parent brokenly, " but I can't help it. It is my fault that I should let you do that."

" No, no, it isn't," said Sebastian. " You couldn't help it. Does mother know anything about it ? "

" Yes, she knows," he returned. " Jennie and George just came up where I was and told me. I didn't know anything about it until just now," and he began to cry again.

" Well, don't you feel badly," went on Bass, the finest part of his nature coming to the surface. " I'll be all right. Just you go back to work now, and don't worry. I'll be all right."

" How did you hurt your eye ? " asked the father, looking at him with red eyes.

" Oh, I had a little wrestling match with the man who nabbed me," said the boy, smiling bravely. " I thought I could get away."

" You shouldn't do that, Sebastian," said the father. " It may go harder with you on that account. When does your case come up ? "

" In the morning, they told me," said Bass. " Nine o'clock."

Gerhardt stayed with his son for some time, and discussed the question of bail, fine, and the dire possibility of a jail sentence without arriving at any definite conclusion. Finally he was persuaded by Bass to go away, but the departure was the occasion for another outburst of feeling ; he was led away shaking and broken with emotion.

" It's pretty tough," said Bass to himself as he was led back to his cell. He was thinking solely of his father. " I wonder what ma will think."

The thought of this touched him tenderly. " I wish I'd knocked the dub over the first crack," he said. " What a fool I was not to get away."

## CHAPTER VII

GERHARDT was in despair; he did not know any one to whom he could appeal between the hours of two and nine o'clock in the morning. He went back to talk with his wife, and then to his post of duty. What was to be done? He could think of only one friend who was able, or possibly willing to do anything. This was the glass manufacturer, Hammond; but he was not in the city. Gerhardt did not know this, however.

When nine o'clock came, he went alone to the court, for it was thought advisable that the others should stay away. Mrs. Gerhardt was to hear immediately what happened. He would come right back.

When Sebastian was lined up inside the dock he had to wait a long time, for there were several prisoners ahead of him. Finally his name was called, and the boy was pushed forward to the bar. "Stealing coal, Your Honour, and resisting arrest," explained the officer who had arrested him.

The magistrate looked at Sebastian closely; he was unfavourably impressed by the lad's scratched and wounded face.

"Well, young man," he said, "what have you to say for yourself? How did you get your black eye?"

Sebastian looked at the judge, but did not answer.

"I arrested him," said the detective. "He was on one of the company's cars. He tried to break away from me, and when I held him he assaulted me. This man here was a witness," he added, turning to the railroad hand who had helped him.

"Is that where he struck you?" asked the Court, observing the detective's swollen jaw.

"Yes, sir," he returned, glad of an opportunity to be further revenged.

"If you please," put in Gerhardt, leaning forward, "he is my boy. He was sent to get the coal. He——"

"We don't mind what they pick up around the yard,"

interrupted the detective, " but he was throwing it off the cars to half a dozen others."

" Can't you earn enough to keep from taking coal off the coal cars ? " asked the Court ; but before either father or son had time to answer he added, " What is your business ? "

" Car builder," said Sebastian.

" And what do you do ? " he questioned, addressing Gerhardt.

" I am watchman at Miller's furniture factory."

" Um," said the court, feeling that Sebastian's attitude remained sullen and contentious. " Well, this young man might be let off on the coal-stealing charge, but he seems to be somewhat too free with his fists. Columbus is altogether too rich in that sort of thing. Ten dollars."

" If you please," began Gerhardt, but the court officer was already pushing him away.

" I don't want to hear any more about it," said the judge. " He's stubborn, anyhow. What's the next case ? "

Gerhardt made his way over to his boy, abashed and yet very glad it was no worse. Somehow, he thought, he could raise the money. Sebastian looked at him solicitously as he came forward.

" It's all right," said Bass soothingly. " He didn't give me half a chance to say anything."

" I'm only glad it wasn't more," said Gerhardt nervously. " We will try and get the money."

Going home to his wife, Gerhardt informed the troubled household of the result. Mrs. Gerhardt stood white and yet relieved, for ten dollars seemed something that might be had. Jennie heard the whole story with open mouth and wide eyes. It was a terrible blow to her. Poor Bass ! He was always so lively and good-natured. It seemed awful that he should be in jail.

Gerhardt went hurriedly to Hammond's fine residence, but he was not in the city. He thought then of a lawyer by the name of Jenkins, whom he knew in a casual way, but Jenkins was not at his office. There were several grocers and coal merchants whom he knew well enough, but he owed them money. Pastor Wundt might let him have it, but the agony such a disclosure to that worthy would entail held him back. He did call on one or two acquaintances, but these, surprised

at the unusual and peculiar request, excused themselves. At
four o'clock he returned home, weary and exhausted.

"I don't know what to do," he said despairingly. "If I
could only think."

Jennie thought of Brander, but the situation had not
accentuated her desperation to the point where she could
brave her father's opposition and his terrible insult to the
Senator, so keenly remembered, to go and ask. Her watch
had been pawned a second time, and she had no other means
of obtaining money.

The family council lasted until half-past ten, but still there
was nothing decided. Mrs. Gerhardt persistently and mono-
tonously turned one hand over in the other and stared at the
floor. Gerhardt ran his hand through his reddish brown hair
distractedly. "It's no use," he said at last. "I can't think
of anything."

"Go to bed, Jennie," said her mother solicitously; "get
the others to go. There's no use their sitting up. I may think
of something. You go to bed."

Jennie went to her room, but the very thought of repose was
insupportable. She had read in the paper, shortly after her
father's quarrel with the Senator, that the latter had departed
for Washington. There had been no notice of his return.
Still he might be in the city. She stood before a short, narrow
mirror that surmounted a shabby bureau, thinking. Her
sister Veronica, with whom she slept, was already composing
herself to dreams. Finally a grim resolution fixed itself in her
consciousness. She would go and see Senator Brander. If
*he* were in town he would help Bass. Why shouldn't she—
he loved her. He had asked over and over to marry her. Why
should she not go and ask him for help?

She hesitated a little while, then hearing Veronica breathing
regularly, she put on her hat and jacket, and noiselessly opened
the door into the sitting-room to see if any one were stirring.

There was no sound save that of Gerhardt rocking nervously
to and fro in the kitchen. There was no light save that of her
own small room-lamp and a gleam from under the kitchen door.
She turned and blew the former out—then slipped quietly to
the front door, opened it and stepped out into the night.

A waning moon was shining, and a hushed sense of growing
life filled the air, for it was nearing spring again. As Jennie

hurried along the shadowy streets—the arc light had not yet been invented—she had a sinking sense of fear ; what was this rash thing she was about to do ? How would the Senator receive her ? What would he think ? She stood stock-still, wavering and doubtful ; then the recollection of Bass in his night cell came over her again, and she hurried on.

The character of the Capitol Hotel was such that it was not difficult for a woman to find ingress through the ladies' entrance to the various floors of the hotel at any hour of the night. The hotel, not unlike many others of the time, was in no sense loosely conducted, but its method of supervision in places was lax. Any person could enter, and, by applying at a rear entrance to the lobby, gain the attention of the clerk. Otherwise not much notice was taken of those who came and went.

When she came to the door it was dark save for a low light burning in the entry-way. The distance to the Senator's room was only a short way along the hall of the second floor. She hurried up the steps, nervous and pale, but giving no other outward sign of the storm that was surging within her. When she came to his familiar door she paused ; she feared that she might not find him in his room ; she trembled again to think that he might be there. A light shone through the transom, and, summoning all her courage, she knocked. A man coughed and bestirred himself.

His surprise as he opened the door knew no bounds. " Why, Jennie ! " he exclaimed. " How delightful ! I was thinking of you. Come in—come in."

He welcomed her with an eager embrace.

" I was coming out to see you, believe me, I was. I was thinking all along how I could straighten this matter out. And now you come. But what's the trouble ? "

He held her at arm's length and studied her distressed face. The fresh beauty of her seemed to him like cut lilies wet with dew.

He felt a great surge of tenderness.

" I have something to ask you," she at last brought herself to say. " My brother is in jail. We need ten dollars to get him out, and I didn't know where else to go."

" My poor child ! " he said, chafing her hands. " Where else should you go ? Haven't I told you always to come to me ? Don't you know, Jennie, I would do anything in the world for you ? "

"Yes," she gasped.

"Well, then, don't worry about that any more. But won't fate ever cease striking at you, poor child? How did your brother come to get in jail?"

"They caught him throwing coal down from the cars," she replied.

"Ah!" he replied, his sympathies touched and awakened. Here was this boy arrested and fined for what fate was practically driving him to do. Here was this girl pleading with him at night, in his room, for what to her was a great necessity—ten dollars; to him, a mere nothing. "I will arrange about your brother," he said quickly. "Don't worry. I can get him out in half an hour. You sit here now and be comfortable until I return."

He waved her to his easy-chair beside a large lamp, and hurried out of the room.

Brander knew the sheriff who had personal supervision of the county jail. He knew the judge who had administered the fine. It was but a five minutes' task to write a note to the judge asking him to revoke the fine, for the sake of the boy's character, and send it by a messenger to his home. Another ten minutes' task to go personally to the jail and ask his friend, the sheriff, to release the boy then and there.

"Here is the money," he said. "If the fine is revoked you can return it to me. Let him go now."

The sheriff was only too glad to comply. He hastened below to personally supervise the task, and Bass, a very much astonished boy, was set free. No explanations were vouchsafed him.

"That's all right now," said the turnkey. "You're at liberty. Run along home and don't let them catch you at anything like that again."

Bass went his way wondering, and the ex-Senator returned to his hotel trying to decide just how this delicate situation should be handled. Obviously Jennie had not told her father of her mission. She had come as a last resource. She was now waiting for him in his room.

There are crises in all men's lives when they waver between the strict fulfilment of justice and duty and the great possibilities for personal happiness which another line of conduct seems to assure. And the dividing line is not always marked and clear. He knew that the issue of taking her, even as his wife, was made difficult by the senseless opposition of her father. The opinion of the world brought up still another complication. Supposing he should take her openly, what would the world say ? She was a significant type emotionally, that he knew. There was something there—artistically, temperamentally, which was far and beyond the keenest suspicion of the herd. He did not know himself quite what it was, but he felt a largeness of feeling not altogether squared with intellect, or perhaps better yet, experience, which was worthy of any man's desire. " This remarkable girl," he thought, seeing her clearly in his mind's eye.

Meditating as to what he should do, he returned to his hotel, and the room. As he entered he was struck anew with her beauty, and with the irresistible appeal of her personality. In the glow of the shaded lamp she seemed a figure of marvellous potentiality.

" Well," he said, endeavouring to appear calm, " I have looked after your brother. He is out."

She rose.

" Oh," she exclaimed, clasping her hands and stretching her arms out toward him. There were tears of gratefulness in her eyes.

He saw them and stepped close to her. " Jennie, for heaven's sake don't cry," he entreated. " You angel ! You sister of mercy ! To think you should have to add tears to your other sacrifices."

He drew her to him, and then all the caution of years deserted him. There was a sense both of need and of fulfilment in his mood. At last, in spite of other losses, fate had brought him what he most desired—love, a woman whom he could love. He took her in his arms, and kissed her again and again.

The English Jefferies has told us that it requires a hundred and fifty years to make a perfect maiden. " From all enchanted things of earth and air, this preciousness has been drawn. From the south wind that breathed a century and a half over the green wheat ; from the perfume of the growing grasses waving over heavy-laden clover and laughing veronica, hiding the green-finches, baffling the bee ; from rose-lined hedge, woodbine, and cornflower, azure blue, where yellowing wheat stalks crowd up under the shadow of green firs. All the devious brooklets' sweetness where the iris stays the sunlight ; all the wild woods hold of beauty ; all the broad hills of thyme and freedom—thrice a hundred years repeated.

"A hundred years of cowslips, bluebells, violets ; purple spring and golden autumn ; sunshine, shower, and dewy mornings ; the night immortal ; all the rhythm of time unrolling. A chronicle unwritten and past all power of writing ; who shall preserve a record of the petals that fell from the roses a century ago ? The swallows to the house-tops three hundred times—think of that ! Thence she sprang, and the world yearns toward her beauty as to flowers that are past. The loveliness of seventeen is centuries old. That is why passion is almost sad."

If you have understood and appreciated the beauty of harebells three hundred times repeated ; if the quality of the roses, of the music, of the ruddy mornings and evenings of the world has ever touched your heart ; if all beauty were passing, and you were given these things to hold in your arms before the world slipped away, would you give them up ?

## CHAPTER VIII

THE significance of the material and spiritual changes which sometimes overtake us are not very clear at the time. A sense of shock, a sense of danger, and then apparently we subside to old ways, but the change has come. Never again, here or elsewhere, will we be the same. Jennie, pondering after the subtle emotional turn which her evening's sympathetic expedition had taken, was lost in a vague confusion of emotions. She had no definite realisation of what social and physical changes this new relationship to the Senator might entail. She was not conscious as yet of that shock which the possibility of maternity, even under the most favourable conditions, must bring to the average woman. Her present attitude was one of surprise, wonder, uncertainty ; and at the same time she experienced a genuine feeling of quiet happiness. Brander was a good man ; now he was closer to her than ever. He loved her. Because of this new relationship a change in her social condition was to inevitably follow. Life was to be radically different from now on—was different at this moment. Brander assured her over and over of his enduring affection.

" I tell you, Jennie," he repeated, as she was leaving, " I don't want you to worry. This emotion of mine got the best of me, but I'll marry you. I've been carried off my feet, but I'll make it up to you. Go home and say nothing at all. Caution your brother, if it isn't too late. Keep your own counsel, and I will marry you and take you away. I can't do it right now. I don't want to do it here. But I'm going to Washington, and I'll send for you. And here "—he reached for his purse and took from it a hundred dollars, practically all he had with him, " take that. I'll send you more to-morrow. You're my girl now—remember that. You belong to me."

He embraced her tenderly.

She went out into the night, thinking. No doubt he would do as he said. She dwelt, in imagination, upon the possibilities of a new and fascinating existence. Of course he would marry her. Think of it! She would go to Washington—that far-off place. And her father and mother—they would not need to work so hard any more. And Bass, and Martha—she fairly glowed as she recounted to herself the many ways in which she could help them all.

A block away she waited for Brander, who accompanied her to her own gate, and waited while she made a cautious reconnaissance. She slipped up the steps and tried the door. It was open. She paused a moment to indicate to her lover that she was safe, and entered. All was silent within. She slipped to her own room and heard Veronica breathing. She went quietly to where Bass slept with George. He was in bed, stretched out as if asleep. When she entered he asked, " Is that you, Jennie ? "

" Yes."

" Where have you been ? "

" Listen," she whispered. " Have you seen papa and mamma ? "

" Yes."

" Did they know I had gone out ? "

" Ma did. She told me not to ask after you. Where have you been ? "

" I went to see Senator Brander for you."

" Oh, that was it. They didn't say why they let me out."

" Don't tell any one," she pleaded. " I don't want any one to know. You know how papa feels about him."

" All right," he replied. But he was curious as to what the ex-Senator thought, what he had done, and how she had appealed to him. She explained briefly, then she heard her mother come to the door.

" Jennie," she whispered.

Jennie went out.

" Oh, why did you go ? " she asked.

" I couldn't help it, ma," she replied. " I thought I must do something."

" Why did you stay so long ? "

" He wanted to talk to me," she answered evasively.

Her mother looked at her nervously, wanly.

" I have been so afraid, oh, so afraid. Your father went to your room, but I said you were asleep. He locked the front

door, but I opened it again. When Bass came in he wanted
to call you, but I persuaded him to wait until morning."

Again she looked wistfully at her daughter.

" I'm all right, mamma," said Jennie encouragingly. " I'll
tell you all about it to-morrow. Go to bed. How does he
think Bass got out ? "

" He doesn't know. He thought maybe they just let him
go because he couldn't pay the fine."

Jennie laid her hand lovingly on her mother's shoulder.

" Go to bed," she said.

She was already years older in thought and act. She felt
as though she must help her mother now as well as herself.

The days which followed were ones of dreamy uncertainty
to Jennie. She went over in her mind these dramatic events
time and time and time and again. It was not such a difficult
matter to tell her mother that the Senator had talked again of
marriage, that he proposed to come and get her after his next
trip to Washington, that he had given her a hundred dollars
and intended to give her more, but of that other matter—the
one all-important thing, she could not bring herself to speak.
It was too sacred. The balance of the money that he had
promised her arrived by messenger the following day, four
hundred dollars in bills, with the admonition that she should
put it in a local bank. The ex-Senator explained that he
was already on his way to Washington, but that he would come
back or send for her. " Keep a stout heart," he wrote. " There
are better days in store for you."

Brander was gone, and Jennie's fate was really in the balance.
But her mind still retained all of the heart-innocence, and
unsophistication of her youth ; a certain gentle wistfulness
was the only outward change in her demeanour. He would
surely send for her. There was the mirage of a distant country
and wondrous scenes looming up in her mind. She had a
little fortune in the bank, more than she had ever dreamed of,
with which to help her mother. There were natural, girlish
anticipations of good still holding over, which made her less
apprehensive than she could otherwise possibly have been.
All nature, life, possibility was in the balance. It might turn
good, or ill, but with so inexperienced a soul it would not be
entirely evil until it was so.

How a mind under such uncertain circumstances could

retain so comparatively placid a vein is one of those marvels which find their explanation in the inherent trustfulness of the spirit of youth. It is not often that the minds of men retain the perceptions of their younger days. The marvel is not that one should thus retain, but that any should ever lose them. Go the world over, and after you have put away the wonder and tenderness of youth what is there left ? The few sprigs of green that sometimes invade the barrenness of your materialism, the few glimpses of summer which flash past the eye of the wintry soul, the half hours off during the long tedium of burrowing, these reveal to the hardened earth-seeker the universe which the youthful mind has with it always. No fear and no favour ; the open fields and the light upon the hills ; morning, noon, night ; stars, the bird-calls, the water's purl—these are the natural inheritance of the mind of the child. Men call it poetic, those who are hardened fanciful. In the days of their youth it was natural, but the receptiveness of youth has departed, and they cannot see.

How this worked out in her personal actions was to be seen only in a slightly accentuated wistfulness, a touch of which was in every task. Sometimes she would wonder that no letter came, but at the same time she would recall the fact that he had specified a few weeks, and hence the six that actually elapsed did not seem so long.

In the meanwhile the distinguished ex-Senator had gone light-heartedly to his conference with the President, he had joined in a pleasant round of social calls, and he was about to pay a short country visit to some friends in Maryland, when he was seized with a slight attack of fever, which confined him to his room for a few days. He felt a little irritated that he should be laid up just at this time, but never suspected that there was anything serious in his indisposition. Then the doctor discovered that he was suffering from a virulent form of typhoid, the ravages of which took away his senses for a time and left him very weak. He was thought to be convalescing, however, when just six weeks after he had last parted with Jennie, he was seized with a sudden attack of heart failure and never regained consciousness. Jennie remained blissfully ignorant of his illness, and did not even see the heavy-typed headlines of the announcement of his death until Bass came home that evening.

" Look here, Jennie," he said excitedly, " Brander's dead ! "
He held up the newspaper, on the first column of which was
printed in heavy block type :

### DEATH OF EX-SENATOR BRANDER

Sudden Passing of Ohio's Distinguished Son.
Succumbs to Heart Failure at the Arlington, in
Washington.

Recent attack of typhoid, from which he was thought to be
recovering, proves fatal.   Notable phases of a remarkable career.

Jennie looked at it in blank amazement.   " Dead ? " she
exclaimed.

" There it is in the paper," returned Bass, his tone being
that of one who is imparting a very interesting piece of news.
" He died at ten o'clock this morning."

## CHAPTER IX

JENNIE took the paper with but ill-concealed trembling, and went into the adjoining room. There she stood by the front window and looked at it again, a sickening sensation of dread holding her as though in a trance.

" He is dead," was all that her mind could formulate for the time, and as she stood there the voice of Bass recounting the fact to Gerhardt in the adjoining room sounded in her ears. " Yes, he is dead," she heard him say ; and once again she tried to get some conception of what it meant to her. But her mind seemed a blank.

A moment later Mrs. Gerhardt joined her. She had heard Bass's announcement, and had seen Jennie leave the room, but her trouble with Gerhardt over the Senator had caused her to be careful of any display of emotion. No conception of the real state of affairs ever having crossed her mind, she was only interested in seeing how Jennie would take this sudden annihilation of her hopes.

" Isn't it too bad ? " she said, with real sorrow. " To think that he should have to die just when he was going to do so much for you—for us all."

She paused, expecting some word of agreement, but Jennie remained unwontedly dumb.

" I wouldn't feel badly," continued Mrs. Gerhardt. " It can't be helped. He meant to do a good deal, but you mustn't think of that now. It's all over, and it can't be helped, you know."

She paused again, and still Jennie remained motionless and mute. Mrs. Gerhardt, seeing how useless her words were, concluded that Jennie wished to be alone, and she went away.

Still Jennie stood there, and now, as the real significance of the news began to formulate itself into consecutive thought, she began to realise the wretchedness of her position, its helplessness. She went into her bedroom and sat down upon the side of the bed, from which position she saw a very pale, distraught face staring at her from out of the small mirror. She looked at it uncertainly; could that really be her own countenance? "I'll have to go away," she thought, and began, with the courage of despair, to wonder what refuge would be open to her.

In the meantime the evening meal was announced, and, to maintain appearances, she went out and joined the family; the naturalness of her part was very difficult to sustain. Gerhardt observed her subdued condition without guessing the depth of emotion which it covered. Bass was too much interested in his own affairs to pay particular attention to anybody.

During the days that followed Jennie pondered over the difficulties of her position and wondered what she should do. Money she had, it was true; but no friends, no experience, no place to go. She had always lived with her family. She began to feel unaccountable sinkings of spirit, nameless and formless fears seemed to surround and haunt her. Once when she arose in the morning she felt an uncontrollable desire to cry, and frequently thereafter this feeling would seize upon her at the most inopportune times. Mrs. Gerhardt began to note her moods, and one afternoon she resolved to question her daughter.

"Now you must tell me what's the matter with you," she said quietly. "Jennie, you must tell your mother everything."

Jennie, to whom confession had seemed impossible, under the sympathetic persistence of her mother, broke down at last and made the fatal confession. Mrs. Gerhardt stood there, too dumb with misery to give vent to a word.

"Oh!" she said at last, a great wave of self-accusation sweeping over her, "it is all my fault. I might have known. But we'll do what we can." She broke down and sobbed aloud.

After a time she went back to the washing she had to do, and stood over her tub rubbing and crying. The tears ran down her cheeks and dropped into the suds. Once in a while she stopped and tried to dry her eyes with her apron, but they soon filled again.

Now that the first shock had passed, there came the vivid consciousness of ever-present danger. What would Gerhardt do if he learned the truth? He had often said that if ever one of his daughters should act like some of those he knew he would turn her out of doors. " She should not stay under my roof ! " he had exclaimed.

"I'm so afraid of your father," Mrs. Gerhardt often said to Jennie in this intermediate period. " I don't know what he'll say."

" Perhaps I'd better go away," suggested her daughter.

" No," she said ; " he needn't know just yet. Wait awhile." But in her heart of hearts she knew that the evil day could not be long postponed.

One day, when her own suspense had reached such a pitch that it could no longer be endured, Mrs. Gerhardt sent Jennie away with the children, hoping to be able to tell her husband before they returned. All the morning she fidgeted about, dreading the opportune moment and letting him retire to his slumber without speaking. When afternoon came she did not go out to work, because she could not leave with her painful duty unfulfilled. Gerhardt arose at four, and still she hesitated, knowing full well that Jennie would soon return and that the specially prepared occasion would then be lost. It is almost certain that she would not have had the courage to say anything if he himself had not brought up the subject of Jennie's appearance.

" She doesn't look well," he said. " There seems to be something the matter with her."

" Oh," began Mrs. Gerhardt, visibly struggling with her fears, and moved to make an end of it at any cost, " Jennie is in trouble. I don't know what to do. She——"

Gerhardt, who had unscrewed a door-lock and was trying to mend it, looked up sharply from his work.

" What do you mean ? " he asked.

Mrs. Gerhardt had her apron in her hands at the time, her nervous tendency to roll it coming upon her. She tried to summon sufficient courage to explain, but fear mastered her completely ; she lifted the apron to her eyes and began to cry.

Gerhardt looked at her and rose. He was a man with the Calvin type of face, rather spare, with skin sallow and discoloured as the result of age and work in the wind and rain. When he was surprised or angry sparks of light glittered in his eyes. He frequently pushed his hair back when he was troubled, and almost invariably walked the floor ; just now he looked alert and dangerous.

" What is that you say ? " he inquired in German, his voice straining to a hard note. " In trouble—has some one——" He paused and flung his hand upward. " Why don't you speak ? " he demanded.

" I never thought," went on Mrs. Gerhardt, frightened, and yet following her own train of thought, " that anything like that would happen to her. She was such a good girl. Oh ! " she concluded, " to think he should ruin Jennie."

" By thunder ! " shouted Gerhardt, giving way to a fury of feeling, " I thought so ! Brander ! Ha ! Your fine man ! That comes of letting her go running around at nights, buggy-riding, walking the streets. I thought so. God in heaven !——"

He broke from his dramatic attitude and struck out in a fierce stride across the narrow chamber, turning like a caged animal.

" Ruined ! " he exclaimed. " Ruined ! Ha ! So he has ruined her, has he ? "

Suddenly he stopped like an image jerked by a string. He was directly in front of Mrs. Gerhardt, who had retired to the table at the side of the wall, and was standing there pale with fear.

" He is dead now ! " he shouted, as if this fact had now first occurred to him. " He is dead ! "

He put both hands to his temples, as if he feared his brain would give way, and stood looking at her, the mocking irony of the situation seeming to burn in his brain like fire.

" Dead ! " he repeated, and Mrs. Gerhardt, fearing for the reason of the man, shrank still farther away, her wits taken up rather with the tragedy of the figure he presented than with the actual substance of his woe.

" He intended to marry her," she pleaded nervously. " He would have married her if he had not died."

" Would have ! " shouted Gerhardt, coming out of his trance at the sound of her voice. " Would have ! That's a fine thing to talk about now. Would have ! The hound ! May his soul burn in hell—the dog ! Ah, God, I hope— I hope— If I were not a Christian——" He clenched his hands, the awfulness of his passion shaking him like a leaf.

Mrs. Gerhardt burst into tears, and her husband turned away, his own feelings far too intense for him to have any sympathy with her. He walked to and fro, his heavy step shaking the kitchen floor. After a time he came back, a new phase of the dread calamity having offered itself to his mind.

" When did this happen ? " he demanded.

" I don't know," returned Mrs. Gerhardt, too terror-stricken to tell the truth. " I only found it out the other day."

" You lie ! " he exclaimed in his excitement. " You were always shielding her. It is your fault that she is where she is. If you had let me have my way there would have been no cause for our trouble to-night.

" A fine ending," he went on to himself. " A fine ending. My boy gets into jail ; my daughter walks the streets and gets herself talked about ; the neighbours come to me with open remarks about my children ; and now this scoundrel ruins her. By the God in heaven, I don't know what has got into my children !

" I don't know how it is," he went on, unconsciously commiserating himself. " I try, I try ! Every night I pray that the Lord will let me do right, but it is no use. I might work and work. My hands—look at them—are rough with work. All my life I have tried to be an honest man. Now—now——" His voice broke, and it seemed for a moment as if he would give way to tears. Suddenly he turned on his wife, the major passion of anger possessing him.

" You are the cause of this," he exclaimed. " You are the sole cause. If you had done as I told you to do this would not have happened. No, you wouldn't do that. She must go out ! out !! out !!! She has become a street-walker, that's what she has become. She has set herself right to go to hell. Let her go. I wash my hands of the whole thing. This is enough for me."

He made as if to go off to his little bedroom, but he had no sooner reached the door than he came back.

" She shall get out ! " he said electrically. " She shall not stay under my roof ! To-night ! At once ! I will not let her enter my door again. I will show her whether she will disgrace me or not ! "

" You mustn't turn her out on the streets to-night," pleaded Mrs. Gerhardt. " She has no place to go."

" To-night!" he repeated. " This very minute! Let her find a home. She did not want this one. Let her get out now. We will see how the world treats her." He walked out of the room, inflexible resolution fixed upon his rugged features.

At half-past five, when Mrs. Gerhardt was tearfully going about the duty of getting supper, Jennie returned. Her mother started when she heard the door open, for now she knew the storm would burst afresh. Her father met her on the threshold.

" Get out of my sight!" he said savagely. " You shall not stay another hour in my house. I don't want to see you any more. Get out!"

Jennie stood before him, pale, trembling a little, and silent. The children she had brought home with her crowded about in frightened amazement. Veronica and Martha, who loved her dearly, began to cry.

" What's the matter?" George asked, his mouth open in wonder.

" She shall get out," reiterated Gerhardt. " I don't want her under my roof. If she wants to be a street-walker, let her be one, but she shall not stay here. Pack your things," he added, staring at her.

Jennie had no word to say, but the children cried loudly.

" Be still," said Gerhardt. " Go into the kitchen."

He drove them all out and followed stubbornly himself.

Jennie went quietly to her room. She gathered up her few little belongings and began, with tears, to put them into a valise her mother brought her. The little girlish trinkets that she had accumulated from time to time she did not take. She saw them, but thought of her younger sisters, and let them stay. Martha and Veronica would have assisted her, but their father forbade them to go.

At six o'clock Bass came in, and seeing the nervous assembly in the kitchen, inquired what the trouble was.

Gerhardt looked at him grimly, but did not answer.

" What's the trouble?" insisted Bass. " What are you all sitting around for?"

" He is driving Jennie away," whispered Mrs. Gerhardt tearfully.

"What for ? " asked Bass, opening his eyes in astonishment.

" I shall tell you what for," broke in Gerhardt, still speaking in German. " Because she's a street walker, that's what for. She goes and gets herself ruined by a man thirty years older than she is, a man old enough to be her father. Let her get out of this. She shall not stay here another minute."

Bass looked about him, and the children opened their eyes. All felt clearly that something terrible had happened, even the little ones. None but Bass understood.

"What do you want to send her out to-night for ? " he inquired. " This is no time to send a girl out on the streets. Can't she stay here until morning ? "

" No," said Gerhardt.

" He oughtn't to do that," put in the mother.

" She goes now," said Gerhardt. " Let that be an end of it."

" Where is she going to go ? " insisted Bass.

" I don't know," Mrs. Gerhardt interpolated weakly.

Bass looked around, but did nothing until Mrs. Gerhardt motioned him toward the front door when her husband was not looking.

" Go in !  Go in ! " was the import of her gesture.

Bass went in, and then Mrs. Gerhardt dared to leave her work and follow. The children stayed awhile, but, one by one, even they slipped away, leaving Gerhardt alone. When he thought that time enough had elapsed he arose.

In the interval Jennie had been hastily coached by her mother.

Jennie should go to a private boarding-house somewhere and send back her address. Bass should not accompany her, but she should wait a little way up the street, and he would follow. When her father was away the mother might get to see her, or Jennie could come home. All else must be postponed until they could meet again.

While the discussion was still going on, Gerhardt came in.

" Is she going ? " he asked harshly.

" Yes," answered Mrs. Gerhardt, with her first and only note of defiance.

Bass said, " What's the hurry ? "  But Gerhardt frowned too mightily for him to venture on any further remonstrances.

Jennie entered, wearing her one good dress and carrying her valise. There was fear in her eyes, for she saw passing through a fiery ordeal, but she had become a woman. The strength of love was with her, the support of patience and the ruling sweetness of sacrifice. Silently she kissed her mother, while tears fell fast. Then she turned, and the door closed upon her as she went forth to a new life.

## CHAPTER X

THE world into which Jennie was thus unduly thrust forth was that in which virtue has always vainly struggled since time immemorial; for virtue is the wishing well and the doing well unto others. Virtue is that quality of generosity which offers itself willingly for another's service, and, being this, it is held by society to be nearly worthless. Sell yourself cheaply and you shall be used lightly and trampled under foot. Hold yourself dearly, however unworthily, and you will be respected. Society in the mass, lacks woefully in the matter of discrimination. Its one criterion is the opinion of others. Its one test that of self-preservation. Has he preserved his fortune? Has she preserved her purity? Only in rare instances and with rare individuals does there seem to be any guiding light from within.

Jennie had not sought to hold herself dear. Innate feeling in her made for self-sacrifice. She could not be readily corrupted by the world's selfish lessons on how to preserve oneself from the evil to come.

It is in such supreme moments that growth is greatest. It comes as with a vast surge, this feeling of strength and sufficiency. We may still tremble, the fear of doing wretchedly may linger, but we grow. Flashes of inspiration come to guide the soul. In nature there is no outside. When we are cast from a group or a condition we have still the companion-ship of all that is. Nature is not ungenerous. Its winds and stars are fellows with you. Let the soul be but gentle and receptive, and this vast truth will come home—not in set phrases, perhaps, but as a feeling, a comfort, which, after all, is the last essence of knowledge. In the universe peace is wisdom.

Jennie had hardly turned from the door when she was over-taken by Bass. "Give me your grip," he said; and then seeing that she was dumb with unutterable feeling, he added, "I think I know where I can get you a room."

He led the way to the southern part of the city, where they

were not known, and up to the door of an old lady whose parlour clock had been recently purchased from the instalment firm by whom he was now employed. She was not well off, he knew, and had a room to rent.

" Is that room of yours still vacant ? " he asked.

" Yes," she said, looking at Jennie.

" I wish you'd let my sister have it. We're moving away, and she can't go yet."

The old lady expressed her willingness, and Jennie was soon temporarily installed.

" Don't worry now," said Bass, who felt rather sorry for her. " This'll blow over. Ma said I should tell you not to worry. Come up to-morrow when he's gone."

Jennie said she would, and, after giving her further oral encouragement, he arranged with the old lady about board, and took his leave.

" It's all right now," he said encouragingly as he went out. " You'll come out all right. Don't worry. I've got to go back, but I'll come around in the morning."

He went away, and the bitter stress of it blew lightly over his head, for he was thinking that Jennie had made a mistake. This was shown by the manner in which he had asked her questions as they had walked together, and that in the face of her sad and doubtful mood.

" What'd you want to do that for ? " and " Didn't you ever think what you were doing ? " he persisted.

" Please don't ask me to-night," Jennie had said, which put an end to the sharpest form of his queries. She had no excuse to offer and no complaint to make. If any blame attached, very likely it was hers. His own misfortune and the family's and her sacrifice were alike forgotten.

Left alone in her strange abode, Jennie gave way to her saddened feelings. The shock and shame of being banished from her home overcame her, and she wept. Although of a naturally long-suffering and uncomplaining disposition, the catastrophic wind-up of all her hopes was too much for her. What was this element in life that could seize and overwhelm one as does a great wind ? Why this sudden intrusion of death to shatter all that had seemed most promising in life ?

As she thought over the past, a very clear recollection of

the details of her long relationship with Brander came back to her, and for all her suffering she could only feel a loving affection for him.    After all, he had not deliberately willed her any harm.    His kindness, his generosity—these things had been real.    He had been essentially a good man, and she was sorry— more for his sake than for her own—that his end had been so untimely.

These cogitations, while not at all reassuring, at least served to pass the night away, and the next morning Bass stopped on his way to work to say that Mrs. Gerhardt wished her to come home that same evening.    Gerhardt would not be present, and they could talk it over.    She spent the day lonesomely enough, but when night fell her spirits brightened, and at a quarter of eight she set out.

There was not much of comforting news to tell her. Gerhardt was still in a direfully angry and outraged mood. He had already decided to throw up his place on the following Saturday and go to Youngstown.    Any place was better than Columbus after this ; he could never expect to hold up his head here again.    Its memories were odious.    He would go away now, and if he succeeded in finding work the family should follow, a decision which meant the abandoning of the little home.    He was not going to try to meet the mortgage on the house—he could not hope to.

At the end of the week Gerhardt took his leave, Jennie returned home, and for a time at least there was a restoration of the old order, a condition which, of course, could not endure.

Bass saw it.    Jennie's trouble and its possible consequences weighed upon him disagreeably.    Columbus was no place to stay.    Youngstown was no place to go.    If they should all move away to some larger city it would be much better.

He pondered over the situation, and hearing that a manu-facturing boom was on in Cleveland, he thought it might be wise to try his luck there.    If he succeeded, the others might follow.    If Gerhardt still worked on in Youngstown, as he was now doing, and the family came to Cleveland, it would save Jennie from being turned out in the streets.

Bass waited a little while before making up his mind, but finally announced his purpose.

" I believe I'll go up to Cleveland," he said to his mother one evening as she was getting supper.

"Why?" she asked, looking up uncertainly. She was rather afraid that Bass would desert her.

"I think I can get work there," he returned. "We oughtn't to stay in this darned old town."

"Don't swear," she returned reprovingly.

"Oh, I know," he said, "but it's enough to make any one swear. We've never had anything but rotten luck here. I'm going to go, and maybe if I get anything we can all move. We'd be better off if we'd get some place where people don't know us. We can't be anything here."

Mrs. Gerhardt listened with a strong hope for a betterment of their miserable life creeping into her heart. If Bass would only do this. If he would go and get work, and come to her rescue, as a strong bright young son might, what a thing it would be! They were in the rapids of a life which was moving toward a dreadful calamity. If only something would happen.

"Do you think you could get something to do?" she asked interestedly.

"I ought to," he said. "I've never looked for a place yet that I didn't get it. Other fellows have gone up there and done all right. Look at the Millers."

He shoved his hands into his pockets and looked out the window.

"Do you think you could get along until I try my hand up there?" he asked.

"I guess we could," she replied. "Papa's at work now and we have some money that, that——" she hesitated to name the source, so ashamed was she of their predicament.

"Yes, I know," said Bass, grimly.

"We won't have to pay any rent here before fall and then we'll have to give it up anyhow," she added.

She was referring to the mortgage on the house, which fell due the next September and which unquestionably could not be met. "If we could move away from here before then, I guess we could get along."

"I'll do it," said Bass determinedly. "I'll go."

Accordingly, he threw up his place at the end of the month, and the day after he left for Cleveland.

## CHAPTER XI

THE incidents of the days that followed, relating as they did peculiarly to Jennie, were of an order which the morality of our day has agreed to taboo.

Certain processes of the all-mother, the great artificing wisdom of the power that works and weaves in silence and in darkness, when viewed in the light of the established opinion of some of the little individuals created by it, are considered very vile. We turn our faces away from the creation of life as if that were the last thing that man should dare to interest himself in, openly.

It is curious that a feeling of this sort should spring up in a world whose very essence is generative, the vast process dual, and where wind, water, soil, and light alike minister to the fruition of that which is all that we are. Although the whole earth, not we alone, is moved by passions hymeneal, and everything terrestrial has come into being by the one common road, yet there is that ridiculous tendency to close the eyes and turn away the head as if there were something unclean in nature itself. "Conceived in iniquity and born in sin," is the unnatural interpretation put upon the process by the extreme religionist, and the world, by its silence, gives assent to a judgment so marvellously warped.

Surely there is something radically wrong in this attitude. The teachings of philosophy and the deductions of biology should find more practical applications in the daily reasoning of man. No process is vile, no condition is unnatural. The accidental variation from a given social practice does not necessarily entail sin. No poor little earthling, caught in the enormous grip of chance, and so swerved from the established customs of men, could possibly be guilty of that depth of vileness which the attitude of the world would seem to predicate so inevitably.

Jennie was now to witness the unjust interpretation of that wonder of nature, which, but for Brander's death, might have been consecrated and hallowed as one of the ideal functions of life. Although herself unable to distinguish the separateness of this from every other normal process of life, yet was she made to feel, by the actions of all about her, that degradation was her portion and sin the foundation as well as the condition of her state. Almost, not quite, it was sought to extinguish the affection, the consideration the care which, afterward, the world would demand of her, for her child. Almost, not quite, was the budding and essential love looked upon as evil. Although her punishment was neither the gibbet nor the jail of a few hundred years before, yet the ignorance and immobility of the human beings about her made it impossible for them to see anything in her present condition, but a vile and premeditated infraction of the social code, the punishment of which was ostracism. All she could do now was to shun the scornful gaze of men, and to bear in silence the great change that was coming upon her. Strangely enough, she felt no useless remorse, no vain regrets. Her heart was pure, and she was conscious that it was filled with peace. Sorrow there was, it is true, but only a mellow phase of it, a vague uncertainty and wonder, which would sometimes cause her eyes to fill with tears.

You have heard the wood-dove calling in the lone stillness of the summertime ; you have found the unheeded brooklet singing and babbling where no ear comes to hear. Under dead leaves and snow-banks the delicate arbutus unfolds its simple blossom, answering some heavenly call for colour. So, too, this other flower of womanhood.

Jennie was left alone, but, like the wood-dove, she was a voice of sweetness in the summertime. Going about her household duties, she was content to wait, without a murmur, the fulfilment of that process for which, after all, she was but the sacrificial implement. When her duties were lightest she was content to sit in quiet meditation, the marvel of life holding her as in a trance. When she was hardest pressed to aid her mother, she would sometimes find herself quietly singing, the pleasure of work lifting her out of herself. Always she was content to face the future with a serene and unfaltering courage. It is not so with all women. Nature is unkind in permitting the minor type to bear a child at all. The larger natures in their maturity welcome motherhood, see in it the immense possibilities of racial fulfilment, and find joy and satisfaction in being the hand-maiden of so immense a purpose.

Jennie, a child in years, was potentially a woman physically and mentally, but not yet come into rounded conclusions as to life and her place in it. The great situation which had forced her into this anomalous position was from one point of view a tribute to her individual capacity. It proved her courage, the largeness of her sympathy, her willingness to sacrifice for what she considered a worthy cause. That it resulted in an unexpected consequence which placed upon her a larger and more complicated burden, was due to the fact that her sense of self-protection had not been commensurate with her emotions. There were times when the prospective coming of the child gave her a sense of fear and confusion, because she did not know, but that the child might eventually reproach her ; but there was always that saving sense of eternal justice in life which would not permit her to be utterly crushed. To her way of thinking, people were not intentionally cruel. Vague thoughts of sympathy and divine goodness permeated her soul. Life at worst or best was beautiful—had always been so.

These thoughts did not come to her all at once, but through the months during which she watched and waited. It was a wonderful thing to be a mother, even under these untoward conditions. She felt that she would love this child, would be a good mother to it if life permitted. That was the problem—what would life permit ?

There were many things to be done—clothes to be made ; certain provisions of hygiene and diet to be observed. One of her fears was that Gerhardt might unexpectedly return, but he did not. The old family doctor who had nursed the various members of the Gerhardt family through their multitudinous ailments—Doctor Ellwanger—was taken into consultation, and he gave sound and practical advice. Despite his Lutheran upbringing, the practice of medicine in a large and kindly way had led him to the conclusion that there are more things in heaven and earth than are dreamed of in our philosophies and in our small neighbourhood relationships. " So it is," he observed to Mrs. Gerhardt when she confided to him nervously what the trouble was. " Well, you mustn't worry. These things happen in more places than you think. If you knew as much about life as I do, and about your neighbours, you would not cry. Your girl will be all right. She is very healthy. She can go away somewhere afterward, and people will never know. Why should you worry about what your neighbours think. It is not so uncommon as you imagine."

Mrs. Gerhardt marvelled. He was such a wise man. It gave her a little courage. As for Jennie, she listened to his advice with interest and without fear. She wanted things not so much for herself as for her child, and she was anxious to do whatever she was told. The doctor was curious to know who the father was ; when informed he lifted his eyes. " Indeed," he commented. " That ought to be a bright baby."

There came the final hour when the child was ushered into the world. It was Doctor Ellwanger who presided, assisted by the mother, who, having brought forth six herself, knew exactly what to do. There was no difficulty, and at the first cry of the new-born infant there awakened in Jennie a tremendous yearning toward it. This was *her* child ! It was weak and feeble—a little girl, and it needed her care. She took it to her breast, when it had been bathed and swaddled, with a tremendous sense of satisfaction and joy. This was her child, her little girl. She wanted to live to be able to work for it, and rejoiced, even in her weakness, that she was so strong. Doctor Ellwanger predicted a quick recovery. He thought two weeks would be the outside limit of her need to stay in bed. As a matter of fact, in ten days she was up and about, as vigorous and healthy as ever. She had been born with strength and with that nurturing quality which makes the ideal mother.

The great crisis had passed, and now life went on much as before. The children, outside of Bass, were too young to understand fully, and had been deceived by the story that Jennie was married to Senator Brander, who had died. They did not know that a child was coming until it was there. The neighbours were feared by Mrs. Gerhardt, for they were ever watchful and really knew all. Jennie would never have braved this local atmosphere except for the advice of Bass, who, having secured a place in Cleveland some time before, had written that he thought when she was well enough it would be advisable for the whole family to seek a new start in Cleveland. Things were flourishing there. Once away they would never hear of their present neighbours and Jennie could find something to do. So she stayed at home.

## CHAPTER XII

BASS was no sooner in Cleveland than the marvel of that growing city was sufficient to completely restore his equanimity of soul and to stir up new illusions as to the possibility of rehabilitation for himself and his family. "If only they could come here," he thought. "If only they could all get work and do right." Here was no evidence of any of their recent troubles, no acquaintance who could suggest by their mere presence the troubles of the past. All was business, all activity. The very turning of the corner seemed to rid one of old times and crimes. It was as if a new world existed in every block.

He soon found a place in a cigar store, and, after working a few weeks, he began to write home the cheering ideas he had in mind. Jennie ought to come as soon as she was able, and then, if she found something to do, the others might follow. There was plenty of work for girls of her age. She could live in the same house with him temporarily; or maybe they could take one of the fifteen-dollar-a-month cottages that were for rent. There were big general furnishing houses, where one could buy everything needful for a small house on very easy monthly terms. His mother could come and keep house for them. They would be in a clean, new atmosphere, unknown and untalked about. They could start life all over again; they could be decent, honourable, prosperous.

Filled with this hope and the glamour which new scenes and new environment invariably throw over the unsophisticated mind, he wrote a final letter, in which he suggested that Jennie should come at once. This was when the baby was six months old. There were theatres here, he said, and beautiful streets. Vessels from the lakes came into the heart of the city. It was a wonderful city, and growing very fast. It was thus that the new life appealed to him.

The effect which all this had upon Mrs. Gerhardt, Jennie, and the rest of the family was phenomenal. Mrs. Gerhardt, long weighed upon by the misery which Jennie's error had entailed, was for taking measures for carrying out this plan at once. So buoyant was her natural temperament that she was completely carried away by the glory of Cleveland, and already saw fulfilled therein not only her own desires for a nice home, but the prosperous advancement of her children. " Of course they could get work," she said. Bass was right. She had always wanted Gerhardt to go to some large city, but he would not. Now it was necessary, and they would go and become better off than they ever had been.

And Gerhardt did take this view of the situation. In answer to his wife's letter he wrote that it was not advisable for him to leave his place, but if Bass saw a way for them, it might be a good thing to go. He was the more ready to acquiesce in the plan for the simple reason that he was half distracted with the worry of supporting the family and of paying the debts already outstanding. Every week he laid by five dollars out of his salary, which he sent in the form of a postal order to Mrs. Gerhardt. Three dollars he paid for board, and fifty cents he kept for spending money, church dues, a little tobacco and occasionally a glass of beer. Every week he put a dollar and a half in a little iron bank against a rainy day. His room was a bare corner in the topmost loft of the mill. To this he would ascend after sitting alone on the doorstep of the mill in this lonely, forsaken neighbourhood, until nine o'clock of an evening ; and here, amid the odour of machinery wafted up from the floor below, by the light of a single tallow candle, he would conclude his solitary day, reading his German paper, folding his hands and thinking, kneeling by an open window in the shadow of the night, to say his prayers, and silently stretching himself to rest. Long were the days, dreary the prospect. Still he lifted his hands in utmost faith to God, praying that his sins might be forgiven and that he might be vouchsafed a few more years of comfort and of happy family life.

So the momentous question was finally decided. There was the greatest longing and impatience among the children, and Mrs. Gerhardt shared their emotions in a suppressed way. Jennie was to go first, as Bass had suggested ; later on they would all follow.

When the hour came for Jennie's departure there was great excitement in the household.

" How long you going to be 'fore you send for us? " was Martha's inquiry, several times repeated.

" Tell Bass to hurry up," said the eager George.

" I want to go to Cleveland, I want to go to Cleveland," Veronica was caught singing to herself.

" Listen to her," exclaimed George, sarcastically.

" Aw, you hush up," was her displeased rejoinder.

When the final hour came, however, it required all of Jennie's strength to go through with the farewells. Though everything was being done in order to bring them together again under better conditions, she could not help feeling depressed. Her little one, now six months old, was being left behind. The great world was to her one undiscovered bourne. It frightened her.

" You mustn't worry, Ma," she found courage enough to say. " I'll be all right. I'll write you just as soon as I get there. It won't be so very long."

But when it came to bending over her baby for the last time her courage went out like a blown lamp. Stooping over the cradle in which the little one was resting, she looked into its face with passionate, motherly yearning.

" Is it going to be a good little girl ? " she cooed.

Then she caught it up into her arms, and hugging it closely to her neck and bosom, she buried her face against its little body. Mrs. Gerhardt saw that she was trembling.

" Come now," she said, coaxingly, " you mustn't carry on so. She will be all right with me. I'll take care of her. If you're going to act this way, you'd better not try to go at all."

Jennie lifted her head, her blue eyes wet with tears, and handed the little one to her mother.

" I can't help it," she said, half crying, half smiling.

Quickly she kissed her mother and the children ; then she hurried out.

As she went down the street with George she looked back and bravely waved her hand. Mrs. Gerhardt responded, noticing how much more like a woman she looked. It had been necessary to invest some of her money in new clothes to wear on the train. She had selected a neat, ready-made suit of brown, which fitted her nicely. She wore the skirt of this with a white shirtwaist, and a sailor hat with a white veil wound around it in such fashion that it could be easily drawn over her face. As she went farther and farther away Mrs. Gerhardt followed her lovingly with her glance ; and when she disappeared from view she said tenderly, through her own tears :

" I'm glad she looked so nice, anyhow."

# CHAPTER XIII

BASS met Jennie at the depôt in Cleveland and talked hopefully of the prospects. " The first thing is to get work," he began while the jingling sounds and the changing odors which the city thrust upon her were confusing and almost benumbing her senses. " Get something to do. It doesn't matter what, so long as you get something. If you don't get more than three or four dollars a week, it will pay the rent. Then, with what George can earn, when he comes, and what Pop sends, we can get along all right. It'll be better than being down in that hole," he concluded.

" Yes," said Jennie, vaguely, her mind so hypnotised by the new display of life about her that she could not bring it forcibly to bear upon the topic under discussion. " I know what you mean. I'll get something."

She was much older now, in understanding if not in years. The ordeal through which she had so recently passed had aroused in her a clearer conception of the responsibilities of life. Her mother was always in her mind, her mother and the children. In particular Martha and Veronica must have a better opportunity to do for themselves than she had had. They should be dressed better ; they ought to be kept longer in school ; they must have more companionship, more opportunity to broaden their lives.

Cleveland, like every other growing city at this time, was crowded with those who were seeking employment. New enterprises were constantly springing up, but those who were seeking to fulfil the duties they provided were invariably in excess of the demand. A stranger coming to the city might walk into a small position of almost any kind on the very day he arrived ; and he might as readily wander in search of employment for weeks and even months. Bass suggested the shops and department stores as a first field in which to inquire. The factories and other avenues of employment were to be her second choice.

" Don't pass a place, though," he had cautioned her, " if

you think there's any chance of getting anything to do. Go right in."

" What must I say ? " asked Jennie, nervously.

" Tell them you want work. You don't care what you do to begin with."

In compliance with this advice, Jennie set out the very first day, and was rewarded by some very chilly experiences. Where-ever she went, no one seemed to want any help. She applied at the stores, the factories, the little shops that lined the outlying thoroughfares, but was always met by a rebuff. As a last resource she turned to housework, although she had hoped to avoid that ; and, studying the want columns, she selected four which seemed more promising than the others. To these she decided to apply. One had already been filled when she arrived, but the lady who came to the door was so taken by her appearance that she invited her in and questioned her as to her ability.

" I wish you had come a little earlier," she said. " I like you better than I do the girl I have taken. Leave me your address, anyhow."

Jennie went away, smiling at her reception. She was not quite so youthful looking as she had been before her recent trouble, but the thinner cheeks and the slightly deeper eyes added to the pensiveness and delicacy of her countenance. She was a model of neatness. Her clothes, all newly cleaned and ironed before leaving home, gave her a fresh and inviting appearance. There was growth coming to her in the matter of height, but already in appearance and intelligence she looked to be a young woman of twenty. Best of all, she was of that naturally sunny disposition, which, in spite of toil and privation kept her always cheerful. Any one in need of a servant-girl or house companion would have been delighted to have had her.

The second place at which she applied was a large residence in Euclid Avenue ; it seemed far too imposing for anything she might have to offer in the way of services, but having come so far she decided to make the attempt. The servant who met her at the door directed her to wait a few moments, and finally ushered her into the boudoir of the mistress of the house on the second floor. The latter, a Mrs. Bracebridge, a prepossessing brunette of the conventionally fashionable type, had a keen eye for feminine values and was impressed rather favourably with Jennie. She talked with her a little while, and finally decided to try her in the general capacity of maid.

" I will give you four dollars a week, and you can sleep here if you wish," said Mrs. Bracebridge.

Jennie explained that she was living with her brother, and would soon have her family with her.

" Oh, very well," replied her mistress. " Do as you like about that. Only I expect you to be here promptly."

She wished her to remain for the day and to begin her duties at once, and Jennie agreed. Mrs. Bracebridge provided her a dainty cap and apron, and then spent some little time in instructing her in her duties. Her principal work would be to wait on her mistress, to brush her hair and to help her dress. She was also to answer the bell, wait on the table if need be, and do any other errand which her mistress might indicate. Mrs. Bracebridge seemed a little hard and formal to her prospective servant, but for all that Jennie admired the dash and go and the obvious executive capacity of her employer.

At eight o'clock that evening Jennie was dismissed for the day. She wondered if she could be of any use in such a household, and marvelled that she had got along as well as she had. Her mistress had set her to cleaning her jewellery and boudoir ornaments as an opening task, and though she had worked steadily and diligently, she had not finished by the time she left. She hurried away to her brother's apartment delighted to be able to report that she had found a situation. Now her mother could come to Cleveland. Now she could have her baby with her. Now they could really begin that new life which was to be so much better and finer and sweeter than anything they had ever had before.

At Bass's suggestion Jennie wrote her mother to come at once, and a week or so later a suitable house was found and rented. Mrs. Gerhardt, with the aid of the children, packed up the simple belongings of the family, including a single vanload of furniture, and at the end of a fortnight they were on their way to the new home.

Mrs. Gerhardt always had had a keen desire for a really comfortable home. Solid furniture, upholstered and trimmed, a thick soft carpet of some warm, pleasing colour, plenty of chairs, settees, pictures, a lounge, and a piano—she had wanted these nice things all her life, but her circumstances had never been good enough for her hopes to be realised. Still she did not despair. Some day, maybe before she died these things would be added to her, and she would be happy. Perhaps her chance was coming now.

Arrived at Cleveland, this feeling of optimism was encouraged by the sight of Jennie's cheerful face. Bass assured her that they would get along all right. He took them out to the house, and George was shown the way to go back to the depôt and have the freight looked after. Mrs. Gerhardt had still fifty dollars left out of the money which Senator Brander had sent to Jennie, and with this a way of getting a little extra furniture on the instalment plan was provided. Bass had already paid the first month's rent, and Jennie had spent her evenings for the last few days in washing the windows and floors of this new house and in getting it into a state of perfect cleanliness. Now, when the first night fell, they had two new mattresses and comfortables spread upon a clean floor ; a new lamp, purchased from one of the near-by stores, a single box, borrowed by Jennie from a grocery store, for cleaning purposes, upon which Mrs. Gerhardt could sit, and some sausages and bread to stay them until morning. They talked and planned for the future until nine o'clock came, when all but Jennie and her mother retired. These two talked on, the burden of responsibilites resting on the daughter. Mrs. Gerhardt had come to feel in a way dependent upon her.

In the course of a week the entire cottage was in order, with a half-dozen pieces of new furniture, a new carpet, and some necessary kitchen utensils. The most disturbing thing was the need of a new cooking-stove, the cost of which added greatly to the bill. The younger children were entered at the public school, but it was decided that George must find some employment. Both Jennie and her mother felt the injustice of this keenly, but knew no way of preventing the sacrifice.

" We will let him go to school next year if we can," said Jennie.

Auspiciously as the new life seemed to have begun, the closeness with which their expenses were matching their income was an ever-present menace. Bass, originally very

generous in his propositions, soon announced that he felt
four dollars a week for his room and board to be a sufficient
contribution from himself.  Jennie gave everything she earned
and protested that she did not stand in need of anything,
so long as the baby was properly taken care of.  George
secured a place as an overgrown cash-boy, and brought in two
dollars and fifty cents a week, all of which, at first, he gladly
contributed.  Later on he was allowed the fifty cents for
himself as being meet and just.  Gerhardt, from his lonely
post of labour, contributed five dollars by mail, always arguing
that a little money ought to be saved in order that his honest
debts back in Columbus might be paid.  Out of this total
income of fifteen dollars a week all of these individuals had
to be fed and clothed, the rent paid, coal purchased, and the
regular monthly instalment of three dollars paid on the
outstanding furniture bill of fifty dollars.

How it was done, those comfortable individuals, who frequently discuss the social aspects of poverty, might well trouble
to inform themselves.  Rent, coal, and light alone consumed
the goodly sum of twenty dollars a month ; food, another
unfortunately necessary item, used up twenty-five more ;
clothes, instalments, dues, occasional items of medicine and
the like, were met out of the remaining eleven dollars—how,
the ardent imagination of the comfortable reader can guess.
It was done, however, and for a time the hopeful members
considered that they were doing fairly well.

During this period the little family presented a picture of
honourable and patient toil, which was interesting to contemplate.  Every day Mrs. Gerhardt, who worked like a servant
and who received absolutely no compensation either in clothes,
amusements, or anything else, arose in the morning while
the others slept, and built the fire.  Then she took up the
task of getting the breakfast.  Often as she moved about
noiselessly in her thin, worn slippers, cushioned with pieces of
newspaper to make them fit, she looked in on Jennie, Bass, and
George, wrapped in their heavy slumbers, and with that
divine sympathy which is born in heaven she wished that
they did not need to rise so early or to work so hard.  Sometimes she would pause before touching her beloved Jennie,
gaze at her white face, so calm in sleep, and lament that life
had not dealt more kindly with her.  Then she would lay her

hand gently upon her shoulder and whisper, " Jennie, Jennie," until the weary sleeper would wake.

When they arose breakfast was always ready. When they returned at night supper was waiting. Each of the children received a due share of Mrs. Gerhardt's attention. The little baby was closely looked after by her. She protested that she needed neither clothes nor shoes so long as one of the children would run errands for her.

Jennie, of all the children, fully understood her mother ; she alone strove, with the fullness of a perfect affection, to ease her burden.

" Ma, you let me do this."

" Now, ma, I'll 'tend to that."

" You go sit down, ma."

These were the every-day expressions of the enduring affection that existed between them. Always there was perfect understanding between Jennie and her mother, and as the days passed this naturally widened and deepened. Jennie could not bear to think of her as being always confined to the house. Daily she thought as she worked of that humble home where her mother was watching and waiting. How she longed to give her those comforts which she had always craved !

## CHAPTER XIV

THE days spent in the employ of the Bracebridge household were of a broadening character. This great house was a school to Jennie, not only in the matter of dress and manners, but as formulating a theory of existence. Mrs. Bracebridge and her husband were the last word in the matter of self-sufficiency, taste in the matter of appointments, care in the matter of dress, good form in the matter of reception, entertainment, and the various usages of social life. Now and then, apropos of nothing save her own mood, Mrs. Bracebridge would indicate her philosophy of life in an epigram.

" Life is a battle, my dear. If you gain anything you will have to fight for it."

" In my judgment it is silly not to take advantage of any aid which will help you to be what you want to be." (This while applying a faint suggestion of rouge.)

" Most people are born silly. They are exactly what they are capable of being. I despise lack of taste ; it is the worst crime."

Most of these worldly-wise counsels were not given directly to Jennie. She overheard them, but to her quiet and reflective mind they had their import. Like seeds fallen upon good ground, they took root and grew. She began to get a faint perception of hierarchies and powers. They were not for her, perhaps, but they were in the world, and if fortune were kind one might better one's state. She worked on, wondering, however, just how better fortune might come to her. Who would have her to wife knowing her history ? How could she ever explain the existence of her child ?

Her child, her child, the one transcendent, gripping theme of joy and fear. If she could only do something for it—sometime somehow !

For the first winter things went smoothly enough. By the closest economy the children were clothed and kept in school, the rent paid, and the instalments met. Once it looked as though there might be some difficulty about the continuance of the home life, and that was when Gerhardt wrote that he would be home for Christmas. The mill was to close down for a short period at that time. He was naturally anxious to see what the new life of his family at Cleveland was like.

Mrs. Gerhardt would have welcomed his return with unalloyed pleasure had it not been for the fear she entertained of his creating a scene. Jennie talked it over with her mother, and Mrs. Gerhardt in turn spoke of it to Bass, whose advice was to brave it out.

"Don't worry," he said ; "he won't do anything about it. I'll talk to him if he says anything."

The scene did occur, but it was not so unpleasant as Mrs. Gerhardt had feared. Gerhardt came home during the afternoon, while Bass, Jennie, and George were at work. Two of the younger children went to the train to meet him. When he entered Mrs. Gerhardt greeted him affectionately, but she trembled for the discovery which was sure to come. Her suspense was not for long. Gerhardt opened the front bedroom door only a few minutes after he arrived. On the white counterpane of the bed was a pretty child, sleeping. He could not but know on the instant whose it was, but he pretended ignorance.

"Whose child is that ? " he questioned.

"It's Jennie's," said Mrs. Gerhardt, weakly.

"When did that come here ? "

"Not so very long ago," answered the mother, nervously.

"I guess she is here, too," he declared, contemptuously, refusing to pronounce her name, a fact which he had already anticipated.

"She's working in a family," returned his wife in a pleading tone. "She's doing so well now. She had no place to go. Let her alone."

Gerhardt had received a light since he had been away. Certain inexplicable thoughts and feelings had come to him in his religious meditations. In his prayers he had admitted to the All-seeing that he might have done differently by his daughter. Yet he could not make up his mind how to treat her for the future. She had committed a great sin ; it was impossible to get away from that.

When Jennie came home that night a meeting was

unavoidable. Gerhardt saw her coming, and pretended to be deeply engaged in a newspaper. Mrs. Gerhardt, who had begged him not to ignore Jennie entirely, trembled for fear he would say or do something which would hurt her feelings.

" She is coming now," she said, crossing to the door of the front room, where he was sitting; but Gerhardt refused to look up. " Speak to her, anyhow," was her last appeal before the door opened; but he made no reply.

When Jennie came in her mother whispered, " He is in the front room."

Jennie paled, put her thumb to her lip and stood irresolute, not knowing how to meet the situation.

" Has he seen ? "

Jennie paused as she realised from her mother's face and nod that Gerhardt knew of the child's existence.

" Go ahead," said Mrs. Gerhardt ; " it's all right. He won't say anything."

Jennie finally went to the door, and, seeing her father, his brow wrinkled as if in serious but not unkindly thought, she hesitated, but made her way forward.

" Papa," she said, unable to formulate a definite sentence.

Gerhardt looked up, his greyish-brown eyes a study under their heavy sandy lashes. At the sight of his daughter he weakened internally; but with the self-adjusted armour of resolve about him he showed no sign of pleasure at seeing her. All the forces of his conventional understanding of morality and his naturally sympathetic and fatherly disposition were battling within him, but, as in so many cases where the average mind is concerned, convention was temporarily the victor.

" Yes," he said.

" Won't you forgive me, Papa ? "

" I do," he returned grimly.

She hesitated a moment, and then stepped forward, for what purpose he well understood.

" There," he said, pushing her gently away, as her lips barely touched his grizzled cheek.

It had been a frigid meeting.

When Jennie went out into the kitchen after this very trying ordeal she lifted her eyes to her waiting mother and tried to make it seem as though all had been well, but her emotional disposition got the better of her.

" Did he make up to you ? " her mother was about to ask ; but the words were only half out of her mouth before her daughter sank down into one of the chairs close to the kitchen table and, laying her head on her arm, burst forth into soft, convulsive, inaudible sobs.

"Now, now," said Mrs. Gerhardt.   " There now, don't cry. What did he say ? "

It was some time before Jennie recovered herself sufficiently to answer.   Her mother tried to treat the situation lightly.

" I wouldn't feel bad," she said.   " He'll get over it.   It's his way."

## CHAPTER XV

THE return of Gerhardt brought forward the child question in all its bearings. He could not help considering it from the standpoint of a grandparent, particularly since it was a human being possessed of a soul. He wondered if it had been baptised. Then he inquired.

"No, not yet," said his wife, who had not forgotten this duty, but had been uncertain whether the little one would be welcome in the faith.

"No, of course not," sneered Gerhardt, whose opinion of his wife's religious devotion was not any too great. "Such carelessness! Such irreligion! That is a fine thing."

He thought it over a few moments, and felt that this evil should be corrected at once.

"It should be baptised," he said. "Why don't she take it and have it baptised?"

Mrs. Gerhardt reminded him that some one would have to stand godfather to the child and there was no way to have the ceremony performed without confessing the fact that it was without a legitimate father.

Gerhardt listened to this, and it quieted him for a few moments, but his religion was something which he could not see put in the background by any such difficulty. How would the Lord look upon quibbling like this? It was not Christian, and it was his duty to attend to the matter. It must be taken, forthwith, to the church, Jennie, himself, and his wife accompanying it as sponsors; or, if he did not choose to condescend thus far to his daughter, he must see that it was baptised when she was not present. He brooded over this difficulty, and finally decided that the ceremony should take place on one of these week-days, between Christmas and New Year's, when Jennie would be at her work. This proposal he broached to his wife, and, receiving her approval, he made his next announcement. "It has no name," he said.

Jennie and her mother had talked over this very matter,

and Jennie had expressed a preference for Vesta. Now her mother made bold to suggest it as her own choice.

" How would Vesta do ? "

Gerhardt heard this with indifference. Secretly he had settled the question in his own mind. He had a name in store, left over from the halcyon period of his youth, and never opportunely available in the case of his own children—Wilhelmina. Of course he had no idea of unbending in the least toward his small granddaughter. He merely liked the name, and the child ought to be grateful to get it. With a far-off, gingery air he brought forward this first offering upon the altar of natural affection, for offering it was, after all.

" That is nice," he said, forgetting his indifference. " But how would Wilhelmina do ? "

Mrs. Gerhardt did not dare cross him when he was thus unconsciously weakening. Her woman's tact came to the rescue.

" We might give her both names," she compromised.

" It makes no difference to me," he replied, drawing back into the shell of opposition from which he had been inadvertently drawn. " Just so she is baptised."

Jennie heard of this with pleasure, for she was anxious that the child should have every advantage, religious or otherwise, that it was possible to obtain. She took great pains to starch and iron the clothes it was to wear on the appointed day.

Gerhardt sought out the minister of the nearest Lutheran church, a round-headed, thick-set theologian of the most formal type to whom he stated his errand.

" Your grandchild ? " inquired the minister.

" Yes," said Gerhardt, " her father is not here."

" So," replied the minister, looking at him curiously.

Gerhardt was not to be disturbed in his purpose. He explained that he and his wife would bring her. The minister, realising the probable difficulty, did not question him further.

" The church cannot refuse to baptise her so long as you, as grandparent, are willing to stand sponsor for her," he said.

Gerhardt came away, hurt by the shadow of disgrace in which he felt himself involved, but satisfied that he had done his duty. Now he would take the child and have it baptised and when that was over his present responsibility would cease.

When it came to the hour of the baptism, however, he found that another influence was working to guide him into greater interest and responsibility. The stern religion with which he was enraptured, its insistence upon a higher law, was there, and he heard again the precepts which had helped to bind him to his own children.

" Is it your intention to educate this child in the knowledge and love of the gospel ? " asked the black-gowned minister, as they stood before him in the silent little church whither they had brought the infant ; he was reading from the form provided for such occasions. Gerhardt answered, " Yes," and Mrs. Gerhardt added her affirmative.

" Do you engage to use all necessary care and diligence, by prayerful instruction, admonition, example, and discipline that this child may renounce and avoid everything that is evil and that she may keep God's will and commandments as declared in His sacred word ? "

A thought flashed through Gerhardt's mind as the words were uttered of how it had fared with his own children. They, too, had been thus sponsored. They too, had heard his solemn pledge to care for their spiritual welfare. He was silent.

" We do," prompted the minister.

" We do," repeated Gerhardt and his wife weakly.

" Do you now dedicate this child by the rite of baptism unto the Lord, who brought it."

" We do."

" And, finally, if you can conscientiously declare before God that the faith to which you have assented is your faith, and that the solemn promises you have made are the serious resolutions of your heart, please to announce the same in the presence of God, by saying ' Yes.' "

" Yes," they replied.

" I baptise thee, Wilhelmina Vesta," concluded the minister, stretching out his hand over her, " in the name of the Father and of the Son and of the Holy Ghost. Let us pray."

Gerhardt bent his grey head and followed with humble reverence the beautiful invocation which followed :

" Almighty and everlasting God ! we adore Thee as the great Parent of the children of men, as the Father of our spirits and the Former of our bodies. We praise Thee for giving existence to this infant and for preserving her until this day. We bless Thee that she is called to virtue and glory, that she has now been dedicated to Thee, and brought within the pale of the Christian Church. We thank Thee that by the Gospel of the Son she is furnished with everything necessary to her spiritual happiness ; that it supplies light for her mind and comfort for her heart, encouragement and power to discharge her duty, and the precious hope of mercy and immortality to sustain and make her faithful. And we beseech Thee, O most merciful God, that this child may be enlightened and sanctified from her early years by the Holy Spirit, and be everlastingly saved by Thy mercy. Direct and bless Thy servants who are intrusted with the care of her in the momentous work of her education. Inspire them with just conception of the absolute necessity of religious instruction and principles. Forbid that they should ever forget that this offspring belongs to Thee, and that, if through their criminal neglect or bad example Thy reasonable creature be lost, Thou wilt require it at their hands. Give them a deep sense of the divinity of her nature, of the worth of her soul, of the dangers to which she will be exposed, of the honour and felicity to which she is capable of ascending with Thy blessing, and of the ruin in this world and the misery in the world to come which springs from wicked passion and conduct. Give them grace to check the first risings of forbidden inclinations in her breast, to be her defence against the temptations incident to childhood and youth, and, as she grows up, to enlarge her understanding and to lead her to an acquaintance with Thee and with Jesus Christ, whom Thou hast sent. Give them grace to cultivate in her heart a supreme reverence and love for Thee, a grateful attachment to the Gospel of Thy Son, her Saviour, a due regard for all its ordinances and institutions, a temper of kindness and good-will to all mankind, and an invincible love of sincerity and truth. Help them to watch continually over her with tender solicitude, to be studious, that by their conversation and deportment her heart may not be corrupted, and at all times to set before her such an example that she may safely tread in their footsteps. If it please Thee to prolong her days on earth, grant that she may prove an honour and a comfort to her parents and friends, be useful in the world, and find in Thy Providence an unfailing defence and support.

Whether she live, let her live to Thee ; or whether she die, let her die to Thee. And, at the great day of account, may she and her parents meet each other with rapture and rejoice together in Thy redeeming love, through Jesus Christ, forever and ever, Amen."

As this solemn admonition was read a feeling of obligation descended upon the grandfather of this little outcast ; a feeling that he was bound to give the tiny creature lying on his wife's arm the care and attention which God in His sacrament had commanded. He bowed his head in utmost reverence, and when the service was concluded and they left the silent church he was without words to express his feelings. Religion was a consuming thing with him. God was a person, a dominant reality. Religion was not a thing of mere words or of interesting ideas to be listened to on Sunday, but a strong, vital expression of the Divine Will handed down from a time when men were in personal contact with God. Its fulfilment was a matter of joy and salvation with him, the one consolation of a creature sent to wander in a vale whose explanation was not here but in heaven. Slowly Gerhardt walked on, and as he brooded on the words and the duties which the sacrament involved the shade of lingering disgust that had possessed him when he had taken the child to church disappeared and a feeling of natural affection took its place. However much the daughter had sinned, the infant was not to blame. It was a helpless, puling, tender thing, demanding his sympathy and his love. Gerhardt felt his heart go out to the little child, and yet he could not yield his position all in a moment.

" That is a nice man," he said of the minister to his wife as they walked along, rapidly softening in his conception of his duty.

" Yes, he was," agreed Mrs. Gerhardt timidly.

" It's a good-sized little church," he continued.

" Yes."

Gerhardt looked around him, at the street, the houses, the show of brisk life on this sunshiny, winter's day, and then finally at the child that his wife was carrying.

" She must be heavy," he said, in his characteristic German. " Let me take her."

Mrs. Gerhardt, who was rather weary, did not refuse.

" There ! " he said, as he looked at her and then fixed her

comfortably upon his shoulder. "Let us hope she proves worthy of all that has been done to-day."

Mrs. Gerhardt listened, and the meaning in his voice interpreted itself plainly enough. The presence of the child in the house might be the cause of recurring spells of depression and unkind words, but there would be another and greater influence restraining him. There would always be her soul to consider. He would never again be utterly unconscious of her soul.

# CHAPTER XVI

DURING the remainder of Gerhardt's stay he was shy in Jennie's presence and endeavoured to act as though he were unconscious of her existence. When the time came for parting, he even went away without bidding her good-bye, telling his wife she might do that for him; but after he was actually on his way back to Youngstown he regretted the omission. "I might have bade her good-bye," he thought to himself as the train rumbled heavily along. But it was too late.

For the time being the affairs of the Gerhardt family drifted. Jennie continued her work with Mrs. Bracebridge. Sebastian fixed himself firmly in his clerkship in the cigar store. George was promoted to the noble sum of three dollars, and then three-fifty. It was a narrow, humdrum life the family led. Coal, groceries, shoes, and clothing were the uppermost topics of their conversation; every one felt the stress and strain of trying to make ends meet.

That which worried Jennie most, and there were many things which weighed upon her sensitive soul, was the outcome of her own life—not so much for herself as for her baby and the family. She could not really see where she fitted in. "Who would have me?" she asked herself over and over. "How was she to dispose of Vesta in the event of a new love affair?" Such a contingency was quite possible. She was young, good-looking, and men were inclined to flirt with her, or rather to attempt it. The Bracebridges entertained many masculine guests, and some of them had made unpleasant overtures to her.

"My dear, you're a very pretty girl," said one old rake of fifty-odd when she knocked at his door one morning to give him a message from his hostess.

"I beg your pardon," she said, confusedly, and coloured.

"Indeed, you're quite sweet. And you needn't beg my pardon. I'd like to talk to you some time."

He attempted to chuck her under the chin, but Jennie

hurried away. She would have reported the matter to her mistress but a nervous shame deterred her. "Why would men always be doing this?" she thought. Could it be because there was something innately bad about her, an inward corruption that attracted its like?

It is a curious characteristic of the non-defensive disposition that it is like a honey-jar to flies. Nothing is brought to it and much is taken away. Around a soft, yielding, unselfish disposition men swarm naturally. They sense this generosity, this non-protective attitude from afar. A girl like Jennie is like a comfortable fire to the average masculine mind; they gravitate to it, seek its sympathy, yearn to possess it. Hence she was annoyed by many unwelcome attentions.

One day there arrived from Cincinnati a certain Lester Kane, the son of a wholesale carriage builder of great trade distinction in that city and elsewhere throughout the country, who was wont to visit this house frequently in a social way. He was a friend of Mrs. Bracebridge more than of her husband, for the former had been raised in Cincinnati and as a girl had visited at his father's house. She knew his mother, his brother and sisters and to all intents and purposes socially had always been considered one of the family.

"Lester's coming to-morrow, Henry," Jennie heard Mrs. Bracebridge tell her husband. "I had a wire from him this noon. He's such a scamp. I'm going to give him the big east front room upstairs. Be sociable and pay him some attention. His father was so good to me."

"I know it," said her husband calmly. "I like Lester. He's the biggest one in that family. But he's too indifferent. He doesn't care enough."

"I know, but he's so nice. I do think he's one of the nicest men I ever knew."

"I'll be decent to him. Don't I always do pretty well by your people?"

"Yes, pretty well."

"Oh, I don't know about that," he replied dryly.

When this notable person arrived Jennie was prepared to see some one of more than ordinary importance, and she was not disappointed. There came into the reception-hall to greet her mistress a man of perhaps thirty-six years of age, above the medium in height, clear-eyed, firm-jawed, athletic, direct, and vigorous. He had a deep, resonant voice that carried clearly everywhere ; people somehow used to stop and listen whether they knew him or not. He was simple and abrupt in his speech.

" Oh, there you are," he began. " I'm glad to see you again. How's Mr. Bracebridge ? How's Fannie ? "

He asked his questions forcefully, whole-heartedly, and his hostess answered with an equal warmth. " I'm glad to see you, Lester," she said. " George will take your things upstairs. Come up into my room. It's more comfy. How are grandpa and Louise ? "

He followed her up the stairs, and Jennie, who had been standing at the head of the stairs listening, felt the magnetic charm of his personality. It seemed, why she could hardly say, that a real personage had arrived. The house was cheerier. The attitude of her mistress was much more complaisant. Everybody seemed to feel that something must be done for this man.

Jennie went about her work, but the impression persisted ; his name ran in her mind. Lester Kane. And he was from Cincinnati. She looked at him now and then on the sly, and felt, for the first time in her life, an interest in a man on his own account. He was so big, so handsome, so forceful. She wondered what his business was. At the same time she felt a little dread of him. Once she caught him looking at her with a steady, incisive stare. She quailed inwardly, and took the first opportunity to get out of his presence. Another time he tried to address a few remarks to her, but she pretended that her duties called her away. She knew that often his eyes were on her when her back was turned, and it made her nervous. She wanted to run away from him, although there was no very definite reason why she should do so.

As a matter of fact, this man, so superior to Jennie in wealth, education, and social position, felt an instinctive interest in her unusual personality. Like the others, he was attracted by the peculiar softness of her disposition and her pre-eminent femininity. There was that about her which suggested the luxury of love. He felt as if somehow she could be reached— why, he could not have said. She did not bear any outward marks of her previous experience. There were no evidences of coquetry about her, but still he " felt that he might."

He was inclined to make the venture on his first visit, but business called him away; he left after four days and was absent from Cleveland for three weeks. Jennie thought he was gone for good, and she experienced a queer sense of relief as well as of regret. Then, suddenly, he returned. He came apparently unexpectedly, explaining to Mrs. Bracebridge that business interests again demanded his presence in Cleveland. As he spoke he looked at Jennie sharply, and she felt as if somehow his presence might also concern her a little.

On this second visit she had various opportunities of seeing him, at breakfast, where she sometimes served, at dinner, when she could see the guests at the table from the parlour or sitting-room, and at odd times when he came to Mrs. Bracebridge's boudoir to talk things over. They were very friendly.

"Why don't you settle down, Lester, and get married?" Jennie heard her say to him the second day he was there. "You know it's time."

"I know," he replied, "but I'm in no mood for that. I want to browse around a little while yet."

"Yes, I know about your browsing. You ought to be ashamed of yourself. Your father is really worried."

He chuckled amusedly. "Father doesn't worry much about me. He has got all he can attend to to look after the business."

Jennie looked at him curiously. She scarcely understood what she was thinking, but this man drew her. If she had realised in what way she would have fled his presence then and there.

Now he was more insistent in his observation of her—addressed an occasional remark to her—engaged her in brief, magnetic conversations. She could not help answering him—he was pleasing to her. Once he came across her in the hall on the second floor searching in a locker for some linen. They were all alone, Mrs. Bracebridge having gone out to do some morning shopping and the other servants being below stairs. On this occasion he made short work of the business. He approached her in a commanding, unhesitating, and thoroughly determined way.

"I want to talk to you," he said. "Where do you live?"

"I—I——" she stammered, and blanched perceptibly. "I live out on Lorrie Street."

"What number?" he questioned, as though she were compelled to tell him.

She quailed and shook inwardly. "Thirteen fourteen," she replied mechanically.

He looked into her big, soft-blue eyes with his dark, vigorous brown ones. A flash that was hypnotic, significant, insistent passed between them.

"You belong to me," he said. "I've been looking for you. When can I see you?"

"Oh, you mustn't," she said, her fingers going nervously to her lips. "I can't see you—I—I——"

"Oh, I mustn't, mustn't I? Look here"—he took her arm and drew her slightly closer—"you and I might as well understand each other right now. I like you. Do you like me? Say?"

She looked at him, her eyes wide, filled with wonder, with fear, with a growing terror.

"I don't know," she gasped, her lips dry.

"Do you?" He fixed her grimly, firmly with his eyes.

"I don't know."

"Look at me," he said.

"Yes," she replied.

He pulled her to him quickly. "I'll talk to you later," he said, and put his lips masterfully to hers.

She was horrified, stunned, like a bird in the grasp of a cat; but through it all something tremendously vital and insistent was speaking to her. He released her with a short laugh. "We won't do any more of this here, but, remember, you belong to me," he said, as he turned and walked nonchalantly down the hall. Jennie, in sheer panic, ran to her mistress's room and locked the door behind her.

## CHAPTER XVII

THE shock of this sudden encounter was so great to Jennie that she was hours in recovering herself. At first she did not understand clearly just what had happened. Out of clear sky, as it were, this astonishing thing had taken place. She had yielded herself to another man. Why ? Why ? she asked herself, and yet within her own consciousness there was an answer. Though she could not explain her own emotions, she belonged to him temperamentally and he belonged to her.

There is a fate in love and a fate in fight. This strong, intellectual bear of a man, son of a wealthy manufacturer, stationed, so far as material conditions were concerned, in a world immensely superior to that in which Jennie moved, was, nevertheless, instinctively, magnetically, and chemically drawn to this poor serving-maid. She was his natural affinity, though he did not know it—the one woman who answered somehow the biggest need of his nature. Lester Kane had known all sorts of women, rich and poor, the highly bred maidens of his own class, the daughters of the proletariat, but he had never yet found one who seemed to combine for him the traits of an ideal woman—sympathy, kindliness of judgment, youth, and beauty. Yet this ideal remained fixedly seated in the back of his brain—when the right woman appeared he intended to take her. He had the notion that, for purposes of marriage, he ought perhaps to find this woman on his own plane. For purposes of temporary happiness he might take her from anywhere, leaving marriage, of course, out of the question. He had no idea of making anything like a serious proposal to a servant-girl. But Jennie was different. He had never seen a servant quite like her. And she was lady-like and lovely without appearing to know it. Why, this girl was a rare flower. Why shouldn't he try to seize her ? Let us be just to Lester Kane ; let us try to understand him and his position. Not every mind is to be estimated by the weight of a single folly ; not every personality is to be judged by the drag of a single passion. We live in an age in which the impact of

materialised forces is well-nigh irresistible : the spiritual
nature is overwhelmed by the shock.  The tremendous and
complicated development of our material civilisation, the
multiplicity, and variety of our social forms, the depth, subtlety,
and sophistry of our imaginative impressions, gathered,
remultiplied, and disseminated by such agencies as the railroad,
the express and the post office, the telephone, the telegraph,
the newspaper, and, in short, the whole machinery of social
intercourse—these elements of existence combine to produce
what may be termed a kaleidoscopic glitter, a dazzling and
confusing phantasmagoria of life that wearies and stultifies the
mental and moral nature.  It induces a sort of intellectual
fatigue through which we see the ranks of the victims of
insomnia, melancholia, and insanity constantly recruited.
Our modern brain-pan does not seem capable as yet of receiving,
sorting, and storing the vast army of facts and impressions which
present themselves daily.  The white light of publicity is too
white.  We are weighed upon by too many things.  It is as
if the wisdom of the infinite were struggling to beat itself into
finite and cup-big minds.

Lester Kane was the natural product of these untoward
conditions.  His was a naturally observing mind, Rabelaisian
in its strength and tendencies, but confused by the multiplicity
of things, the vastness of the panorama of life, the glitter of
its details, the unsubstantial nature of its forms, the uncertainty
of their justification.  Born a Catholic, he was no longer a
believer in the divine inspiration of Catholicism ; raised a
member of the social elect, he had ceased to accept the fetish
that birth and station presuppose any innate superiority ;
brought up as the heir to a comfortable fortune and expected
to marry in his own sphere, he was by no means sure that he
wanted marriage on any terms.  Of course the conjugal state
was an institution.  It was established.  Yes, certainly.
But what of it ?  The whole nation believed in it.  True, but
other nations believed in polygamy.  There were other
questions that bothered him—such questions as the belief in
a single deity or ruler of the universe, and whether a republican,
monarchial, or aristocratic form of government were best.  In
short, the whole body of things material, social, and spiritual
had come under the knife of his mental surgery and had been
left but half dissected.  Life was not proved to him.  Not a

single idea of his, unless it were the need of being honest, was finally settled. In all other things he wavered, questioned, procrastinated, leaving to time and to the powers back of the universe the solution of the problem that vexed him. Yes, Lester Kane was the natural product of a combination of elements—religious, commercial, social—modified by that pervading atmosphere of liberty in our national life which is productive of almost uncounted freedom of thought and action. Thirty-six years of age, and apparently a man of vigorous, aggressive, and sound personality, he was, nevertheless, an essentially animal-man, pleasantly veneered by education and environment. Like the hundreds of thousands of Irishmen who in his father's day had worked on the railroad tracks, dug in the mines, picked and shovelled in the ditches, and carried up bricks and mortar on the endless structures of a new land, he was strong, hairy, axiomatic, and witty.

" Do you want me to come back here next year ? " he had asked of Brother Ambrose, when, in his seventeenth year, that ecclesiastical member was about to chastise him for some school-boy misdemeanour.

The other stared at him in astonishment. " Your father will have to look after that," he replied.

" Well, my father won't look after it," Lester returned. " If you touch me with that whip I'll take things into my own hands. I'm not committing any punishable offences, and I'm not going to be knocked around any more."

Words, unfortunately, did not avail in this case, but a good vigorous Irish-American wrestle did, in which the whip was broken and the discipline of the school so far impaired that he was compelled to take his clothes and leave. After that he looked his father in the eye and told him that he was not going to school any more.

" I'm perfectly willing to jump in and work," he explained. " There's nothing in a classical education for me. Let me go into the office, and I guess I'll pick up enough to carry me through."

Old Archibald Kane, keen, single-minded, of unsullied commercial honour, admired his son's determination, and did not attempt to coerce him.

" Come down to the office," he said ; " perhaps there is something you can do."

Entering upon a business life at the age of eighteen, Lester had worked faithfully, rising in his father's estimation, until now he had come to be, in a way, his personal representative. Whenever there was a contract to be entered upon, an important move to be decided, or a representative of the manufactory to be sent anywhere to consumate a deal, Lester was the agent selected. His father trusted him implicitly, and so diplomatic and earnest was he in the fulfilment of his duties that this trust had never been impaired.

"Business is business," was a favourite axiom with him, and the very tone in which he pronounced the words was a reflex of his character and personality.

There were molten forces in him, flames which burst forth now and then in spite of the fact that he was sure that he had them under control. One of these impulses was a taste for liquor, of which he was perfectly sure he had the upper hand. He drank but very little, he thought, and only, in a social way, among friends ; never to excess. Another weakness lay in his sensual nature ; but here again he believed he was the master. If he chose to have irregular relations with women, he was capable of deciding where the danger point lay. If men were only guided by a sense of the brevity inherent in all such relationships there would not be so many troublesome consequences growing out of them. Finally, he flattered himself that he had a grasp upon a right method of living, a method which was nothing more than a quiet acceptance of social conditions as they were, tempered by a little personal judgment as to the right and wrong of individual conduct. Not to fuss and fume, not to cry out about anything, not to be mawkishly sentimental ; to be vigorous and sustain your personality intact—such was his theory of life, and he was satisfied that it was a good one.

As to Jennie, his original object in approaching her had been purely selfish. But now that he had asserted his masculine prerogatives, and she had yielded, at least in part, he began to realise that she was no common girl, no toy of the passing hour.

There is a time in some men's lives when they unconsciously begin to view feminine youth and beauty not so much in relation to the ideal happiness, but rather with regard to the social conventions by which they are environed.

"Must it be ? " they ask themselves, in speculating concerning the possibility of taking a maiden to wife, " that I shall be compelled to swallow the whole social code, make a covenant with society, sign a pledge of abstinence, and give to another a life interest in all my affairs, when I know too well that I am but taking to my arms a variable creature like myself, whose wishes are apt to become insistent and burdensome in proportion to the decrease of her beauty and interest ? " These are the men, who, unwilling to risk the manifold contingencies of an authorised connection, are led to consider the advantages of a less-binding union, a temporary companionship. They seek to seize the happiness of life without paying the cost of their indulgence. Later on, they think, the more definite and conventional relationship may be established without reproach or the necessity of radical readjustment.

Lester Kane was past the youthful love period, and he knew it. The innocence and unsophistication of younger ideals had gone. He wanted the comfort of feminine companionship, but he was more and more disinclined to give up his personal liberty in order to obtain it. He would not wear the social shackles if it were possible to satisfy the needs of his heart and nature and still remain free and unfettered. Of course he must find the right woman, and in Jennie he believed that he had discovered her. She appealed to him on every side ; he had never known anybody quite like her. Marriage was not only impossible but unnecessary. He had only to say " Come " and she must obey ; it was her destiny.

Lester thought the matter over calmly, dispassionately. He strolled out to the shabby street where she lived ; he looked at the humble roof that sheltered her. Her poverty, her narrow and straightened environment touched his heart. Ought he not to treat her generously, fairly, honourably ? Then the remembrance of her marvellous beauty swept over him and changed his mood. No, he must possess her if he could—to-day, quickly, as soon as possible. It was in that frame of mind that he returned to Mrs. Bracebridge's home from his visit to Lorrie Street.

# CHAPTER XVIII

JENNIE was now going through the agony of one who has a varied and complicated problem to confront. Her baby, her father, her brothers, and her sisters all rose up to confront her. What was this thing that she was doing ? Was she allowing herself to slip into another wretched, unsanctified relationship ? How was she to explain to her family about this man ? He would not marry her, that was sure, if he knew all about her. He would not marry her, anyhow, a man of his station and position. Yet here she was parleying with him. What ought she to do ? She pondered over the problem until evening, deciding first that it was best to run away, but remembering painfully that she had told him where she lived. Then she resolved that she would summon up her courage and refuse him—tell him she couldn't, wouldn't have anything to do with him. This last solution of the difficulty seemed simple enough—in his absence. And she would find work where he could not follow her up so easily. It all seemed simple enough as she put on her things in the evening to go home.

Her agressive lover, however, was not without his own conclusion in this matter. Since leaving Jennie he had thought concisely and to the point. He came to the decision that he must act at once. She might tell her family, she might tell Mrs. Bracebridge, she might leave the city. He wanted to know more of the conditions which surrounded her, and there was only one way to do that—talk to her. He must persuade her to come and live with him. She would, he thought. She admitted that she liked him. That soft, yielding note in her character which had originally attracted him seemed to presage that he could win her without much difficulty, if he wished to try. He decided to do so, anyhow, for truly he desired her greatly.

At half-past five he returned to the Bracebridge home to see if she were still there. At six he had an opportunity to say to her, unobserved, " I am going to walk home with you. Wait for me at the next corner, will you ? "

" Yes," she said, a sense of compulsion to do his bidding seizing her. She explained to herself afterward that she ought to talk to him, that she must tell him finally of her decision not to see him again, and this was as good an opportunity as any. At half-past six he left the house on a pretext—a forgotten engagement—and a little after seven he was waiting for her in a closed carriage near the appointed spot. He was calm, absolutely satisfied as to the result, and curiously elated beneath a sturdy, shock-proof exterior. It was as if he breathed some fragrant perfume, soft, grateful, entrancing.

A few minutes after eight he saw Jennie coming along. The flare of the gas-lamp was not strong, but it gave sufficient light for his eyes to make her out. A wave of sympathy passed over him, for there was a great appeal in her personality. He stepped out as she neared the corner and confronted her. " Come," he said, " and get in this carriage with me. I'll take you home."

" No," she replied. " I don't think I ought to."

" Come with me. I'll take you home. It's a better way to talk."

Once more that sense of dominence on his part, that power of compulsion. She yielded, feeling all the time that she should not ; he called out to the cabman, " Anywhere for a little while." When she was seated beside him he began at once.

" Listen to me, Jennie, I want you. Tell me something about yourself."

" I have to talk to you," she replied, trying to stick to her original line of defence.

" About what ? " he inquired, seeking to fathom her expression in the half light.

" I can't go on this way," she murmured nervously. " I can't act this way. You don't know how it all is. I shouldn't have done what I did this morning. I mustn't see you any more. Really I mustn't."

" You didn't do what you did this morning," he remarked, paradoxically, seizing on that one particular expression. " I did that. And as for seeing me any more, I'm going to see you." He seized her hand. " You don't know me, but I

like you. I'm crazy about you, that's all. You belong to me.
Now listen. I'm going to have you. Are you going to come
to me ? "

"No, no, no ! " she replied in an agonised voice. " I can't
do anything like that, Mr. Kane. Please listen to me. It
can't be. You don't know. Oh, you don't know. I can't
do what you want. I don't want to. I couldn't, even if I
wanted to. You don't know how things are. But I don't
want to do anything wrong. I mustn't. I can't. I won't.
Oh, no ! no !! no !!! Please let me go home."

He listened to this troubled, feverish outburst with
sympathy, with even a little pity.

"What do you mean by you can't ? " he asked, curiously.

"Oh, I can't tell you," she replied. "Please don't ask
me. You oughtn't to know. But I mustn't see you any
more. It won't do any good."

"But you like me," he retorted.

"Oh yes, yes, I do. I can't help that. But you mustn't
come near me any more. Please don't."

He turned his proposition over in his mind with the solemnity
of a judge. He knew that this girl liked him—loved him really,
brief as their contact had been. And he was drawn to her,
perhaps not irrevocably, but with exceeding strength. What
prevented her from yielding, especially since she wanted to ?
He was curious.

"See here, Jennie," he replied. "I hear what you say.
I don't know what you mean by ' can't ' if you want to. You
say you like me. Why can't you come to me ? You're my
sort. We will get along beautifully together. You're suited
to me temperamentally. I'd like to have you with me. What
makes you say you can't come ? "

"I can't," she replied. "I can't. I don't want to. I
oughtn't. Oh, please don't ask me any more. You don't
know. I can't tell you why." She was thinking of her baby.

The man had a keen sense of justice and fair play. Above
all things he wanted to be decent in his treatment of people.
In this case he intended to be tender and considerate, and yet
he must win her. He turned this over in his mind.

"Listen to me," he said finally, still holding her hand.
" I may not want you to do anything immediately. I want
you to think it over. But you belong to me. You say you

care for me. You admitted that this morning. I know you
do. Now why should you stand out against me ? I like you,
and I can do a lot of things for you. Why not let us be good
friends now ? Then we can talk the rest of this over later."

"But I mustn't do anything wrong," she insisted. "I
don't want to. Please don't come near me any more. I can't
do what you want."

"Now, look here," he said. "You don't mean that. Why
did you say you liked me ? Have you changed your mind ?
Look at me." (She had lowered her eyes.) "Look at me !
You haven't, have you ? "

"Oh no, no, no," she half sobbed, swept by some force
beyond her control.

"Well, then, why stand out against me ? I love you, I
tell you—I'm crazy about you. That's why I came back this
time. It was to see you ! "

"Was it ? " asked Jennie, surprised.

"Yes, it was. And I would have come again and again if
necessary. I tell you I'm crazy about you. I've got to have
you. Now tell me you'll come with me."

"No, no, no," she pleaded. "I can't. I must work.
I want to work. I don't want to do anything wrong. Please
don't ask me. You mustn't. You must let me go. Really
you must. I can't do what you want."

"Tell me, Jennie," he said, changing the subject. "What
does your father do ? "

"He's a glass-blower.",

"Here in Cleveland ? "

"No, he works in Youngstown."

"Is your mother alive ? "

"Yes, sir."

"You live with her ? "

"Yes, sir."

He smiled at the " sir." " Don't say ' sir ' to me, sweet ! "
he pleaded in his gruff way. "And don't insist on the *Mr.*
Kane. I'm not ' mister ' to you any more. You belong to
me, little girl, me." And he pulled her close to him.

"Please don't, Mr. Kane," she pleaded. "Oh, please
don't. I can't ! I can't ! You mustn't."

But he sealed her lips with his own.

"Listen to me, Jennie," he repeated, using his favourite

expression. "I tell you you belong to me. I like you better every moment. I haven't had a chance to know you. I'm not going to give you up. You've got to come to me eventually. And I'm not going to have you working as a lady's maid. You can't stay in that place except for a little while. I'm going to take you somewhere else. And I'm going to leave you some money, do you hear? You have to take it."

At the word money she quailed and withdrew her hand.

"No, no, no!" she repeated. "No, I won't take it."

"Yes, you will. Give it to your mother. I'm not trying to buy you. I know what you think. But I'm not. I want to help you. I want to help your family. I know where you live. I saw the place to-day. How many are there of you?"

"Six," she answered faintly.

"The families of the poor," he thought.

"Well, you take this from me," he insisted, drawing a purse from his coat. "And I'll see you very soon again. There's no escape, sweet."

"No, no," she protested. "I won't. I don't need it. No, you mustn't ask me."

He insisted further, but she was firm, and finally he put the money away.

"One thing is sure, Jennie, you're not going to escape me," he said soberly. "You'll have to come to me eventually. Don't you know you will? Your own attitude shows that. I'm not going to leave you alone."

"Oh, if you knew the trouble you're causing me."

"I'm not causing you any real trouble, am I?" he asked. "Surely not."

"Yes. I can never do what you want."

"You will! You will!" he exclaimed eagerly, the bare thought of this prize escaping him heightening his passion. "You'll come to me." And he drew her close in spite of all her protests.

"There," he said when, after the struggle, that mystic something between them spoke again, and she relaxed. Tears were in her eyes, but he did not see them. "Don't you see how it is? You like me too."

"I can't," she repeated, with a sob.

Her evident distress touched him. "You're not crying, little girl, are you?" he asked.

She made no answer.

" I'm sorry," he went on. " I'll not say anything more to-night. We're almost at your home. I'm leaving to-morrow, but I'll see you again. Yes, I will, sweet. I can't give you up now. I'll do anything in reason to make it easy for you, but I can't, do you hear ? "

She shook her head.

" Here's where you get out," he said, as the carriage drew up near the corner. He could see the evening lamp gleaming behind the Gerhardt cottage curtains.

" Good-bye," he said as she stepped out.

" Good-bye," she murmured.

" Remember," he said, " this is just the beginning."

" Oh no, no ! " she pleaded.

He looked after her as she walked away.

" The beauty ! " he exclaimed.

Jennie stepped into the house weary, discouraged, ashamed. What had she done ? There was no denying that she had compromised herself irretrievably. He would come back.

He would come back. And he had offered her money. That was the worst of all.

## CHAPTER XIX

THE inconclusive nature of this interview, exciting as it was, did not leave any doubt in either Lester Kane's or Jennie's mind; certainly this was not the end of the affair. Kane knew that he was deeply fascinated. This girl was lovely. She was sweeter than he had had any idea of. Her hesitancy, her repeated protests, her gentle "no, no, no" moved him as music might. Depend upon it, this girl was for him, and he would get her. She was too sweet to let go. What did he care about what his family or the world might think?

It was curious that Kane held the well-founded idea that in time Jennie would yield to him physically, as she had already done spiritually. Just why he could not say. Something about her—a warm womanhood, a guileless expression of countenance—intimated a sympathy toward sex relationship which had nothing to do with hard, brutal immorality. She was the kind of a woman who was made for a man—one man. All her attitude toward sex was bound up with love, tenderness, service. When the one man arrived she would love him and she would go to him. That was Jennie as Lester understood her. He felt it. She would yield to him because he was the one man.

On Jennie's part there was a great sense of complication and of possible disaster. If he followed her of course he would learn all. She had not told him about Brander, because she was still under the vague illusion that, in the end, she might escape. When she left him she knew that he would come back. She knew, in spite of herself that she wanted him to do so. Yet she felt that she must not yield, she must go on leading her straitened, humdrum life. This was her punishment for having made a mistake. She had made her bed, and she must lie on it.

The Kane family mansion at Cincinnati to which Lester returned after leaving Jennie was an imposing establishment, which contrasted strangely with the Gerhardt home. It was a great, rambling, two-storey affair, done after the manner of the French châteaux, but in red brick and brownstone. It was set down, among flowers and trees, in an almost park-like enclosure, and its very stones spoke of a splendid dignity and of a refined luxury. Old Archibald Kane, the father, had amassed a tremendous fortune, not by grabbing and brow-beating and unfair methods, but by seeing a big need and filling it. Early in life he had realised that America was a growing country. There was going to be a big demand for vehicles—wagons, carriages, drays—and he knew that some one would have to supply them. Having founded a small wagon industry, he had built it up into a great business ; he made good wagons, and he sold them at a good profit. It was his theory that most men were honest ; he believed that at bottom they wanted honest things, and if you gave them these they would buy of you, and come back and buy again and again, until you were an influential and rich man. He believed in the measure " heaped full and running over." All through his life and now in his old age he enjoyed the respect and approval of every one who knew him. " Archibald Kane," you would hear his competitors say, " Ah, there is a fine man. Shrewd, but honest. He's a big man."

This man was the father of two sons and three daughters, all healthy, all good-looking, all blessed with exceptional minds, but none of them so generous and forceful as their long-living and big-hearted sire. Robert, the eldest, a man forty years of age, was his father's right-hand man in financial matters, having a certain hard incisiveness which fitted him for the somewhat sordid details of business life. He was of medium height, of a rather spare build, with a high-forehead, slightly inclined to baldness, bright, liquid-blue eyes, an eagle nose, and thin, firm, even lips. He was a man of few words, rather slow to action and of deep thought. He sat close to his father as vice-president of the big company which occupied two whole blocks in an outlying section of the city. He was a strong man—a coming man, as his father well knew.

Lester, the second boy, was his father's favourite. He was not by any means the financier that Robert was, but he had a larger vision of the subtleties that underlie life. He was softer, more human, more good-natured about everything. And, strangely enough, old Archibald admired and trusted him. He knew he had the bigger vision. Perhaps he turned to

Robert when it was a question of some intricate financial problem, but Lester was the most loved as a son.

Then there was Amy, thirty-two years of age, married, handsome, the mother of one child—a boy ; Imogene, twenty-eight, also married, but as yet without children, and Louise, twenty-five, single, the best-looking of the girls, but also the coldest and most critical. She was the most eager of all for social distinction, the most vigorous of all in her love of family prestige, the most desirous that the Kane family should outshine every other. She was proud to think that the family was so well placed socially, and carried herself with an air and a hauteur which was sometimes amusing, sometimes irritating to Lester ! He liked her—in a way she was his favourite sister—but he thought she might take herself with a little less seriousness and not do the family standing any harm.

Mrs. Kane, the mother, was a quiet, refined woman, sixty years of age, who, having come up from comparative poverty with her husband, cared but little for social life. But she loved her children and her husband, and was naïvely proud of their position and attainments. It was enough for her to shine only in their reflected glory. A good woman, a good wife, and a good mother.

Lester arrived at Cincinnati early in the evening, and drove at once to his home. An old Irish servitor met him at the door.

" Ah, Mr. Lester," he began, joyously, " sure I'm glad to see you back. I'll take your coat. Yes, yes, it's been fine weather we're having. Yes, yes, the family's all well. Sure your sister Amy is just after leavin' the house with the boy. Your mother's upstairs in her room. Yes, yes."

Lester smiled cheerily and went up to his mother's room. In this, which was done in white and gold and overlooked the garden to the south and east, sat Mrs. Kane, a subdued, graceful, quiet woman, with smoothly laid grey hair. She looked up when the door opened, laid down the volume that she had been reading, and rose to greet him.

" There you are, Mother," he said, putting his arms around her and kissing her. " How are you ? "

" Oh, I'm just about the same, Lester. How have you been ? "

" Fine. I was up with the Bracebridges for a few days

again. I had to stop off in Cleveland to see Parsons. They all asked after you."

"How is Minnie ? "

"Just the same. She doesn't change any that I can see. She's just as interested in entertaining as she ever was."

"She's a bright girl," remarked his mother, recalling Mrs. Bracebridge as a girl in Cincinnati. "I always liked her. She's so sensible."

"She hasn't lost any of that, I can tell you," replied Lester significantly. Mrs. Kane smiled and went on to speak of various family happenings. Imogene's husband was leaving for St. Louis on some errand. Robert's wife was sick with a cold. Old Zwingle, the yard watchman at the factory, who had been with Mr. Kane for over forty years, had died. Her husband was going to the funeral. Lester listened dutifully, albeit a trifle absently.

Lester, as he walked down the hall, encountered Louise. "Smart," was the word for her. She was dressed in a beaded black silk dress, fitting close to her form, with a burst of rubies at her throat which contrasted effectively with her dark complexion and black hair. Her eyes were black and piercing.

"Oh, there you are, Lester," she exclaimed. "When did you get in ? Be careful how you kiss me. I'm going out, and I'm all fixed, even to the powder on my nose. Oh, you bear ! " Lester had gripped her firmly and kissed her soundly. She pushed him away with her strong hands.

"I didn't brush much of it off," he said. "You can always dust more on with that puff of yours." He passed on to his own room to dress for dinner. Dressing for dinner was a custom that had been adopted by the Kane family in the last few years. Guests had become so common that in a way it was a necessity, and Louise, in particular, made a point of it. To-night Robert was coming, and Mr. and Mrs. Burnett, old friends of his father and mother, and so, of course, the meal would be a formal one. Lester knew that his father was around somewhere, but he did not trouble to look him up now. He was thinking of his last two days in Cleveland and wondering when he would see Jennie again.

## CHAPTER XX

A S Lester came downstairs after making his toilet he found his father in the library reading.

"Hello, Lester," he said, looking up from his paper over the top of his glasses and extending his hand. "Where do you come from?"

"Cleveland," replied his son, shaking hands heartily, and smiling.

"Robert tells me you've been to New York."

"Yes, I was there."

"How did you find my old friend Arnold?"

"Just about the same," returned Lester. "He doesn't look any older."

"I suppose not," said Archibald Kane genially, as if the report were a compliment to his own hardy condition. "He's been a temperate man. A fine old gentleman."

He led the way back to the sitting-room where they chatted over business and home news until the chime of the clock in the hall warned the guests upstairs that dinner had been served.

Lester sat down in great comfort amid the splendours of the great Louis Quinze dining-room. He liked this homey home atmosphere—his mother and father and his sisters—the old family friends. So he smiled and was exceedingly genial.

Louise announced that the Leverings were going to give a dance on Tuesday, and inquired whether he intended to go.

"You know I don't dance," he returned dryly. "Why should I go?"

"Don't dance. Won't dance, you mean. You're getting too lazy to move. If Robert is willing to dance occasionally I think you might."

"Robert's got it on me in lightness," Lester replied, airily.

"And politeness," retorted Louise.

"Be that as it may," said Lester.

"Don't try to stir up a fight, Louise," observed Robert, sagely.

After dinner they adjourned to the library, and Robert talked with his brother a little on business. There were some contracts coming up for revision. He wanted to see what suggestions Lester had to make. Louise was going to a party, and the carriage was now announced. " So you are not coming ? " she asked, a trifle complainingly.

" Too tired," said Lester lightly. " Make my excuses to Mrs. Knowles."

" Letty Pace asked about you the other night," Louise called back from the door.

" Kind," replied Lester. " I'm greatly obliged."

" She's a nice girl, Lester," put in his father, who was standing near the open fire. " I only wish you would marry her and settle down. You'd have a good wife in her."

" She's charming," testified Mrs. Kane.

" What is this ? " asked Lester jocularly—" a conspiracy ? You know I'm not strong on the matrimonial business."

" And I well know it," replied his mother semi-seriously. " I wish you were."

Lester changed the subject. He really could not stand for this sort of thing any more, he told himself. And as he thought his mind wandered back to Jennie and her peculiar " Oh no, no ! " There was some one that appealed to him. That was a type of womanhood worth while. Not sophisticated, not self-seeking, not watched over and set like a man-trap in the path of men, but a sweet little girl—sweet as a flower, who was without anybody, apparently, to watch over her. That night in his room he composed a letter, which he dated a week later, because he did not want to appear too urgent and because he could not again leave Cincinnati for at least two weeks.

" My Dear Jennie,

"Although it has been a week, and I have said nothing, I have not forgotten you—believe me. Was the impression I gave of myself very bad ? I will make it better from now on, for I love you, little girl—I really do. There is a flower on my table which reminds me of you very much—white, delicate, beautiful. Your personality, lingering with me, is just that. You are the essence of everything beautiful to me. It is in your power to strew flowers in my path if you will.

" But what I want to say here is that I shall be in Cleveland on the

18th, and I shall expect to see you. I arrive Thursday night, and I want you to meet me in the ladies' parlour of the Dornton at noon Friday. Will you ? You can lunch with me.

"You see, I respect your suggestion that I should not call. (I will not—on condition.) These separations are dangerous to good friendship. Write me that you will. I throw myself on your generosity. But I can't take ' no ' for an answer, not now.

"With a world of affection.

"LESTER KANE."


He sealed the letter and addressed it. "She's a remarkable girl in her way," he thought. "She really is."

## CHAPTER XXI

THE arrival of this letter, coming after a week of silence and after she had had a chance to think, moved Jennie deeply. What did she want to do ? What ought she to do ? How did she truly feel about this man ? Did she sincerely wish to answer his letter ? If she did so, what should she say ? Heretofore all her movements, even the one in which she had sought to sacrifice herself for the sake of Bass in Columbus, had not seemed to involve any one but herself. Now, there seemed to be others to consider—her family, above all, her child. The little Vesta was now eighteen months of age ; she was an interesting child ; her large, blue eyes and light hair giving promise of a comeliness which would closely approximate that of her mother, while her mential traits indicated a clear and intelligent mind. Mrs. Gerhardt had become very fond of her. Gerhardt had unbended so gradually that his interest was not even yet clearly discernible, but he had a distinct feeling of kindliness toward her. And this readjustment of her father's attitude had aroused in Jennie an ardent desire to so conduct herself that no pain should ever come to him again. Any new folly on her part would not only be base ingratitude to her father, but would tend to injure the prospects of her little one. Her life was a failure, she fancied, but Vesta's was a thing apart ; she must do nothing to spoil it. She wondered whether it would not be better to write Lester and explain everything. She had told him that she did not wish to do wrong. Suppose she went on to inform him that she had a child, and beg him to leave her in peace. Would he obey her ? She doubted it. Did she really want him to take her at her word ?

The need of making this confession was a painful thing to Jennie. It caused her to hesitate, to start a letter in which she tried to explain, and then to tear it up. Finally, fate intervened in the sudden home-coming of her father, who had been seriously injured by an accident at the glass-works in Youngstown where he worked.

It was on a Wednesday afternoon, in the latter part of August, when a letter came from Gerhardt. But instead of the customary fatherly communication, written in German and enclosing the regular weekly remittance of five dollars, there was only a brief note, written by another hand, and explaining that the day before Gerhardt had received a severe burn on both hands, due to the accidental overturning of a dipper of molten glass. The letter added that he would be home the next morning.

"What do you think of that?" exclaimed William, his mouth wide open.

"Poor papa!" said Veronica, tears welling up in her eyes.

Mrs. Gerhardt sat down, clasped her hands in her lap, and stared at the floor. "Now, what to do?" she nervously exclaimed. The possibility that Gerhardt was disabled for life opened long vistas of difficulties which she had not the courage to contemplate.

Bass came home at half-past six and Jennie at eight. The former heard the news with an astonished face.

"Gee! that's tough, isn't it?" he exclaimed. "Did the letter say how bad he was hurt?"

"No," replied Mrs. Gerhardt.

"Well, I wouldn't worry about it," said Bass easily. "It won't do any good. We'll get along somehow. I wouldn't worry like that if I were you."

The truth was, he wouldn't, because his nature was wholly different. Life did not rest heavily upon his shoulders. His brain was not large enough to grasp the significance and weigh the results of things.

"I know," said Mrs. Gerhardt, endeavouring to recover herself. "I can't help it, though. To think that just when we were getting along fairly well this new calamity should be added. It seems sometimes as if we were under a curse. We have so much bad luck."

When Jennie came her mother turned to her instinctively; here was her one stay.

"What's the matter, ma?" asked Jennie as she opened the door and observed her mother's face. "What have you been crying about?"

Mrs. Gerhardt looked at her, and then turned half away.

" Pa's had his hands burned," put in Bass solemnly. " He'll be home to-morrow."

Jennie turned and stared at him. " His hands burned ! " she exclaimed.

" Yes," said Bass.

" How did it happen ? "

" A pot of glass was turned over."

Jennie looked at her mother, and her eyes dimmed with tears. Instinctively she ran to her and put her arms around her.

" Now, don't you cry, ma," she said, barely able to control herself. " Don't you worry. I know how you feel, but we'll get along. Don't cry now." Then her own lips lost their evenness, and she struggled long before she could pluck up courage to contemplate this new disaster. And now without volition upon her part there leaped into her consciousness a new and subtly persistent thought. What about Lester's offer of assistance now ? What about his declaration of love ? Somehow it came back to her—his affection, his personality, his desire to help her, his sympathy, so like that which Brander had shown when Bass was in jail. Was she doomed to a second sacrifice ? Did it really make any difference ? Wasn't her life a failure already ? She thought this over as she looked at her mother sitting there so silent, haggard, and distraught. " What a pity," she thought, " that her mother must always suffer ! Wasn't it a shame that she could never have any real happiness ? "

" I wouldn't feel so badly," she said, after a time. " Maybe pa isn't burned so badly as we think. Did the letter say he'd be home in the morning ? "

" Yes," said Mrs. Gerhardt, recovering herself.

They talked more quietly from now on, and gradually, as the details were exhausted, a kind of dumb peace settled down upon the household.

" One of us ought to go to the train to meet him in the morning," said Jennie to Bass. " I will. I guess Mrs. Bracebridge won't mind."

" No," said Bass gloomily, " you mustn't. I can go."

He was sour at this new fling of fate, and he looked his feelings ; he stalked off gloomily to his room and shut himself in. Jennie and her mother saw the others off to bed, and then sat out in the kitchen talking.

" I don't see what's to become of us now," said Mrs. Gerhardt at last, completely overcome by the financial complications which this new calamity had brought about. She looked so weak and helpless that Jennie could hardly contain herself.

" Don't worry, mamma dear," she said, softly, a peculiar resolve coming into her heart. The world was wide. There was comfort and ease in it scattered by others with a lavish hand. Surely, surely misfortune could not press so sharply but that they could live !

She sat down with her mother, the difficulties of the future seeming to approach with audible and ghastly steps.

" What do you suppose will become of us now ? " repeated her mother, who saw how her fanciful conception of this Cleveland home had crumbled before her eyes.

" Why," said Jennie, who saw clearly and knew what could be done, " it will be all right. I wouldn't worry about it. Something will happen. We'll get something."

She realised, as she sat there, that fate had shifted the burden of the situation to her. She must sacrifice herself ; there was no other way.

Bass met his father at the railway station in the morning. He looked very pale, and seemed to have suffered a great deal. His cheeks were slightly sunken and his bony profile appeared rather gaunt. His hands were heavily bandaged, and altogether he presented such a picture of distress that many stopped to look at him on the way home from the station.

" By chops," he said to Bass, " that was a burn I got. I thought once I couldn't stand the pain any longer. Such pain I had ! Such pain ! By chops ! I will never forget it."

He related just how the accident had occurred, and said that he did not know whether he would ever be able to use his hands again. The thumb on his right hand and the first two fingers on the left had been burned to the bone. The latter had been amputated at the first joint—the thumb he might save, but his hands would be in danger of being stiff.

" By chops ! " he added, " just at the time when I needed the money most. Too bad ! Too bad ! "

When they reached the house, and Mrs. Gerhardt opened the door, the old mill-worker, conscious of her voiceless sympathy, began to cry. Mrs. Gerhardt sobbed also. Even Bass lost control of himself for a moment or two, but quickly recovered. The other children wept, until Bass called a halt on all of them.

" Don't cry now," he said cheeringly. " What's the use of crying ? It isn't so bad as all that. You'll be all right again. We can get along."

Bass's words had a soothing effect, temporarily, and, now that her husband was home, Mrs. Gerhardt recovered her composure. Though his hands were bandaged, the mere fact that he could walk and was not otherwise injured was some consolation. He might recover the use of his hands and be able to undertake light work again. Anyway, they would hope for the best.

When Jennie came home that night she wanted to run to her father and lay the treasury of her services and affection at his feet, but she trembled lest he might be as cold to her as formerly.

Gerhardt, too, was troubled. Never had he completely recovered from the shame which his daughter had brought upon him. Although he wanted to be kindly, his feelings were so tangled that he hardly knew what to say or do.

" Papa," said Jennie, approaching him timidly.

Gerhardt looked confused and tried to say something natural, but it was unavailing. The thought of his helplessness, the knowledge of her sorrow and of his own responsiveness to her affection—it was all too much for him ; he broke down again and cried helplessly.

" Forgive me, papa," she pleaded, " I'm so sorry. Oh, I'm so sorry."

He did not attempt to look at her, but in the swirl of feeling that their meeting created he thought that he could forgive, and he did.

" I have prayed," he said brokenly. " It is all right."

When he recovered himself he felt ashamed of his emotion, but a new relationship of sympathy and of understanding had been established. From that time, although there was always a great reserve between them, Gerhardt tried not to ignore her completely, and she endeavoured to show him the simple affection of a daughter, just as in the old days.

But while the household was again at peace, there were other cares and burdens to be faced. How were they to get along now with five dollars taken from the weekly budget, and with the cost of Gerhardt's presence added ? Bass might have contributed more of his weekly earnings, but he did not feel called upon to do it.   And so the small sum of nine dollars weekly must meet as best it could the current expenses of rent, food, and coal, to say nothing of incidentals, which now began to press very heavily.   Gerhardt had to go to a doctor to have his hands dressed daily.   George needed a new pair of shoes. Either more money must come from some source or the family must beg for credit and suffer the old tortures of want.   The situation crystallised the half-formed resolve in Jennie's mind.

Lester's letter had been left unanswered.   The day was drawing near.   Should she write ?   He would help them. Had he not tried to force money on her ?   She finally decided that it was her duty to avail herself of this proffered assistance. She sat down and wrote him a brief note.   She would meet him as he had requested, but he would please not come to the house.   She mailed the letter, and then waited, with mingled feelings of trepidation and thrilling expectancy, the arrival of the fateful day.

## CHAPTER XXII

THE fatal Friday came, and Jennie stood face to face with this new and overwhelming complication in her modest scheme of existence. There was really no alternative, she thought. Her own life was a failure. Why go on fighting? If she could make her family happy, if she could give Vesta a good education, if she could conceal the true nature of this older story and keep Vesta in the background—perhaps, perhaps —well, rich men had married poor girls before this, and Lester was very kind, he certainly liked her. At seven o'clock she went to Mrs. Bracebridge's ; at noon she excused herself on the pretext of some work for her mother and left the house for the hotel.

Lester, leaving Cincinnati a few days earlier than he expected, had failed to receive her reply ; he arrived at Cleveland feeling sadly out of tune with the world. He had a lingering hope that a letter from Jennie might be awaiting him at the hotel, but there was no word from her. He was a man not easily wrought up, but to-night he felt depressed, and so went gloomily up to his room and changed his linen. After supper he proceeded to drown his dissatisfaction in a game of billiards with some friends, from whom he did not part until he had taken very much more than his usual amount of alcoholic stimulant. The next morning he arose with a vague idea of abandoning the whole affair, but as the hours elapsed and the time of his appointment drew near he decided that it might not be unwise to give her one last chance. She might come. Accordingly, when it still lacked a quarter of an hour of the time, he went down into the parlour. Great was his delight when he beheld her sitting in a chair and waiting—the outcome of her acquiescence. He walked briskly up, a satisfied, gratified smile on his face.

" So you did come after all," he said, gazing at her with the look of one who has lost and recovered a prize. " What do you mean by not writing me? I thought from the way you neglected me that you had made up your mind not to come at all."

" I did write," she replied.

" Where ? "

" To the address you gave me. I wrote three days ago."

" That explains it. It came too late. You should have written me before. How have you been ? "

" Oh, all right," she replied.

" You don't look it ! " he said. " You look worried. What's the trouble, Jennie ? Nothing gone wrong out at your house, has there ? "

It was a fortuitous question. He hardly knew why he had asked it. Yet it opened the door to what she wanted to say.

" My father's sick," she replied.

" What's happened to him ? "

" He burned his hands at the glass-works. We've been terribly worried. It looks as though he would not be able to use them any more."

She paused, looking the distress she felt, and he saw plainly that she was facing a crisis.

" That's too bad," he said. " That certainly is. When did this happen ? "

" Oh, almost three weeks ago now."

" It certainly is bad. Come into lunch, though. I want to talk with you. I've been wanting to get a better understanding of your family affairs ever since I left." He led the way into the dining-room and selected a secluded table. He tried to divert her mind by asking her to order the luncheon, but she was too worried and too shy to do so and he had to make out the menu by himself. Then he turned to her with a cheering air. " Now, Jennie," he said, " I want you to tell me all about your family. I got a little something of it last time, but I want to get it straight. Your father, you said, was a glass-blower by trade. Now he can't work any more at that, that's obvious."

" Yes," she said.

" How many other children are there ? "

" Six."

" Are you the oldest ? "

" No, my brother Sebastian is. He's twenty-two."

" And what does he do ? "

" He's a clerk in a cigar store."

" Do you know how much he makes ? "

" I think it's twelve dollars," she replied thoughtfully.

" And the other children ? "

" Martha and Veronica don't do anything yet. They're too young. My brother George works at Wilson's. He's a cash-boy. He gets three dollars and a half."

" And how much do you make ? "

" I make four."

He stopped, figuring up mentally just what they had to live on. " How much rent do you pay ? " he continued.

" Twelve dollars."

" How old is your mother ? "

" She's nearly fifty now."

He turned a fork in his hands back and forth ; he was thinking earnestly.

" To tell you the honest truth, I fancied it was something like that, Jennie," he said. " I've been thinking about you a lot. Now, I know. There's only one answer to your problem, and it isn't such a bad one, if you'll only believe me." He paused for an inquiry, but she made none. Her mind was running on her own difficulties.

" Don't you want to know ? " he inquired.

" Yes," she answered mechanically.

" It's me," he replied. " You have to let me help you. I wanted to last time. Now you have to ; do you hear ? "

" I thought I wouldn't," she said simply.

" I knew what you thought," he replied. " That's all over now. I'm going to 'tend to that family of yours. And I'll do it right now while I think of it."

He drew out his purse and extracted several ten and twenty-dollar bills—two hundred and fifty dollars in all. " I want you to take this," he said. " It's just the beginning. I will see that your family is provided for from now on. Here, give me your hand."

" Oh no," she said. " Not so much. Don't give me all that."

" Yes," he replied. " Don't argue. Here. Give me your hand."

She put it out in answer to the summons of his eyes, and he shut her fingers on the money, pressing them gently at the same time. " I want you to have it, sweet. I love you, little girl. I'm not going to see you suffer, nor any one belonging to you."

Her eyes looked a dumb thankfulness, and she bit her lips.

" I don't know how to thank you," she said.

" You don't need to," he replied. " The thanks are all the other way—believe me."

He paused and looked at her, the beauty of her face holding him. She looked at the table, wondering what would come next.

" How would you like to leave what you're doing and stay at home ? " he asked. " That would give you your freedom day times."

" I couldn't do that," she replied. " Papa wouldn't allow it. He knows I ought to work."

" That's true enough," he said. " But there's so little in what you're doing. Good heavens ! Four dollars a week ! I would be glad to give you fifty times that sum if I thought there was any way in which you could use it." He idly thrummed the cloth with his fingers.

" I couldn't," she said. " I hardly know how to use this. They'll suspect. I'll have to tell mamma."

From the way she said it he judged there must be some bond of sympathy between her and her mother which would permit of a confidence such as this. He was by no means a hard man, and the thought touched him. But he would not relinquish his purpose.

" There's only one thing to be done, as far as I can see," he went on very gently. " You're not suited for the kind of work you're doing. You're too refined. I object to it. Give it up and come with me down to New York ; I'll take good care of you. I love you and want you. As far as your family is concerned, you won't have to worry about them any more. You can take a nice home for them and furnish it in any style you please. Wouldn't you like that ? "

He paused, and Jennie's thoughts reverted quickly to her mother, her dear mother. All her life long Mrs. Gerhardt had been talking of this very thing—a nice home. If they could just have a larger house, with good furniture and a yard filled with trees, how happy she would be. In such a home she would be free of the care of rent, the discomfort of poor furniture, the wretchedness of poverty; she would be so happy. She hesitated there while his keen eye followed her in spirit, and he saw what a power he had set in motion. It had been a happy inspiration—the suggestion of a decent home for the family. He waited a few minutes longer, and then said:

"Well, wouldn't you better let me do that?"

"It would be very nice," she said, "but it can't be done now. I couldn't leave home. Papa would want to know all about where I was going. I wouldn't know what to say."

"Why couldn't you pretend that you are going down to New York with Mrs. Bracebridge?" he suggested. "There couldn't be any objection to that, could there?"

"Not if they didn't find out," she said, her eyes opening in amazement. "But if they should!"

"They won't," he replied calmly. "They're not watching Mrs. Bracebridge's affairs. Plenty of mistresses take their maids on long trips. Why not simply tell them you're invited to go—have to go—and then go?"

"Do you think I could?" she inquired.

"Certainly," he replied. "What is there peculiar about that?"

She thought it over, and the plan did seem feasible. Then she looked at this man and realised that relationship with him meant possible motherhood for her again. The tragedy of giving birth to a child—ah, she could not go through that a second time, at least under the same conditions. She could not bring herself to tell him about Vesta, but she must voice this insurmountable objection.

"I——" she said, formulating the first word of her sentence, and then stopping.

"Yes," he said. "I—what?"

"I——" She paused again.

He loved her shy ways, her sweet, hesitating lips.

"What is it, Jennie?" he asked helpfully. "You're so delicious. Can't you tell me?"

Her hand was on the table. He reached over and laid his strong brown one on top of it.

"I couldn't have a baby," she said, finally, and looked down.

He gazed at her, and the charm of her frankness, her innate decency under conditions so anomalous, her simple unaffected recognition of the primal facts of life lifted her to a plane in his esteem which she had not occupied until that moment.

"You're a great girl, Jennie," he said. "You're wonderful. But don't worry about that. It can be arranged. You don't need to have a child unless you want to, and I don't want you to."

He saw the question written in her wondering, shamed face.

"It's so," he said. "You believe me, don't you? You think I know, don't you?"

"Yes," she faltered.

"Well, I do. But anyway, I wouldn't let any trouble come to you. I'll take you away. Besides, I don't want any children. There wouldn't be any satisfaction in that proposition for me at this time. I'd rather wait. But there won't be—don't worry."

"Yes," she said faintly. Not for worlds could she have met his eyes.

"Look here, Jennie," he said, after a time. "You care for me, don't you? You don't think I'd sit here and plead with you if I didn't care for you? I'm crazy about you, and that's the literal truth. You're like wine to me. I want you to come with me. I want you to do it quickly. I know how difficult this family business is, but you can arrange it. Come with me down to New York. We'll work out something later. I'll meet your family. We'll pretend a courtship, anything you like—only come now."

"You don't mean right away, do you?" she asked, startled.

"Yes, to-morrow if possible. Monday sure. You can arrange it. Why, if Mrs. Bracebridge asked you you'd go fast enough, and no one would think anything about it. Isn't that so?"

"Yes," she admitted slowly.

"Well, then, why not now?"

"It's always so much harder to work out a falsehood," she replied thoughtfully.

"I know it, but you can come. Won't you?"

"Won't you wait a little while?" she pleaded. "It's so very sudden. I'm afraid."

"Not a day, sweet, that I can help. Can't you see how I feel? Look in my eyes. Will you?"

"Yes," she replied sorrowfully, and yet with a strange thrill of affection. "I will."

## CHAPTER XXIII

THE business of arranging for this sudden departure was really not so difficult as it first appeared. Jennie proposed to tell her mother the whole truth, and there was nothing to say to her father except that she was going with Mrs. Bracebridge at the latter's request. He might question her, but he really could not doubt. Before going home that afternoon she accompanied Lester to a department store, where she was fitted out with a trunk, a suit-case, and a travelling suit and hat. Lester was very proud of his prize. "When we get to New York I am going to get you some real things," he told her. "I am going to show you what you can be made to look like." He had all the purchased articles packed in the trunk and sent to his hotel. Then he arranged to have Jennie come there and dress Monday for the trip which began in the afternoon.

When she came home Mrs. Gerhardt, who was in the kitchen, received her with her usual affectionate greeting. "Have you been working very hard?" she asked. "You look tired."

"No," she said, "I'm not tired. It isn't that. I just don't feel good."

"What's the trouble?"

"Oh, I have to tell you something, mamma. It's so hard." She paused, looking inquiringly at her mother, and then away.

"Why, what is it?" asked her mother nervously. So many things had happened in the past that she was always on the alert for some new calamity. "You haven't lost your place, have you?"

"No," replied Jennie, with an effort to maintain her mental poise, "but I'm going to leave it."

"No!" exclaimed her mother. "Why?"

"I'm going to New York."

Her mother's eyes opened widely. "Why, when did you decide to do that?" she inquired.

" To-day."

" You don't mean it ! "

" Yes, I do, mamma. Listen. I've got something I want to tell you. You know how poor we are. There isn't any way we can make things come out right. I have found some one who wants to help us. He says he loves me, and he wants me to go to New York with him Monday. I've decided to go."

" Oh, Jennie ! " exclaimed her mother. " Surely not ! You wouldn't do anything like that after all that's happened. Think of your father."

" I've thought it all out," went on Jennie, firmly. " It's really for the best. He's a good man. I know he is. He has lots of money. He wants me to go with him, and I'd better go. He will take a new house for us when we come back and help us to get along. No one will ever have me as a wife— you know that. It might as well be this way. He loves me. And I love him. Why shouldn't I go ? "

" Does he know about Vesta ? " asked her mother cautiously.

" No," said Jennie guiltily. " I thought I'd better not tell him about her. She oughtn't to be brought into it if I can help it."

" I'm afraid you're storing up trouble for yourself, Jennie," said her mother. " Don't you think he is sure to find it out some time ? "

" I thought maybe that she could be kept here," suggested Jennie, " until she's old enough to go to school. Then maybe I could send her somewhere."

" She might," assented her mother ; " but don't you think it would be better to tell him now ? He won't think any the worse of you."

" It isn't that. It's her," said Jennie passionately. " I don't want her to be brought into it."

Her mother shook her head. " Where did you meet him ? " she inquired.

" At Mrs. Bracebridge's."

" How long ago ? "

" Oh, it's been almost two months now."

" And you never said anything about him," protested Mrs. Gerhardt reproachfully.

" I didn't know that he cared for me this way," said Jennie defensively.

" Why didn't you wait and let him come out here first ? " asked her mother. " It will make things so much easier. You can't go and not have your father find out."

" I thought I'd say I was going with Mrs. Bracebridge. Papa can't object to my going with her."

" No," agreed her mother thoughtfully.

The two looked at each other in silence. Mrs. Gerhardt, with her imaginative nature, endeavoured to formulate some picture of this new and wonderful personality that had come into Jennie's life. He was wealthy ; he wanted to take Jennie ; he wanted to give them a good home. What a story !

"And he gave me this," put in Jennie, who, with some instinctive psychic faculty, had been following her mother's mood. She opened her dress at the neck, and took out the two hundred and fifty dollars ; she placed the money in her mother's hands.

The latter stared at it wide-eyed. Here was the relief for all her woes—food, clothes, rent, coal—all done up in one small package of green and yellow bills. If there were plenty of money in the house Gerhardt need not worry about his burned hands ; George and Martha and Veronica could be clothed in comfort and made happy. Jennie could dress better ; there would be a future education for Vesta.

" Do you think he might ever want to marry you ? " asked her mother finally.

" I don't know," replied Jennie, " he might. I know he loves me."

" Well," said her mother after a long pause, " if you're going to tell your father you'd better do it right away. He'll think it's strange as it is."

Jennie realised that she had won. Her mother had acquiesced from sheer force of circumstances. She was sorry, but somehow it seemed to be for the best. " I'll help you out with it," her mother had concluded, with a little sigh.

The difficulty of telling this lie was very great for Mrs. Gerhardt, but she went through the falsehood with a seeming nonchalance which allayed Gerhardt's suspicions. The children were also told, and when, after the general discussion,

Jennie repeated the falsehood to her father it seemed natural enough.

" How long do you think you'll be gone ? " he inquired.

" About two or three weeks," she replied.

" That's a nice trip," he said. " I came through New York in 1844. It was a small place then compared to what it is now."

Secretly he was pleased that Jennie should have this fine chance. Her employer must like her.

When Monday came Jennie bade her parents good-bye and left early, going straight to the Dornton, where Lester awaited her.

" So you came," he said gaily, greeting her as she entered the ladies' parlour.

" Yes," she said simply.

" You are my niece," he went on. " I have engaged a room for you near mine. I'll call for the key, and you go dress. When you're ready I'll have the trunk sent to the depôt. The train leaves at one o'clock."

She went to her room and dressed, while he fidgeted about, read, smoked, and finally knocked at her door.

She replied by opening to him, fully clad.

" You look charming," he said with a smile.

She looked down, for she was nervous and distraught. The whole process of planning, lying, nerving herself to carry out her part had been hard on her. She looked tired and worried.

" Not grieving, are you ? " he asked, seeing how things stood.

" No-o," she replied.

" Come now, sweet. You mustn't feel this way. It's coming out all right." He took her in his arms and kissed her, and they strolled down the hall. He was astonished to see how well she looked in even these simple clothes—the best she had ever had.

They reached the depôt after a short carriage ride. The accommodations had been arranged for before hand, and Kane had allowed just enough time to make the train. When they settled themselves in a Pullman state-room it was with a keen sense of satisfaction on his part. Life looked rosy. Jennie was beside him. He had succeeded in what he had started out to do. So might it always be.

As the train rolled out of the depôt and the long reaches

of the fields succeeded Jennie studied them wistfully. There were the forests, leafless and bare ; the wide, brown fields, wet with the rains of winter ; the low farm-houses sitting amid flat stretches of prairie, their low roofs making them look as if they were hugging the ground. The train roared past little hamlets, with cottages of white and yellow and drab, their roofs blackened by frost and rain. Jennie noted one in particular which seemed to recall the old neighbourhood where they used to live at Columbus ; she put her handkerchief to her eyes and began silently to cry.

"I hope you're not crying, are you, Jennie ? " said Lester, looking up suddenly from the letter he had been reading. "Come, come," he went on as he saw a faint tremor shaking her. "This won't do. You have to do better than this. You'll never get along if you act that way."

She made no reply, and the depth of her silent grief filled him with strange sympathies.

"Don't cry," he continued soothingly ; "everything will be all right. I told you that. You needn't worry about anything."

Jennie made a great effort to recover herself, and began to dry her eyes.

"You don't want to give way like that," he continued. "It doesn't do you any good. I know how you feel about leaving home, but tears won't help it any. It isn't as if you were going away for good, you know. Besides, you'll be going back shortly. You care for me, don't you, sweet ? I'm something ? "

"Yes," she said, and managed to smile back at him.

Lester returned to his correspondence and Jennie fell to thinking of Vesta. It troubled her to realise that she was keeping this secret from one who was already very dear to her. She knew that she ought to tell Lester about the child, but she shrank from the painful necessity. Perhaps later on she might find the courage to do it.

"I'll have to tell him something," she thought with a sudden upwelling of feeling as regarded the seriousness of this duty. "If I don't do it soon and I should go and live with him and he should find it out he would never forgive me. He might turn me out, and then where would I go ? I have no home now. What would I do with Vesta ? "

She turned to contemplate him, a premonitory wave of terror sweeping over her, but she only saw that imposing and comfort-loving soul quietly reading his letters, his smoothly shaved red cheek and comfortable head and body looking anything but militant or like an avenging Nemesis. She was just withdrawing her gaze when he looked up.

" Well, have you washed all your sins away ? " he inquired merrily.

She smiled faintly at the allusion. The touch of fact in it made it slightly piquant.

" I expect so," she replied.

He turned to some other topic, while she looked out of the window, the realisation that one impulse to tell him had proved unavailing dwelling in her mind. " I'll have to do it shortly," she thought, and consoled herself with the idea that she would surely find courage before long.

Their arrival in New York the next day raised the important question in Lester's mind as to where he should stop. New York was a very large place, and he was not in much danger of encountering people who would know him, but he thought it just as well not to take chances. Accordingly he had the cabman drive them to one of the more exclusive apartment hotels, where he engaged a suite of rooms ; and they settled themselves for a stay of two or three weeks.

This atmosphere into which Jennie was now plunged was so wonderful, so illuminating, that she could scarcely believe this was the same world that she had inhabited before. Kane was no lover of vulgar display. The appointments with which he surrounded himself were always simple and elegant. He knew at a glance what Jennie needed, and bought for her with discrimination and care. And Jennie, a woman, took a keen pleasure in the handsome gowns and pretty fripperies that he lavished upon her. Could this be really Jennie Gerhardt, the washerwoman's daughter, she asked herself, as she gazed in her mirror at the figure of a girl clad in blue velvet, with yellow French lace at her throat and upon her arms ? Could these be her feet, clad in soft shapely shoes at ten dollars a pair, these her hands adorned with flashing jewels ? What wonderful good fortune she was enjoying ! And Lester had promised that her mother would share in it. Tears sprang to her eyes at the thought. The dear mother, how she loved her !

It was Lester's pleasure in these days to see what he could do to make her look like some one truly worthy of him. He exercised his most careful judgment, and the result surprised even himself. People turned in the halls, in the dining-rooms, and on the street to gaze at Jennie.

" A stunning woman that man has with him," was a frequent comment.

Despite her altered state Jennie did not lose her judgment of life or her sense of perspective or proportion. She felt as though life were tentatively loaning her something which would be taken away after a time. There was no pretty vanity in her bosom. Lester realised this as he watched her. " You're a big woman, in your way," he said. " You'll amount to something. Life hasn't given you much of a deal up to now."

He wondered how he could justify this new relationship to his family, should they chance to hear about it. If he should decide to take a home in Chicago or St. Louis (there was such a thought running in his mind) could he maintain it secretly ? Did he want to ? He was half persuaded that he really, truly loved her.

As the time drew near for their return he began to counsel her as to her future course of action. " You ought to find some way of introducing me, as an acquaintance, to your father," he said. " It will ease matters up. I think I'll call. Then if you tell him you're going to marry me he'll think nothing of it." Jennie thought of Vesta, and trembled inwardly. But perhaps her father could be induced to remain silent.

Lester had made the wise suggestion that she should retain the clothes she had worn in Cleveland in order that she might wear them home when she reached there. " There won't be any trouble about this other stuff," he said. " I'll have it cared for until we make some other arrangement." It was all very simple and easy ; he was a master strategist.

Jennie had written her mother almost daily since she had been East. She had enclosed little separate notes to be read by Mrs. Gerhardt only. In one she explained Lester's desire to call, and urged her mother to prepare the way by telling her father that she had met some one who liked her. She spoke of the difficulty concerning Vesta, and her mother at once began to plan a campaign to have Gerhardt hold his peace. There must be no hitch now. Jennie must be given an opportunity to better herself. When she returned there was great rejoicing. Of course she could not go back to her work, but Mrs. Gerhardt explained that Mrs. Bracebridge had given Jennie a few weeks' vacation in order that she might look for something better, something at which she could make more money.

## CHAPTER XXIV

THE problem of the Gerhardt family and its relationship to himself comparatively settled, Kane betook himself to Cincinnati and to his business duties. He was heartily interested in the immense plant, which occupied two whole blocks in the outskirts of the city, and its conduct and development was as much a problem and a pleasure to him as to either his father or his brother. He liked to feel that he was a vital part of this great and growing industry. When he saw freight cars going by on the railroads labelled " The Kane Manufacturing Company—Cincinnati " or chanced to notice displays of the company's products in the windows of carriage sales companies in the different cities he was conscious of a warm glow of satisfaction. It was something to be a factor in an institution so stable, so distinguished, so honestly worth while. This was all very well, but now Kane was entering upon a new phase of his personal existence—in a word, there was Jennie. He was conscious as he rode toward his home city that he was entering on a relationship which might involve disagreeable consequences. He was a little afraid of his father's attitude ; above all, there was his brother Robert.

Robert was cold and conventional in character ; an excellent business man ; irreproachable in both his public and in his private life. Never overstepping the strict boundaries of legal righteousness, he was neither warm-hearted nor generous —in fact, he would turn any trick which could be speciously, or at best necessitously, recommended to his conscience. How he reasoned Lester did not know—he could not follow the ramifications of a logic which could combine hard business tactics with moral rigidity, but somehow his brother managed to do it. " He's got a Scotch Presbyterian conscience mixed with an Asiatic perception of the main chance." Lester once told somebody, and he had the situation accurately measured. Nevertheless he could not rout his brother from his positions nor defy him, for he had the public conscience with him. He was in line with convention practically, and perhaps sophisticatedly.

The two brothers were outwardly friendly; inwardly they were far apart. Robert liked Lester well enough personally, but he did not trust his financial judgment, and, temperamentally, they did not agree as to how life and its affairs should be conducted. Lester had a secret contempt for his brother's chill, persistent chase of the almighty dollar. Robert was sure that Lester's easy-going ways were reprehensible, and bound to create trouble sooner or later. In the business they did not quarrel much—there was not so much chance with the old gentleman still in charge—but there were certain minor differences constantly cropping up which showed which way the wind blew. Lester was for building up trade through friendly relationship, concessions, personal contact, and favours. Robert was for pulling everything tight, cutting down the cost of production, and offering such financial inducements as would throttle competition.

The old manufacturer always did his best to pour oil on these troubled waters, but he foresaw an eventual clash. One or the other would have to get out or perhaps both. " If only you two boys could agree ! " he used to say.

Another thing which disturbed Lester was his father's attitude on the subject of marriage—Lester's marriage, to be specific. Archibald Kane never ceased to insist on the fact that Lester ought to get married, and that he was making a big mistake in putting it off. All the other children, save Louise, were safely married. Why not his favourite son ? It was doing him injury morally, socially, commercially, that he was sure of.

" The world expects it of a man in your position," his father had argued from time to time. " It makes for social solidity and prestige. You ought to pick out a good woman and raise a family. Where will you be when you get to my time of life if you haven't any children, any home ? "

" Well, if the right woman came along," said Lester, " I suppose I'd marry her. But she hasn't come along. What do you want me to do ? Take anybody ? "

" No, not anybody, of course, but there are lots of good women. You can surely find some one if you try. There's that Pace girl. What about her ? You used to like her. I wouldn't drift on this way, Lester ; it can't come to any good."

His son would only smile. " There, father, let it go now.

I'll come around some time, no doubt. I've got to be thirsty when I'm led to water."

The old gentleman gave over, time and again, but it was a sore point with him. He wanted his son to settle down and be a real man of affairs.

The fact that such a situation as this might militate against any permanent arrangement with Jennie was obvious even to Lester at this time. He thought out his course of action carefully. Of course he would not give Jennie up, whatever the possible consequences. But he must be cautious ; he must take no unnecessary risks. Could he bring her to Cincinnati ? What a scandal if it were ever found out ! Could he install her in a nice home somewhere near the city ? The family would probably eventually suspect something. Could he take her along on his numerous business journeys ? This first one to New York had been successful. Would it always be so ? He turned the question over in his mind. The very difficulty gave it zest. Perhaps St. Louis, or Pittsburg, or Chicago would be best after all. He went to these places frequently, and particularly to Chicago. He decided finally that it should be Chicago if he could arrange it. He could always make excuses to run up there, and it was only a night's ride. Yes, Chicago was best. The very size and activity of the city made concealment easy. After two weeks' stay at Cincinnati, Lester wrote Jennie that he was coming to Cleveland soon, and she answered that she thought it would be all right for him to call and see her. Her father had been told about him. She had felt it unwise to stay about the house, and so had secured a position in a store at four dollars a week. He smiled as he thought of her working, and yet the decency and energy of it appealed to him. "She's all right," he said. "She's the best I've come across yet."

He ran up to Cleveland the following Saturday, and, calling at her place of business, he made an appointment to see her that evening. He was anxious that his introduction, as her beau , should be gotten over with as quickly as possible. When he did call the shabbiness of the house and the manifest poverty of the family rather disgusted him, but somehow Jennie seemed as sweet to him as ever. Gerhardt came in the front-room, after he had been there a few minutes, and shook hands with him, as did also Mrs. Gerhardt, but Lester paid little attention to them. The old German appeared to him to be merely commonplace—the sort of man who was hired by hundreds in common capacities in his father's factory. After some desultory conversation Lester suggested to Jennie that they should go for a drive. Jennie put on her hat, and together they departed. As a matter of fact, they went to an apartment which he had hired for the storage of her clothes. When she returned at eight in the evening the family considered it nothing amiss.

## CHAPTER XXV

A MONTH later Jennie was able to announce that Lester intended to marry her. His visits had of course paved the way for this, and it seemed natural enough. Only Gerhardt seemed a little doubtful. He did not know just how this might be. Perhaps it was all right. Lester seemed a fine enough man in all conscience, and really, after Brander, why not ? If a United States Senator could fall in love with Jennie, why not a business man ? There was just one thing—the child. "Has she told him about Vesta ? " he asked his wife.

" No," said Mrs. Gerhardt, " not yet."

" Not yet, not yet. Always something underhanded. Do you think he wants her if he knows ? That's what comes of such conduct in the first place. Now she has to slip around like a thief. The child cannot even have an honest name."

Gerhardt went back to his newspaper reading and brooding. His life seemed a complete failure to him and he was only waiting to get well enough to hunt up another job as watchman. He wanted to get out of this mess of deception and dishonesty.

A week or two later Jennie confided to her mother that Lester had written her to join him in Chicago. He was not feeling well, and could not come to Cleveland. The two women explained to Gerhardt that Jennie was going away to be married to Mr. Kane. Gerhardt flared up at this, and his suspicions were again aroused. But he could do nothing but grumble over the situation ; it would lead to no good end, of that he was sure.

When the day came for Jennie's departure she had to go without saying farewell to her father. He was out looking for work until late in the afternoon, and before he had returned she had been obliged to leave for the station. " I will write a note to him when I get there," she said. She kissed her baby over and over. " Lester will take a better house for us soon," she went on hopefully. " He wants us to move." The night train bore her to Chicago ; the old life had ended and the new one had begun.

The curious fact should be recorded here that, although Lester's generosity had relieved the stress upon the family finances, the children and Gerhardt were actually none the wiser. It was easy for Mrs. Gerhardt to deceive her husband as to the purchase of necessities and she had not as yet indulged in any of the fancies which an enlarged purse permitted. Fear deterred her. But, after Jennie had been in Chicago for a few days, she wrote to her mother saying that Lester wanted them to take a new home. This letter was shown to Gerhardt, who had been merely biding her return to make a scene. He frowned, but somehow it seemed an evidence of regularity. If he had not married her why should he want to help them? Perhaps Jennie was well married after all. Perhaps she really had been lifted to a high station in life, and was now able to help the family. Gerhardt almost concluded to forgive her everything once and for all.

The end of it was that a new house was decided upon, and Jennie returned to Cleveland to help her mother move. Together they searched the streets for a nice, quiet neighbourhood, and finally found one. A house of nine rooms, with a yard, which rented for thirty dollars, was secured and suitably furnished. There were comfortable fittings for the dining-room and sitting-room, a handsome parlour set and bedroom sets complete for each room. The kitchen was supplied with every convenience, and there was even a bathroom, a luxury the Gerhardts had never enjoyed before. Altogether the house was attractive, though plain, and Jennie was happy to know that her family could be comfortable in it.

When the time came for the actual moving Mrs. Gerhardt was fairly beside herself with joy, for was not this the realisation of her dreams? All through the long years of her life she had been waiting, and now it had come. A new house, new furniture, plenty of room—things finer than she had ever even imagined—think of it! Her eyes shone as she looked at the new beds and tables and bureaus and whatnots. " Dear, dear, isn't this nice! " she exclaimed. " Isn't it beautiful! " Jennie smiled and tried to pretend satisfaction without emotion, but there were tears in her eyes. She was so glad for her mother's sake. She could have kissed Lester's feet for his goodness to her family.

The day the furniture was moved in Mrs. Gerhardt, Martha,

and Veronica were on hand to clean and arrange things. At the sight of the large rooms and pretty yard, bare enough in winter, but giving promise of a delightful greenness in spring, and the array of new furniture standing about in excelsior, the whole family fell into a fever of delight. Such beauty, such spaciousness! George rubbed his feet over the new carpets and Bass examined the quality of the furniture critically. " Swell," was his comment. Mrs. Gerhardt roved to and fro like a person in a dream. She could not believe that these bright bedrooms, this beautiful parlour, this handsome dining-room were actually hers.

Gerhardt came last of all. Although he tried hard not to show it, he, too, could scarcely refrain from enthusiastic comment. The sight of an opal-globed chandelier over the dining-room table was the finishing touch.

" Gas, yet ! " he said.

He looked grimly around, under his shaggy eyebrows, at the new carpets under his feet, the long oak extension table covered with a white cloth and set with new dishes, at the pictures on the walls, the bright, clean kitchen. He shook his head. " By chops, it's fine ! " he said. " It's very nice. Yes, it's very nice. We want to be careful now not to break anything. It's so easy to scratch things up, and then it's all over."

Yes, even Gerhardt was satisfied.

## CHAPTER XXVI

IT would be useless to chronicle the events of the three years that followed—events and experiences by which the family grew from an abject condition of want to a state of comparative self-reliance, based, of course, on the obvious prosperity of Jennie and the generosity (through her) of her distant husband. Lester was seen now and then, a significant figure, visiting Cleveland, and sometimes coming out to the house where he occupied with Jennie the two best rooms of the second floor. There were hurried trips on her part—in answer to telegraph messages—to Chicago, to St. Louis, to New York. One of his favourite pastimes was to engage quarters at the great resorts—Hot Springs, Mt. Clemens, Saratoga—and for a period of a week or two at a stretch enjoy the luxury of living with Jennie as his wife. There were other times when he would pass through Cleveland only for the privilege of seeing her for a day. All the time he was aware that he was throwing on her the real burden of a rather difficult situation, but he did not see how he could remedy it at this time. He was not sure as yet that he really wanted to. They were getting along fairly well.

The attitude of the Gerhardt family toward this condition of affairs was peculiar. At first, in spite of the irregularity of it, it seemed natural enough. Jennie said she was married. No one had seen her marriage certificate, but she said so, and she seemed to carry herself with the air of one who holds that relationship. Still, she never went to Cincinnati, where his family lived, and none of his relatives ever came near her. Then, too, his attitude, in spite of the money which had first blinded them, was peculiar. He really did not carry himself like a married man. He was so indifferent. There were weeks in which she appeared to receive only perfunctory notes. There were times when she would only go away for a few days to meet him. Then there were the long periods in which she absented herself—the only worthwhile testimony toward a real relationship, and that, in a way, unnatural.

Bass, who had grown to be a young man of twenty-five, with some business judgment and a desire to get out in the world, was suspicious. He had come to have a pretty keen knowledge of life, and intuitively he felt that things were not right. George, nineteen, who had gained a slight foothold in a wall-paper factory and was looking forward to a career in that field, was also restless. He felt that something was wrong. Martha, seventeen, was still in school, as were William and Veronica. Each was offered an opportunity to study indefinitely; but there was unrest with life. They knew about Jennie's child. The neighbours were obviously drawing conclusions for themselves. They had few friends. Gerhardt himself finally concluded that there was something wrong, but he had let himself into this situation, and was not in much of a position now to raise an argument. He wanted to ask her at times—proposed to make her do better if he could—but the worst had already been done. It depended on the man now, he knew that.

Things were gradually nearing a state where a general up-heaval would have taken place had not life stepped in with one of its fortuitous solutions. Mrs. Gerhardt's health failed. Although stout and formerly of a fairly active disposition, she had of late years become decidedly sedentary in her habits and grown weak, which, coupled with a mind naturally given to worry, and weighed upon as it had been by a number of serious and disturbing ills, seemed now to culminate in a slow but very certain case of systemic poisoning. She became decidedly sluggish in her motions, wearied more quickly at the few tasks left for her to do, and finally complained to Jennie that it was very hard for her to climb stairs. "I'm not feeling well," she said. "I think I'm going to be sick."

Jennie now took alarm and proposed to take her to some near-by watering-place, but Mrs. Gerhardt wouldn't go. "I don't think it would do any good," she said. She sat about or went driving with her daughter, but the fading autumn scenery depressed her. "I don't like to get sick in the fall," she said. "The leaves coming down make me think I am never going to get well."

"Oh, ma, how you talk!" said Jennie; but she felt frightened, nevertheless.

How much the average home depends upon the mother was

seen when it was feared the end was near. Bass, who had thought of getting married and getting out of this atmosphere, abandoned the idea temporarily. Gerhardt, shocked and greatly depressed, hung about like one expectant of and greatly awed by the possibility of disaster. Jennie, too inexperienced in death to feel that she could possibly lose her mother, felt as if somehow her living depended on her. Hoping in spite of all opposing circumstances, she hung about, a white figure of patience, waiting and serving.

The end came one morning after a month of illness and several days of unconsciousness, during which silence reigned in the house and all the family went about on tiptoe. Mrs. Gerhardt passed away with her dying gaze fastened on Jennie's face for the last few minutes of consciousness that life vouchsafed her. Jennie stared into her eyes with a yearning horror. " Oh, mamma ! mamma ! " she cried. " Oh, no, no ! "

Gerhardt came running in from the yard, and, throwing himself down by the bedside, wrung his bony hands in anguish. " I should have gone first ! " he cried. " I should have gone first ! "

The death of Mrs. Gerhardt hastened the final breaking up of the family. Bass was bent on getting married at once, having had a girl in town for some time. Martha, whose views of life had broadened and hardened, was anxious to get out also. She felt that a sort of stigma attached to the home—to herself, in fact, so long as she remained there. Martha looked to the public schools as a source of income ; she was going to be a teacher. Gerhardt alone scarcely knew which way to turn. He was again at work as a night watchman. Jennie found him crying one day alone in the kitchen, and immediately burst into tears herself. " Now, papa ! " she pleaded, " it isn't as bad as that. You will always have a home—you know that— as long as I have anything. You can come with me."

" No, no," he protested. He really did not want to go with her. " It isn't that," he continued. " My whole life comes to nothing."

It was some little time before Bass, George and Martha finally left, but, one by one, they got out, leaving Jennie, her father, Veronica, and William, and one other—Jennie's child. Of course Lester knew nothing of Vesta's parentage, and curiously enough he had never seen the little girl. During the short periods in which he deigned to visit the house—two or three days at most—Mrs. Gerhardt took care that Vesta was kept in the background.  There was a playroom on the top floor, and also a bedroom there, and concealment was easy.  Lester rarely left his rooms, he even had his meals served to him in what might have been called the living-room of the suite. He was not at all inquisitive or anxious to meet any one of the other members of the family.  He was perfectly willing to shake hands with them or to exchange a few perfunctory words, but perfunctory words only.  It was generally understood that the child must not appear, and so it did not.

There is an inexplicable sympathy between old age and childhood, an affinity which is as lovely as it is pathetic.  During that first year in Lorrie Street, when no one was looking, Gerhardt often carried Vesta about on his shoulders and pinched her soft, red cheeks.  When she got old enough to walk he it was who, with a towel fastened securely under her arms, led her patiently around the room until she was able to take a few steps of her own accord.  When she actually reached the point where she could walk he was the one who coaxed her to the effort, shyly, grimly, but always lovingly.  By some strange leading of fate this stigma on his family's honour, this blotch on conventional morality, had twined its helpless baby fingers about the tendons of his heart.  He loved this little outcast ardently, hopefully.  She was the one bright ray in a narrow, gloomy life, and Gerhardt early took upon himself the responsibility of her education in religious matters.  Was it not he who had insisted that the infant should be baptised ?

" Say, ' Our Father,' " he used to demand of the lisping infant when he had her alone with him.

" ' Ow Fowvaw,' " was her vowel-like interpretation of his words.

" ' Who art in heaven.' "

" ' OOh ah in aven,' " repeated the child.

" Why do you teach her so early ? " pleaded Mrs. Gerhardt, overhearing the little one's struggles with stubborn consonants and vowels.

" Because I want she should learn the Christian faith," returned Gerhardt determinedly.  " She ought to know her prayers.  If she don't begin now she never will know them."

Mrs. Gerhardt smiled.  Many of her husband's religious

idiosyncrasies were amusing to her. At the same time she liked to see this sympathetic interest he was taking in the child's upbringing. If he were only not so hard, so narrow at times. He made himself a torment to himself and to every one else.

On the earliest bright morning of returning spring he was wont to take her for her first little journeys in the world. "Come, now," he would say, "we will go for a little walk."

"Walk," chirped Vesta.

"Yes, walk," echoed Gerhardt.

Mrs. Gerhardt would fasten on one of her little hoods, for in these days Jennie kept Vesta's wardrobe beautifully replete. Taking her by the hand, Gerhardt would issue forth, satisfied to drag first one foot and then the other in order to accommodate his gait to her toddling steps.

One beautiful May day, when Vesta was four years old, they started on one of their walks. Everywhere nature was budding and bourgeoning; the birds twittering their arrival from the south; the insects making the best of their brief span of life. Sparrows chirped in the road; robins strutted upon the grass; bluebirds built in the eaves of the cottages. Gerhardt took a keen delight in pointing out the wonders of nature to Vesta, and she was quick to respond. Every new sight and sound interested her.

"Ooh!—ooh!" exclaimed Vesta, catching sight of a low, flashing touch of red as a robin lighted upon a twig nearby Her hand was up, and her eyes were wide open.

"Yes," said Gerhardt, as happy as if he himself had but newly discovered this marvellous creature. "Robin. Bird. Robin. Say robin."

"Wobin," said Vesta.

"Yes, robin," he answered. "It is going to look for a worm now. We will see if we cannot find its nest. I think I saw a nest in one of these trees."

He plodded peacefully on, seeking to rediscover an old abandoned nest that he had observed on a former walk. "Here it is," he said at last, coming to a small and leafless tree, in which a winter-beaten remnant of a home was still clinging. "Here, come now, see," and he lifted the baby up at arm's length.

"See," said Gerhardt, indicating the wisp of dead grasses with his free hand, "nest. That is a bird's nest. See!"

" Ooh ! " repeated Vesta, imitating his pointing finger with one of her own.  " Ness—ooh ! "

" Yes," said Gerhardt, putting her down again.  " That was a *wren's* nest.  They have all gone now.  They will not come any more."

Still further they plodded, he unfolding the simple facts of life, she wondering with the wide wonder of a child.  When they had gone a block or two he turned slowly about as if the end of the world had been reached.

" We must be going back ! " he said.

And so she had come to her fifth year, growing in sweetness, intelligence, and vivacity.  Gerhardt was fascinated by the questions she asked, the puzzles she pronounced.  " Such a girl ! " he would exclaim to his wife.  " What is it she doesn't want to know ?  ' Where is God ?  What does He do ?  Where does He keep His feet ? ' she asks me.  I gotta laugh sometimes."  From rising in the morning, to dress her to laying her down at night after she had said her prayers, she came to be the chief solace and comfort of his days.  Without Vesta, Gerhardt would have found his life hard indeed to bear.

## CHAPTER XXVII

FOR three years now Lester had been happy in the companionship of Jennie. Irregular as the connection might be in the eyes of the church and of society, it had brought him peace and comfort, and he was perfectly satisfied with the outcome of the experiment. His interest in the social affairs of Cincinnati was now practically *nil*, and he had consistently refused to consider any matrimonial proposition which had himself as the object. He looked on his father's business organisation as offering a real chance for himself if he could get control of it ; but he saw no way of doing so. Robert's interests were always in the way, and, if anything, the two brothers were farther apart than ever in their ideas and aims. Lester had thought once or twice of entering some other line of business or of allying himself with another carriage company, but he did not feel that he could conscientiously do this. Lester had his salary—fifteen thousand a year as secretary and treasurer of the company (his brother was vice-president)—and about five thousand from some outside investments. He had not been so lucky or so shrewd in speculation as Robert had been ; aside from the principal which yielded his five thousand, he had nothing. Robert, on the other hand, was unquestionably worth between three and four hundred thousand dollars, in addition to his future interest in the business, which both brothers shrewdly suspected would be divided somewhat in their favour. Robert and Lester would get a fourth each, they thought ; their sisters a sixth. It seemed natural that Kane senior should take this view, seeing that the brothers were actually in control and doing the work. Still, there was no certainty. The old gentleman might do anything or nothing. The probabilities were that he would be very fair and liberal. At the same time, Robert was obviously beating Lester in the game of life. What did Lester intend to do about it ?

There comes a time in every thinking man's life when he pauses and " takes stock " of his condition ; when he asks himself how it fares with his individuality as a whole, mental, moral, physical, material. This time comes after the first heedless flights of youth have passed, when the initiative and more powerful efforts have been made, and he begins to feel the uncertainty of results and final values which attaches itself to everything. There is a deadening thought of uselessness which creeps into many men's minds—the thought which has been best expressed by the Preacher in Ecclesiastes.

Yet Lester strove to be philosophical. " What difference does it make ? " he used to say to himself, " whether I live at the White House, or here at home, or at the Grand Pacific ? " But in the very question was the implication that there were achievements in life which he had failed to realise in his own career. The White House represented the rise and success of a great public character. His home and the Grand Pacific were what had come to him without effort.

He decided for the time being—it was about the period of the death of Jennie's mother—that he would make some effort to rehabilitate himself. He would cut out idling—these numerous trips with Jennie had cost him considerable time. He would make some outside investments. If his brother could find avenues of financial profit, so could he. He would endeavour to assert his authority—he would try to make himself of more importance in the business, rather than let Robert gradually absorb everything. Should he forsake Jennie? —that thought also came to him. She had no claim on him. She could make no protest. Somehow he did not see how it could be done. It seemed cruel, useless ; above all (though he disliked to admit it ) it would be uncomfortable for himself. He liked her—loved her, perhaps, in a selfish way. He didn't see how he could desert her very well.

Just at this time he had a really serious difference with Robert. His brother wanted to sever relations with an old and well established paint company in New York, which had manufactured paints especially for the house, and invest in a new concern in Chicago, which was growing and had a promising future. Lester, knowing the members of the Eastern firm, their reliability, their long and friendly relations with the house, was in opposition. His father at first seemed to agree with Lester. But Robert argued out the question in his cold, logical way, his blue eyes fixed uncompromisingly upon his brother's face. "We can't go on forever," he said, "standing by old friends, just because father here has dealt with them, or you like them. We must have a change. The business must be stiffened up ; we're going to have more and stronger competition."

"It's just as father feels about it," said Lester at last. "I have no deep feeling in the matter. It won't hurt me one way or the other. You say the house is going to profit eventually. I've stated the arguments on the other side."

"I'm inclined to think Robert is right," said Archibald Kane calmly. "Most of the things he has suggested so far have worked out."

Lester coloured. "Well, we won't have any more discussion about it then," he said. He rose and strolled out of the office.

The shock of this defeat, coming at a time when he was considering pulling himself together, depressed Lester considerably. It wasn't much but it was a straw, and his father's remark about his brother's business acumen was even more irritating. He was beginning to wonder whether his father would discriminate in any way in the distribution of the property. Had he heard anything about his entanglement with Jennie ? Had he resented the long vacations he had taken from business ? It did not appear to Lester that he could be justly chargeable with either incapacity or indifference, so far as the company was concerned. He had done his work well. He was still the investigator of propositions put up to the house, the student of contracts, the trusted adviser of his father and mother—but he was being worsted. Where would it end ? He thought about this, but could reach no conclusion.

Later in this same year Robert came forward with a plan for reorganisation in the executive department of the business. He proposed that they should build an immense exhibition and storage warehouse on Michigan Avenue in Chicago, and transfer a portion of their completed stock there. Chicago was more central than Cincinnati. Buyers from the West and country merchants could be more easily reached and dealt with there. It would be a big advertisement for the house, a magnificent evidence of its standing and prosperity. Kane senior and Lester immediately approved of this. Both saw its advantages. Robert suggested that Lester should undertake

the construction of the new buildings. It would probably
be advisable for him to reside in Chicago a part of the time.

The idea appealed to Lester, even though it took him away
from Cincinnati, largely if not entirely. It was dignified and
not unrepresentative of his standing in the company. He
could live in Chicago and he could have Jennie with him.
The scheme he had for taking an apartment could now be
arranged without difficulty. He voted yes. Robert smiled.
" I'm sure we'll get good results from this all around," he said.

As construction work was soon to begin, Lester decided to
move to Chicago immediately. He sent word for Jennie to
meet him, and together they selected an apartment on the
North Side, a very comfortable suite of rooms on a side street
near the lake, and he had it fitted up to suit his taste. He
figured that living in Chicago he could pose as a bachelor. He
would never need to invite his friends to his rooms. There
were his offices, where he could always be found, his clubs and
the hotels. To his way of thinking the arrangement was
practically ideal.

Of course Jennie's departure from Cleveland brought
the affairs of the Gerhardt family to a climax. Probably
the home would be broken up, but Gerhardt himself took the
matter philosophically. He was an old man, and it did not
matter much where he lived. Bass, Martha, and George
were already taking care of themselves. Veronica and William
were still in school, but some provision could be made for
boarding them with a neighbour. The one real concern of
Jennie and Gerhardt was Vesta. It was Gerhardt's natural
thought that Jennie must take the child with her. What else
should a mother do ?

" Have you told him yet ? " he asked her, when the day of
her contemplated departure had been set.

" No ; but I'm going to soon," she assured him.

" Always soon," he said.

He shook his head. His throat swelled.

" It's too bad," he went on. " It's a great sin. God will
punish you, I'm afraid. The child needs some one. I'm
getting old—otherwise I would keep her. There is no one
here all day now to look after her right, as she should be."
Again he shook his head.

" I know," said Jennie weakly. " I'm going to fix it now

I'm going to have her live with me soon. I won't neglect her—you know that."

"But the child's name," he insisted. "She should have a name. Soon in another year she goes to school. People will want to know who she is. It can't go on forever like this."

Jennie understood well enough that it couldn't. She was crazy about her baby. The heaviest cross she had to bear was the constant separations and the silence she was obliged to maintain about Vesta's very existence. It did seem unfair to the child, and yet Jennie did not see clearly how she could have acted otherwise. Vesta had good clothes, everything she needed. She was at least comfortable. Jennie hoped to give her a good education. If only she had told the truth to Lester in the first place. Now it was almost too late, and yet she felt that she had acted for the best. Finally she decided to find some good woman or family in Chicago who would take charge of Vesta for a consideration. In a Swedish colony to the west of La Salle Avenue she came across an old lady who seemed to embody all the virtues she required—cleanliness, simplicity, honesty. She was a widow, doing work by the day, but she was glad to make an arrangement by which she should give her whole time to Vesta. The latter was to go to kindergarten when a suitable one should be found. She was to have toys and kindly attention, and Mrs. Oslen was to inform Jennie of any change in the child's health. Jennie proposed to call every day, and she thought that sometimes, when Lester was out of town, Vesta might be brought to the apartment. She had had her with her at Cleveland, and he had never found out anything.

The arrangements completed, Jennie returned at the first opportunity to Cleveland to take Vesta away. Gerhardt, who had been brooding over his approaching loss, appeared most solicitous about her future. "She should grow up to be a fine girl," he said. "You should give her a good education—she is so smart." He spoke of the advisability of sending her to a Lutheran school and church, but Jennie was not so sure of that. Time and association with Lester had led her to think that perhaps the public school was better than any private institution. She had no particular objection to the church, but she no longer depended upon its teachings as a guide in the affairs of life. Why should she ?

The next day it was necessary for Jennie to return to Chicago. Vesta, excited and eager, was made ready for the journey. Gerhardt had been wandering about, restless as a lost spirit, while the process of dressing was going on ; now that the hour had actually struck he was doing his best to control his feelings. He could see that the five-year-old child had no conception of what it meant to him. She was happy and self-interested, chattering about the ride and the train.

" Be a good little girl," he said, lifting her up and kissing her. " See that you study your catechism and say your prayers. And you won't forget the grandpa—what ?——" He tried to go on, but his voice failed him.

Jennie, whose heart ached for her father, choked back her emotion. " There," she said, " if I'd thought you were going to act like that——" She stopped.

" Go," said Gerhardt, manfully, " go. It is best this way." And he stood solemnly by as they went out of the door. Then he turned back to his favourite haunt, the kitchen, and stood there staring at the floor. One by one they were leaving him— Mrs. Gerhardt, Bass, Martha, Jennie, Vesta. He clasped his hands together, after his old-time fashion, and shook his head again and again. " So it is ! So it is ! " he repeated. " They all leave me. All my life goes to pieces."

## CHAPTER XXVIII

DURING the three years in which Jennie and Lester had been associated there had grown up between them a strong feeling of mutual sympathy and understanding. Lester truly loved her in his own way. It was a strong, self-satisfying, determined kind of way, based solidly on a big natural foundation, but rising to a plane of genuine spiritual affinity. The yielding sweetness of her character both attracted and held him. She was true, and good, and womanly to the very centre of her being ; he had learned to trust her, to depend upon her, and the feeling had but deepened with the passing of the years.

On her part Jennie had sincerely, deeply, truly learned to love this man. At first when he had swept her off her feet, overawed her soul, and used her necessity as a chain wherewith to bind her to him, she was a little doubtful, a little afraid of him, although she had always liked him. Now, however, by living with him, by knowing him better, by watching his moods, she had come to love him. He was so big, so vocal, so handsome. His point of view and opinions of anything and everything were so positive. His pet motto, " Hew to the line, let the chips fall where they may," had clung in her brain as something immensely characteristic. Apparently he was not afraid of anything—God, man, or devil. He used to look at her, holding her chin between the thumb and fingers of his big brown hand, and say : " You're sweet, all right, but you need courage and defiance. You haven't enough of those things." And her eyes would meet his in dumb appeal. " Never mind," he would add, " you have other things." And then he would kiss her.

One of the most appealing things to Lester was the simple way in which she tried to avoid exposure of her various social and educational shortcomings. She could not write very well, and once he found a list of words he had used written out on a piece of paper with the meanings opposite. He smiled, but he liked her better for it. Another time in the Southern hotel in St. Louis he watched her pretending a loss of appetite because she thought that her lack of table manners was being observed by near-by diners. She could not always be sure of the right forks and knives, and the strange-looking dishes bothered her ; how did one eat asparagus and artichokes.

"Why don't you eat something ? " he asked good-naturedly. "You're hungry, aren't you ? "

"Not very."

"You must be. Listen, Jennie. I know what it is. You mustn't feel that way. Your manners are all right. I wouldn't bring you here if they weren't. Your instincts are all right. Don't be uneasy. I'd tell you quick enough when there was anything wrong." His brown eyes held a friendly gleam.

She smiled gratefully. " I do feel a little nervous at times," she admitted.

"Don't," he repeated. " You're all right. Don't worry. I'll show you." And he did.

By degrees Jennie grew into an understanding of the usages and customs of comfortable existence. All that the Gerhardt family had ever had were the bare necessities of life. Now she was surrounded with whatever she wanted—trunks, clothes, toilet articles, the whole varied equipment of comfort—and while she liked it all, it did not upset her sense of proportion and her sense of the fitness of things. There was no element of vanity in her, only a sense of joy in privilege and opportunity. She was grateful to Lester for all that he had done and was doing for her. If only she could hold him—always !

The details of getting Vesta established once adjusted, Jennie settled down into the routine of home life. Lester, busy about his multitudinous affairs, was in and out. He had a suite of rooms reserved for himself at the Grand Pacific, which was then the exclusive hotel of Chicago, and this was his ostensible residence. His luncheon and evening appointments were kept at the Union Club. An early patron of the telephone, he had one installed in the apartment, so that he could reach Jennie quickly and at any time. He was home two or three nights a week, sometimes oftener. He insisted at first on Jennie having a girl of general housework, but acquiesced in the more sensible arrangement which she suggested later of letting some one come in to do the cleaning. She liked to work around her own home. Her natural industry and love of order prompted this feeling.

Lester liked his breakfast promptly at eight in the morning. He wanted dinner served nicely at seven. Silverware, cut glass, imported china—all the little luxuries of life appealed to him. He kept his trunks and wardrobe at the apartment.

During the first few months everything went smoothly. He was in the habit of taking Jennie to the theatre now and then, and if he chanced to run across an acquaintance he always introduced her as Miss Gerhardt. When he registered her as his wife it was usually under an assumed name ; where there was no danger of detection he did not mind using his own signature. Thus far there had been no difficulty or unpleasantness of any kind.

The trouble with this situation was that it was criss-crossed with the danger and consequent worry which the deception in regard to Vesta had entailed, as well as with Jennie's natural anxiety about her father and the disorganised home. Jennie feared, as Veronica hinted, that she and William would go to live with Martha, who was installed in a boarding-house in Cleveland, and that Gerhardt would be left alone. He was such a pathetic figure to her, with his injured hands and his one ability—that of being a watchman—that she was hurt to think of his being left alone. Would he come to her ? She knew that he would not—feeling as he did at present. Would Lester have him—she was not sure of that. If he came Vesta would have to be accounted for. So she worried.

The situation in regard to Vesta was really complicated. Owing to the feeling that she was doing her daughter a great injustice, Jennie was particularly sensitive in regard to her, anxious to do a thousand things to make up for the one great duty that she could not perform. She daily paid a visit to the home of Mrs. Oslen, always taking with her toys, candy, or whatever came into her mind as being likely to interest and please the child. She liked to sit with Vesta and tell her stories of fairy and giant, which kept the little girl wide-eyed. At last she went so far as to bring her to the apartment, when Lester was away visiting his parents, and she soon found it possible, during his several absences, to do this regularly. After that, as time went on and she began to know his habits, she became more bold—although bold is scarcely the word to use in connection with Jennie. She became venturesome much as a mouse might ; she would risk Vesta's presence on the

assurance of even short absences—two or three days.    She
even got into the habit of keeping a few of Vesta's toys at the
apartment, so that she could have something to play with
when she came.

During these several visits from her child Jennie could not
but realise the lovely thing life would be were she only an
honoured wife and a happy mother.    Vesta was a most observant
little girl.    She could by her innocent childish questions give
a hundred turns to the dagger of self-reproach which was
already planted deeply in Jennie's heart.

" Can I come to live with you ? " was one of her simplest
and most frequently repeated questions.    Jennie would reply
that mamma could not have her just yet, but that very soon
now, just as soon as she possibly could, Vesta should come to
stay always.

" Don't you know just when ? " Vesta would ask.

" No, dearest, not just when.    Very soon now.    You won't
mind waiting a little while.    Don't you like Mrs. Olsen ? "

" Yes," replied Vesta ; " but then she ain't got any nice
things now.    She's just got old things."    And Jennie, stricken
to the heart, would take Vesta to the toy shop, and load her
down with a new assortment of playthings.

Of course Lester was not in the least suspicious.    His
observation of things relating to the home were rather casual.
He went about his work and his pleasures believing Jennie
to be the soul of sincerity and good-natured service, and it
never occurred to him that there was anything underhanded
in her actions.    Once he did come home sick in the afternoon
and found her absent—an absence which endured from two
o'clock to five.    He was a little irritated and grumbled on her
return, but his annoyance was as nothing to her astonishment
and fright when she found him there.    She blanched at the
thought of his suspecting something, and explained as best
she could.    She had gone to see her washerwoman.    She was
slow about her marketing.    She didn't dream he was there.
She was sorry, too, that her absence had lost her an opportunity
to serve him.    It showed her what a mess she was likely to
make of it all.

It happened that about three weeks after the above occurrence Lester had occasion to return to Cincinnati for a week,
and during this time Jennie again brought Vesta to the flat ;

for four days there was the happiest goings on between the mother and child.

Nothing would have come of this little reunion had it not been for an oversight on Jennie's part, the far-reaching effects of which she could only afterward regret. This was the leaving of a little toy lamb under the large leather divan in the front room, where Lester was wont to lie and smoke. A little bell held by a thread of blue ribbon was fastened about its neck, and this tinkled feebly whenever it was shaken. Vesta, with the unaccountable freakishness of children had deliberately dropped it behind the divan, an action which Jennie did not notice at the time. When she gathered up the various playthings after Vesta's departure she overlooked it entirely, and there it rested, its innocent eyes still staring upon the sunlit regions of toyland, when Lester returned.

That same evening, when he was lying on the divan, quietly enjoying his cigar and his newspaper, he chanced to drop the former, fully lighted. Wishing to recover it before it should do any damage, he leaned over and looked under the divan. The cigar was not in sight, so he rose and pulled the lounge out, a move which revealed to him the little lamb still standing where Vesta had dropped it. He picked it up, turning it over and over, and wondering how it had come there.

A lamb! It must belong to some neighbour's child in whom Jennie had taken an interest, he thought. He would have to go and tease her about this.

Accordingly he held the toy jovially before him, and, coming out into the dining-room, where Jennie was working at the sideboard, he exclaimed in a mock solemn voice, " Where did this come from ? "

Jennie, who was totally unconscious of the existence of this evidence of her duplicity, turned, and was instantly possessed with the idea that he had suspected all and was about to visit his just wrath upon her. Instantly the blood flamed in her cheeks and as quickly left them.

" Why, why ! " she stuttered, " it's a little toy I bought."

" I see it is," he returned genially, her guilty tremor not escaping his observation, but having at the same time no explicable significance to him. " It's frisking around a mighty lone sheepfold."

He touched the little bell at its throat, while Jennie stood there, unable to speak. It tinkled feebly, and then he looked at her again. His manner was so humorous that she could tell he suspected nothing. However, it was almost impossible for her to recover her self-possession.

" What's ailing you ? " he asked.

" Nothing," she replied.

" You look as though a lamb was a terrible shock to you."

" I forgot to take it out from there, that was all," she went on blindly.

" It looks as though it has been played with enough," he added more seriously, and then seeing that the discussion was evidently painful to her, he dropped it. The lamb had not furnished him the amusement that he had expected.

Lester went back into the front room, stretched himself out and thought it over. Why was she nervous ? What was there about a toy to make her grow pale ? Surely there was no harm in her harbouring some youngster of the neighbourhood when she was alone—having it come in and play. Why should she be so nervous ? He thought it over, but could come to no conclusion.

Nothing more was said about the incident of the toy lamb. Time might have wholly effaced the impression from Lester's memory had nothing else intervened to arouse his suspicions ; but a mishap of any kind seems invariably to be linked with others which follow close upon its heels.

One evening when Lester happened to be lingering about the flat later than usual the door bell rang, and, Jennie being busy in the kitchen, Lester went himself to open the door. He was greeted by a middle-aged lady, who frowned very nervously upon him, and inquired in broken Swedish accents for Jennie.

" Wait a moment," said Lester ; and stepping to the rear door he called her.

Jennie came, and seeing who the visitor was, she stepped nervously out in the hall and closed the door after her. The action instantly struck Lester as suspicious. He frowned and determined to inquire thoroughly into the matter. A moment later Jennie reappeared. Her face was white and her fingers seemed to be nervously seeking something to seize upon.

" What's the trouble ? " he inquired, the irritation he had felt the moment before giving his voice a touch of gruffness.

" I've to go out for a little while," she at last managed to reply.

" Very well," he assented unwillingly. " But you can tell me what's the trouble with you, can't you ? Where do you have to go ? "

" I—I," began Jennie, stammering. " I—have——"

" Yes," he said grimly.

" I have to go on an errand," she stumbled on. " I—I can't wait. I'll tell you when I come back, Lester. Please don't ask me now."

She looked vainly at him, her troubled countenance still marked by preoccupation and anxiety to get away, and Lester, who had never seen this look of intense responsibility in her before, was moved and irritated by it.

" That's all right," he said, " but what's the use of all this secrecy ? Why can't you come out and tell what's the matter with you ? What's the use of this whispering behind doors ? Where do you have to go ? "

He paused, checked by his own harshness, and Jennie who was intensely wrought up by the information she had received, as well as the unwonted verbal castigation she was now enduring, rose to an emotional state never reached by her before.

" I will, Lester, I will," she exclaimed. " Only not now. I haven't time. I'll tell you everything when I come back. Please don't stop me now."

She hurried to the adjoining chamber to get her wraps, and Lester, who had even yet no clear conception of what it all meant, followed her stubbornly to the door.

" See here," he exclaimed in his vigorous, brutal way, " you're not acting right. What's the matter with you ? I want to know."

He stood in the doorway, his whole frame exhibiting the pugnacity and settled determination of a man who is bound to be obeyed. Jennie, troubled and driven to bay, turned at last.

" It's my child, Lester," she exclaimed. " It's dying. I haven't time to talk. Oh, please don't stop me. I'll tell you everything when I come back."

" Your child ! " he exclaimed. " What the hell are you talking about ? "

" I couldn't help it," she returned. " I was afraid—I

should have told you long ago. I meant to only—only—Oh, let me go now, and I'll tell you all when I come back!"

He stared at her in amazement; then he stepped aside, unwilling to force her any further for the present. "Well, go ahead," he said quietly. "Don't you want some one to go along with you?"

"No," she replied. "Mrs. Oslen is right here. I'll go with her."

She hurried forth, white-faced, and he stood there, pondering. Could this be the woman he had thought he knew? Why, she had been deceiving him for years. Jennie! The white-faced! The simple.

He choked a little as he muttered.

"Well, I'll be damned!"

## CHAPTER XXIX

THE reason why Jennie had been called was nothing more than one of those infantile seizures the coming and result of which no man can predict two hours beforehand. Vesta had been seriously taken with membranous croup only a few hours before, and the development since had been so rapid that the poor old Swedish mother was half frightened to death herself, and hastily despatched a neighbour to say that Vesta was very ill and Mrs. Kane was to come at once. This message, delivered as it was in a very nervous manner by one whose only object was to bring her, and induced the soul-racking fear of death in Jennie and caused her to brave the discovery of Lester in the manner described. Jennie hurried on anxiously, her one thought being to reach her child before the arm of death could interfere and snatch it from her, her mind weighed upon by a legion of fears. What if it should already be too late when she got there ; what if Vesta already should be no more. Instinctively she quickened her pace and as the street lamps came and receded in the gloom she forgot all the sting of Lester's words, all fear that he might turn her out and leave her alone in a great city with a little child to care for, and remembered only the fact that her Vesta was very ill, possibly dying, and that she was the direct cause of the child's absence from her ; that perhaps but for the want of her care and attention Vesta might be well to-night.

" If I can only get there," she kept saying to herself ; and then, with that frantic unreason which is the chief characteristic of the instinct-driven mother : " I might have known that God would punish me for my unnatural conduct. I might have known—I might have known."

When she reached the gate she fairly sped up the little walk and into the house, where Vesta was lying pale, quiet, and weak, but considerably better. Several Swedish neighbours and a middle-aged physician were in attendance, all of whom looked at her curiously as she dropped beside the child's bed and spoke to her.

Jennie's mind had been made up. She had sinned, and sinned grievously, against her daughter, but now she would make amends so far as possible. Lester was very dear to her, but she would no longer attempt to deceive him in anything, even if he left her—she felt an agonised stab, a pain at the thought—she must still do the one right thing. Vesta must not be an outcast any longer. Her mother must give her a home. Where Jennie was, there must Vesta be.

Sitting by the bedside in this humble Swedish cottage, Jennie realised the fruitlessness of her deception, the trouble and pain it had created in her home, the months of suffering it had given her with Lester, the agony it had heaped upon her this night—and to what end ? The truth had been discovered anyhow. She sat there and meditated, not knowing what next was to happen, while Vesta quieted down, and then went soundly to sleep.

Lester, after recovering from the first heavy import of this discovery, asked himself some perfectly natural questions. " Who was the father of the child ?   How old was it ?   How did it chance to be in Chicago, and who was taking care of it ? He could ask, but he could not answer ; he knew absolutely nothing.

Curiously, now, as he thought, his first meeting with Jennie at Mrs. Bracebridge's came back to him. What was it about her then that had attracted him ? What made him think, after a few hours' observation, that he could seduce her to his will ? What was it—moral looseness, or weakness, or what ? There must have been art in the sorry affair, the practised art of the cheat, and, in deceiving such a confiding nature as his, she had done even more than practise deception—she had been ungrateful.

Now the quality of ingratitude was a very objectionable thing to Lester—the last and most offensive trait of a debased nature, and to be able to discover a trace of it in Jennie was very disturbing. It is true that she had not exhibited it in any other way before—quite to the contrary—but nevertheless he saw strong evidences of it now, and it made him very bitter in his feeling toward her. How could she be guilty of any such conduct toward him ? Had he not picked her up out of nothing, so to speak, and befriended her ?

He moved from his chair in this silent room and began to

pace slowly to and fro, the weightiness of this subject exercising to the full his power of decision. She was guilty of a misdeed which he felt able to condemn. The original concealment was evil; the continued deception more. Lastly, there was the thought that her love after all had been divided, part for him, part for the child, a discovery which no man in his position could contemplate with serenity. He moved irritably as he thought of it, shoved his hands in his pockets and walked to and fro across the floor.

That a man of Lester's temperament should consider himself wronged by Jennie merely because she had concealed a child whose existence was due to conduct no more irregular than was involved later in the yielding of herself to him was an example of those inexplicable perversions of judgment to which the human mind, in its capacity of keeper of the honour of others, seems permanently committed. Lester, aside from his own personal conduct (for men seldom judge with that in the balance), had faith in the ideal that a woman should reveal herself completely to the one man with whom she is in love; and the fact that she had not done so was a grief to him. He had asked her once tentatively about her past. She begged him not to press her. That was the time she should have spoken of any child. Now—he shook his head.

His first impulse, after he had thought the thing over, was to walk out and leave her. At the same time he was curious to hear the end of this business. He did put on his hat and coat, however, and went out, stopping at the first convenient saloon to get a drink. He took a car and went down to the club, strolling about the different rooms and chatting with several people whom he encountered. He was restless and irritated; and finally, after three hours of meditation, he took a cab and returned to his apartment.

The distraught Jennie, sitting by her sleeping child, was at last made to realise, by its peaceful breathing that all danger was over. There was nothing more that she could do for Vesta, and now the claims of the home that she had deserted began to reassert themselves, the promise to Lester and the need of being loyal to her duties unto the very end. Lester might possibly be waiting for her. It was just probable that he wished to hear the remainder of her story before breaking with her entirely. Although anguished and frightened by the certainty, as she deemed it, of his forsaking her, she nevertheless felt that it was no more than she deserved—a just punishment for all her misdoings.

When Jennie arrived at the flat it was after eleven, and the hall light was already out. She first tried the door, and then inserted her key. No one stirred, however, and, opening the door, she entered in the expectation of seeing Lester sternly confronting her. He was not there, however. The burning gas had merely been an oversight on his part. She glanced quickly about, but seeing only the empty room, she came instantly to the other conclusion, that he had forsaken her—and so stood there, a meditative, helpless figure.

" Gone ! " she thought.

At this moment his footsteps sounded on the stairs. He came in with his derby hat pulled low over his broad forehead, close to his sandy eyebrows, and with his overcoat buttoned up closely about his neck. He took off the coat without looking at Jennie and hung it on the rack. Then he deliberately took off his hat and hung that up also. When he was through he turned to where she was watching him with wide eyes.

" I want to know about this thing now from beginning to end," he began. " Whose child is that ? "

Jennie wavered a moment, as one who might be going to take a leap in the dark, then opened her lips mechanically and confessed :

" It's Senator Brander's."

" Senator Brander ! " echoed Lester, the familiar name of the dead but still famous statesman ringing with shocking and unexpected force in his ears. " How did you come to know him ? "

" We used to do his washing for him," she rejoined simply— " my mother and I."

Lester paused, the baldness of the statements issuing from her sobering even his rancorous mood. " Senator Brander's child," he thought to himself. So that great representative of the interests of the common people was the undoer of her— a self-confessed washerwoman's daughter. A fine tragedy of low life all this was.

" How long ago was this ? " he demanded, his face the picture of a darkling mood.

" It's been nearly six years now," she returned.

He calculated the time that had elapsed since he had known her, and then continued :

" How old is the child ? "

" She's a little over five."

Lester moved a little. The need for serious thought made his tone more peremptory but less bitter.

" Where have you been keeping her all this time ? "

" She was at home until you went to Cincinnati last spring. I went down and brought her then."

" Was she there the times I came to Cleveland ? "

" Yes," said Jennie ; " but I didn't let her come out anywhere where you could see her."

" I thought you said you told your people that you were married," he exclaimed, wondering how this relationship of the child to the family could have been adjusted.

" I did," she replied, " but I didn't want to tell you about her. They thought all the time I intended to."

" Well, why didn't you ? "

" Because I was afraid."

" Afraid of what ? "

" I didn't know what was going to become of me when I went with you, Lester. I didn't want to do her any harm if I could help it. I was ashamed, afterward ; when you said you didn't like children I was afraid."

" Afraid I'd leave you ? "

" Yes."

He stopped, the simplicity of her answers removing a part of the suspicion of artful duplicity which had originally weighed upon him. After all, there was not so much of that in it as mere wretchedness of circumstance and cowardice of morals. What a family she must have ! What queer non-moral natures they must have to have brooked any such a combination of affairs ! " Didn't you know that you'd be found out in the long run ? " he at last demanded. " Surely you might have seen that you couldn't raise her that way. Why didn't you tell me in the first place ? I wouldn't have thought anything of it then."

" I know," she said. " I wanted to protect her."

" Where is she now ? " he asked.

Jennie explained.

She stood there, the contradictory aspect of these questions and of his attitude puzzling even herself.   She did try to explain them after a time, but all Lester could gain was that she had blundered along without any artifice at all—a condition that was so manifest that, had he been in any other position than that he was, he might have pitied her.   As it was, the revelation concerning Brander was hanging over him, and he finally returned to that.

" You say your mother used to do washing for him.   How did you come to get in with him ? "

Jennie, who until now had borne his questions with unmoving pain, winced at this.   He was now encroaching upon the period that was by far the most distressing memory of her life.   What he had just asked seemed to be a demand upon her to make everything clear.

" I was so young, Lester," she pleaded.   " I was only eighteen. I didn't know.   I used to go to the hotel where he was stopping and get his laundry, and at the end of the week I'd take it to him again."

She paused, and as he took a chair, looking as if he expected to hear the whole story, she continued : " We were so poor. He used to give me money to give to my mother.  I didn't know."

She paused again, totally unable to go on, and he, seeing that it would be impossible for her to explain without prompting, took up his questioning again—eliciting by degrees the whole pitiful story.   Brander had intended to marry her.   He had written to her, but before he could come to her he died.

The confession was complete.   It was followed by a period of five minutes, in which Lester said nothing at all ; he put his arm on the mantel and stared at the wall, while Jennie waited, not knowing what would follow—not wishing to make a single plea.   The clock ticked audibly.   Lester's face betrayed no sign of either thought or feeling.   He was now quite calm, quite sober, wondering what he should do.   Jennie was before him as the criminal at the bar.   He, the righteous, the moral, the pure of heart, was in the judgment seat.   Now to sentence her—to make up his mind what course of action he should pursue.

It was a disagreeable tangle, to be sure, something that a man of his position and wealth really ought not to have anything to do with.   This child, the actuality of it, put an almost unbearable face upon the whole matter—and yet he was not quite prepared to speak. He turned after a time, the silvery tinkle of the French clock on the mantel striking three and causing him to become aware of Jennie, pale, uncertain, still standing as she had stood all this while.

" Better go to bed," he said at last, and fell again to pondering this difficult problem.

But Jennie continued to stand there wide-eyed, expectant, ready to hear at any moment his decision as to her fate. She waited in vain, however. After a long time of musing he turned and went to the clothes-rack near the door.

" Better go to bed," he said, indifferently. " I'm going out."

She turned instinctively, feeling that even in this crisis there was some little service that she might render, but he did not see her. He went out, vouchsafing no further speech.

She looked after him, and as his footsteps sounded on the stair she felt as if she were doomed and hearing her own death-knell. What had she done ? What would he do now ? She stood there a dissonance of despair, and when the lower door clicked moved her hand out of the agony of her suppressed hopelessness.

" Gone ! " she thought. " Gone ! "

In the light of a late dawn she was still sitting there pondering, her state far too urgent for idle tears.

## CHAPTER XXX

THE sullen, philosophic Lester was not so determined upon his future course of action as he appeared to be. Stern as was his mood, he did not see, after all, exactly what grounds he had for complaint. And yet the child's existence complicated matters considerably. He did not like to see the evidence of Jennie's previous misdeeds walking about in the shape of a human being ; but, as a matter of fact, he admitted to himself that long ago he might have forced Jennie's story out of her if he had gone about it in earnest. She would not have lied, he knew that. At the very outset he might have demanded the history of her past. He had not done so ; well, now it was too late. The one thing it did fix in his mind was that it would be useless to ever think of marrying her. It couldn't be done, not by a man in his position. The best solution of the problem was to make reasonable provision for Jennie and then leave her. He went to his hotel with his mind made up, but he did not actually say to himself that he would do it at once.

It is an easy thing for a man to theorise in a situation of this kind, quite another to act. Our comforts, appetites and passions grow with usage, and Jennie was not only a comfort, but an appetite, with him. Almost four years of constant association had taught him so much about her and himself that he was not prepared to let go easily or quickly. It was too much of a wrench. He could think of it bustling about the work of a great organisation during the daytime, but when night came it was a different matter. He could be lonely, too, he discovered much to his surprise, and it disturbed him.

One of the things that interested him in this situation was Jennie's early theory that the intermingling of Vesta with him and her in this new relationship would injure the child. Just how did she come by that feeling, he wanted to know ? His place in the world was better than hers, yet it dawned on him after a time that there might have been something in her point of view. She did not know who he was or what he would do with her. He might leave her shortly. Being uncertain, she wished to protect her baby. That wasn't so bad. Then again, he was curious to know what the child was like. The daughter of a man like Senator Brander might be somewhat of an infant. He was a brilliant man and Jennie was a charming woman. He thought of this, and while it irritated him, it aroused his curiosity. He ought to go back and see the child —he was really entitled to a view of it—but he hesitated because of his own attitude in the beginning. It seemed to him that he really ought to quit, and here he was parleying with himself.

The truth was that he couldn't. These years of living with Jennie had made him curiously dependent upon her. Who had ever been so close to him before ? His mother loved him, but her attitude toward him had not so much to do with real love as with ambition. His father—well, his father was a man, like himself. All of his sisters were distinctly wrapped up in their own affairs ; Robert and he were temperamentally uncongenial. With Jennie he had really been happy, he had truly lived. She was necessary to him ; the longer he stayed away from her the more he wanted her. He finally decided to have a straight-out talk with her, to arrive at some sort of understanding. She ought to get the child and take care of it. She must understand that he might eventually want to quit. She ought to be made to feel that a definite change had taken place, though no immediate break might occur. That same evening he went out to the apartment. Jennie heard him enter, and her heart began to flutter. Then she took her courage in both hands, and went to meet him.

" There's just one thing to be done about this as far as I can see," began Lester, with characteristic directness. " Get the child and bring her here where you can take care of her. There's no use leaving her in the hands of strangers."

" I will, Lester," said Jennie submissively. " I always wanted to."

" Very well, then, you'd better do it at once." He took an evening newspaper out of his pocket and strolled toward one of the front windows ; then he turned to her. " You and I might as well understand each other, Jennie," he went on. " I can see how this thing came about. It was a piece of foolishness on my part not to have asked you before, and made you tell me.  It was silly for you to conceal it, even if you didn't want the child's life mixed with mine.  You might have known that it couldn't be done.  That's neither here nor there, though, now.  The thing that I want to point out is that one can't live and hold a relationship such as ours without confidence. You and I had that, I thought.  I don't see my way clear to ever hold more than a tentative relationship with you on this basis.  The thing is too tangled.  There's too much cause for scandal."

" I know," said Jennie.

" Now, I don't propose to do anything hasty.  For my part I don't see why things can't go on about as they are—certainly for the present—but I want you to look the facts in the face."

Jennie sighed.  " I know, Lester," she said, " I know."

He went to the window and stared out.  There were some trees in the yard, where the darkness was settling.  He wondered how this would really come out, for he liked a home atmosphere.  Should he leave the apartment and go to his club ?

" You'd better get the dinner," he suggested, after a time, turning toward her irritably ; but he did not feel so distant as he looked.  It was a shame that life could not be more decently organised.  He strolled back to his lounge, and Jennie went about her duties.  She was thinking of Vesta, of her ungrateful attitude toward Lester, of his final decision never to marry her.  So that was how one dream had been wrecked by folly.

She spread the table, lighted the pretty silver candles, made his favourite biscuit, put a small leg of lamb in the oven to roast, and washed some lettuce-leaves for a salad.  She had been a diligent student of a cook-book for some time, and she had learned a good deal from her mother.  All the time she was wondering how the situation would work out.  He would leave her eventually—no doubt of that.  He would go away and marry some one else.

" Oh, well," she thought finally, " he is not going to leave me right away—that is something.  And I can bring Vesta here." She sighed as she carried the things to the table.  If life would only give her Lester and Vesta together—but that hope was over.

## CHAPTER XXXI

THERE was peace and quiet for some time after this storm. Jennie went the next day and brought Vesta away with her. The joy of the reunion between mother and child made up for many other worries. "Now I can do by her as I ought," she thought; and three or four times during the day she found herself humming a little song.

Lester came only occasionally at first. He was trying to make himself believe that he ought to do something toward reforming his life—toward bringing about that eventual separation which he had suggested. He did not like the idea of a child being in this apartment—particularly that particular child. He fought his way through a period of calculated neglect, and then began to return to the apartment more regularly. In spite of all its drawbacks, it was a place of quiet, peace, and very notable personal comfort.

During the first days of Lester's return it was difficult for Jennie to adjust matters so as to keep the playful, nervous, almost uncontrollable child from annoying the staid, emphatic, commercial-minded man. Jennie gave Vesta a severe talking to the first night Lester telephoned that he was coming, telling her that he was a very bad-tempered man who didn't like children, and that she mustn't go near him. "You mustn't talk," she said. "You mustn't ask questions. Let mamma ask you what you want. And don't reach, ever."

Vesta agreed solemnly, but her childish mind hardly grasped the full significance of the warning.

Lester came at seven. Jennie, who had taken great pains to array Vesta as attractively as possible, had gone into her bedroom to give her own toilet a last touch. Vesta was supposedly in the kitchen. As a matter of fact, she had followed her mother to the door of the sitting-room, where now she could be plainly seen. Lester hung up his hat and coat, then, turning, he caught his first glimpse. The child looked very sweet—he admitted that at a glance. She was arrayed in a blue-dotted, white flannel dress, with a soft roll collar and cuffs, and the costume was completed by white stockings and shoes. Her corn-coloured ringlets hung gaily about her face. Blue eyes, rosy lips, rosy cheeks completed the picture. Lester stared, almost inclined to say something, but restrained himself. Vesta shyly retreated.

When Jennie came out he commented on the fact that Vesta had arrived. " Rather sweet-looking child," he said. " Do you have much trouble in making her mind ? "

" Not much," she returned.

Jennie went on to the dining-room, and Lester overheard a scrap of their conversation.

" Who are he ? " asked Vesta.

" Sh ! That's your Uncle Lester. Didn't I tell you you mustn't talk ? "

" Are he your uncle ? "

" No, dear. Don't talk now. Run into the kitchen."

" Are he only my uncle ? "

" Yes. Now run along."

" All right."

In spite of himself Lester had to smile.

What might have followed if the child had been homely, misshapen, peevish, or all three, can scarcely be conjectured. Had Jennie been less tactful, even in the beginning, he might have obtained a disagreeable impression. As it was, the natural beauty of the child, combined with the mother's gentle diplomacy in keeping her in the background, served to give him that fleeting glimpse of innocence and youth which is always pleasant. The thought struck him that Jennie had been the mother of a child all these years ; she had been separated from it for months at a time ; she had never even hinted at its existence, and yet her affection for Vesta was obviously great. " It's queer," he said. " She's a peculiar woman."

One morning Lester was sitting in the parlour reading his paper when he thought he heard something stir. He turned, and was surprised to see a large blue eye fixed upon him through the crack of a neighbouring door—the effect was most disconcerting. It was not like the ordinary eye, which, under such embarrassing circumstances, would have been immediately withdrawn ; it kept its position with deliberate boldness. He turned his paper solemnly and looked again. There was the eye. He turned it again. Still was the eye present.

He crossed his legs and looked again. Now the eye was gone.

This little episode, unimportant in itself, was yet informed with the saving grace of comedy, a thing to which Lester was especially responsive. Although not in the least inclined to relax his attitude of aloofness, he found his mind, in the minutest degree, tickled by the mysterious appearance; the corners of his mouth were animated by a desire to turn up. He did not give way to the feeling, and stuck by his paper, but the incident remained very clearly in his mind. The young wayfarer had made her first really important impression upon him.

Not long after this Lester was sitting one morning at breakfast, calmly eating his chop and conning his newspaper, when he was aroused by another visitation—this time not quite so simple. Jennie had given Vesta her breakfast, and set her to amuse herself alone until Lester should leave the house. Jennie was seated at the table, pouring out the coffee, when Vesta suddenly appeared, very business-like in manner, and marched through the room. Lester looked up, and Jennie coloured and arose.

" What is it, Vesta ? " she inquired, following her.

By this time, however, Vesta had reached the kitchen, secured a little broom, and returned, a droll determination lighting her face.

" I want my little broom," she exclaimed and marched sedately past, at which manifestation of spirit Lester again twitched internally, this time allowing the slightest suggestion of a smile to play across his mouth.

The final effect of this intercourse was gradually to break down the feeling of distaste Lester had for the child, and to establish in its place a sort of tolerant recognition of her possibilities as a human being.

The developments of the next six months were of a kind to further relax the strain of opposition which still existed in Lester's mind. Although not at all resigned to the somewhat tainted atmosphere in which he was living, he yet found himself so comfortable that he could not persuade himself to give it up. It was too much like a bed of down. Jennie was too worshipful. The condition of unquestioned liberty, so far as all his old social relationships were concerned, coupled with the privilege of quiet, simplicity, and affection in the home was too inviting. He lingered on, and began to feel that perhaps it would be just as well to let matters rest as they were.

During this period his friendly relations with the little Vesta insensibly strengthened. He discovered that there was a real flavour of humour about Vesta's doings, and so came to watch for its development. She was forever doing something interesting, and although Jennie watched over her with a care that was in itself a revelation to him, nevertheless Vesta managed to elude every effort to suppress her and came straight home with her remarks. Once, for example, she was sawing away at a small piece of meat upon her large plate with her big knife, when Lester remarked to Jennie that it might be advisable to get her a little breakfast set.

" She can hardly handle these knives."

" Yes," said Vesta instantly. " I need a little knife. My hand is just so very little."

She held it up. Jennie, who never could tell what was to follow, reached over and put it down, while Lester with difficulty restrained a desire to laugh.

Another morning, not long after, she was watching Jennie put the lumps of sugar in Lester's cup, when she broke in with, " I want two lumps in mine, mamma."

" No, dearest," replied Jennie, " you don't need any in yours. You have milk to drink."

" Uncle Lester has two," she protested.

" Yes," returned Jennie ; " but you're only a little girl. Besides you mustn't say anything like that at the table. It isn't nice."

" Uncle Lester eats too much sugar," was her immediate rejoinder, at which that fine gourmet smiled broadly.

" I don't know about that," he put in, for the first time deigning to answer her directly. " That sounds like the fox and grapes to me." Vesta smiled back at him, and now that the ice was broken she chattered on unrestrainedly. One thing led to another, and at last Lester felt as though, in a way, the little girl belonged to him ; he was willing even that she should share in such opportunities as his position and wealth might make possible—provided, of course, that he stayed with Jennie, and that they worked out some arrangement which would not put him hopelessly out of touch with the world which was back of him, and which he had to keep constantly in mind

## CHAPTER XXXII

THE following spring the show-rooms and warehouse were completed, and Lester removed his office to the new building. Heretofore, he had been transacting all his business affairs at the Grand Pacific and the club. From now on he felt himself to be firmly established in Chicago—as if that was to be his future home. A large number of details were thrown upon him—the control of a considerable office force, and the handling of various important transactions. It took away from him the need of travelling, that duty going to Amy's husband, under the direction of Robert. The latter was doing his best to push his personal interests, not only through the influence he was bringing to bear upon his sisters, but through his reorganisation of the factory. Several men whom Lester was personally fond of were in danger of elimination. But Lester did not hear of this, and Kane senior was inclined to give Robert a free hand. Age was telling on him. He was glad to see some one with a strong policy come up and take charge. Lester did not seem to mind. Apparently he and Robert were on better terms than ever before.

Matters might have gone on smoothly enough were it not for the fact that Lester's private life with Jennie was not a matter which could be permanently kept under cover. At times he was seen driving with her by people who knew him in a social and commercial way. He was for brazening it out on the ground that he was a single man, and at liberty to associate with anybody he pleased. Jennie might be any young woman of good family in whom he was interested. He did not propose to introduce her to anybody if he could help it, and he always made it a point to be a fast traveller in driving, in order that others might not attempt to detain and talk to him. At the theatre, as has been said, she was simply " Miss Gerhardt."

The trouble was that many of his friends were also keen observers of life. They had no quarrel to pick with Lester's conduct. Only he had been seen in other cities, in times past, with this same woman. She must be some one whom he was maintaining irregularly. Well, what of it ? Wealth and youthful spirits must have their fling. Rumours came to Robert, who, however, kept his own counsel. If Lester wanted to do this sort of thing, well and good. But there must come a time when there would be a show-down.

This came about in one form about a year and a half after Lester and Jennie had been living in the north side apartment. It so happened that, during a stretch of inclement weather in the fall, Lester was seized with a mild form of grip. When he felt the first symptoms he thought that his indisposition would be a matter of short duration, and tried to overcome it by taking a hot bath and a liberal dose of quinine. But the infection was stronger than he counted on ; by morning he was flat on his back, with a severe fever and a splitting headache.

His long period of association with Jennie had made him incautious. Policy would have dictated that he should betake himself to his hotel and endure his sickness alone. As a matter of fact, he was very glad to be in the house with her. He had to call up the office to say that he was indisposed and would not be down for a day or so ; then he yielded himself comfortably to her patient ministrations.

Jennie, of course, was delighted to have Lester with her, sick or well. She persuaded him to see a doctor and have him prescribe. She brought him potions of hot lemonade, and bathed his face and hands in cold water over and over. Later, when he was recovering, she made him appetising cups of beef-tea or gruel.

It was during this illness that the first real contretemps occurred. Lester's sister Louise, who had been visiting friends in St. Paul, and who had written him that she might stop off to see him on her way, decided upon an earlier return than she had originally planned. While Lester was sick at his apartment she arrived in Chicago. Calling up the office, and finding that he was not there and would not be down for several days, she asked where he could be reached.

" I think he is at his rooms in the Grand Pacific," said an incautious secretary. " He's not feeling well." Louise, a little disturbed, telephoned to the Grand Pacific, and was told that Mr. Kane had not been there for several days—did not, as a matter of fact, occupy his rooms more than one or two days a week. Piqued by this, she telephoned his club.

It so happened that at the club there was a telephone boy who had called up the apartment a number of times for Lester himself. He had not been cautioned not to give its number—as a matter of fact, it had never been asked for by any one else. When Louise stated that she was Lester's sister, and was anxious to find him, the boy replied, " I think he lives at 19, Schiller Place."

" Whose address is that you're giving ? " inquired a passing clerk.

" Mr. Kane's."

" Well, don't be giving out addresses. Don't you know that yet ? "

The boy apologised, but Louise had hung up the receiver and was gone.

About an hour later, curious as to this third residence of her brother, Louise arrived at Schiller Place. Ascending the steps—it was a two-apartment house—she saw the name of Kane on the door leading to the second floor. Ringing the bell, she was opened to by Jennie, who was surprised to see so fashionably attired a young woman.

" This is Mr. Kane's apartment, I believe," began Louise, condescendingly, as she looked in at the open door behind Jennie. She was a little surprised to meet a young woman, but her suspicions were as yet only vaguely aroused.

" Yes," replied Jennie.

" He's sick, I believe. I'm his sister. May I come in ? "

Jennie, had she had time to collect her thoughts, would have tried to make some excuse, but Louise, with the audacity of her birth and station, swept past before Jennie could say a word. Once inside Louise looked about her inquiringly. She found herself in the sitting-room, which gave into the bedroom where Lester was lying. Vesta happened to be playing in one corner of the room, and stood up to eye the new-comer. The open bedroom showed Lester quite plainly lying in bed, a window to the left of him, his eyes closed.

" Oh, there you are, old fellow ! " exclaimed Louise. " What's ailing you ? " she hurried on.

Lester, who at the sound of her voice had opened his eyes, realised in an instant how things were. He pulled himself up on one elbow, but words failed him.

"Why, hello, Louise," he finally forced himself to say, "Where did you come from ? "

"St. Paul. I came back sooner than I thought," she answered lamely, a sense of something wrong irritating her. "I had a hard time finding you, too. Who's your——" she was about to say "pretty housekeeper," but turned to find Jennie dazedly gathering up certain articles in the adjoining room and looking dreadfully distraught.

Lester cleared his throat hopelessly.

His sister swept the place with an observing eye. It took in the home atmosphere, which was both pleasing and suggestive. There was a dress of Jennie's lying across a chair, in a familiar way, which caused Miss Kane to draw herself up warily. She looked at her brother, who had a rather curious expression in his eyes—he seemed slightly nonplussed, but cool and defiant.

"You shouldn't have come out here," said Lester finally, before Louise could give vent to the rising question in her mind.

"Why shouldn't I ? " she exclaimed, angered at the brazen confession. "You're my brother, aren't you ? Why should you have any place that I couldn't come. Well, I like that—and from you to me."

"Listen, Louise," went on Lester, drawing himself up further on one elbow. "You know as much about life as I do. There is no need of our getting into an argument. I didn't know you were coming, or I would have made other arrangements."

"Other arrangements, indeed," she sneered. "I should think as much. The idea ! "

She was greatly irritated to think that she had fallen into this trap ; it was really disgraceful of Lester.

"I wouldn't be so haughty about it," he declared, his colour rising. "I'm not apologising to you for my conduct. I'm saying I would have made other arrangements, which is a very different thing from begging your pardon. If you don't want to be civil, you needn't."

"Why, Lester Kane ! " she exclaimed, her cheeks flaming. "I thought better of you, honestly I did. I should think you would be ashamed of yourself living here in open——" she paused without using the word—" and our friends scattered all over the city. It's terrible ! I thought you had more sense of decency and consideration."

"Decency nothing," he flared. "I tell you I'm not apologising to you. If you don't like this you know what you can do."

"Oh!" she exclaimed. "This from my own brother! And for the sake of that creature! Whose child is that?" she demanded, savagely and yet curiously.

"Never mind, it's not mine. If it were it wouldn't make any difference. I wish you wouldn't busy yourself about my affairs."

Jennie, who had been moving about the dining-room beyond the sitting-room, heard the cutting references to herself. She winced with pain.

"Don't flatter yourself. I won't any more," retorted Louise. "I should think, though, that you, of all men, would be above anything like this—and that with a woman so obviously beneath you. Why, I thought she was——" she was again going to add "your housekeeper," but she was interrupted by Lester, who was angry to the point of brutality.

"Never mind what you thought she was," he growled. "She's better than some who do the so-called superior thinking. I know what you think. It's neither here nor there, I tell you. I'm doing this, and I don't care what you think. I have to take the blame. Don't bother about me."

"Well, I won't, I assure you," she flung back. "It's quite plain that your family means nothing to you. But if you had any sense of decency, Lester Kane, you would never let your sister be trapped into coming into a place like this. I'm disgusted, that's all, and so will the others be when they hear of it."

She turned on her heel and walked scornfully out, a withering look being reserved for Jennie, who had unfortunately stepped near the door of the dining-room. Vesta had disappeared. Jennie came in a little while later and closed the door. She knew of nothing to say. Lester, his thick hair pushed back from his vigorous face, leaned back moodily on his pillow. "What a devilish trick of fortune," he thought. Now she would go home and tell it to the family. His father would know, and his mother. Robert, Imogene, Amy—all would hear. He would have no explanation to make—she had seen. He stared at the wall meditatively.

Meanwhile Jennie, moving about her duties, also found food

for reflection. So this was her real position in another woman's eyes. Now she could see what the world thought. This family was as aloof from her as if it lived on another planet. To his sisters and brothers, his father and mother, she was a bad woman, a creature far beneath him socially, far beneath him mentally and morally, a creature of the streets. And she had hoped somehow to rehabilitate herself in the eyes of the world. It cut her as nothing before had ever done. The thought tore a great, gaping wound in her sensibilities. She was really low and vile in her—Louise's—eyes, in the world's eyes, basically so in Lester's eyes. How could it be otherwise ? She went about numb and still, but the ache of defeat and disgrace was under it all. Oh, if she could only see some way to make herself right with the world, to live honourably, to be decent. How could that possibly be brought about ? It ought to be—she knew that. But how ?

# CHAPTER XXXIII

OUTRAGED in her family pride, Louise lost no time in returning to Cincinnati, where she told the story of her discovery, embellished with many details. According to her, she was met at the door by a "silly-looking, white-faced woman," who did not even offer to invite her in when she announced her name, but stood there "looking just as guilty as a person possibly could." Lester also had acted shamefully, having outbrazened the matter to her face. When she had demanded to know whose the child was he had refused to tell her. "It isn't mine," was all he would say.

"Oh dear, oh dear!" exclaimed Mrs. Kane, who was the first to hear the story. "My son, my Lester! How could he have done it!"

"And such a creature!" exclaimed Louise emphatically, as though the words needed to be reiterated to give them any shadow of reality.

"I went there solely because I thought I could help him," continued Louise. "I thought when they said he was indisposed that he might be seriously ill. How should I have known?"

"Poor Lester!" exclaimed her mother. "To think he would come to anything like that!"

Mrs. Kane turned the difficult problem over in her mind and, having no previous experiences whereby to measure it, telephoned for old Archibald, who came out from the factory and sat through the discussion with a solemn countenance. So Lester was living openly with a woman of whom they had never heard. He would probably be as defiant and indifferent as his nature was strong. The standpoint of parental authority was impossible. Lester was a centralised authority in himself, and if any overtures for a change of conduct were to be made, they would have to be very diplomatically executed.

Archibald Kane returned to the manufactory sore and disgusted, but determined that something ought to be done. He held a consultation with Robert, who confessed that he had heard disturbing rumours from time to time, but had not wanted to say anything. Mrs. Kane suggested that Robert might go to Chicago, and have a talk with Lester.

" He ought to see that this thing, if continued, is going to do him irreparable damage," said Mr. Kane. " He cannot hope to carry it off successfully. Nobody can. He ought to marry her or he ought to quit. I want you to tell him that for me."

" All well and good," said Robert, " but who's going to convince him ? I'm sure I don't want the job."

" I hope to," said old Archibald, " eventually ; but you'd better go up and try, anyhow. It can't do any harm. He might come to his senses."

" I don't believe it," replied Robert. " He's a strong man. You see how much good talk does down here. Still, I'll go if it will relieve your feelings any. Mother wants it."

" Yes, yes," said his father distractedly, " better go."

Accordingly Robert went. Without allowing himself to anticipate any particular measure of success in this venture, he rode pleasantly into Chicago confident in the reflection that he had all the powers of morality and justice on his side.

Upon Robert's arrival, the third morning after Louise's interview, he called up the warerooms, but Lester was not there. He then telephoned to the house, and tactfully made an appointment. Lester was still indisposed, but he preferred to come down to the office, and he did. He met Robert in his cheerful, nonchalant way, and together they talked business for a time. Then followed a pregnant silence.

" Well, I suppose you know what brought me up here." began Robert tentatively.

" I think I could make a guess at it," Lester replied.

" They were all very much worried over the fact that you were sick—mother particularly. You're not in any danger of having a relapse, are you ? "

" I think not."

" Louise said there was some sort of a peculiar *ménage* she ran into up here. You're not married, are you ? "

" No."

" The young woman Louise saw is just——" Robert waved his hand expressively.

Lester nodded.

" I don't want to be inquisitive, Lester. I didn't come up for that. I'm simply here because the family felt that I ought to come. Mother was so very much distressed that I couldn't do less than see you for her sake——" he paused, and Lester, touched by the fairness and respect of his attitude, felt that mere courtesy at least made some explanation due.

" I don't know that anything I can say will help matters much," he replied thoughtfully. " There's really nothing to be said. I have the woman and the family has its objections. The chief difficulty about the thing seems to be the bad luck in being found out."

He stopped, and Robert turned over the substance of this worldly reasoning in his mind. Lester was very calm about it. He seemed, as usual, to be most convincingly sane.

" You're not contemplating marrying her, are you ? " queried Robert hesitatingly.

" I hadn't come to that," answered Lester coolly.

They looked at each other quietly for a moment, and then Robert turned his glance to the distant scene of the city.

" It's useless to ask whether you are seriously in love with her, I suppose," ventured Robert.

" I don't know whether I'd be able to discuss that divine afflatus with you or not," returned Lester, with a touch of grim humour. " I have never experienced the sensation myself. All I know is that the lady is very pleasing to me."

" Well, it's all a question of your own well-being and the family's, Lester," went on Robert, after another pause. " Morality doesn't seem to figure in it anyway—at least you and I can't discuss that together. Your feelings on that score naturally relate to you alone. But the matter of your own personal welfare seems to me to be substantial enough ground to base a plea on. The family's feelings and pride are also fairly important. Father's the kind of a man who sets more store by the honour of his family than most men. You know that as well as I do, of course."

" I know how father feels about it," returned Lester. " The whole business is as clear to me as it is to any of you, though off-hand I don't see just what's to be done about it. These matters aren't always of a day's growth, and they can't be settled in a day. The girl's here. To a certain extent I'm responsible that she is here. While I'm not willing to go into details, there's always more in these affairs than appears on the court calendar."

"Of course I don't know what your relations with her have been," returned Robert, "and I'm not curious to know, but it does look like a bit of injustice all around, don't you think—unless you intend to marry her ?" This last was put forth as a feeler.

"I might be willing to agree to that, too," was Lester's baffling reply, "if anything were to be gained by it. The point is, the woman is here, and the family is in possession of the fact. Now if there is anything to be done I have to do it. There isn't anybody else who can act for me in this matter."

Lester lapsed into a silence, and Robert rose and paced the floor, coming back after a time to say : "You say you haven't any idea of marrying her—or rather you haven't come to it. I wouldn't, Lester. It seems to me you would be making the mistake of your life, from every point of view. I don't want to orate, but a man of your position has so much to lose ; you can't afford to do it. Aside from family considerations, you have too much at stake. You'd be simply throwing your life away——"

He paused, with his right hand held out before him, as was customary when he was deeply in earnest, and Lester felt the candour and simplicity of this appeal. Robert was not criticising him now. He was making an appeal to him, and this was somewhat different.

The appeal passed without comment, however, and then Robert began on a new tack, this time picturing old Archibald's fondness for Lester and the hope he had always entertained that he would marry some well-to-do Cincinnati girl, Catholic, if agreeable to him, but at least worthy of his station. And Mrs. Kane felt the same way ; surely Lester must realise that.

"I know just how all of them feel about it," Lester interrupted at last, "but I don't see that anything's to be done right now."

"You mean that you don't think it would be policy for you to give her up just at present ?"

"I mean that she's been exceptionally good to me, and that I'm morally under obligations to do the best I can by her. What that may be, I can't tell."

"To live with her ?" inquired Robert coolly.

" Certainly not to turn her out bag and baggage if she has been accustomed to live with me," replied Lester. Robert sat down again, as if he considered his recent appeal futile.

" Can't family reasons persuade you to make some amicable arrangements with her and let her go ? "

" Not without due consideration of the matter ; no."

" You don't think you could hold out some hope that the thing will end quickly—something that would give me a reasonable excuse for softening down the pain of it to the family ? "

" I would be perfectly willing to do anything which would take away the edge of this thing for the family, but the truth's the truth, and I can't see any room for equivocation between you and me. As I've said before, these relationships are involved with things which make it impossible to discuss them— unfair to me, unfair to the woman. No one can see how they are to be handled, except the people that are in them, and even they can't always see. I'd be a damned dog to stand up here and give you my word to do anything except the best I can."

Lester stopped, and now Robert rose and paced the floor again, only to come back after a time and say, " You don't think there's anything to be done just at present ? "

" Not at present."

" Very well, then, I expect I might as well be going. I don't know that there's anything else we can talk about."

" Won't you stay and take lunch with me ? I think I might manage to get down to the hotel if you'll stay."

" No, thank you," answered Robert. " I believe I can make that one o'clock train for Cincinnati. I'll try, anyhow."

They stood before each other now, Lester pale and rather flaccid, Robert, clear, wax-like, well-knit, and shrewd, and one could see the difference time had already made. Robert was the clean, decisive man, Lester the man of doubts. Robert was the spirit of business energy and integrity embodied, Lester the spirit of commercial self-sufficiency, looking at life with an uncertain eye. Together they made a striking picture, which was none the less powerful for the thoughts that were now running through their minds.

" Well," said the older brother, after a time, " I don't suppose there is anything more I can say. I had hoped to make you feel just as we do about this thing, but of course you are your own best judge of this. If you don't see it now, nothing I could say would make you. It strikes me as a very bad move on your part though."

Lester listened. He said nothing, but his face expressed an unchanged purpose.

Robert turned for his hat, and they walked to the office door together.

" I'll put the best face I can on it," said Robert, and walked out.

## CHAPTER XXXIV

IN this world of ours the activities of animal life seem to be limited to a plane or circle, as if that were an inherent necessity to the creatures of a planet which is perforce compelled to swing about the sun. A fish, for instance, may not pass out of the circle of the seas without courting annihilation; a bird may not enter the domain of the fishes without paying for it dearly. From the parasites of the flowers to the monsters of the jungle and the deep we see clearly the circumscribed nature of their movements—the emphatic manner in which life has limited them to a sphere; and we are content to note the ludicrous and invariably fatal results which attend any effort on their part to depart from their environment.

In the case of man, however, the operation of this theory of limitations has not as yet been so clearly observed. The laws governing our social life are not so clearly understood as to permit of a clear generalisation. Still, the opinions, pleas, and judgments of society serve as boundaries which are none the less real for being intangible. When men or women err— that is, pass out from the sphere in which they are accustomed to move—it is not as if the bird had intruded itself into the water, or the wild animal into the haunts of man. Annihilation is not the immediate result. People may do no more than elevate their eyebrows in astonishment, laugh sarcastically, lift up their hands in protest. And yet so well defined is the sphere of social activity that he who departs from it is doomed. Born and bred in this environment, the individual is practically unfitted for any other state. He is like a bird accustomed to a certain density of atmosphere, and which cannot live comfortably at either higher or lower level.

Lester sat down in his easy-chair by the window after his brother had gone and gazed ruminatively out over the flourishing city. Yonder was spread out before him, life with its concomitant phases of energy, hope, prosperity, and pleasure, and here he was suddenly struck by a wind of misfortune and blown

aside for the time being—his prospects and purposes dissipated.
Could he continue as cheerily in the paths he had hitherto
pursued ?   Would not his relations with Jennie be necessarily
affected by this sudden tide of opposition ?   Was not his own
home now a thing of the past so far as his old easy-going
relationship was concerned ?   All the atmosphere of unstained
affection would be gone out of it now.  That hearty look of
approval which used to dwell in his father's eye—would it be
there any longer ?   Robert, his relations with the manufactory, everything that was a part of his old life, had been
affected by this sudden intrusion of Louise.

"It's unfortunate," was all that he thought to himself,
and therewith turned from what he considered senseless
brooding to the consideration of what, if anything, was to be
done.

"I'm thinking I'd take a run up to Mt. Clemens to-morrow,
or Thursday anyhow, if I feel strong enough," he said to
Jennie after he had returned.  "I'm not feeling as well as I
might.  A few days will do me good."  He wanted to get
off by himself and think.  Jennie packed his bag for him at the
given time, and he departed, but he was in a sullen, meditative
mood.

During the week that followed he had ample time to think
it all over, the result of his cogitations being that there was
no need of making a decisive move at present.  A few weeks
more, one way or the other, could not make any practical
difference.  Neither Robert nor any other member of the
family was at all likely to seek another conference with him.
His business relations would necessarily go on as usual, since
they were coupled with the welfare of the manufactory ;
certainly no attempt to coerce him would be attempted.
But the consciousness that he was at hopeless variance with his
family weighed upon him.  "Bad business," he meditated—
"bad business."  But he did not change.

For the period of a whole year this unsatisfactory state of
affairs continued.  Lester did not go home for six months ;
then an important business conference demanding his presence,
he appeared and carried it off quite as though nothing important
had happened.  His mother kissed him affectionately, if a
little sadly ; his father gave him his customary greeting, a
hearty handshake ; Robert, Louise, Amy, Imogene, concertedly,

though without any verbal understanding, agreed to ignore the one real issue. But the feeling of estrangement was there, and it persisted. Hereafter his visits to Cincinnati were as few and far between as he could possibly make them.

## CHAPTER XXXV

IN the meantime Jennie had been going through a moral crisis of her own. For the first time in her life, aside from the family attitude, which had afflicted her greatly, she realised what the world thought of her. She was bad—she knew that. She had yielded on two occasions to the force of circumstances which might have been fought out differently. If only she had had more courage ! If she did not always have this haunting sense of fear ! If she could only make up her mind to do the right thing ! Lester would never marry her. Why should he ? She loved him, but she could leave him, and it would be better for him. Probably her father would live with her if she went back to Cleveland. He would honour her for at last taking a decent stand. Yet the thought of leaving Lester was a terrible one to her—he had been so good. As for her father, she was not sure whether he would receive her or not.

After the tragic visit of Louise she began to think of saving a little money, laying it aside as best she could from her allowance. Lester was generous and she had been able to send home regularly fifteen dollars a week to maintain the family— as much as they had lived on before, without any help from the outside. She spent twenty dollars to maintain the table, for Lester required the best of everything—fruit, meats, desserts, liquors, and what not. The rent was fifty-five dollars, with clothes and extras a varying sum. Lester gave her fifty dollars a week, but somehow it had all gone. She thought how she might economise but this seemed wrong. Better go without taking anything, if she were going, was the thought that came to her. It was the only decent thing to do.

She thought over this week after week, after the advent of Louise, trying to nerve herself to the point where she could speak or act. Lester was consistently generous and kind, but she felt at times that he himself might wish it. He was thoughtful, abstracted. Since the scene with Louise it seemed to her that he had been a little different. If she could only say to him that she was not satisfied with the way she was living, and then leave. But he himself had plainly indicated after his discovery of Vesta that her feelings on that score could not matter so very much to him, since he thought the presence of the child would definitely interfere with his ever marrying her. It was her presence he wanted on another basis. And he was so forceful, she could not argue with him very well. She decided if she went it would be best to write a letter and tell him why. Then maybe when he knew how she felt he would forgive her and think nothing more about it.

The condition of the Gerhardt family was not improving. Since Jennie had left Martha had married. After several years of teaching in the public schools of Cleveland she had met a young architect, and they were united after a short engagement. Martha had been always a little ashamed of her family, and now, when this new life dawned, she was anxious to keep the connection as slight as possible. She barely notified the members of the family of the approaching marriage—Jennie not at all—and to the actual ceremony she invited only Bass and George. Gerhardt, Veronica, and William resented the slight. Gerhardt ventured upon no comment. He had had too many rebuffs. But Veronica was angry. She hoped that life would give her an opportunity to pay her sister off. William, of course, did not mind particularly. He was interested in the possibilities of becoming an electrical engineer, a career which one of his school-teachers had pointed out to him as being attractive and promising.

Jennie heard of Martha's marriage after it was all over, a note from Veronica giving her the main details. She was glad from one point of view, but realised that her brothers and sisters were drifting away from her.

A little while after Martha's marriage Veronica and William went to reside with George, a break which was brought about by the attitude of Gerhardt himself. Ever since his wife's death and the departure of the other children he had been subject to moods of profound gloom, from which he was not easily aroused. Life, it seemed, was drawing to a close for him, although he was only sixty-five years of age. The earthly ambitions he had once cherished were gone for ever. He saw Sebastian, Martha, and George out in the world practically ignoring him, contributing nothing at all to a home which should never have taken a dollar from Jennie. Veronica and William were restless. They objected to leaving school and going to work, apparently preferring to live on money which Gerhardt had long since concluded was not being come by honestly. He was now pretty well satisfied as to the true relations of Jennie and Lester. At first he had believed them to be married, but the way Lester had neglected Jennie for long periods, the humbleness with which she ran at his beck and call, her fear of telling him about Vesta—somehow it all pointed to the same thing. She had not been married at home. Gerhardt had never had sight of her marriage certificate. Since she was away she might have been married, but he did not believe it.

The real trouble was that Gerhardt had grown intensely morose and crotchety, and it was becoming impossible for young people to live with him. Veronica and William felt it. They resented the way in which he took charge of the expenditures after Martha left. He accused them of spending too much on clothes and amusements, he insisted that a smaller house should be taken, and he regularly sequestered a part of the money which Jennie sent, for what purpose they could hardly guess. As a matter of fact, Gerhardt was saving as much as possible in order to repay Jennie eventually. He thought it was sinful to go on in this way, and this was his one method, outside of his meagre earnings, to redeem himself. If his other children had acted rightly by him he felt that he would not now be left in his old age the recipient of charity from one, who, despite her other good qualities, was certainly not leading a righteous life. So they quarrelled.

It ended one winter month when George agreed to receive his complaining brother and sister on condition that they should get something to do. Gerhardt was nonplussed for a moment, but invited them to take the furniture and go their way. His generosity shamed them for the moment ; they even tentatively invited him to come and live with them, but this he would not do. He would ask the foreman of the mill he watched for the privilege of sleeping in some out-of-the-way garret. He was always liked and trusted. And this would save him a little money.

So in a fit of pique he did this, and there was seen the spectacle of an old man watching through a dreary season of nights, in a lonely trafficless neighbourhood while the city pursued its gaiety elsewhere. He had a wee small corner in the topmost loft of a warehouse away from the tear and grind of the factory proper. Here Gerhardt slept by day. In the afternoon he would take a little walk, strolling toward the business centre, or out along the banks of the Cuyahoga, or the lake. As a rule his hands were below his back, his brow bent in meditation. He would even talk to himself a little—an occasional " By chops ! " or " So it is " being indicative of his dreary mood. At dusk he would return, taking his stand at the lonely gate which was his post of duty. His meals he secured at a nearby workingmen's boarding-house, such as he felt he must have.

The nature of the old German's reflections at this time were of a peculiarly subtle and sombre character. What was this thing—life ? What did it all come to after the struggle, and the worry, and the grieving ? Where does it all go to ? People die ; you hear nothing more from them. His wife, now, she had gone. Where had her spirit taken its flight ?

Yet he continued to hold some strongly dogmatic convictions. He believed there was a hell, and that people who sinned would go there. How about Mrs. Gerhardt ? How about Jennie ? He believed that both had sinned woefully. He believed that the just would be rewarded in heaven. But who were the just ? Mrs. Gerhardt had not had a bad heart. Jennie was the soul of generosity. Take his son Sebastian. Sebastian was a good boy, but he was cold, and certainly indifferent to his father. Take Martha—she was ambitious, but obviously selfish. Somehow the children outside of Jennie, seemed self-centred. Bass walked off when he got married, and did nothing more for anybody. Martha insisted that she needed all she made to live on. George had contributed for a little while, but had finally refused to help out. Veronica and William had been content to live on Jennie's money so long as he would allow it, and yet they knew it was not right. His very existence, was it not a commentary on the selfishness of his children ? And he was getting so old. He shook his head. Mystery of mysteries. Life was truly strange, and dark, and uncertain. Still he did not want to go and live with any of his children. Actually they were not worthy of him—none but Jennie, and she was not good. So he grieved.

This woeful condition of affairs was not made known to Jennie for some time. She had been sending her letters to Martha, but, on her leaving, Jennie had been writing directly to Gerhardt. After Veronica's departure Gerhardt wrote to Jennie saying that there was no need of sending any more money. Veronica and William were going to live with George. He himself had a good place in a factory, and would live there a little while. He returned her a moderate sum that he had saved—one hundred and fifteen dollars—with the word that he would not need it.

Jennie did not understand, but as the others did not write, she was not sure but what it might be all right—her father was so determined. But by degrees, however, a sense of what it really must mean overtook her—a sense of something wrong, and she worried, hesitating between leaving Lester and going to see about her father, whether she left him or not. Would he come with her ? Not here certainly. If she were married, yes, possibly. If she were alone—probably. Yet if she did not get some work which paid well they would have a difficult time. It was the same old problem. What could she do ? Nevertheless, she decided to act. If she could get five or six dollars a week they could live. This hundred and fifteen dollars which Gerhardt had saved would tide them over the worst difficulties perhaps.

## CHAPTER XXXVI

THE trouble with Jennie's plan was that it did not definitely take into consideration Lester's attitude. He did care for her in an elemental way, but he was hedged about by the ideas of the conventional world in which he had been reared. To say that he loved her well enough to take her for better or worse—to legalise her anomalous position and to face the world bravely with the fact that he had chosen a wife who suited him—was perhaps going a little too far, but he did really care for her, and he was not in a mood, at this particular time, to contemplate parting with her for good.

Lester was getting along to that time of life when his ideas of womanhood were fixed and not subject to change. Thus far, on his own plane and within the circle of his own associates, he had met no one who appealed to him as did Jennie. She was gentle, intelligent, gracious, a handmaiden to his every need ; and he had taught her the little customs of polite society, until she was as agreeable a companion as he cared to have. He was comfortable, he was satisfied—why seek further.

But Jennie's restlessness increased day by day. She tried writing out her views, and started a half dozen letters before she finally worded one which seemed, partially at least, to express her feelings. It was a long letter for her, and it ran as follows :

" LESTER DEAR,

" When you get this I won't be here, and I want you not to think harshly of me until you have read it all. I am taking Vesta and leaving, and I think it is really better that I should. Lester, I ought to do it. You know when you met me we were very poor, and my condition was such that I didn't think any good man would ever want me. When you came along and told me you loved me I was hardly able to think just what I ought to do. You made me love you, Lester, in spite of myself.

" You know I told you that I oughtn't to do anything wrong any more and that I wasn't good, but somehow when you were near me I couldn't think just right, and I didn't see just how I was to get away from you. Papa was sick at home that time, and there was hardly anything in the house to eat. We were all doing so poorly. My brother George didn't have good shoes, and mamma was so worried. I have often thought, Lester, if mamma had not been compelled to worry so much she might be alive to-day. I thought if you liked me and I really liked you—I love you, Lester—maybe it wouldn't make so much difference about me. You know you told me right away you would like to help my family, and I felt that maybe that would be the right thing to do. We were so terribly poor.

"Lester, dear, I am ashamed to leave you this way; it seems so mean, but if you knew how I have been feeling these days you would forgive me. Oh, I love you, Lester, I do, I do. But for months past —ever since your sister came—I felt that I was doing wrong, and that I oughtn't to go on doing it, for I know how terribly wrong it is. It was wrong for me ever to have anything to do with Senator Brander, but I was such a girl then—I hardly knew what I was doing. It was wrong of me not to tell you about Vesta when I first met you, though I thought I was doing right when I did it. It was terribly wrong of me to keep her here all that time concealed, Lester, but I was afraid of you then —afraid of what you would say and do. When your sister Louise came it all came over me somehow, clearly, and I have never been able to think right about it since. It can't be right, Lester, but I don't blame you. I blame myself.

"I don't ask you to marry me, Lester. I know how you feel about me and how you feel about your family, and I don't think it would be right. They would never want you to do it, and it isn't right that I should ask you. At the same time I know I oughtn't to go on living this way. Vesta is getting along where she understands everything. She thinks you are her really truly uncle. I have thought of it all so much. I have thought a number of times that I would try to talk to you about it, but you frighten me when you get serious, and I don't seem to be able to say what I want to. So I thought if I could just write you this and then go you would understand. You do, Lester, don't you? You won't be angry with me? I know it's for the best for you and for me. I ought to do it. Please forgive me, Lester, please; and don't think of me any more. I will get along. But I love you—oh yes, I do—and I will never be grateful enough for all you have done for me. I wish you all the luck that can come to you. Please forgive me, Lester. I love you, yes I do. I love you.

" Jennie.

"P.S. I expect to go to Cleveland with papa. He needs me. He is all alone. But don't come for me, Lester. It's best that you shouldn't."

She put this in an envelope, sealed it, and, having hidden it in her bosom, for the time being, awaited the hour when she could conveniently take her departure.

It was several days before she could bring herself to the actual execution of the plan, but one afternoon, Lester, having telephoned that he would not be home for a day or two, she packed some necessary garments for herself and Vesta in several trunks, and sent for an expressman. She thought of telegraphing her father that she was coming; but, seeing he had no home, she thought it would be just as well to go and find him. George and Veronica had not taken all the furniture. The major portion of it was in storage—so Gerhardt had written. She might take that and furnish a little home or flat. She was ready for the end, waiting for the expressman, when the door opened and in walked Lester.

For some unforeseen reason he had changed his mind. He was not in the least psychic or intuitional, but on this occasion his feelings had served him a peculiar turn. He had thought of going for a day's duck-shooting with some friends in the Kankakee Marshes south of Chicago, but had finally changed his mind; he even decided to go out to the house early. What prompted this he could not have said.

As he neared the house he felt a little peculiar about coming home so early; then at the sight of the two trunks standing in the middle of the room he stood dumbfounded. What did it mean—Jennie dressed and ready to depart? And Vesta in a similar condition? He stared in amazement, his brown eyes keen in inquiry.

" Where are you going ? " he asked.

" Why—why—" she began, falling back. " I was going away."

" Where to ? "

" I thought I would go to Cleveland," she replied.

" What for ? "

" Why—why—I meant to tell you, Lester, that I didn't think I ought to stay here any longer this way. I didn't think it was right. I thought I'd tell you, but I couldn't. I wrote you a letter."

" A letter," he exclaimed. " What the deuce are you talking about ? Where is the letter ? "

" There," she said, mechanically pointing to a small

centre-table where the letter lay conspicuous on a large book.

"And you were really going to leave me, Jennie, with just a letter?" said Lester, his voice hardening a little as he spoke. "I swear to heaven you are beyond me. What's the point?" He tore open the envelope and looked at the beginning. "Better send Vesta from the room," he suggested

She obeyed. Then she came back and stood there pale and wide-eyed, looking at the wall, at the trunks, and at him. Lester read the letter thoughtfully. He shifted his position once or twice, then dropped the paper on the floor.

"Well, I'll tell you, Jennie," he said finally, looking at her curiously and wondering just what he was going to say. Here again was his chance to end this relationship if he wished. He couldn't feel that he did wish it, seeing how peacefully things were running. They had gone so far together it seemed ridiculous to quit now. He truly loved her—there was no doubt of that. Still he did not want to marry her—could not very well. She knew that. Her letter said as much. "You have this thing wrong," he went on slowly. "I don't know what comes over you at times, but you don't view the situation right. I've told you before that I can't marry you—not now, anyhow. There are too many big things involved in this, which you don't know anything about. I love you, you know that. But my family has to be taken into consideration, and the business. You can't see the difficulties raised on these scores, but I can. Now I don't want you to leave me. I care too much about you. I can't prevent you, of course. You can go if you want to. But I don't think you ought to want to. You don't really, do you? Sit down a minute."

Jennie, who had been counting on getting away without being seen, was now thoroughly nonplussed. To have him begin a quiet argument—a plea as it were. It hurt her. He, Lester, pleading with her, and she loved him so.

She went over to him, and he took her hand.

"Now, listen," he said. "There's really nothing to be gained by your leaving me at present. Where did you say you were going?"

"To Cleveland," she replied.

"Well, how did you expect to get along?"

"I thought I'd take papa, if he'd come with me—he's alone now—and get something to do, maybe."

"Well, what can you do, Jennie, different from what you ever have done? You wouldn't expect to be a lady's maid again, would you? Or clerk in a store?"

"I thought I might get some place as a housekeeper," she suggested. She had been counting up her possibilities, and this was the most promising idea that had occurred to her.

"No, no," he grumbled, shaking his head. "There's nothing to that. There's nothing in this whole move of yours except a notion. Why, you won't be any better off morally than you are right now. You can't undo the past. It doesn't make any difference, anyhow. I can't marry you now. I might in the future, but I can't tell anything about that, and I don't want to promise anything. You're not going to leave me though with my consent, and if you were going I wouldn't have you dropping back into any such thing as you're contemplating. I'll make some provision for you. You don't really want to leave me, do you, Jennie?"

Against Lester's strong personality and vigorous protest Jennie's own conclusions and decisions went to pieces. Just the pressure of his hand was enough to upset her. Now she began to cry.

"Don't cry, Jennie," he said. "This thing may work out better than you think. Let it rest for a while. Take off your things. You're not going to leave me any more, are you?"

"No-o-o!" she sobbed.

He took her in his lap. "Let things rest as they are," he went on. "It's a curious world. Things can't be adjusted in a minute. They may work out. I'm putting up with some things myself that I ordinarily wouldn't stand for."

He finally saw her restored to comparative calmness, smiling sadly through her tears.

"Now you put those things away," he said genially, pointing to the trunks. "Besides, I want you to promise me one thing."

"What's that?" asked Jennie.

"No more concealment of anything, do you hear? No more thinking out things for yourself, and acting without my knowing anything about it. If you have anything on your mind, I want you to come out with it. I'm not going to eat you! Talk to me about whatever is troubling you. I'll help you solve it, or, if I can't, at least there won't be any concealment between us."

" I know, Lester," she said earnestly, looking him straight in the eyes.  " I promise I'll never conceal anything any more —truly I won't.  I've been afraid, but I won't be now.  You can trust me."

" That sounds like what you ought to be," he replied.  " I know you will."    And he let her go.

A few days later, and in consequence of this agreement, the future of Gerhardt came up for discussion.  Jennie had been worrying about him for several days ; now it occurred to her that this was something to talk over with Lester.   Accordingly, she explained one night at dinner what had happened in Cleveland.  " I know he is very unhappy there all alone," she said, " and I hate to think of it.  I was going to get him if I went back to Cleveland.  Now I don't know what to do about it."

" Why don't you send him some money ? " he inquired.

" He won't take any more money from me, Lester," she explained.  " He thinks I'm not good—not acting right.  He doesn't believe I'm married."

" He has pretty good reason, hasn't he ? " said Lester calmly.

" I hate to think of him sleeping in a factory.  He's so old and lonely."

" What's the matter with the rest of the family in Cleveland ?  Won't they do anything for him ?  Where's your brother Bass ? "

" I think maybe they don't want him, he's so cross," she said simply.

" I hardly know what to suggest in that case," smiled Lester. " The old gentleman oughtn't to be so fussy."

" I know," she said, " but he's old now, and he has had so much trouble."

Lester ruminated for a while, toying with his fork.  " I'll tell you what I've been thinking, Jennie," he said finally. " There's no use living this way any longer, if we're going to stick it out.  I've been thinking that we might take a house out in Hyde Park.  It's something of a run from the office, but I'm not much for this apartment life.  You and Vesta would be better off for a yard.  In that case you might bring your father on to live with us. He couldn't do any harm pottering about ; indeed, he might help keep things straight."

" Oh, that would just suit papa, if he'd come," she replied. " He loves to fix things, and he'd cut the grass and look after the furnace. But he won't come unless he's sure I'm married."

" I don't know how that could be arranged unless you could show the old gentleman a marriage certificate. He seems to want something that can't be produced very well. A steady job he'd have running the furnace of a country house," he added meditatively.

Jennie did not notice the grimness of the jest. She was too busy thinking what a tangle she had made of her life. Gerhardt would not come now, even if they had a lovely home to share with him. And yet he ought to be with Vesta again. She would make him happy.

She remained lost in a sad abstraction, until Lester, following the drift of her thoughts, said : " I don't see how it can be arranged. Marriage certificate blanks aren't easily procurable. It's bad business—a criminal offence to forge one, I believe. I wouldn't want to be mixed up in that sort of thing."

" Oh, I don't want you to do anything like that, Lester. I'm just sorry papa is so stubborn. When he gets a notion you can't change him."

" Suppose we wait until we get settled after moving," he suggested. " Then you can go to Cleveland and talk to him personally. You might be able to persuade him." He liked her attitude toward her father. It was so decent that he rather wished he could help her carry out her scheme. While not very interesting, Gerhardt was not objectionable to Lester, and if the old man wanted to do the odd jobs around a big place, why not ?

## CHAPTER XXXVII

THE plan for a residence in Hyde Park was not long in taking shape. After several weeks had passed, and things had quieted down again, Lester invited Jennie to go with him to South Hyde Park to look for a house. On the first trip they found something which seemed to suit admirably—an old-time home of eleven large rooms, set in a lawn fully two hundred feet square and shaded by trees which had been planted when the city was young. It was ornate, homelike, peaceful. Jennie was fascinated by the sense of space and country, although depressed by the reflection that she was not entering her new home under the right auspices. She had vaguely hoped that in planning to go away she was bringing about a condition under which Lester might have come after her and married her. Now all that was over. She had promised to stay, and she would have to make the best of it. She suggested that they would never know what to do with so much room, but he waved that aside. "We will very likely have people in now and then," he said. "We can furnish it up anyhow, and see how it looks." He had the agent make out a five-year lease, with an option for renewal, and set at once the forces to work to put the establishment in order.

The house was painted and decorated, the lawn put in order, and everything done to give the place a trim and satisfactory appearance. There was a large, comfortable library and sitting-room, a big dining-room, a handsome reception hall, a parlour, a large kitchen, serving-room, and in fact, all the ground-floor essentials of a comfortable home. On the second floor were bedrooms, baths, and the maid's room. It was all very comfortable and harmonious, and Jennie took an immense pride and pleasure in getting things in order.

Immediately after moving in, Jennie, with Lester's permission, wrote to her father asking him to come to her. She did not say that she was married, but left it to be inferred. She descanted on the beauty of the neighbourhood, the size of the yard, and the manifold conveniences of the establishment. "It is so very nice," she added, "you would like it, papa. Vesta is here and goes to school every day. Won't you come and stay with us? It's so much better than living in a factory. And I would like to have you so."

Gerhardt read this letter with a solemn countenance. Was it really true? Would they be taking a larger house if they were not permanently united? After all these years and all this lying? Could he have been mistaken? Well, it was high time—but should he go? He had lived alone this long time now—should he go to Chicago and live with Jennie? Her appeal did touch him, but somehow he decided against it. That would be too generous an acknowledgment of the fact that there had been fault on his side as well as on hers.

Jennie was disappointed at Gerhardt's refusal. She talked it over with Lester, and decided that she would go on to Cleveland and see him. Accordingly, she made the trip, hunted up the factory, a great rumbling furniture concern in one of the poorest sections of the city, and inquired at the office for her father. The clerk directed her to a distant warehouse, and Gerhardt was informed that a lady wished to see him. He crawled out of his humble cot and came down, curious as to who it could be. When Jennie saw him in his dusty, baggy clothes, his hair grey, his eyebrows shaggy, coming out of the dark door, a keen sense of the pathetic moved her again. "Poor papa!" she thought. He came toward her, his inquisitorial eye softened a little by his consciousness of the affection that had inspired her visit. "What are you come for?" he asked cautiously.

"I want you to come home with me, papa," she pleaded yearningly. "I don't want you to stay here any more. I can't think of you living alone any longer."

"So," he said, nonplussed, "that brings you?"

"Yes," she replied; "Won't you? Don't stay here."

"I have a good bed," he explained by way of apology for his state.

"I know," she replied, "but we have a good home now and Vesta is there. Won't you come? Lester wants you to."

"Tell me one thing," he demanded. "Are you married?"

"Yes," she replied, lying hopelessly. "I have been married a long time. You can ask Lester when you come." She could scarcely look him in the face, but she managed somehow, and he believed her.

"Well," he said, "it is time."

"Won't you come, papa?" she pleaded.

He threw out his hands after his characteristic manner. The urgency of her appeal touched him to the quick. "Yes, I come," he said, and turned; but she saw by his shoulders what was happening. He was crying.

"Now, papa?" she pleaded.

For answer he walked back into the dark warehouse to get his things.

## CHAPTER XXXVIII

GERHARDT, having become an inmate of the Hyde Park home, at once bestirred himself about the labours which he felt instinctively concerned him. He took charge of the furnace and the yard, outraged at the thought that good money should be paid to any outsider when he had nothing to do. The trees, he declared to Jennie, were in a dreadful condition. If Lester would get him a pruning knife and a saw he would attend to them in the spring. In Germany they knew how to care for such things, but these Americans were so shiftless. Then he wanted tools and nails, and in time all the closets and shelves were put in order. He found a Lutheran Church almost two miles away, and declared that it was better than the one in Cleveland. The pastor, of course, was a heaven-sent son of divinity. And nothing would do but that Vesta must go to church with him regularly.

Jennie and Lester settled down into the new order of living with some misgivings; certain difficulties were sure to arise On the North Side it had been easy for Jennie to shun neighbours and say nothing. Now they were occupying a house of some pretensions; their immediate neighbours would feel it their duty to call, and Jennie would have to play the part of an experienced hostess. She and Lester had talked this situation over. It might as well be understood here, he said, that they were husband and wife. Vesta was to be introduced as Jennie's daughter by her first marriage, her husband, a Mr. Stover (her mother's maiden name), having died immediately after the child's birth. Lester, of course, was the stepfather. This particular neighbourhood was so far from the fashionable heart of Chicago that Lester did not expect to run into many of his friends. He explained to Jennie the ordinary formalities of social intercourse, so that when the first visitor called Jennie might be prepared to receive her. Within a fortnight this first visitor arrived in the person of Mrs. Jacob Stendahl, a woman of considerable importance in this particular section. She lived five doors from Jennie—the houses of the neighbourhood were all set in spacious lawns—and drove up in her carriage, on her return from her shopping, one afternoon.

" Is Mrs. Kane in ? " she asked of Jeannette, the new maid.

" I think so, mam," answered the girl. " Won't you let me have your card ? "

The card was given and taken to Jennie, who looked at it curiously.

When Jennie came into the parlour Mrs. Stendahl, a tall dark, inquisitive-looking woman, greeted her most cordially.

" I thought I would take the liberty of intruding on you," she said most winningly. " I am one of your neighbours. I live on the other side of the street, some few doors up. Perhaps you have seen the house—the one with the white stone gate-posts."

" Oh, yes indeed," replied Jennie. " I know it well. Mr. Kane and I were admiring it the first day we came out here."

" I know of your husband, of course, by reputation. My husband is connected with the Wilkes Frog and Switch Company."

Jennie bowed her head. She knew that the latter concern must be something important and profitable from the way in which Mrs. Stendahl spoke of it.

" We have lived here quite a number of years, and I know how you must feel coming as a total stranger to a new section of the city. I hope you will find time to come in and see me some afternoon. I shall be most pleased. My regular reception day is Thursday."

" Indeed I shall," answered Jennie, a little nervously, for the ordeal was a trying one. " I appreciate your goodness in calling. Mr. Kane is very busy as a rule, but when he is at home I am sure he would be most pleased to meet you and your husband."

" You must both come over some evening," replied Mrs. Stendahl. " We lead a very quiet life. My husband is not much for social gatherings. But we enjoy our neighbourhood friends."

Jennie smiled her assurances of good-will. She accompanied Mrs. Stendahl to the door, and shook hands with her. " I'm so glad to find you so charming," observed Mrs. Stendahl frankly.

" Oh, thank you," said Jennie flushing a little. " I'm sure I don't deserve so much praise."

" Well, now I will expect you some afternoon. Good-bye," and she waved a gracious farewell.

" That wasn't so bad," thought Jennie as she watched Mrs. Stendahl drive away. " She is very nice, I think. I'll tell Lester about her."

Among the other callers were a Mr. and Mrs. Carmichael Burke, a Mrs. Hanson Field, and a Mrs. Timothy Ballinger— all of whom left cards, or stayed to chat a few minutes. Jennie found herself taken quite seriously as a woman of importance, and she did her best to support the dignity of her position. And, indeed, she did exceptionally well. She was most hospitable and gracious. She had a kindly smile and a manner wholly natural ; she succeeded in making a most favourable impression. She explained to her guests that she had been living on the North Side until recently, that *her husband*, Mr. Kane, had long wanted to have a home in Hyde Park, that her father and daughter were living here, and that Lester was the child's stepfather. She said she hoped to repay all these nice attentions and to be a good neighbour.

Lester heard about these calls in the evening, for he did not care to meet these people. Jennie came to enjoy it in a mild way. She liked making new friends, and she was hoping that something definite could be worked out here which would make Lester look upon her as a good wife and an ideal companion. Perhaps, some day, he might really want to marry her.

First impressions are not always permanent, as Jennie was soon to discover. The neighbourhood had accepted her perhaps a little too hastily, and now rumours began to fly about. A Mrs. Sommerville, calling on Mrs. Craig, one of Jennie's near neighbours, intimated that she knew who Lester was—" oh, yes, indeed. You know, my dear," she went on, " his reputation is just a little——" she raised her eyebrows and her hand at the same time.

" You don't say ! " commented her friend curiously. " He looks like such a staid, conservative person."

" Oh, no doubt, in a way, he is," went on Mrs. Sommerville. " His family is of the very best. There was some young woman he went with—so my husband tells me. I don't know whether this is the one or not, but she was introduced as a Miss Gorwood, or some such name as that, when they were living together as husband and wife on the North Side."

"Tst! Tst! Tst!" clicked Mrs. Craig with her tongue at this astonishing news. "You don't tell me! Come to think of it, it must be the same woman. Her father's name is Gerhardt."

"Gerhardt!" exclaimed Mrs. Sommerville. "Yes, that's the name. It seems to me that there was some earlier scandal in connection with her—at least there was a child. Whether he married her afterward or not, I don't know. Anyhow, I understand his family will not have anything to do with her."

"How very interesting!" exclaimed Mrs. Craig. "And to think he should have married her afterward, if he really did. I'm sure you can't tell with whom you're coming in contact these days, can you?"

"It's so true. Life does get badly mixed at times. She appears to be a charming woman."

"Delightful!" exclaimed Mrs. Craig. "Quite naïve. I was really taken with her."

"Well, it may be," went on her guest, "that this isn't the same woman after all. I may be mistaken."

"Oh, I hardly think so. Gerhardt! She told me they had been living on the North Side."

"Then I'm sure it's the same person. How curious that you should speak of her!"

"It is, indeed," went on Mrs. Craig, who was speculating as to what her attitude toward Jennie should be in the future.

Other rumours came from other sources. There were people who had seen Jennie and Lester out driving on the North Side, who had been introduced to her as Miss Gerhardt, who knew what the Kane family thought. Of course her present position, the handsome house, the wealth of Lester, the beauty of Vesta—all these things helped to soften the situation. She was apparently too circumspect, too much the good wife and mother, too really nice to be angry with; but she had a past, and that had to be taken into consideration.

An opening bolt of the coming storm fell upon Jennie one day when Vesta, returning from school, suddenly asked: "Mamma, who was my papa?"

"His name was Stover, dear," replied her mother, struck at once by the thought that there might have been some criticism—that some one must have been saying something. "Why do you ask?"

"Where was I born?" continued Vesta, ignoring the last inquiry, and interested in clearing up her own identity.

"In Columbus, Ohio, pet. Why?"

"Anita Ballinger said I didn't have any papa, and that you weren't ever married when you had me. She said I wasn't a really, truly girl at all—just a nobody. She made me so mad I slapped her."

Jennie's face grew rigid. She sat staring straight before her. Mrs. Ballinger had called, and Jennie had thought her peculiarly gracious and helpful in her offer of assistance, and now her little daughter had said this to Vesta. Where did the child hear it?

"You mustn't pay any attention to her, dearie," said Jennie at last. "She doesn't know. Your papa was Mr. Stover, and you were born in Columbus. You mustn't fight other little girls. Of course they say nasty things when they fight—sometimes things they don't really mean. Just let her alone and don't go near her any more. Then she won't say anything to you."

It was a lame explanation, but it satisfied Vesta for the time being. "I'll slap her if she tries to slap me," she persisted.

"You mustn't go near her, pet, do you hear? Then she can't try to slap you," returned her mother. "Just go about your studies, and don't mind her. She can't quarrel with you if you don't let her."

Vesta went away leaving Jennie brooding over her words. The neighbours were talking. Her history was becoming gossip. How had they found out.

It is one thing to nurse a single thrust, another to have the wound opened from time to time by additional stabs. One day Jennie, having gone to call on Mrs. Hanson Field, who was her immediate neighbour, met a Mrs. Williston Baker, who was there taking tea. Mrs. Baker knew of the Kanes, of Jennie's history on the North Side, and the attitude of the Kane family. She was a thin, vigorous, intellectual woman, somewhat on the order of Mrs. Bracebridge, and very careful of her social connections. She had always considered Mrs. Field a woman of the same rigid circumspectness of attitude, and when she found Jennie calling there she was outwardly calm but inwardly irritated. "This is Mrs. Kane, Mrs. Baker," said Mrs. Field, introducing her guests with a smiling countenance. Mrs. Baker looked at Jennie ominously.

" Mrs. Lester Kane ? " she inquired.

" Yes," replied Mrs. Field

" Indeed," she went on freezingly. " I've heard a great deal about Mrs.——" accenting the word—" Mrs. Lester Kane."

She turned to Mrs. Field, ignoring Jennie completely, and started an intimate conversation in which Jennie could have no possible share. Jennie stood helplessly by, unable to formulate a thought which would be suitable to so trying a situation. Mrs. Baker soon announced her departure, although she had intended to stay longer. " I can't remain another minute," she said ; " I promised Mrs. Neil that I would step in to see her to-day. I'm sure I've bored you enough already as it is."

She walked to the door, not troubling to look at Jennie until she was nearly out of the room. Then she looked in her direction, and gave her a frigid nod.

" We meet such curious people now and again," she observed finally to her hostess as she swept away.

Mrs Field did not feel able to defend Jennie, for she herself was in no notable social position, and was endeavouring, like every other middle-class woman of means, to get along. She did not care to offend Mrs. Williston Baker, who was socially so much more important than Jennie. She came back to where Jennie was sitting, smiling apologetically, but she was a little bit flustered. Jennie was out of countenance, of course. Presently she excused herself and went home. She had been cut deeply by the slight offered her, and she felt that Mrs. Field realised that she had made a mistake in ever taking her up. There would be no additional exchange of visits there— that she knew. The old hopeless feeling came over her that her life was a failure. It couldn't be made right, if it could, it wouldn't be. Lester was not inclined to marry her and put her right.

Time went on and matters remained very much as they were. To look at this large house, with its smooth lawn and well-grown trees, its vines clambering about the pillars of the veranda and interlacing themselves into a transparent veil of green ; to see Gerhardt pottering about the yard, Vesta coming home from school, Lester leaving in the morning in his smart trap—one would have said that here is peace and plenty, no shadow of unhappiness hangs over this charming home.

And as a matter of fact existence with Lester and Jennie did run smoothly. It is true that the neighbours did not call any more, or only a very few of them, and there was no social life to speak of; but the deprivation was hardly noticed; there was so much in the home life to please and interest. Vesta was learning to play the piano, and to play quite well. She had a good ear for music. Jennie was a charming figure in blue, lavender, and olive-green house-gowns as she went about her affairs, sewing, dusting, getting Vesta off to school, and seeing that things generally were put to rights. Gerhardt busied himself about his multitudinous duties, for he was not satisfied unless he had his hands into all the domestic economies of the household. One of his self-imposed tasks was to go about the house after Lester, or the servants, turning out the gas-jets or electric-light bulbs which might accidentally have been left burning. That was a sinful extravagance.

Again, Lester's expensive clothes, which he carelessly threw aside after a few month's use, were a source of woe to the thrifty old German. Moreover, he grieved over splendid shoes discarded because of a few wrinkles in the leather or a slightly run down heel or sole. Gerhardt was for having them repaired, but Lester answered the old man's querulous inquiry as to what was wrong " with them shoes " by saying that they weren't comfortable any more.

" Such extravagance ! " Gerhardt complained to Jennie. " Such waste ! No good can come of anything like that. It will mean want one of these days."

" He can't help it, papa," Jennie excused. " That's the way he was raised."

" Ha ! A fine way to be raised. These Americans, they know nothing of economy. They ought to live in Germany awhile. Then they would know what a dollar can do."

Lester heard something of this through Jennie, but he only smiled. Gerhardt was amusing to him.

Another grievance was Lester's extravagant use of matches. He had the habit of striking a match, holding it while he talked, instead of lighting his cigar, and then throwing it away. Some-times he would begin to light a cigar two or three minutes before he would actually do so, tossing aside match after match.

There was a place out in one corner of the veranda where he
liked to sit of a spring or summer evening, smoking and throwing
away half-burned matches.   Jennie would sit with him, and a
vast number of matches would be lit and flung out on the lawn.
At one time, while engaged in cutting the grass, Gerhardt
found, to his horror, not a handful, but literally boxes of half-
burned match-sticks lying unconsumed and decaying under
the fallen blades.   He was discouraged, to say the least.   He
gathered up this damning evidence in a newspaper and carried
it back into the sitting-room where Jennie was sewing.

"See here, what I find!" he demanded.   "Just look at
that!   That man, he has no more sense of economy than a—
than a——" the right term failed him.   "He sits and smokes,
and this is the way he uses matches.   Five cents a box they
cost—five cents.   How can a man hope to do well and carry
on like that, I like to know.   Look at them."

Jennie looked.   She shook her head.   "Lester is extravagant," she said.

Gerhardt carried them to the basement.   At least they
should be burned in the furnace.   He would have used them
as lighters for his own pipe, sticking them in the fire to catch
a blaze, only old newspapers were better, and he had stacks
of these—another evidence of his lord and master's wretched,
spendthrift disposition.   It was a sad world to work in.   Almost
everything was against him.   Still he fought as valiantly as
he could against waste and shameless extravagance.   His own
economies were rigid.   He would wear the same suit of black—
cut down from one of Lester's expensive investments of years
before—every Sunday for a couple of years.   Lester's shoes,
by a little stretch of the imagination, could be made to seem
to fit, and these he wore.   His old ties also—the black ones—
they were fine.   If he could have cut down Lester's shirts he
would have done so; he did make over the underwear, with the
friendly aid of the cook's needle.   Lester's socks, of course,
were just right.   There was never any expense for Gerhardt's
clothing.

The remaining stock of Lester's discarded clothing—shoes,
shirts, collars, suits, ties, and what not—he would store away
for weeks and months, and then, in a sad and gloomy frame of
mind, he would call in a tailor, or an old-shoe man, or a ragman,
and dispose of the lot at the best price he could.   He learned

that all second-hand clothes men were sharks ; that there was no use in putting the least faith in the protests of any rag dealer or old-shoe man. They all lied. They all claimed to be very poor, when as a matter of fact they were actually rolling in wealth. Gerhardt had investigated these stories ; he had followed them up ; he had seen what they were doing with the things he sold them.

" Scoundrels ! " he declared. " They offer me ten cents for a pair of shoes, and then I see them hanging out in front of their places marked two dollars. Such robbery ! My God ! They could afford to give me a dollar."

Jennie smiled It was only to her that he complained, for he could expect no sympathy from Lester. So far as his own meagre store of money was concerned, he gave the most of it to his beloved church, where he was considered to be a model of propriety, honesty, faith—in fact, the embodiment of all the virtues.

And so, for all the ill winds that were beginning to blow socially, Jennie was now leading the dream years of her existence. Lester, in spite of the doubts which assailed him at times as to the wisdom of his career, was invariably kind and considerate, and he seemed to enjoy his home life.

" Everything all right ? " she would ask when he came in of an evening.

" Sure ! " he would answer, and pinch her chin or cheek.

She would follow him in while Jeannette, always alert, would take his coat and hat. In the winter-time they would sit in the library before the big grate-fire. In the spring, summer, or fall Lester preferred to walk out on the porch, one corner of which commanded a sweeping view of the lawn and the distant street, and light his before-dinner cigar. Jennie would sit on the side of his chair and stroke his head. " Your hair is not getting the least bit thin, Lester ; aren't you glad ? " she would say ; or, " Oh, see how your brow is wrinkled now. You mustn't do that. You didn't change your tie, mister, this morning. Why didn't you ? I laid one out for you."

" Oh, I forgot," he would answer, or he would cause the wrinkles to disappear, or laughingly predict that he would soon be getting bald if he wasn't so now.

In the drawing-room or library, before Vesta and Gerhardt, she was not less loving, though a little more circumspect.

She loved odd puzzles like pigs in clover, the spider's hole, baby billiards, and the like. Lester shared in these simple amusements. He would work by the hour, if necessary, to make a difficult puzzle come right. Jennie was clever at solving these mechanical problems. Sometimes she would have to show him the right method, and then she would be immensely pleased with herself. At other times she would stand behind him watching, her chin on his shoulder, her arms about his neck. He seemed not to mind—indeed, he was happy in the wealth of affection she bestowed. Her cleverness, her gentleness, her tact created an atmosphere which was immensely pleasing ; above all her youth and beauty appealed to him. It made him feel young, and if there was one thing Lester objected to, it was the thought of drying up into an aimless old age. " I want to keep young, or die young," was one of his pet remarks ; and Jennie came to understand. She was glad that she was so much younger now for his sake.

Another pleasant feature of the home life was Lester's steadily increasing affection for Vesta. The child would sit at the big table in the library in the evening conning her books, while Jennie would sew, and Gerhardt would read his interminable list of German Lutheran papers. It grieved the old man that Vesta should not be allowed to go to a German Lutheran parochial school, but Lester would listen to nothing of the sort. " We'll not have any thick-headed German training in this," he said to Jennie, when she suggested that Gerhardt had complained. " The public schools are good enough for any child. You tell him to let her alone."

There were really some delightful hours among the four. Lester liked to take the little seven-year-old school-girl between his knees and tease her. He liked to invert the so-called facts of life, to propound its paradoxes, and watch how the child's budding mind took them. " What's water ? " he would ask ; and being informed that it was " what we drink," he would stare and say, " That's so, but what is it ? Don't they teach you any better than that ? "

" Well, it is what we drink, isn't it ? " persisted Vesta.

" The fact that we drink it doesn't explain what it is," he would retort. " You ask your teacher what water is " ; and then he would leave her with this irritating problem troubling her young soul.

Food, china, her dress, anything was apt to be brought back to its chemical constituents, and he would leave her to struggle with these dark suggestions of something else back of the superficial appearance of things until she was actually in awe of him. She had a way of showing him how nice she looked before she started to school in the morning, a habit that arose because of his constant criticism of her appearance. He wanted her to look smart, he insisted on a big bow of blue ribbon for her hair, he demanded that her shoes be changed from low quarter to high boots with the changing character of the seasons and that her clothing be carried out on a colour scheme suited to her complexion and disposition.

"That child's light and gay by disposition. Don't put anything sombre on her," he once remarked.

Jennie had come to realise that he must be consulted in this, and would say, "Run to your papa and show him how you look."

Vesta would come and turn briskly around before him, saying, "See."

"Yes. You're all right. Go on"; and on she would go.

He grew so proud of her that on Sundays and some week-days when they drove he would always have her in between them. He insisted that Jennie send her to dancing-school, and Gerhardt was beside himself with rage and grief. "Such irreligion!" he complained to Jennie. "Such devil's fol-de-rol. Now she goes to dance. What for ? To make a no-good out of her—a creature to be ashamed of ? "

"Oh, no, papa," replied Jennie. "It isn't as bad as that. This is an awful nice school. Lester says she has to go."

"Lester, Lester; that man ! A fine lot he knows about what is good for a child. A card-player, a whisky-drinker ! "

"Now, hush, papa; I won't have you talk like that," Jennie would reply warmly. "He's a good man, and you know it."

"Yes, yes, a good man. In some things, maybe. Not in this. No."

He went away groaning. When Lester was near he said nothing, and Vesta could wind him around her finger.

"Oh you," she would say, pulling at his arm or rubbing his grizzled cheek. There was no more fight in Gerhardt when Vesta did this. He lost control of himself—something welled up and choked his throat. " Yes, I know how you do," he would exclaim.

Vesta would tweak his ear.

" Stop now ! " he would say. " That is enough."

It was noticeable, however, that she did not have to stop unless she herself willed it. Gerhardt adored the child, and she could do anything with him ; he was always her devoted servitor.

## CHAPTER XXXIX

DURING this period the dissatisfaction of the Kane family with Lester's irregular habit of life grew steadily stronger. That it could not help but become an open scandal, in the course of time, was sufficiently obvious to them. Rumours were already going about. People seemed to understand in a wise way, though nothing was ever said directly. Kane senior could scarcely imagine what possessed his son to fly in the face of conventions in this manner. If the woman had been some one of distinction—some sorceress of the stage, or of the world of art, or letters, his action would have been explicable if not commendable, but with this creature of very ordinary capabilities, as Louise had described her, this putty-faced nobody—he could not possibly understand it.

Lester was his son, his favourite son; it was too bad that he had not settled down in the ordinary way. Look at the women in Cincinnati who knew him and liked him. Take Letty Pace, for instance. Why in the name of common sense had he not married her ? She was good looking, sympathetic, talented. The old man grieved bitterly, and then, by degrees, he began to harden. It seemed a shame that Lester should treat him so. It wasn't natural, or justifiable, or decent. Archibald Kane brooded over it until he felt that some change ought to be enforced, but just what it should be he could not say. Lester was his own boss, and he would resent any criticism of his actions. Apparently, nothing could be done.

Certain changes helped along an approaching dénouement. Louise married not many months after her very disturbing visit to Chicago, and then the home property was fairly empty except for visiting grandchildren. Lester did not attend the wedding, though he was invited. For another thing, Mrs. Kane died, making a readjustment of the family will necessary. Lester came home on this occasion, grieved to think he had lately seen so little of his mother—that he had caused her so much pain—but he had no explanation to make. His father thought at the time of talking to him, but put it off because of his obvious gloom.  He went back to Chicago, and there were more months of silence.

After Mrs. Kane's death and Louise's marriage, the father went to live with Robert, for his three grandchildren afforded him his greatest pleasure in his old age.  The business, except for the final adjustment which would come after his death, was in Robert's hands.  The latter was consistently agreeable to his sisters and their husbands and to his father, in view of the eventual control he hoped to obtain.  He was not a sycophant in any sense of the word, but a shrewd, cold business man, far shrewder than his brother gave him credit for.  He was already richer than any two of the other children put together, but he chose to keep his counsel and to pretend modesty of fortune.  He realised the danger of envy, and preferred a Spartan form of existence, putting all the emphasis on inconspicuous but very ready and very hard cash.  While Lester was drifting Robert was working—working all the time.

Robert's scheme for eliminating his brother from participation in the control of the business was really not very essential, for his father, after long brooding over the details of the Chicago situation, had come to the definite conclusion that any large share of his property ought not to go to Lester.  Obviously, Lester was not so strong a man as he had thought him to be.  Of the two brothers, Lester might be the bigger intellectually or sympathetically—artistically and socially there was no comparison—but Robert got commercial results in a silent, effective way.  If Lester was not going to pull himself together at this stage of the game, when would he ?  Better leave his property to those who would take care of it.  Archibald Kane thought seriously of having his lawyer revise his will in such a way that, unless Lester should reform, he would be cut off with only a nominal income.  But he decided to give Lester one more chance—to make a plea, in fact, that he should abandon his false way of living, and put himself on a sound basis before the world.  It wasn't too late.  He really had a great future.  Would he deliberately choose to throw it away ?  Old Archibald wrote Lester that he would like to have a talk with him at his convenience, and within the lapse of thirty-six hours Lester was in Cincinnati.

" I thought I'd have one more talk with you, Lester, on a

subject that's rather difficult for me to bring up," began the elder Kane. " You know what I'm referring to ? "

" Yes, I know," replied Lester, calmly.

" I used to think, when I was much younger, that my son's matrimonial ventures would never concern me, but I changed my views on that score when I got a little farther along. I began to see through my business connections how much the right sort of a marriage helps a man, and then I got rather anxious that my boys should marry well. I used to worry about you, Lester, and I'm worrying yet. This recent connection you've made has caused me no end of trouble. It worried your mother up to the very last. It was her one great sorrow. Don't you think you have gone far enough with it ? The scandal has reached down here. What it is in Chicago I don't know, but it can't be a secret. That can't help the house in business there. It certainly can't help you. The whole thing has gone on so long that you have injured your prospects all around, and yet you continue. Why do you ? "

" I suppose because I love her," Lester replied.

" You can't be serious in that," said his father. " If you had loved her, you'd have married her in the first place. Surely you wouldn't take a woman and live with her as you have with this woman for years, disgracing her and yourself, and still claim that you love her. You may have a passion for her, but it isn't love."

" How do you know I haven't married her ? " inquired Lester coolly. He wanted to see how his father would take to that idea.

" You're not serious ! " The old gentleman propped himself up on his arms and looked at him.

" No, I'm not," replied Lester, " but I might be. I might marry her."

" Impossible ! " exclaimed his father vigorously. " I can't believe it. I can't believe a man of your intelligence would do a thing like that, Lester. Where is your judgment ? Why, you've lived in open adultery with her for years, and now you talk of marrying her. Why, in heaven's name, if you were going to do anything like that, didn't you do it in the first place ? Disgrace your parents, break your mother's heart, injure the business, become a public scandal, and then marry the cause of it ? I don't believe it."

Old Archibald got up.

"Don't get excited, father," said Lester quickly. "We won't get anywhere that way. I say I might marry her. She's not a bad woman, and I wish you wouldn't talk about her as you do. You've never seen her. You know nothing about her.

"I know enough," insisted old Archibald, determinedly. "I know that no good woman would act as she has done. Why, man, she's after your money. What else could she want? It's as plain as the nose on your face."

"Father," said Lester, his voice lowering ominously, "why do you talk like that? You never saw the woman. You wouldn't know her from Adam's off ox. Louise comes down here and gives an excited report, and you people swallow it whole. She isn't as bad as you think she is, and I wouldn't use the language you're using about her if I were you. You're doing a good woman an injustice, and you won't, for some reason, be fair."

"Fair! Fair!" interrupted Archibald. "Talk about being fair. Is it fair to me, to your family, to your dead mother to take a woman of the streets and live with her? Is it——"

"Stop now, father," exclaimed Lester, putting up his hand. "I warn you. I won't listen to talk like that. You're talking about the woman that I'm living with—that I may marry. I love you, but I won't have you saying things that aren't so. She isn't a woman of the streets. You know, as well as you know anything, that I wouldn't take up with a woman of that kind. We'll have to discuss this in a calmer mood, or I won't stay here. I'm sorry. I'm awfully sorry. But I won't listen to any such language as that."

Old Archibald quieted himself. In spite of his opposition, he respected his son's point of view. He sat back in his chair and stared at the floor. "How was he to handle this thing?" he asked himself.

"Are you living in the same place?" he finally inquired.

"No, we've moved out to Hyde Park. I've taken a house out there."

"I hear there's a child. Is that yours?"

"No."

"Have you any children of your own?"

"No."

"Well, that's a God's blessing."

Lester merely scratched his chin.

" And you insist you will marry her ? " Archibald went on.

" I didn't say that," replied his son. " I said I might."

" Might ! Might ! " exclaimed his father, his anger bubbling again. " What a tragedy ! You with your prospects ! Your outlook ! How do you suppose I can seriously contemplate entrusting any share of my fortune to a man who has so little regard for what the world considers as right and proper ? Why, Lester, this carriage business, your family, your personal reputation appear to be as nothing at all to you. I can't understand what has happened to your pride. It seems like some wild, impossible fancy."

" It's pretty hard to explain, father, and I can't do it very well. I simply know that I'm in this affair, and that I'm bound to see it through. It may come out all right. I may not marry her—I may. I'm not prepared now to say what I'll do. You'll have to wait. I'll do the best I can."

Old Archibald merely shook his head disapprovingly.

" You've made a bad mess of this, Lester," he said finally. " Surely you have. But I suppose you are determined to go your way. Nothing that I have said appears to move you."

" Not now, father. I'm sorry."

" Well, I warn you, then, that, unless you show some consideration for the dignity of your family and the honour of your position it will make a difference in my will. I can't go on countenancing this thing, and not be a party to it morally and every other way. I won't do it. You can leave her, or you can marry her. You certainly ought to do one or the other. If you leave her, everything will be all right. You can make any provision for her you like. I have no objection to that. I'll gladly pay whatever you agree to. You will share with the rest of the children, just as I had planned. If you marry her it will make a difference. Now do as you please. But don't blame me. I love you. I'm your father. I'm doing what I think is my bounden duty. Now you think that over and let me know."

Lester sighed. He saw how hopeless this argument was. He felt that his father probably meant what he said, but how could he leave Jennie, and justify himself to himself ? Would his father really cut him off ? Surely not. The old gentleman loved him even now—he could see it. Lester felt troubled and distressed ; this attempt at coercion irritated him. The idea—he, Lester Kane, being made to do such a thing—to throw Jennie down. He stared at the floor.

Old Archibald saw that he had let fly a telling bullet.

" Well," said Lester finally, " there's no use of our discussing it any further now—that's certain, isn't it ? I can't say what I'll do. I'll have to take time and think. I can't decide this offhand."

The two looked at each other. Lester was sorry for the world's attitude and for his father's keen feeling about the affair. Kane senior was sorry for his son, but he was determined to see the thing through. He wasn't sure whether he had converted Lester or not, but he was hopeful. Maybe he would come around yet.

" Good-bye, father," said Lester, holding out his hand. " I think I'll try and make that two-ten train. There isn't anything else you wanted to see me about ? "

" No."

The old man sat there after Lester had gone, thinking deeply. What a twisted career ! What an end to great possibilities ? What a foolhardy persistence in evil and error ! He shook his head. Robert was wiser. He was the one to control a business. He was cool and conservative. If Lester were only like that. He thought and thought. It was a long time before he stirred. And still, in the bottom of his heart, his erring son continued to appeal to him.

# CHAPTER XL

LESTER returned to Chicago. He realised that he had offended his father seriously, how seriously he could not say. In all his personal relations with old Archibald he had never seen him so worked up. But even now Lester did not feel that the breach was irreparable ; he hardly realised that it was necessary for him to act decisively if he hoped to retain his father's affection and confidence. As for the world at large, what did it matter how much people talked or what they said. He was big enough to stand alone. But was he ? People turn so quickly from weakness or the shadow of it. To get away from failure—even the mere suspicion of it—that seems to be a subconscious feeling with the average man and woman ; we all avoid non-success as though we fear that it may prove contagious. Lester was soon to feel the force of this prejudice.

One day Lester happened to run across Berry Dodge, the millionaire head of Dodge, Holbrook & Kingsbury, a firm that stood in the dry-goods world, where the Kane Company stood in the carriage world. Dodge had been one of Lester's best friends. He knew him as intimately as he knew Henry Bracebridge, of Cleveland, and George Knowles, of Cincinnati. He visited at his handsome home on the North Shore Drive, and they met constantly in a business and social way. But since Lester had moved out to Hyde Park, the old intimacy had lapsed. Now they came face to face on Michigan Avenue near the Kane building.

" Why, Lester, I'm glad to see you again," said Dodge. He extended a formal hand, and seemed just a little cool. " I hear you've gone and married since I saw you."

" No, nothing like that," replied Lester, easily, with the air of one who prefers to be understood in the way of the world sense.

" Why so secret about it, if you have ? " asked Dodge, attempting to smile, but with a wry twist to the corners of his mouth. He was trying to be nice, and to go through a difficult situation gracefully. " We fellows usually make a fuss about that sort of thing. You ought to let your friends know."

"Well," said Lester, feeling the edge of the social blade that was being driven into him, "I thought I'd do it in a new way. I'm not much for excitement in that direction, anyhow."

"It is a matter of taste, isn't it ? " said Dodge a little absently. "You're living in the city, of course ? "

"In Hyde Park."

"That's a pleasant territory. How are things otherwise ? " And he deftly changed the subject before waving him a perfunctory farewell.

Lester missed at once the inquiries which a man like Dodge would have made if he had really believed that he was married. Under ordinary circumstances his friend would have wanted to know a great deal about the new Mrs. Kane. There would have been all those little familiar touches common to people living on the same social plane. Dodge would have asked Lester to bring his wife over to see them, would have definitely promised to call. Nothing of the sort happened, and Lester noticed the significant omission.

It was the same with the Burnham Moores, the Henry Aldriches, and a score of other people whom he knew equally well. Apparently they all thought that he had married and settled down. They were interested to know where he was living, and they were rather disposed to joke him about being so very secretive on the subject, but they were not willing to discuss the supposed Mrs. Kane. He was beginning to see that this move of his was going to tell against him notably.

One of the worst stabs—it was the cruellest because, in a way, it was the most unintentional—he received from an old acquaintance, Will Whitney, at the Union Club. Lester was dining there one evening, and Whitney met him in the main reading-room as he was crossing from the cloak-room to the cigar-stand. The latter was a typical society figure, tall, lean, smooth-faced, immaculately garbed, a little cynical, and to-night a little the worse for liquor. "Hi, Lester ! " he called out, "what's this talk about a *ménage* of yours out in Hyde Park ? Say, you're going some. How are you going to explain all this to your wife when you get married ? "

"I don't have to explain it," replied Lester irritably. "Why should you be so interested in my affairs ? You're not living in a stone house, are you ? "

" Say, ha ! ha ! that's pretty good now, isn't it ? You didn't marry that little beauty you used to travel around with on the North Side, did you ? Eh, now ! Ha, ha ! Well, I swear. You married ! You didn't, now, did you ? "

" Cut it out, Whitney," said Lester roughly. " You're talking wild."

" Pardon, Lester," said the other aimlessly, but sobering. " I beg your pardon. Remember, I'm just a little warm. Eight whisky-sours straight in the other room there. Pardon. I'll talk to you some time when I'm all right. See, Lester ? Eh ! Ha ! ha ! I'm a little loose, that's right. Well, so long ! Ha ! ha ! "

Lester could not get over that cacaphonous " ha ! ha ! " It cut him, even though it came from a drunken man's mouth. " That little beauty you used to travel with on the North Side. You didn't marry her, did you ? " He quoted Whitney's impertinences resentfully. George ! But this was getting a little rough ! He had never endured anything like this before —he, Lester Kane. It set him thinking. Certainly he was paying dearly for trying to do the kind thing by Jennie.

## CHAPTER XLI

BUT worse was to follow. The American public likes gossip about well-known people, and the Kanes were wealthy and socially prominent. The report was that Lester, one of its principal heirs, had married a servant girl. He, an heir to millions! Could it be possible? What a piquant morsel for the newspapers! Very soon the paragraphs began to appear. A small society paper, called the *South Side Budget*, referred to him anonymously as "the son of a famous and wealthy carriage manufacturer of Cincinnati," and outlined briefly what it knew of the story. "Of Mrs.——" it went on, sagely, "not so much is known, except that she once worked in a well-known Cleveland society family as a maid and was, before that, a working-girl in Columbus, Ohio. After such a picturesque love-affair in high society who shall say that romance is dead?"

Lester saw this item. He did not take the paper, but some kind soul took good care to see that a copy was marked and mailed to him. It irritated him greatly, for he suspected at once that it was a scheme to blackmail him. But he did not know exactly what to do about it. He preferred, of course, that such comments should cease, but he also thought that if he made any effort to have them stopped he might make matters worse. So he did nothing. Naturally, the paragraph in the *Budget* attracted the attention of other newspapers. It sounded like a good story, and one Sunday editor, more enterprising than the others, conceived the notion of having this romance written up. A full-page Sunday story with a scare-head such as "Sacrifices Millions for His Servant Girl Love," pictures of Lester, Jennie, the house at Hyde Park, the Kane manufactory at Cincinnati, the warehouse on Michigan Avenue—certainly, such a display would make a sensation. The Kane Company was not an advertiser in any daily or Sunday paper. The newspaper owed him nothing. If Lester had been forewarned he might have put a stop to the whole business by putting an advertisement in the paper or appealing to the publisher.

He did not know, however, and so was without power to prevent the publication. The editor made a thorough job of the business. Local newspaper men in Cincinnati, Cleveland, and Columbus were instructed to report by wire whether anything of Jennie's history was known in their city. The Bracebridge family in Cleveland was asked whether Jennie had ever worked there. A garbled history of the Gerhardts was obtained from Columbus. Jennie's residence on the North Side, for several years prior to her supposed marriage, was discovered and so the whole story was nicely pieced together. It was not the idea of the newspaper editor to be cruel or critical, but rather complimentary. All the bitter things, such as the probable illegitimacy of Vesta, the suspected immorality of Lester and Jennie in residing together as man and wife, the real grounds of the well-known objections of his family to the match, were ignored. The idea was to frame up a Romeo and Juliet story in which Lester should appear as an ardent, self-sacrificing lover, and Jennie as a poor and lovely working-girl, lifted to great financial and social heights by the devotion of her millionaire lover. An exceptional newspaper artist was engaged to make scenes depicting the various steps of the romance and the whole thing was handled in the most approved yellow-journal style. There was a picture of Lester obtained from his Cincinnati photographer for a consideration ; Jennie had been surreptitiously " snapped " by a staff artist while she was out walking.

And so, apparently out of a clear sky, the story appeared— highly complimentary, running over with sugary phrases, but with all the dark, sad facts looming up in the background. Jennie did not see it at first. Lester came across the page accidentally, and tore it out. He was stunned and chagrined beyond words. " To think the damned newspaper would do that to a private citizen who was quietly minding his own business ! " he thought. He went out of the house, the better to conceal his deep inward mortification. He avoided the more populous parts of the town, particularly the downtown section, and rode far out on Cottage Grove Avenue to the open prairie. He wondered, as the trolley-car rumbled along, what his friends were thinking—Dodge, and Burnham Moore, and Henry Aldrich, and the others. This was a smash, indeed. The best he could do was to put a brave face on it and say nothing, or else wave it off with an indifferent motion of the hand.   One thing was sure—he would prevent further comment. He returned to the house calmer, his self-poise restored, but he was eager for Monday to come in order that he might get in touch with his lawyer, Mr. Watson.   But when he did see Mr. Watson it was soon agreed between the two men that it would be foolish to take any legal action.   It was the part of wisdom to let the matter drop.   " But I won't stand for anything more," concluded Lester.

" I'll attend to that," said the lawyer, consolingly.

Lester got up.   " It's amazing—this damned country of ours ! " he exclaimed.   " A man with a little money hasn't any more privacy than a public monument."

" A man with a little money," said Mr. Watson, " is just like a cat with a bell around its neck.   Every rat knows exactly where it is and what it is doing."

" That's an apt simile," assented Lester, bitterly.

Jennie knew nothing of this newspaper story for several days.   Lester felt that he could not talk it over, and Gerhardt never read the wicked Sunday newspapers.   Finally, one of Jennie's neighbourhood friends, less tactful than the others, called her attention to the fact of its appearance by announcing that she had seen it.   Jennie did not understand at first.   " A story about me ? " she exclaimed.

" You and Mr. Kane, yes," replied her guest.   " Your love romance."

Jennie coloured swiftly.   " Why, I hadn't seen it," she said. " Are you sure it was about us ? "

" Why, of course," laughed Mrs. Stendahl.   " How could I be mistaken ?   I have the paper over at the house.   I'll send Marie over with it when I get back.   You look very sweet in your picture."

Jennie winced.

" I wish you would," she said, weakly.

She was wondering where they had secured her picture, what the article said.   Above all, she was dismayed to think of its effect upon Lester.   Had he seen the article ?   Why had he not spoken to her about it ?

The neighbour's daughter brought over the paper, and Jennie's heart stood still as she glanced at the title-page. There it all was—uncompromising and direct.   How dreadfully conspicuous the headline—" This Millionaire Fell in Love With This Lady's Maid," which ran between a picture of Lester on the left and Jennie on the right. There was an additional caption which explained how Lester, son of the famous carriage family of Cincinnati, had sacrificed great social opportunity and distinction to marry his heart's desire. Below were scattered a number of other pictures—Lester addressing Jennie in the mansion of Mrs. Bracebridge, Lester standing with her before an imposing and conventional-looking parson, Lester driving with her in a handsome victoria, Jennie standing beside the window of an imposing mansion (the fact that it was a mansion being indicated by most sumptuous-looking hangings) and gazing out on a very modest working-man's cottage pictured in the distance. Jennie felt as though she must die for very shame. She did not so much mind what it meant to her, but Lester, Lester, how must he feel ? And his family ? Now they would have another club with which to strike him and her. She tried to keep calm about it, to exert emotional control, but again the tears would rise, only this time they were tears of opposition to defeat. She did not want to be hounded this way. She wanted to be let alone. She was trying to do right now. Why couldn't the world help her, instead of seeking to push her down ?

## CHAPTER XLII

THE fact that Lester had seen this page was made perfectly clear to Jennie that evening, for he brought it home himself, having concluded, after mature deliberation, that he ought to. He had told her once that there was to be no concealment between them, and this thing, coming so brutally to disturb their peace, was nevertheless a case in point. He had decided to tell her not to think anything of it—that it did not make much difference, though to him it made all the difference in the world. The effect of this chill history could never be undone. The wise—and they included all his social world and many who were not of it—could see just how he had been living. The article which accompanied the pictures told how he had followed Jennie from Cleveland to Chicago, how she had been coy and distant and that he had to court her a long time to win her consent. This was to explain their living together on the North Side. Lester realised that this was an asinine attempt to sugar-coat the true story and it made him angry. Still he preferred to have it that way rather than in some more brutal vein. He took the paper out of his pocket when he arrived at the house, spreading it on the library table. Jennie, who was close by, watched him, for she knew what was coming.

" Here's something that will interest you, Jennie," he said dryly, pointing to the array of text and pictures.

" I've already seen it, Lester," she said wearily. " Mrs. Stendahl showed it to me this afternoon. I was wondering whether you had."

" Rather high-flown description of my attitude, isn't it ? I didn't know I was such an ardent Romeo."

" I'm awfully sorry, Lester," said Jennie, reading behind the dry face of humour the serious import of this affair to him. She had long since learned that Lester did not express his real feeling, his big ills in words. He was inclined to jest and make light of the inevitable, the inexorable. This light comment merely meant " this matter cannot be helped, so we will make the best of it."

" Oh, don't feel badly about it," he went on. " It isn't anything which can be adjusted now. They probably meant well enough. We just happen to be in the limelight."

" I understand," said Jennie, coming over to him. " I'm sorry, though, anyway." Dinner was announced a moment later and the incident was closed.

But Lester could not dismiss the thought that matters were getting in a bad way. His father had pointed it out to him rather plainly at the last interview, and now this newspaper notoriety had capped the climax. He might as well abandon his pretension to intimacy with his old world. It would have none of him, or at least the more conservative part of it would not. There were a few bachelors, a few gay married men, some sophisticated women, single and married, who saw through it all and liked him just the same, but they did not make society. He was virtually an outcast, and nothing could save him but to reform his ways ; in other words, he must give up Jennie once and for all.

But he did not want to do this. The thought was painful to him—objectionable in every way. Jennie was growing in mental acumen. She was beginning to see things quite as clearly as he did. She was not a cheap, ambitious, climbing creature. She was a big woman and a good one. It would be a shame to throw her down, and besides she was good-looking. He was forty-six and she was twenty-nine ; and she looked twenty-four or five. It is an exceptional thing to find beauty, youth, compatibility, intelligence, your own point of view—softened and charmingly emotionalised—in another. He had made his bed, as his father had said. He had better lie on it.

It was only a little while after this disagreeable newspaper incident that Lester had word that his father was quite ill and failing ; it might be necessary for him to go to Cincinnati at any moment. Pressure of work was holding him pretty close when the news came that his father was dead. Lester, of course, was greatly shocked and grieved, and he returned to Cincinnati in a retrospective and sorrowful mood. His father had been a great character to him—a fine and interesting old gentleman entirely aside from his relationship to him as his son.  He remembered him now dandling him upon his knee as a child, telling him stories of his early life in Ireland, and of his subsequent commercial struggle when he was a little older, impressing the maxims of his business career and his commercial wisdom on him as he grew to manhood.  Old Archibald had been radically honest.  It was to him that Lester owed his instincts for plain speech and direct statement of fact.  " Never lie," was Archibald's constant, reiterated statement.  " Never try to make a thing look different from what it is to you.  It's the breath of life—truth—it's the basis of real worth, while commercial success—it will make a notable character of any one who will stick to it."  Lester believed this.  He admired his father intensely for his rigid insistence on truth, and now that he was really gone he felt sorry.  He wished he might have been spared to be reconciled to him.  He half fancied that old Archibald would have liked Jennie if he had known her.  He did not imagine that he would ever have had the opportunity to straighten things out, although he still felt that Archibald would have liked her.

When he reached Cincinnati it was snowing, a windy, blustery snow.  The flakes were coming down thick and fast.  The traffic of the city had a muffled sound.  When he stepped down from the train he was met by Amy, who was glad to see him in spite of all their past differences.  Of all the girls she was the most tolerant.  Lester put his arms about her, and kissed her.

" It seems like old times to see you, Amy," he said, " your coming to meet me this way.  How's the family ?  I suppose they're all here.  Well, poor father, his time had to come.  Still, he lived to see everything that he wanted to see.  I guess he was pretty well satisfied with the outcome of his efforts."

" Yes," replied Amy, " and since mother died he was very lonely."

They rode up to the house in kindly good feeling, chatting of old times and places.  All the members of the immediate family, and the various relatives, were gathered in the old family mansion.  Lester exchanged the customary condolences with the others, realising all the while that his father had lived long enough.  He had had a successful life, and had fallen like a ripe apple from the tree.  Lester looked at him where he lay in the great parlour, in his black coffin, and a feeling of the old-time affection swept over him. He smiled at the clean-cut, determined, conscientious face.

" The old gentleman was a big man all the way through," he said to Robert, who was present. " We won't find a better figure of a man soon."

" We will not," said his brother, solemnly.

After the funeral it was decided to read the will at once. Louise's husband was anxious to return to Buffalo; Lester was compelled to be in Chicago. A conference of the various members of the family was called for the second day after the funeral, to be held at the offices of Messrs. Knight, Keatley and O'Brien, counsellors of the late manufacturer.

As Lester rode to the meeting he had the feeling that his father had not acted in any way prejudicial to his interests. It had not been so very long since they had had their last conversation; he had been taking his time to think about things, and his father had given him time. He always felt that he had stood well with the old gentleman, except for his alliance with Jennie. His business judgment had been valuable to the company. Why should there be any discrimination against him? He really did not think it possible.

When they reached the offices of the law firm, Mr. O'Brien, a short, fussy, albeit comfortable-looking little person, greeted all the members of the family and the various heirs and assigns with a hearty handshake. He had been personal counsel to Archibald Kane for twenty years. He knew his whims and idiosyncrasies, and considered himself very much in the light of a father confessor. He liked all the children, Lester especially.

" Now I believe we are all here," he said, finally, extracting a pair of large horn reading-glasses from his coat pocket and looking sagely about. " Very well. We might as well proceed to business. I will just read the will without any preliminary remarks."

He turned to his desk, picked up a paper lying upon it, cleared his throat, and began.

It was a peculiar document, in some respects, for it began with all the minor bequests; first, small sums to old employees, servants, and friends. It then took up a few institutional bequests, and finally came to the immediate family, beginning with the girls. Imogene, as a faithful and loving daughter was left a sixth of the stock of the carriage company and a fourth of the remaining properties of the deceased, which roughly aggregated (the estate—not her share) about eight hundred thousand dollars. Amy and Louise were provided for in exactly the same proportion. The grandchildren were given certain little bonuses for good conduct, when they should come of age. Then it took up the cases of Robert and Lester.

" Owing to certain complications which have arisen in the affairs of my son Lester," it began, " I deem it my duty to make certain conditions which shall govern the distribution of the remainder of my property, to wit : One-fourth of the stock of the Kane Manufacturing Company and one-fourth of the remainder of my various properties, real, personal, moneys, stocks and bonds, to go to my beloved son Robert, in recognition of the faithful performance of his duty, and one-fourth of the stock of the Kane Manufacturing Company and the remaining fourth of my various properties, real, personal, moneys, stocks and bonds, to be held in trust by him for the benefit of his brother Lester, until such time as such conditions as may hereinafter be set forth shall have been complied with. And it is my wish and desire that my children shall concur in his direction of the Kane Manufacturing Company, and of such other interests as are entrusted to him, until such time as he shall voluntarily relinquish such control, or shall indicate another arrangement which shall be better."

Lester swore under his breath. His cheeks changed colour, but he did not move. He was not inclined to make a show. It appeared that he was not even mentioned separately.

The conditions " hereinafter set forth " dealt very fully with his case, however, though they were not read aloud to the family at the time, Mr. O'Brien stating that this was in accordance with their father's wish. Lester learned immediately afterward that he was to have ten thousand a year for three years, during which time he had the choice of doing either one of two things : First, he was to leave Jennie, if he had not already married her, and so bring his life into moral conformity with the wishes of his father. In this event Lester's share of the estate was to be immediately turned over to him. Secondly, he might elect to marry Jennie, if he had not already done so, in which case the ten thousand a year, specifically set aside to him for three years, was to be continued for life—but for his life only. Jennie was not to have anything of it after his death. The ten thousand in question represented the annual interest on two hundred shares of L.S. and M.S. stock which were also to be held in trust until his decision had been reached and their final disposition effected. If Lester refused to marry Jennie, or to leave her, he was to have nothing at all after the three years were up. At Lester's death the stock on which his interest was drawn was to be divided pro rata among the surviving members of the family. If any heir or assign contested the will, his or her share was thereby forfeited entirely.

It was astonishing to Lester to see how thoroughly his father had taken his case into consideration. He half suspected, on reading these conditions, that his brother Robert had had something to do with the framing of them, but of course he could not be sure. Robert had not given any direct evidence of enmity.

" Who drew this will ? " he demanded of O'Brien, a little later.

" Well, we all had a hand in it," replied O'Brien, a little shamefacedly. " It was a very difficult document to draw up. You know, Mr. Kane, there was no budging your father. He was adamant. He has come very near defeating his own wishes in some of these clauses. Of course, you know, we had nothing to do with its spirit. That was between you and him. I hated very much to have to do it."

" Oh, I understand all that ! " said Lester. " Don't let that worry you."

Mr. O'Brien was very grateful.

During the reading of the will Lester had sat as stolid as an ox.

He got up after a time, as did the others, assuming an air of nonchalance. Robert, Amy, Louise and Imogene all felt shocked, but not exactly, not unqualifiedly regretful. Certainly Lester had acted very badly. He had given his father great provocation.

" I think the old gentleman has been a little rough in this," said Robert, who had been sitting next him. " I certainly did not expect him to go as far as that. So far as I am concerned some other arrangement would have been satisfactory."

Lester smiled grimly. " It doesn't matter," he said.

Imogene, Amy, and Louise were anxious to be consolatory, but they did not know what to say. Lester had brought it all on himself. " I don't think papa acted quite right, Lester," ventured Amy, but Lester waved her away almost gruffly.

" I can stand it," he said.

He figured out, as he stood there, what his income would be in case he refused to comply with his father's wishes. Two hundred shares of L.S. and M.S., in open market, were worth a little over one thousand each. They yielded from five to six per cent., sometimes more, sometimes less. At this rate he would have ten thousand a year, not more.

The family gathering broke up, each going his way, and Lester returned to his sister's house. He wanted to get out of the city quickly, gave business as an excuse to avoid lunching with any one, and caught the earliest train back to Chicago. As he rode he meditated.

So this was how much his father really cared for him! Could it really be so ? He, Lester Kane, ten thousand a year, for only three years, and then longer only on condition that he married Jennie ! " Ten thousand a year," he thought, " and that for three years ! Good Lord ! Any smart clerk can earn that. To think he should have done that to me ! "

## CHAPTER XLIII

THIS attempt at coercion was the one thing which would definitely set Lester in opposition to his family, at least for the time being. He had realised clearly enough of late that he had made a big mistake ; first in not having married Jennie, thus avoiding scandal ; and in the second place in not having accepted her proposition at the time when she wanted to leave him. There were no two ways about it, he had made a mess of this business. He could not afford to lose his fortune entirely. He did not have enough money of his own. Jennie was unhappy, he could see that. Why shouldn't she be ? He was unhappy. Did he want to accept the shabby ten thousand a year, even if he were willing to marry her ? Finally, did he want to lose Jennie, to have her go out of his life once and for all ? He could not make up his mind ; the problem was too complicated.

When Lester returned to his home, after the funeral, Jennie saw at once that something was amiss with him, something beyond a son's natural grief for his father's death was weighing upon his spirits. What was it, she wondered. She tried to draw near to him sympathetically, but his wounded spirit could not be healed so easily. When hurt in his pride he was savage and sullen—he could have struck any man who irritated him. She watched him interestedly, wishing to do something for him, but he would not give her his confidence. He grieved, and she could only grieve with him.

Days passed, and now the financial situation which had been created by his father's death came up for careful consideration. The factory management had to be reorganised. Robert would have to be made president, as his father wished. Lester's own relationship to the business would have to come up for adjudication. Unless he changed his mind about Jennie, he was not a stockholder. As a matter of fact, he was not anything. To continue to be secretary and treasurer, it was necessary that he should own at least one share of the company's stock. Would Robert give him any ? Would Amy, Louise,

or Imogene ?  Would they sell him any ?  Would the other
members of the family care to do anything which would infringe
on Robert's prerogatives under the will ?  They were all rather
unfriendly to Lester at present, and he realised that he was
facing a ticklish situation.  The solution was—to get rid of
Jennie.  If he did that he would not need to be begging for
stock.  If he didn't, he was flying in the face of his father's
last will and testament.  He turned the matter over in his
mind slowly and deliberately.  He could quite see how things
were coming out.  He must abandon either Jennie or his
prospects in life.  What a dilemma !

Despite Robert's assertion, that so far as he was concerned
another arrangement would have been satisfactory, he was
really very well pleased with the situation ; his dreams were
slowly nearing completion.  Robert had long had his plans
perfected, not only for a thorough reorganisation of the company
proper, but for an extension of the business in the direction
of a combination of carriage companies.  If he could get two
or three of the larger organisations in the East and West to
join with him, selling costs could be reduced, over-production
would be avoided, and the general expenses could be materially
scaled down.  Through a New York representative, he had
been picking up stock in outside carriage companies for some
time and he was almost ready to act.  In the first place he
would have himself elected president of the Kane Company,
and since Lester was no longer a factor, he could select Amy's
husband as vice-president, and possibly some one other than
Lester as secretary and treasurer.  Under the conditions of
the will, the stock and other properties set aside temporarily
for Lester, in the hope that he would come to his senses, were
to be managed and voted by Robert.  His father had meant,
obviously, that he, Robert, should help him coerce his brother.
He did not want to appear mean, but this was such an easy way.
It gave him a righteous duty to perform.  Lester must come
to his senses or he must let Robert run the business to suit
himself.

Lester, attending to his branch duties in Chicago, foresaw
the drift of things.  He realised now that he was permanently
out of the company, a branch manager at his brother's sufferance,
and the thought irritated him greatly.  Nothing had been said
by Robert to indicate that such a change had taken place—

things went on very much as before—but Robert's suggestions were now obviously law. Lester was really his brother's employee at so much a year. It sickened his soul.

There came a time, after a few weeks, when he felt as if he could not stand this any longer. Hitherto he had been a free and independent agent. The approaching annual stockholder's meeting which hitherto had been a one-man affair and a formality, his father doing all the voting, would be now a combination of voters, his brother presiding, his sisters very likely represented by their husbands, and he not there at all. It was going to be a great come-down, but as Robert had not said anything about offering to give or sell him any stock which would entitle him to sit as a director or hold any official position in the company, he decided to write and resign. That would bring matters to a crisis. It would show his brother that he felt no desire to be under obligations to him in any way or to retain anything which was not his—and gladly so—by right of ability and the desire of those with whom he was associated. If he wanted to move back into the company by deserting Jennie he would come in a very different capacity from that of branch manager. He dictated a simple, straightforward business letter, saying :

" DEAR ROBERT,
        " I know the time is drawing near when the company must be reorganised under your direction. Not having any stock, I am not entitled to sit as a director, or to hold the joint position of secretary and treasurer. I want you to accept this letter as formal notice of my resignation from both positions, and I want to have your directors consider what disposition should be made of this position and my services. I am not anxious to retain the branch-managership as a branch-managership merely ; at the same time I do not want to do anything which will embarrass you in your plans for the future. You see by this that I am not ready to accept the proposition laid down in father's will—at least, not at present. I would like a definite understanding of how you feel in this matter. Will you write and let me know ?
                                        . " Yours,
                                            " LESTER."

Robert, sitting in his office at Cincinnati, considered this letter gravely. It was like his brother to come down to " brass tacks." If Lester were only as cautious as he was straightforward and direct, what a man he would be ! But there was no guile in the man—no subtlety. He would never do a snaky thing—and Robert knew, in his own soul, that to succeed greatly one must. " You have to be ruthless at times—you have to be subtle," Robert would say to himself. " Why not face the facts to yourself when you are playing for big stakes ? " He would, for one, and he did.

Robert felt that although Lester was a tremendously decent fellow and his brother, he wasn't pliable enough to suit his needs. He was too outspoken, too inclined to take issue. If Lester yielded to his father's wishes, and took possession of his share of the estate, he would become, necessarily, an active partner in the affairs of the company. Lester would be a barrier in Robert's path. Did Robert want this ? Decidedly he did not. He much preferred that Lester should hold fast to Jennie, for the present at least, and so be quietly shelved by his own act.

After long consideration, Robert dictated a politic letter. He hadn't made up his mind yet just what he wanted to do. He did not know what his sisters' husbands would like. A consultation would have to be held. For his part, he would be very glad to have Lester remain as secretary and treasurer, if it could be arranged. Perhaps it would be better to let the matter rest for the present.

Lester cursed. What did Robert mean by beating around the bush ? He knew well enough how it could be arranged. One share of stock would be enough for Lester to qualify. Robert was afraid of him—that was the basic fact. Well, he would not retain any branch-managership, depend on that. He would resign at once. Lester accordingly wrote back, saying that he had considered all sides, and had decided to look after some interests of his own, for the time being. If Robert could arrange it, he would like to have some one come on to Chicago and take over the branch agency. Thirty days would be time enough. In a few days came a regretful reply, saying that Robert was awfully sorry, but that if Lester was determined he did not want to interfere with any plans he might have in view. Imogene's husband, Jefferson Midgely, had long thought he would like to reside in Chicago. He would undertake the work for the time being.

Lester smiled. Evidently Robert was making the best of a

very subtle situation. Robert knew that he, Lester, could sue and tie things up, and also that he would be very loath to do so. The newspapers would get hold of the whole story. This matter of his relationship to Jennie was in the air, anyhow. He could best solve the problem by leaving her. So it all came back to that.

## CHAPTER XLIV

FOR a man of Lester's years—he was now forty-six—to be tossed out in the world without a definite connection, even though he did have a present income (including this new ten thousand) of fifteen thousand a year, was a disturbing and discouraging thing. He realised now that, unless he made some very fortunate and profitable arrangements in the near future, his career was virtually at an end. Of course he could marry Jennie. That would give him the ten thousand for the rest of his life, but it would also end his chance of getting his legitimate share of the Kane estate. Again, he might sell out the seventy-five thousand dollars' worth of moderate interest-bearing stocks, which now yielded him about five thousand, and try a practical investment of some kind—say a rival carriage company. But did he want to jump in, at this stage of the game, and begin a running fight on his father's old organisation ? Moreover, it would be a hard row to hoe. There was the keenest rivalry for business as it was, with the Kane Company very much in the lead. Lester's only available capital was his seventy-five thousand dollars. Did he want to begin in a picayune, obscure way ? It took money to get a foothold in the carriage business as things were now.

The trouble with Lester was that, while blessed with a fine imagination and considerable insight, he lacked the ruthless, narrow-minded insistence on his individual superiority which is a necessary element in almost every great business success. To be a forceful figure in the business world means, as a rule, that you must be an individual of one idea, and that idea the God-given one that life has destined you for a tremendous future in the particular field you have chosen. It means that one thing, a cake of soap, a new can-opener, a safety razor, or speed-accelerator, must seize on your imagination with tremendous force, burn as a raging flame, and make itself the be-all and end-all of your existence. As a rule, a man needs poverty to help him to this enthusiasm, and youth. The thing he has discovered, and with which he is going to busy himself, must be the door to a thousand opportunities and a thousand joys. Happiness must be beyond or the fire will not burn as brightly as it might—the urge will not be great enough to make a great success.

Lester did not possess this indispensable quality of enthusiasm. Life had already shown him the greater part of its so-called joys. He saw through the illusions that are so often and so noisily labelled pleasure. Money, of course, was essential, and he had already had money—enough to keep him comfortably. Did he want to risk it ? He looked about him thoughtfully. Perhaps he did. Certainly he could not comfortably contemplate the thought of sitting by and watching other people work for the rest of his days.

In the end he decided that he would bestir himself and look into things. He was, as he said to himself, in no hurry ; he was not going to make a mistake. He would first give the trade, the people who were identified with the manufacture and sale of carriages, time to realise that he was out of the Kane Company, for the time being, anyhow, and open to other connections. So he announced that he was leaving the Kane Company and going to Europe, ostensibly for a rest. He had never been abroad, and Jennie, too, would enjoy it. Vesta could be left at home with Gerhardt and a maid, and he and Jennie would travel around a bit, seeing what Europe had to show. He wanted to visit Venice and Baden-Baden, and the great watering-places that had been recommended to him. Cairo and Luxor and the Parthenon had always appealed to his imagination. After he had had his outing he could come back and seriously gather up the threads of his intentions.

The spring after his father died, he put his plan into execution. He had wound up the work of the warerooms and with a pleasant deliberation had studied out a tour. He made Jennie his confidante, and now, having gathered together their travelling comforts they took a steamer from New York to Liverpool. After a few weeks in the British Isles they went to Egypt. From there they came back, through Greece and Italy, into Austria and Switzerland, and then later, through France and Paris, to Germany and Berlin. Lester was diverted by the novelty of the experience and yet he had an uncomfortable feeling that he was wasting his time. Great business enterprises were not built by travellers, and he was not looking for health.

Jennie on the other hand, was transported by what she saw, and enjoyed the new life to the full. Before Luxor and Karnak—places which Jennie had never dreamed existed—she learned of an older civilisation, powerful, complex, complete. Millions of people had lived and died here, believing in other gods, other forms of government, other conditions of existence. For the first time in her life Jennie gained a clear idea of how vast the world is. Now from this point of view—of decayed Greece, of fallen Rome, of forgotten Egypt, she saw how pointless are our minor difficulties, our minor beliefs. Her father's Lutheranism—it did not seem so significant any more ; and the social economy of Columbus, Ohio—rather pointless, perhaps. Her mother had worried so of what people—her neighbours—thought, but here were dead worlds of people, some bad, some good. Lester explained that their differences in standards of morals were due sometimes to climate, sometimes to religious beliefs, and sometimes to the rise of peculiar personalities like Mohammed. Lester liked to point out how small conventions bulked in this, the larger world, and vaguely she began to see. Admitting that she had been bad—locally it was important, perhaps, but in the sum of civilisation, in the sum of big forces, what did it all amount to ? They would be dead after a little while, she and Lester and all these people. Did anything matter except goodness—goodness of heart ? What else was there that was real ?

## CHAPTER XLV

IT was while travelling abroad that Lester came across, first at the Carlton in London and later at Shepheards in Cairo, the one girl, before Jennie, whom it might have been said he truly admired—Letty Pace. He had not seen her for a long time, and she had been Mrs. Malcolm Gerald for nearly four years, and a charming widow for nearly two years more. Malcolm Gerald had been a wealthy man, having amassed a fortune in banking and stock-brokering in Cincinnati, and he had left Mrs. Malcolm Gerald very well off. She was the mother of one child, a little girl, who was safely in charge of a nurse and maid at all times, and she was invariably the picturesque centre of a group of admirers recruited from every capital of the civilised world. Letty Gerald was a talented woman, beautiful, graceful, artistic, a writer of verse, an omnivorous reader, a student of art, and a sincere and ardent admirer of Lester Kane.

In her day she had truly loved him, for she had been a wise observer of men and affairs, and Lester had always appealed to her as a real man. He was so sane, she thought, so calm He was always intolerant of sham, and she liked him for it. He was inclined to wave aside the petty little frivolities of common society conversation, and to talk of simple and homely things. Many and many a time, in years past, they had deserted a dance to sit out on a balcony somewhere, and talk while Lester smoked. He had argued philosophy with her, discussed books, described political and social conditions in other cities—in a word, he had treated her like a sensible human being, and she had hoped and hoped and hoped that he would propose to her. More than once she had looked at his big, solid head with its short growth of hardy brown hair, and wished that she could stroke it. It was a hard blow to her when he finally moved away to Chicago ; at that time she knew nothing of Jennie, but she felt instinctively that her chance of winning him was gone.

Then Malcolm Gerald, always an ardent admirer, proposed

for something like the sixty-fifth time, and she took him. She did not love him, but she was getting along, and she had to marry some one. He was forty-four when he married her, and he lived only four years—just long enough to realise that he had married a charming, tolerant, broad-minded woman. Then he died of pneumonia and Mrs. Gerald was a rich widow, sympathetic, attractive, delightful in her knowledge of the world, and with nothing to do except to live and to spend her money.

She was not inclined to do either indifferently. She had long since had her ideal of a man established by Lester. These whipper-snappers of counts, earls, lords, barons, whom she met in one social world and another (for her friendship and connections had broadened notably with the years), did not interest her a particle. She was terribly weary of the superficial veneer of the titled fortune-hunter whom she met abroad. A good judge of character, a student of men and manners, a natural reasoner along sociologic and psychologic lines, she saw through them and through the civilisation which they repre-sented. "I could have been happy in a cottage with a man I once knew out in Cincinnati," she told one of her titled women friends who had been an American before her marriage. "He was the biggest, cleanest, sanest fellow. If he had proposed to me I would have married him if I had had to work for a living myself."

"Was he so poor?" asked her friend.

"Indeed he wasn't. He was comfortably rich, but that did not make any difference to me. It was the man I wanted."

"It would have made a difference in the long run," said the other.

"You misjudge me," replied Mrs. Gerald. "I waited for him for a number of years, and I know."

Lester had always retained pleasant impressions and kindly memories of Letty Pace, or Mrs. Gerald, as she was now. He had been fond of her in a way, very fond. Why hadn't he married her? He had asked himself that question time and again. She would have made him an ideal wife, his father would have been pleased, everybody would have been delighted. Instead he had drifted and drifted, and then he had met Jennie ; and somehow, after that, he did not want her any more. Now after six years of separation he met her again. He knew she was married. She was vaguely aware he had had some sort of an affair—she had heard that he had subsequently married the woman and was living on the South Side. She did not know of the loss of his fortune. She ran across him first in the Carlton one June evening. The windows were open, and the flowers were blooming everywhere, odorous, with that sense of new life in the air which runs through the world when spring comes back. For the moment she was a little beside herself, Something choked in her throat; but she collected herself and extended a graceful arm and hand.

"Why, Lester Kane," she exclaimed. "How *do* you do! I am so glad. And this is Mrs. Kane? Charmed, I'm sure. It seems truly like a breath of spring to see you again. I hope you'll excuse me, Mrs. Kane, but I'm delighted to see your husband. I'm ashamed to say how many years it is, Lester, since I saw you last! I feel quite old when I think of it. Why, Lester, think; it's been all of six or seven years! And I've been married and had a child, and poor Mr. Gerald has died, and oh, dear, I don't know what all hasn't happened to me."

"You don't look it," commented Lester, smiling. He was pleased to see her again, for they had been good friends. She liked him still—that was evident, and he truly liked her.

Jennie smiled. She was glad to see this old friend of Lester's. This woman, trailing a magnificent yellow lace train over pale, mother-of-pearl satin, her round, smooth arms bare to the shoulder, her corsage cut low and a dark red rose blowing at her waist, seemed to her the ideal of what a woman should be. She liked looking at lovely women quite as much as Lester; she enjoyed calling his attention to them, and teasing him, in the mildest way, about their charms. "Wouldn't you like to run and talk to her, Lester, instead of to me?" she would ask when some particularly striking or beautiful woman chanced to attract her attention. Lester would examine her choice critically, for he had come to know that her judge of feminine charms was excellent. "Oh, I'm pretty well off where I am," he would retort, looking into her eyes; or, jestingly, "I'm not as young as I used to be, or I'd get in tow of that."

"Run on," was her comment. "I'll wait for you."

"What would you do if I really should?"

"Why, Lester, I wouldn't do anything. You'd come back to me, maybe."

" Wouldn't you care ? "

" You know I'd care. But if you felt that you wanted to, I wouldn't try to stop you. I wouldn't expect to be all in all to one man, unless he wanted me to be."

" Where do you get those ideas, Jennie ? " he asked her once, curious to test the breadth of her philosophy.

" Oh, I don't know, why ? "

" They're so broad, so good-natured, so charitable. They're not common, that's sure."

" Why, I don't think we ought to be selfish, Lester. I don't know why. Some women think differently, I know, but a man and a woman ought to want to live together, or they ought not to—don't you think ? It doesn't make so much difference if a man goes off for a little while—just so long as he doesn't stay—if he wants to come back at all."

Lester smiled, but he respected her for the sweetness of her point of view—he had to.

To-night, when she saw this woman so eager to talk to Lester, she realised at once that they must have a great deal in common to talk over ; whereupon she did a characteristic thing. " Won't you excuse me for a little while ? " she asked, smiling. " I left some things uncared for in our rooms. I'll be back."

She went away, remaining in her room as long as she reasonably could, and Lester and Letty fell to discussing old times in earnest. He recounted as much of his experiences as he deemed wise, and Letty brought the history of her life up to date. " Now that you're safely married, Lester," she said daringly, " I'll confess to you that you were the one man I always wanted to have propose to me—and you never did."

" Maybe I never dared," he said, gazing into her superb black eyes, and thinking that perhaps she might know that he was not married. He felt that she had grown more beautiful in every way. She seemed to him now to be an ideal society figure—perfection itself—gracious, natural, witty, the type of woman who mixes and mingles well, meeting each new-comer upon the plane best suited to him or her.

" Yes, you thought ! I know what you thought. Your real thought just left the table."

" Tut, tut, my dear. Not so fast. You don't know what I thought."

" Anyhow, I allow you some credit. She's charming."

"Jennie has her good points," he replied simply.

"And are you happy?"

"Oh, fairly so. Yes, I suppose I'm happy—as happy as any one can be who sees life as it is. You know I'm not troubled with many illusions."

"Not any, I think, kind sir, if I know you."

"Very likely, not any, Letty; but sometimes I wish I had a few. I think I would be happier."

"And I, too, Lester. Really I look on my life as a kind of failure, you know, in spite of the fact that I'm almost as rich as Crœsus—not quite. I think he had some more than I have."

"What talk from you—you, with your beauty and talent, and money—good heavens!"

"And what can I do with it? Travel, talk, shoo away silly fortune-hunters. Oh, dear, sometimes I get so tired!"

Letty looked at Lester. In spite of Jennie, the old feeling came back. Why should she have been cheated of him? They were as comfortable together as old married people, or young lovers. Jennie had had no better claim. She looked at him, and her eyes fairly spoke. He smiled a little sadly.

"Here comes my wife," he said. "We'll have to brace up and talk of other things. You'll find her interesting—really.'

"Yes, I know," she replied, and turned on Jennie a radiant smile.

Jennie felt a faint sense of misgiving. She thought vaguely that this might be one of Lester's old flames. This was the kind of woman he should have chosen—not her. She was suited to his station in life, and he would have been as happy—perhaps happier. Was he beginning to realise it? Then she put away the uncomfortable thought; pretty soon she would be getting jealous, and that would be contemptible.

Mrs. Gerald continued to be most agreeable in her attitude toward the Kanes. She invited them the next day to join her on a drive through Rotten Row. There was a dinner later at Claridge's, and then she was compelled to keep some engagement which was taking her to Paris. She bade them both an affectionate farewell, and hoped that they would soon meet again. She was envious, in a sad way, of Jennie's good fortune. Lester had lost none of his charm for her. If anything, he seemed nicer, more considerate, more wholesome. She wished sincerely that he were free.   And Lester—subconsciously perhaps —was thinking the same thing.

No doubt because of the fact that she was thinking of it, he had been led over mentally all of the things which might have happened if he had married her.   They were so congenial now, philosophically, artistically, practically.   There was a natural flow of conversation between them all the time, like two old comrades among men.   She knew everybody in his social sphere, which was equally hers, but Jennie did not.   They could talk of certain subtle characteristics of life in a way which was not possible between him and Jennie, for the latter did not have the vocabulary.   Her ideas did not flow as fast as those of Mrs. Gerald.   Jennie had actually the deeper, more comprehensive, sympathetic, and emotional note in her nature, but she could not show it in light conversation.   Actually she was living the thing she was, and that was perhaps the thing which drew Lester to her.   Just now, and often in situations of this kind, she seemed at a disadvantage, and she was.   It seemed to Lester for the time being as if Mrs. Gerald would perhaps have been a better choice after all—certainly as good, and he would not now have this distressing thought as to his future.

They did not see Mrs. Gerald again until they reached Cairo. In the gardens about the hotel they suddenly encountered her, or rather Lester did, for he was alone at the time, strolling and smoking.

" Well, this is good luck," he exclaimed.   " Where do you come from ? "

" Madrid, if you please.   I didn't know I was coming until last Thursday.   The Ellicotts are here.   I came over with them.   You know I wondered where you might be.   Then I remembered that you said you were going to Egypt.   Where is your wife ? "

" In her bath, I fancy, at this moment.   This warm weather makes Jennie take to water.   I was thinking of a plunge myself."

They strolled about for a time.   Letty was in light blue silk, with a blue and white parasol held daintily over her shoulder, and looked very pretty.   " Oh, dear ! " she suddenly ejaculated, " I wonder sometimes what I am to do with myself.   I can't loaf always this way.   I think I'll go back to the States to live."

" Why don't you ? "

" What good would it do me ? I don't want to get married. I haven't any one to marry now—that I want." She glanced at Lester significantly, then looked away.

" Oh, you'll find some one eventually," he said, somewhat awkwardly. " You can't escape for long—not with your looks and money."

" Oh, Lester, hush ! "

" All right ! Have it otherwise, if you want. I'm telling you."

" Do you still dance ? " she inquired lightly, thinking of a ball which was to be given at the hotel that evening. He had danced so well a few years before.

" Do I look it ? "

" Now, Lester, you don't mean to say that you have gone and abandoned that last charming art. I still love to dance. Doesn't Mrs. Kane ? "

" No, she doesn't care to. At least she hasn't taken it up. Come to think of it, I suppose that is my fault. I haven't thought of dancing in some time."

It occurred to him that he hadn't been going to functions of any kind much for some time. The opposition his entanglement had generated had put a stop to that.

" Come and dance with me to-night. Your wife won't object. It's a splendid floor. I saw it this morning."

" I'll have to think about that," replied Lester. " I'm not much in practice. Dancing will probably go hard with me at my time of life."

" Oh, hush, Lester," replied Mrs. Gerald. " You make me feel old. Don't talk so sedately. Mercy alive, you'd think you were an old man ! "

" I am in experience, my dear."

" Pshaw, that simply makes us more attractive," replied his old flame.

## CHAPTER XLVI

THAT night after dinner the music was already sounding in the ball-room of the great hotel adjacent to the palm-gardens when Mrs. Gerald found Lester smoking on one of the verandas with Jennie by his side. The latter was in white satin and white slippers, her hair lying a heavy, enticing mass about her forehead and ears. Lester was brooding over the history of Egypt, its successive tides or waves of rather weak-bodied people ; the thin, narrow strip of soil along either side of the Nile that had given these successive waves of population sustenance ; the wonder of heat and tropic life, and this hotel with its modern conveniences and fashionable crowd set down among ancient, soul-weary, almost despairing conditions. He and Jennie had looked this morning on the pyramids. They had taken a trolley to the Sphinx ! They had watched swarms of ragged, half-clad, curiously costumed men and boys moving through narrow, smelly, albeit brightly coloured, lanes and alleys.

"It all seems such a mess to me," Jennie had said at one place. "They are so dirty and oily. I like it, but somehow they seem tangled up, like a lot of worms."

Lester chuckled. "You're almost right. But climate does it. Heat. The tropics. Life is always mushy and sensual under these conditions. They can't help it."

"Oh, I know that. I don't blame them. They're just queer."

To-night he was brooding over this, the moon shining down into the grounds with an exuberant, sensuous luster.

"Well, at last I've found you !" Mrs. Gerald exclaimed. "I couldn't get down to dinner, after all. Our party was so late getting back. I've made your husband agree to dance with me, Mrs. Kane," she went on smilingly. She, like Lester and Jennie, was under the sensuous influence of the warmth, the spring, the moonlight. There were rich odours abroad, floating subtly from groves and gardens ; from the remote distance camel-bells were sounding and exotic cries, " *Ayah !* "

and " *oosh ! oosh !* " as though a drove of strange animals were being rounded up and driven through the crowded streets.

" You're welcome to him," replied Jennie pleasantly. " He ought to dance. I sometimes wish I did."

" You ought to take lessons right away then," replied Lester genially. " I'll do my best to keep you company. I'm not as light on my feet as I was once, but I guess I can get around."

" Oh, I don't want to dance that badly," smiled Jennie. " But you two go on, I'm going upstairs in a little while, anyway."

" Why don't you come sit in the ball-room ? I can't do more than a few rounds. Then we can watch the others," said Lester rising.

" No. I think I'll stay here. It's so pleasant. You go. Take him, Mrs. Gerald."

Lester and Letty strolled away. They made a striking pair—Mrs. Gerald in dark wine-coloured silk, covered with glistening black beads, her shapely arms and neck bare, and a flashing diamond of great size set just above her forehead in her dark hair. Her lips were red, and she had an engaging smile, showing an even row of white teeth between wide, full, friendly lips. Lester's strong, vigorous figure was well set off by his evening clothes, he looked distinguished.

" That is the woman he should have married," said Jennie to herself as he disappeared. She fell into a reverie, going over the steps of her past life. Sometimes it seemed to her now as if she had been living in a dream. At other times she felt as though she were in that dream yet. Life sounded in her ears much as this night did. She heard its cries. She knew its large-mass features. But back of it were subtleties that shaded and changed one into the other like the shifting of dreams. Why had she been so attractive to men ? Why had Lester been so eager to follow her ? Could she have prevented him ? She thought of her life in Columbus, when she carried coal ; to-night she was in Egypt, at this great hotel, the chatelaine of a suite of rooms, surrounded by every luxury, Lester still devoted to her. He had endured so many things for her ! Why ? Was she so wonderful ? Brander had said so. Lester had told her so. Still she felt humble, out of place, holding handfuls of jewels that did not belong to her. Again she experienced that peculiar feeling which had come over her the first time she went to New York with Lester—namely, that this fairy existence could not endure. Her life was fated. Something would happen. She would go back to simple things, to a side street, a poor cottage, to old clothes.

And then as she thought of her home in Chicago, and the attitude of his friends, she knew it must be so. She would never be received, even if he married her. And she could understand why. She could look into the charming, smiling face of this woman who was now with Lester, and see that she considered her very nice, perhaps, but not of Lester's class. She was saying to herself now no doubt as she danced with Lester that he needed some one like her. He needed some one who had been raised in the atmosphere of the things to which he had been accustomed. He couldn't very well expect to find in her, Jennie, the familiarity with, the appreciation of the niceties to, which he had always been accustomed. She understood what they were. Her mind had awakened rapidly to details of furniture, clothing, arrangement, decorations, manner, forms, customs, but—she was not to the manner born.

If she went away Lester would return to his old world, the world of the attractive, well-bred, clever woman who now hung upon his arm. The tears came into Jennie's eyes; she wished, for the moment, that she might die. It would be better so. Meanwhile Lester was dancing with Mrs. Gerald, or sitting out between the waltzes talking over old times, old places, and old friends. As he looked at Letty he marvelled at her youth and beauty. She was more developed than formerly, but still as slender and shapely as Diana. She had strength, too, in this smooth body of hers, and her black eyes were liquid and lusterful.

"I swear, Letty," he said impulsively, "you're really more beautiful than ever. You're exquisite. You've grown younger instead of older."

"You think so?" she smiled, looking up into his face.

"You know I do, or I wouldn't say so. I'm not much on philandering."

"Oh, Lester, you bear, can't you allow a woman just a little coyness? Don't you know we all love to sip our praise, and not be compelled to swallow it in one great mouthful?"

"What's the point?" he asked. "What did I say?"

"Oh, nothing. You're such a bear. You're such a big,

determined, straightforward boy. But never mind. I like you. That's enough, isn't it ? "

" It surely is," he said.

They strolled into the garden as the music ceased, and he squeezed her arm softly. He couldn't help it ; she made him feel as if he owned her. She wanted him to feel that way. She said to herself, as they sat looking at the lanterns in the gardens, that if ever he were free, and would come to her, she would take him. She was almost ready to take him anyhow—only he probably wouldn't. He was so straight-laced, so considerate. He wouldn't, like so many other men she knew, do a mean thing. He couldn't. Finally Lester rose and excused himself. He and Jennie were going farther up the Nile in the morning—toward Karnak and Thebes and the water-washed temples at Phylæ. They would have to start at an unearthly early hour, and he must get to bed.

" When are you going home ? " asked Mrs. Gerald, ruefully.

" In September."

" Have you engaged your passage ? "

" Yes ; we sail from Hamburg on the ninth—the *Fulda*."

" I may be going back in the fall," laughed Letty. " Don't be surprised if I crowd in on the same boat with you. I'm very unsettled in my mind."

" Come along, for goodness sake," replied Lester. " I hope you do. . . . I'll see you to-morrow before we leave." He paused, and she looked at him wistfully.

" Cheer up," he said, taking her hand. " You never can tell what life will do. We sometimes find ourselves right when we thought we were all wrong."

He was thinking that she was sorry to lose him, and he was sorry that she was not in a position to have what she wanted. As for himself, he was saying that here was one solution that probably he would never accept ; yet it was a solution. Why had he not seen this years before ?

" And yet she wasn't as beautiful then as she is now, nor as wise, nor as wealthy." Maybe ! Maybe ! But he couldn't be unfaithful to Jennie nor wish her any bad luck. She had had enough without his willing, and had borne it bravely.

# CHAPTER XLVII

THE trip home did bring another week with Mrs. Gerald, for after mature consideration she had decided to venture to America for a while. Chicago and Cincinnati were her destinations, and she hoped to see more of Lester. Her presence was a good deal of a surprise to Jennie, and it started her thinking again. She could see what the point was. If she were out of the way Mrs. Gerald would marry Lester; that was certain. As it was—well, the question was a complicated one. Letty was Lester's natural mate, so far as birth, breeding, and position went. And yet Jennie felt instinctively that, on the large human side, Lester preferred her. Perhaps time would solve the problem; in the meantime the little party of three continued to remain excellent friends. When they reached Chicago Mrs. Gerald went her way, and Jennie and Lester took up the customary thread of their existence.

On his return from Europe Lester set to work in earnest to find a business opening. None of the big companies made him any overtures, principally because he was considered a strong man who was looking for a control in anything he touched. The nature of his altered fortunes had not been made public. All the little companies that he investigated were having a hand-to-mouth existence, or manufacturing a product which was not satisfactory to him. He did find one company in a small town in northern Indiana which looked as though it might have a future. It was controlled by a practical builder of wagons and carriages—such as Lester's father had been in his day—who, however, was not a good business man. He was making some small money on an investment of fifteen thousand dollars and a plant worth, say, twenty-five thousand. Lester felt that something could be done here if proper methods were pursued and business acumen exercised. It would be slow work. There would never be a great fortune in it. Not in his lifetime. He was thinking of making an offer to the small manufacturer when the first rumours of a carriage trust reached him.

Robert had gone ahead rapidly with his scheme for

reorganising the carriage trade. He showed his competitors how much greater profits could be made through consolidation than through a mutually destructive rivalry. So convincing were his arguments that one by one the big carriage manu-facturing companies fell into line. Within a few months the deal had been pushed through, and Robert found himself president of the United Carriage and Wagon Manufacturers' Association, with a capital stock of ten million dollars, and with assets aggregating nearly three-fourths of that sum at a forced sale. He was a happy man.

While all this was going forward Lester was completely in the dark. His trip to Europe prevented him from seeing three or four minor notices in the newspapers of some of the efforts that were being made to unite the various carriage and wagon manufactories. He returned to Chicago to learn that Jefferson Midgely, Imogene's husband, was still in full charge of the branch and living in Evanston, but because of his quarrel with his family he was in no position to get the news direct. Accident brought it fast enough, however, and that rather irritatingly.

The individual who conveyed this information was none other than Mr. Henry Bracebridge, of Cleveland, into whom he ran at the Union Club one evening after he had been in the city a month.

" I hear you're out of the old company," Bracebridge remarked, smiling blandly.

" Yes," said Lester, " I'm out."

" What are you up to now ? "

" Oh, I have a deal of my own under consideration. I'm thinking something of handling an independent concern."

" Surely you won't run counter to your brother ? He has a pretty good thing in that combination of his."

" Combination ! I hadn't heard of it," said Lester. " I've just got back from Europe."

" Well, you want to wake up, Lester," replied Bracebridge. " He's got the biggest thing in your line. I thought you knew all about it. The Lyman-Winthrop Company, the Myer-Brooks Company, the Woods Company—in fact, five or six of the big companies are all in. Your brother was elected president of the new concern. I dare say he cleaned up a couple of millions out of the deal."

Lester stared. His glance hardened a little.

"Well, that's fine for Robert. I'm glad of it."

Bracebridge could see that he had given him a vital stab.

"Well, so long, old man," he exclaimed. "When you're in Cleveland look us up. You know how fond my wife is of you."

"I know," replied Lester. "By-bye."

He strolled away to the smoking-room, but the news took all the zest out of his private venture. Where would he be with a shabby little wagon company and his brother president of a carriage trust ? Good heavens ! Robert could put him out of business in a year. Why, he himself had dreamed of such a combination as this. Now his brother had done it.

It is one thing to have youth, courage, and a fighting spirit to meet the blows with which fortune often afflicts the talented. It is quite another to see middle age coming on, your principal fortune possibly gone, and avenue after avenue of opportunity being sealed to you on various sides. Jennie's obvious social insufficiency, the quality of newspaper reputation which had now become attached to her, his father's opposition and death, the loss of his fortune, the loss of his connection with the company, his brother's attitude, this trust, all combined in a way to dishearten and discourage him. He tried to keep a brave face—and he had succeeded thus far, he thought, admirably, but this last blow appeared for the time being a little too much. He went home, the same evening that he heard the news, sorely disheartened. Jennie saw it. She realised it, as a matter of fact, all during the evening that he was away. She felt blue and despondent herself. When he came home she saw what it was—something had happened to him. Her first impulse was to say, "What is the matter, Lester ? " but her next and sounder one was to ignore it until he was ready to speak, if ever. She tried not to let him see that she saw, coming as near as she might affectionately without disturbing him.

"Vesta is so delighted with herself to-day," she volunteered by way of diversion. "She has got such nice marks in school."

"That's good," he replied solemnly.

"And she dances beautifully these days. She showed me some of her new dances to-night. You haven't any idea how sweet she looks."

"I'm glad of it," he grumbled. "I always wanted her to

be perfect in that. It's time she was going into some good girl's school, I think."

"And papa gets in such a rage. I have to laugh. She teases him about it—the little imp. She offered to teach him to dance to-night. If he didn't love her so he'd box her ears."

"I can see that," said Lester, smiling. "Him dancing! That's pretty good!"

"She's not the least bit disturbed by his storming, either."

"Good for her," said Lester. He was very fond of Vesta, who was now quite a girl.

So Jennie tripped on until his mood was modified a little, and then some inkling of what had happened came out. It was when they were retiring for the night. "Robert's formulated a pretty big thing in a financial way since we've been away," he volunteered.

"What is it?" asked Jennie, all ears.

"Oh, he's gotten up a carriage trust. It's something which will take in every manufactory of any importance in the country. Bracebridge was telling me that Robert was made president, and that they have nearly eight millions in capital."

"You don't say!" replied Jennie. "Well, then you won't want to do much with your new company, will you?"

"No; there's nothing in that, just now," he said. "Later on I fancy it may be all right. I'll wait and see how this thing comes out. You never can tell what a trust like that will do."

Jennie was intensely sorry. She had never heard Lester complain before. It was a new note. She wished sincerely that she might do something to comfort him, but she knew that her efforts were useless. "Oh, well," she said, "there are so many interesting things in this world. If I were you I wouldn't be in a hurry to do anything, Lester. You have so much time."

She didn't trust herself to say anything more, and he felt that it was useless to worry. Why should he? After all, he had an ample income that was absolutely secure for two years yet. He could have more if he wanted it. Only his brother was moving so dazzlingly onward, while he was standing still—perhaps " drifting " would be the better word. It did seem a pity; worst of all, he was beginning to feel a little uncertain of himself.

# CHAPTER XLVIII

LESTER had been doing some pretty hard thinking, but so far he had been unable to formulate any feasible plan for his re-entrance into active life. The successful organisation of Robert's carriage trade trust had knocked in the head any further thought on his part of taking an interest in the small Indiana wagon manufactory. He could not be expected to sink his sense of pride and place, and enter a petty campaign for business success with a man who was so obviously his financial superior. He had looked up the details of the combination, and he found that Bracebridge had barely indicated how wonderfully complete it was. There were millions in the combine. It would have every little manufacturer by the throat. Should he begin now in a small way and " pike along " in the shadow of his giant brother ? He couldn't see it. It was too ignominious. He would be running around the country trying to fight a new trust, with his own brother as his tolerant rival and his own rightful capital arrayed against him. It couldn't be done. Better sit still for the time being. Something else might show up. If not—well, he had his independent income and the right to come back into the Kane Company if he wished. Did he wish ? The question was always with him.

It was while Lester was in this mood, drifting, that he received a visit from Samuel M. Ross, a real estate dealer, whose great, wooden signs might be seen everywhere on the windy stretches of prairie about the city. Lester had seen Ross once or twice at the Union Club, where he had been pointed out as a daring and successful real estate speculator, and he had noticed his rather conspicuous offices at La Salle and Washington Streets. Ross was a magnetic-looking person of about fifty-years of age, tall, black-bearded, black-eyed, an arched, wide-nostrilled nose, and hair that curled naturally, almost electrically. Lester was impressed with his lithe, cat-like figure, and his long, thin, impressive white hands.

Mr. Ross had a real estate proposition to lay before Mr. Kane.

Of course Mr. Kane knew who he was. And Mr. Ross admitted fully that he knew all about Mr. Kane. Recently, in conjunction with Mr. Norman Yale, of the wholesale grocery firm of Yale, Simpson & Rice, he had developed " Yalewood." Mr. Kane knew of that ?

Yes, Mr. Kane knew of that.

Only within six weeks the last lots in the Ridgewood section of " Yalewood " had been closed out at a total profit of forty-two per cent. He went over a list of other deals in real estate which he had put through, all well-known properties. He admitted frankly that there were failures in the business ; he had had one or two himself. But the successes far out numbered the bad speculations, as every one knew. Now Lester was no longer connected with the Kane Company. He was probably looking for a good investment, and Mr. Ross had a proposition to lay before him. Lester consented to listen, and Mr. Ross blinked his cat-like eyes and started in.

The idea was that he and Lester should enter into a one-deal partnership, covering the purchase and development of a forty-acre tract of land lying between Fifty-fifth, Seventy-first, Halstead Streets, and Ashland Avenue, on the south-west side. There were indications of a genuine real estate boom there—healthy, natural, and permanent. The city was about to pave Fifty-fifth Street. There was a plan to extend the Halstead Street car line far below its present terminus. The Chicago, Burlington & Quincy, which ran near there, would be glad to put a passenger station on the property. The initial cost of the land would be forty thousand dollars which they would share equally. Grading, paving, lighting, tree planting, surveying would cost, roughly, an additional twenty-five thousand. There would be expenses for advertising—say ten per cent. of the total investment for two years, or perhaps three—a total of nineteen thousand five hundred or twenty thousand dollars. All told, they would stand to invest jointly the sum of ninety-five thousand, or possibly one hundred thousand dollars, of which Lester's share would be fifty thousand. Then Mr. Ross began to figure on the profits.

The character of the land, its saleability, and the likelihood of a rise in value could be judged by the property adjacent, the sales that had been made north of Fifty-fifth Street and east of Halstead. Take, for instance, the Mortimer plot, at

Halstead and Fifty-fifth Streets, on the south-east corner. Here was a piece of land that in 1882 was held at forty-five dollars an acre. In 1886 it had risen to five hundred dollars an acre, as attested by its sale to a Mr. John L. Slosson at that time. In 1889, three years later, it had been sold to Mr. Mortimer for one thousand per acre, precisely the figure at which this tract was now offered. It could be parcelled out into lots fifty by one hundred feet at five hundred dollars per lot. Was there any profit in that ?

Lester admitted that there was.

Ross went on, somewhat boastfully, to explain just how real estate profits were made. It was useless for any outsider to rush into the game, and imagine that he could do in a few weeks or years what trained real estate speculators like himself had been working on for a quarter of a century. There was something in prestige, something in taste, something in psychic apprehension. Supposing that they went into the deal, he, Ross, would be the presiding genius. He had a trained staff, he controlled giant contractors, he had friends in the tax office, in the water office, and in the various other city departments which made or marred city improvements. If Lester would come in with him he would make him some money— how much he would not say exactly—fifty thousand dollars at the lowest—one hundred and fifty to two hundred thousand in all likelihood. Would Lester let him go into details, and explain just how the scheme could be worked out ? After a few days of quiet cogitation, Lester decided to accede to Mr. Ross's request ; he would look into this thing.

## CHAPTER XLIX

THE peculiarity of this particular proposition was that it had the basic elements of success. Mr. Ross had the experience and the judgment which were quite capable of making a success of almost anything he undertook. He was in a field which was entirely familiar. He could convince almost any able man if he could get his ear sufficiently long to lay his facts before him.

Lester was not convinced at first, although, generally speaking, he was interested in real estate propositions. He liked land. He considered it a sound investment providing you did not get too much of it. He had never invested in any, or scarcely any, solely because he had not been in a realm where real estate propositions were talked of. As it was he was landless and, in a way, jobless.

He rather liked Mr. Ross and his way of doing business. It was easy to verify his statements, and he did verify them in several particulars. There were his signs out on the prairie stretches, and here were his ads. in the daily papers. It seemed not a bad way at all in his idleness to start and make some money.

The trouble with Lester was that he had reached the time where he was not as keen for details as he had formerly been. All his work in recent years—in fact, from the very beginning—had been with large propositions, the purchasing of great quantities of supplies, the placing of large orders, the discussion of things which were wholesale and which had very little to do with the minor details which make up the special interests of the smaller traders of the world. In the factory his brother Robert had figured the pennies and nickels of labour-cost, had seen to it that all the little leaks were shut off. Lester had been left to deal with larger things, and he had consistently done so. When it came to this particular proposition his interest was in the wholesale phases of it, not the petty details of selling. He could not help seeing that Chicago was a growing city, and that land values must rise. What was now far-out prairie property would soon, in the course of a few years, be well built-up suburban residence territory. Scarcely any land that could be purchased now would fall in value. It might drag in sales or increase, but it couldn't fall. Ross convinced him of this. He knew it of his own judgment to be true.

The several things on which he did not speculate sufficiently were the life or health of Mr. Ross ; the chance that some obnoxious neighbourhood growth would affect the territory he had selected as residence territory ; the fact that difficult money situations might reduce real estate values—in fact, bring about a flurry of real estate liquidation which would send prices crashing down and cause the failure of strong promoters, even such promoters for instance, as Mr. Samuel E. Ross.

For several months he studied the situation as presented by his new guide and mentor, and then, having satisfied himself that he was reasonably safe, decided to sell some of the holdings which were netting him a beggarly six per cent. and invest in this new proposition. The first cash outlay was twenty thousand dollars for the land, which was taken over under an operative agreement between himself and Ross ; this was run indefinitely—so long as there was any of this land left to sell. The next thing was to raise twelve thousand five hundred dollars for improvements, which he did, and then to furnish some twenty-five hundred dollars more for taxes and unconsidered expenses, items which had come up in carrying out the improvement work which had been planned. It seemed that hard and soft earth made a difference in grading costs, that trees would not always flourish as expected, that certain members of the city water and gas departments had to be " seen " and " fixed " before certain other improvements could be effected. Mr. Ross attended to all this, but the cost of the proceedings was something which had to be discussed, and Lester heard it all.

After the land was put in shape, about a year after the original conversation, it was necessary to wait until spring for the proper advertising and booming of the new section ; and this advertising began to call at once for the third payment. Lester disposed of an additional fifteen thousand dollars worth of securities in order to follow this venture to its logical and profitable conclusion.

Up to this time he was rather pleased with his venture. Ross had certainly been thorough and business-like in his handling of the various details. The land was put in excellent shape. It was given a rather attractive title—" Inwood," although, as Lester noted, there was precious little wood anywhere around there. But Ross assured him that people looking for a suburban residence would be attracted by the name ; seeing the vigorous efforts in tree-planting that had been made to provide for shade in the future, they would take the will for the deed. Lester smiled.

The first chill wind that blew upon the infant project came in the form of a rumour that the International Packing Company, one of the big constituent members of the packing house combination at Halstead and Thirty-ninth Streets, had determined to desert the old group and lay out a new packing area for itself. The papers explained that the company intended to go farther south, probably below Fifty-fifth Street and west of Ashland Avenue. This was the territory that was located due west of Lester's property, and the mere suspicion that the packing company might invade the territory was sufficient to blight the prospects of any budding real estate deal.

Ross was beside himself with rage. He decided, after quick deliberation, that the best thing to do would be to boom the property heavily, by means of newspaper advertising, and see if it could not be disposed of before any additional damage was likely to be done to it. He laid the matter before Lester, who agreed that this would be advisable. They had already expended six thousand dollars in advertising, and now the additional sum of three thousand dollars was spent in ten days, to make it appear that " Inwood " was an ideal residence section, equipped with every modern convenience for the home-lover, and destined to be one of the most exclusive and beautiful suburbs of the city. It was " no go." A few lots were sold, but the rumour that the International Packing Company might come was persistent and deadly ; from any point of view, save that of a foreign population neighbourhood, the enterprise was a failure.

To say that Lester was greatly disheartened by this blow is to put it mildly. Practically fifty thousand dollars, two-thirds of all his earthly possessions, outside of his stipulated annual income, was tied up here ; and there were taxes to pay, repairs to maintain, actual depreciation in value to face. He suggested to Ross that the area might be sold at its cost value, or a loan raised on it, and the whole enterprise abandoned; but that experienced real estate dealer was not so sanguine. He had had one or two failures of this kind before. He was superstitious about anything which did not go smoothly from the beginning. If it didn't go it was a hoodoo—a black shadow—and he wanted no more to do with it. Other real estate men, as he knew to his cost, were of the same opinion.

Some three years later the property was sold under the sheriff's hammer. Lester, having put in fifty thousand dollars all told, recovered a trifle more than eighteen thousand; and some of his wise friends assured him that he was lucky in getting off so easily.

## CHAPTER L

WHILE the real estate deal was in progress Mrs. Gerald decided to move to Chicago. She had been staying in Cincinnati for a few months, and had learned a great deal as to the real facts of Lester's irregular mode of life. The question whether or not he was really married to Jennie remained an open one. The garbled details of Jennie's early years, the fact that a Chicago paper had written him up as a young millionaire who was sacrificing his fortune for love of her, the certainty that Robert had practically eliminated him from any voice in the Kane Company, all came to her ears. She hated to think that Lester was making such a sacrifice of himself. He had let nearly a year slip by without doing anything. In two more years his chance would be gone. He had said to her in London that he was without many illusions. Was Jennie one ? Did he really love her, or was he just sorry for her ? Letty wanted very much to find out for sure.

The house that Mrs. Gerald leased in Chicago was a most imposing one on Drexel Boulevard. " I'm going to take a house in your town this winter, and I hope to see a lot of you," she wrote to Lester. " I'm awfully bored with life here in Cincinnati. After Europe it's so—well, you know. I saw Mrs. Knowles on Saturday. She asked after you. You ought to know that you have a loving friend in her. Her daughter is going to marry Jimmy Severance in the spring."

Lester thought of her coming with mingled feelings of pleasure and uncertainty. She would be entertaining largely, of course. Would she foolishly begin by attempting to invite him and Jennie ? Surely not. She must know the truth by this time. Her letter indicated as much. She spoke of seeing a lot of him. That meant that Jennie would have to be eliminated. He would have to make a clean breast of the whole affair to Letty. Then she could do as she pleased about their future intimacy. Seated in Letty's comfortable boudoir one afternoon, facing a vision of loveliness in pale yellow, he decided that he might as well have it out with her. She would understand. Just at this time he was beginning to doubt the outcome of the real estate deal, and consequently he was feeling a little blue, and, as a concomitant, a little confidential. He could not as yet talk to Jennie about his troubles.

"You know, Lester," said Letty, by way of helping him to his confession—the maid had brought tea for her and some brandy and soda for him, and departed—"that I have been hearing a lot of things about you since I've been back in this country. Aren't you going to tell me all about yourself? You know I have your real interests at heart."

"What have you been hearing, Letty?" he asked, quietly.

"Oh, about your father's will for one thing, and the fact that you're out of the company, and some gossip about Mrs. Kane which doesn't interest me very much. You know what I mean. Aren't you going to straighten things out, so that you can have what rightfully belongs to you? It seems to me such a great sacrifice, Lester, unless, of course, you are very much in love. Are you?" she asked archly.

Lester paused and deliberated before replying. "I really don't know how to answer that last question, Letty," he said. "Sometimes I think that I love her; sometimes I wonder whether I do or not. I'm going to be perfectly frank with you. I was never in such a curious position in my life before. You like me so much, and I—well, I don't say what I think of you," he smiled. "But, anyhow, I can talk to you frankly. I'm not married."

"I thought as much," she said, as he paused.

"And I'm not married because I have never been able to make up my mind just what to do about it. When I first met Jennie I thought her the most entrancing girl I had ever laid eyes on."

"That speaks volumes for my charms at that time," interrupted his *vis-a-vis*.

"Don't interrupt me if you want to hear this," he smiled.

"Tell me one thing," she questioned, "and then I won't. Was that in Cleveland?"

"Yes."

"So I heard," she assented.

"There was something about her so——"

" Love at first sight," again interpolated Letty foolishly. Her heart was hurting her. " I know."

" Are you going to let me tell this ? "

" Pardon me, Lester. I can't help a twinge or two."

" Well, anyhow, I lost my head. I thought she was the most perfect thing under the sun, even if she was a little out of my world. This is a democratic country. I thought that I could just take her, and then—well, you know. That is where I made my mistake. I didn't think that would prove as serious as it did. I never cared for any other woman but you before and—I'll be frank—I didn't know whether I wanted to marry you. I thought I didn't want to marry any woman. I said to myself that I could just take Jennie, and then, after a while, when things had quieted down some, we could separate. She would be well provided for. I wouldn't care very much. She wouldn't care. You understand."

" Yes, I understand," replied his confessor.

" Well, you see, Letty, it hasn't worked out that way. She's a woman of a curious temperament. She possesses a world of feeling and emotion. She's not educated in the sense in which we understand that word, but she has natural refinement and tact. She's a good housekeeper. She's an ideal mother. She's the most affectionate creature under the sun. Her devotion to her mother and father was beyond words. Her love for her daughter—she's hers, not mine—is perfect. She hasn't any of the graces of the smart society woman. She isn't quick at repartee. She can't join in any rapid-fire conversation. She thinks rather slowly, I imagine. Some of her big thoughts never come to the surface at all, but you can feel that she is thinking and that she is feeling."

" You pay her a lovely tribute, Lester," said Letty.

" I ought to," he replied. " She's a good woman, Letty ; but, for all that I have said, I sometimes think that it's only sympathy that's holding me."

" Don't be too sure," she said warningly.

" Yes, but I've gone through with a great deal. The thing for me to have done was to have married her in the first place. There have been so many entanglements since, so much rowing and discussion, that I've rather lost my bearings. This will of father's complicates matters. I stand to lose eight hundred thousand if I marry her—really, a great deal more, now that the company has been organised into a trust. I might better say two millions. If I don't marry her, I lose everything outright in about two more years. Of course, I might pretend that I have separated from her, but I don't care to lie. I can't work it out that way without hurting her feelings, and she's been the soul of devotion. Right down in my heart, at this minute, I don't know whether I want to give her up. Honestly, I don't know what the devil to do."

Lester looked, lit a cigar in a far-off, speculative fashion, and looked out of the window.

"Was there ever such a problem ? " questioned Letty, staring at the floor. She rose, after a few moments of silence, and put her hands on his round, solid head. Her yellow, silken house-gown, faintly scented, touched his shoulders. "Poor Lester," she said. "You certainly have tied yourself up in a knot. But it's a Gordian knot, my dear, and it will have to be cut. Why don't you discuss this whole thing with her, just as you have with me, and see how she feels about it ? "

"It seems such an unkind thing to do," he replied.

"You must take some action, Lester dear," she insisted. "You can't just drift. You are doing yourself such a great injustice. Frankly, I can't advise you to marry her ; and I'm not speaking for myself in that, though I'll take you gladly, even if you did forsake me in the first place. I'll be perfectly honest—whether you ever come to me or not—I love you, and always shall love you."

"I know it," said Lester, getting up. He took her hands in his, and studied her face curiously. Then he turned away. Letty paused to get her breath. His action discomposed her.

"But you're too big a man, Lester, to settle down on ten thousand a year," she continued. "You're too much of a social figure to drift. You ought to get back into the social and financial world where you belong. All that's happened won't injure you, if you reclaim your interest in the company. You can dictate your own terms. And if you tell her the truth she won't object, I'm sure. If she cares for you, as you think she does, she will be glad to make this sacrifice. I'm positive of that. You can provide for her handsomely, of course."

"It isn't the money that Jennie wants," said Lester gloomily.

"Well, even if it isn't, she can live without you; and she can live better for having an ample income."

"She will never want if I can help it," he said solemnly.

"You must leave her," she urged, with a new touch of decisiveness. "You must. Every day is precious with you, Lester! Why don't you make up your mind to act at once—to-day, for that matter? Why not?"

"Not so fast," he protested. "This is a ticklish business. To tell you the truth, I hate to do it. It seems so brutal—so unfair. I'm not one to run around and discuss my affairs with other people. I've refused to talk about this to any one heretofore—my father, my mother, any one. But somehow you have always seemed closer to me than any one else, and, since I met you this time, I have felt as though I ought to explain—I have really wanted to. I care for you. I don't know whether you understand how that can be under the circumstances. But I do. You're nearer to me intellectually and emotionally than I thought you were. Don't frown. You want the truth, don't you? Well, there you have it. Now explain me to myself, if you can."

"I don't want to argue with you, Lester," she said softly, laying her hand on his arm. "I merely want to love you. I understand quite well how it has all come about. I'm sorry for myself. I'm sorry for you. I'm sorry——" she hesitated —"for Mrs. Kane. She's a charming woman. I like her. I really do. But she isn't the woman for you, Lester; she really isn't. You need another type. It seems so unfair for us two to discuss her in this way, but really it isn't. We all have to stand on our merits. And I'm satisfied, if the facts in this case were put before her, as you have put them before me, she would see just how it all is, and agree. She can't want to harm you. Why, Lester, if I were in her position I would let you go. I would, truly. I think you know that I would. Any good woman would. It would hurt me, but I'd do it. It will hurt her, but she'll do it. Now, mark you my words, she will. I think I understand her as well as you do—better—for I am a woman. Oh," she said, pausing, "I wish I were in a position to talk to her. I could make her understand."

Lester looked at Letty, wondering at her eagerness. She was beautiful, magnetic, immensely worth while.

"Not so fast," he repeated. "I want to think about this. I have some time yet."

She paused, a little crestfallen but determined.

"This is the time to act," she repeated, her whole soul in her eyes. She wanted this man, and she was not ashamed to let him see that she wanted him.

"Well, I'll think of it," he said uneasily, then, rather hastily, he bade her good-bye and went away.

CHAPTER LI

L ESTER had thought of his predicament earnestly enough,
and he would have been satisfied to act soon if it had
not been that one of those disrupting influences which sometimes complicate our affairs entered into his Hyde Park
domicile. Gerhardt's health began rapidly to fail.

Little by little he had been obliged to give up his various
duties about the place; finally he was obliged to take to his
bed. He lay in his room, devotedly attended by Jennie
and visited constantly by Vesta, and occasionally by Lester.
There was a window not far from his bed, which commanded
a charming view of the lawn and one of the surrounding streets,
and through this he would gaze by the hour, wondering how
the world was getting on without him. He suspected that
Woods, the coachman, was not looking after the horses and
harnesses as well as he should, that the newspaper carrier
was getting negligent in his delivery of the papers, that the
furnace man was wasting coal, or was not giving them enough
heat. A score of little petty worries, which were nevertheless
real enough to him. He knew how a house should be kept.
He was always rigid in his performance of his self-appointed
duties, and he was so afraid that things would not go right.
Jennie made for him a most imposing and sumptuous dressing-
gown of basted wool, covered with dark-blue silk, and bought
him a pair of soft, thick, wool slippers to match, but he did
not wear them often. He preferred to lie in bed, read his
Bible and the Lutheran papers, and ask Jennie how things
were getting along.

" I want you should go down in the basement and see what
that feller is doing. He's not giving us any heat," he would
complain. " I bet I know what he does. He sits down there
and reads, and then he forgets what the fire is doing until
it is almost out. The beer is right there where he can take it.
You should lock it up. You don't know what kind of a man
he is. He may be no good."

Jennie would protest that the house was fairly comfortable,

that the man was a nice, quiet, respectable-looking American —that if he did drink a little beer it would not matter. Gerhardt would immediately become incensed.

"That is always the way," he declared vigorously. "You have no sense of economy. You are always so ready to let things go if I am not there. He is a nice man! How do you know he is a nice man? Does he keep the fire up? No! Does he keep the walks clean? If you don't watch him he will be just like the others, no good. You should go around and see how things are for yourself."

"All right, papa," she would reply in a genial effort to soothe him, "I will. Please don't worry. I'll lock up the beer. Don't you want a cup of coffee now and some toast?"

"No," Gerhardt would sign immediately, "my stomach it don't do right. I don't know how I am going to come out of this."

Dr. Makin, the leading physician of the vicinity, and a man of considerable experience and ability, called at Jennie's request and suggested a few simple things—hot milk, a wine tonic, rest, but he told Jennie that she must not expect too much. "You know he is quite well along in years now. He is quite feeble. If he were twenty years younger we might do a great deal for him. As it is he is quite well off where he is. He may live for some time. He may get up and be around again, and then he may not. We must all expect these things. I have never any care as to what may happen to me. I am too old myself."

Jennie felt sorry to think that her father might die, but she was pleased to think that if he must it was going to be under such comfortable circumstances. Here at least he could have every care.

It soon became evident that this was Gerhardt's last illness, and Jennie thought it her duty to communicate with her brothers and sisters. She wrote Bass that his father was not well, and had a letter from him saying that he was very busy and couldn't come on unless the danger was an immediate one. He went on to say that George was in Rochester, working for a wholesale wallpaper house—the Sheff-Jefferson Company, he thought. Martha and her husband had gone to Boston. Her address was a little suburb named Belmont, just outside the city. William was in Omaha, working for a local electric company. Veronica was married to a man named Albert Sheridan, who was connected with a wholesale drug company in Cleveland. " She never comes to see me," complained Bass, " but I'll let her know." Jennie wrote each one personally. From Veronica and Martha she received brief replies. They were very sorry, and would she let them know if anything happened. George wrote that he could not think of coming to Chicago unless his father was very ill indeed, but that he would like to be informed from time to time how he was getting along. William, as he told Jennie some time afterward, did not get her letter.

The progress of the old German's malady toward final dissolution preyed greatly on Jennie's mind ; for, in spite of the fact that they had been so far apart in times past, they had now grown very close together. Gerhardt had come to realise clearly that his outcast daughter was goodness itself— at least, so far as he was concerned. She never quarrelled with him, never crossed him in any way. Now that he was sick, she was in and out of his room a dozen times in an evening or an afternoon, seeing whether he was " all right," asking how he liked his breakfast, or his lunch, or his dinner. As he grew weaker she would sit by him and read, or do her sewing in his room. One day when she was straightening his pillow he took her hand and kissed it. He was feeling very weak— and despondent. She looked up in astonishment, a lump in her throat. There were tears in his eyes.

" You're a good girl, Jennie," he said brokenly. " You've been good to me. I've been hard and cross, but I'm an old man. You forgive me, don't you ? "

" Oh, papa, please don't," she pleaded, tears welling from her eyes. " You know I have nothing to forgive. I'm the one who has been all wrong."

" No, no," he said ; and she sank down on her knees beside him and cried. He put his thin, yellow hand on her hair. " There, there," he said brokenly, " I understand a lot of things I didn't. We get wiser as we get older."

She left the room, ostensibly to wash her face and hands, and cried her eyes out. Was he really forgiving her at last ? And she had lied to him so ! She tried to be more attentive, but that was impossible. But after this reconciliation he seemed happier and more contented, and they spent a number of happy hours together, just talking. Once he said to her, "You know I feel just like I did when I was a boy. If it wasn't for my bones I could get up and dance on the grass."

Jennie fairly smiled and sobbed in one breath. "You'll get stronger, papa," she said. "You're going to get well. Then I'll take you out driving." She was so glad she had been able to make him comfortable these last few years.

As for Lester, he was affectionate and considerate.

"Well, how is it to-night?" he would ask the moment he entered the house, and he would always drop in for a few minutes before dinner to see how the old man was getting along. "He looks pretty well," he would tell Jennie. "He's apt to live some time yet. I wouldn't worry."

Vesta also spent much time with her grandfather, for she had come to love him dearly. She would bring her books, if it didn't disturb him too much, and recite some of her lessons, or she would leave his door open, and play for him on the piano. Lester had bought her a handsome music-box also, which she would sometimes carry to his room and play for him. At times he wearied of everything and everybody save Jennie; he wanted to be alone with her. She would sit beside him quite still and sew. She could see plainly that the end was only a little way off.

Gerhardt, true to his nature, took into consideration all the various arrangements contingent upon his death. He wished to be buried in the little Lutheran cemetery, which was several miles farther out on the South Side, and he wanted the beloved minister of his church to officiate.

"I want everything plain," he said. "Just my black suit and those Sunday shoes of mine, and that black string tie. I don't want anything else. I will be all right."

Jennie begged him not to talk of it, but he would. One day at four o'clock he had a sudden sinking spell, and at five he was dead. Jennie held his hands, watching his laboured breathing; once or twice he opened his eyes to smile at her. "I don't mind going," he said, in this final hour. "I've done what I could."

"Don't talk of dying, papa," she pleaded.

"It's the end," he said. "You've been good to me. You're a good woman."

She heard no other words from his lips.

The finish which time thus put to this troubled life affected Jennie deeply. Strong in her kindly, emotional relationships, Gerhardt had appealed to her not only as her father, but as a friend and counsellor. She saw him now in his true perspective, a hard-working, honest, sincere old German, who had done his best to raise a troublesome family and lead an honest life. Truly she had been his one great burden, and she had never really dealt truthfully with him to the end. She wondered now if where he was he could see that she had lied. And would he forgive her ? He had called her a good woman.

Telegrams were sent to all the children. Bass wired that he was coming, and arrived the next day. The others wired that they could not come, but asked for details, which Jennie wrote. The Lutheran minister was called in to say prayers and fix the time of the burial service. A fat, smug undertaker was commissioned to arrange all the details. Some few neighbourhood friends called—those who had remained most faithful —and on the second morning following his death the services were held. Lester accompanied Jennie and Vesta and Bass to the little red brick Lutheran church, and sat stolidly through the rather dry services. He listened wearily to the long discourse on the beauties and rewards of a future life and stirred irritably when reference was made to a hell. Bass was rather bored, but considerate. He looked upon his father now much as he would on any other man. Only Jennie wept sympathetically. She saw her father in perspective, the long years of trouble he had had, the days in which he had had to saw wood for a living, the days in which he had lived in a factory loft, the little shabby house they had been compelled to live in in Thirteenth Street, the terrible days of suffering they had spent in Lorrie Street, in Cleveland, his grief over her, his grief over Mrs. Gerhardt, his love and care of Vesta, and finally these last days.

" Oh, he was a good man," she thought. " He meant so well." They sang a hymn. " A Mighty Fortress Is Our God," and then she sobbed.

Lester pulled at her arm. He was moved to the danger-line himself by her grief. " You'll have to do better than this," he whispered. " My God, I can't stand it. I'll have to get up and get out." Jennie quieted a little, but the fact that the last visible ties were being broken between her and her father was almost too much.

At the grave in the Cemetery of the Redeemer, where Lester had immediately arranged to purchase a lot, they saw the plain coffin lowered and the earth shovelled in. Lester looked curiously at the bare trees, the brown dead grass, and the brown soil of the prairie turned up at this simple graveside. There was no distinction to this burial plot. It was commonplace and shabby, a working-man's resting-place, but so long as he wanted it, it was all right. He studied Bass's keen, lean face, wondering what sort of a career he was cutting out for himself. Bass looked to him like some one who would run a cigar store successfully. He watched Jennie wiping her red eyes, and then he said to himself again, " Well, there is something to her." The woman's emotion was so deep, so real. " There's no explaining a good woman," he said to himself.

On the way home, through the wind-swept, dusty streets, he talked of life in general, Bass and Vesta being present. " Jennie takes things too seriously," he said. " She's inclined to be morbid. Life isn't as bad as she makes out with her sensitive feelings. We all have our troubles, and we all have to stand them, some more, some less. We can't assume that any one is so much better or worse off than any one else. We all have our share of troubles."

" I can't help it," said Jennie. " I feel so sorry for some people."

" Jennie always was a little gloomy," put in Bass. He was thinking what a fine figure of a man Lester was, how beautifully they lived, how Jennie had come up in the world. He was thinking that there must be a lot more to her than he had originally thought. Life surely did turn out queer. At one time he thought Jennie was a hopeless failure and no good.

" You ought to try to steel yourself to take things as they come without going to pieces this way," said Lester finally.

Bass thought so too.

Jennie stared thoughtfully out of the carriage window. There was the old house now, large and silent without Gerhardt. Just think, she would never see him any more. They finally turned into the drive and entered the library. Jeannette, nervous and sympathetic, served tea. Jennie went to look after various details. She wondered curiously where she would be when she died.

## CHAPTER LII

THE fact that Gerhardt was dead made no particular difference to Lester, except as it affected Jennie. He had liked the old German for his many sterling qualities, but beyond that he thought nothing of him one way or the other. He took Jennie to a watering-place for ten days to help her recover her spirits, and it was soon after this that he decided to tell her just how things stood with him ; he would put the problem plainly before her. It would be easier now, for Jennie had been informed of the disastrous prospects of the real-estate deal. She was also aware of his continued interest in Mrs. Gerald. Lester did not hesitate to let Jennie know that he was on very friendly terms with her. Mrs. Gerald had, at first, formally requested him to bring Jennie to see her, but she never had called herself, and Jennie understood quite clearly that it was not to be. Now that her father was dead, she was beginning to wonder what was going to become of her ; she was afraid that Lester might not marry her. Certainly he showed no signs of intending to do so.

By one of those curious coincidences of thought, Robert also had reached the conclusion that something should be done. He did not, for one moment, imagine that he could directly work upon Lester—he did not care to try—but he did think that some influence might be brought to bear on Jennie. She was probably amenable to reason. If Lester had not married her already, she must realise full well that he did not intend to do so. Suppose that some responsible third person were to approach her, and explain how things were, including, of course, the offer of an independent income ? Might she not be willing to leave Lester, and end all this trouble ? After all, Lester was his brother, and he ought not to lose his fortune. Robert had things very much in his own hands now, and could afford to be generous. He finally decided that Mr. O'Brien, of Knight, Keatley & O'Brien, would be the proper intermediary, for O'Brien was suave, good-natured, and well-meaning, even if he was a lawyer. He might explain to Jennie very delicately just how the family felt, and how much Lester stood to lose if he continued to maintain his connection with her. If Lester had married Jennie, O'Brien would find it out. A liberal provision would be made for her—say fifty or one hundred thousand, or even one hundred and fifty thousand dollars. He sent for Mr. O'Brien and gave him his instructions. As one of the executors of Archibald Kane's estate, it was really the lawyer's duty to look into the matter of Lester's ultimate decision.

Mr. O'Brien journeyed to Chicago. On reaching the city, he called up Lester, and found out to his satisfaction that he was out of town for the day. He went out to the house in Hyde Park, and sent in his card to Jennie. She came downstairs in a few minutes quite unconscious of the import of his message ; he greeted her most blandly.

" This is Mrs. Kane ? " he asked, with an interlocutory jerk of his head.

" Yes," replied Jennie.

" I am, as you see by my card, Mr. O'Brien, of Knight, Keatley & O'Brien," he began. " We are the attorneys and executors of the late Mr. Kane, your—ah—Mr. Kane's father. You'll think it's rather curious, my coming to you, but under your husband's father's will there were certain conditions stipulated which affect you and Mr. Kane very materially. These provisions are so important that I think you ought to know about them—that is if Mr. Kane hasn't already told you. I—pardon me—but the peculiar nature of them makes me conclude that—possibly—he hasn't." He paused, a very question-mark of a man—every feature of his face an interrogation.

" I don't quite understand," said Jennie. " I don't know anything about the will. If there's anything that I ought to know, I suppose Mr. Kane will tell me. He hasn't told me anything as yet."

" Ah ! " breathed Mr. O'Brien, highly gratified. " Just as I thought. Now, if you will allow me I'll go into the matter briefly. Then you can judge for yourself whether you wish to hear the full particulars. Won't you sit down ? " They had both been standing. Jennie seated herself, and Mr. O'Brien pulled up a chair near to hers.

"Now to begin," he said. "I need not say to you, of course, that there was considerable opposition on the part of Mr. Kane's father, to this—ah—union between yourself and his son."

"I know——" Jennie started to say, but checked herself. She was puzzled, disturbed, and a little apprehensive.

"Before Mr. Kane senior died," he went on, "he indicated to your—ah—to Mr. Lester Kane, that he felt this way. In his will he made certain conditions governing the distribution of his property which made it rather hard for his son, your—ah—husband, to come into his rightful share. Ordinarily, he would have inherited one-fourth of the Kane Manufacturing Company, worth to-day in the neighbourhood of a million dollars, perhaps more ; also one-fourth of the other properties, which now aggregate something like five hundred thousand dollars. I believe Mr. Kane senior was really very anxious that his son should inherit this property. But owing to the conditions which your—ah—which Mr. Kane's father made, Mr. Lester Kane cannot possibly obtain his share, except by complying with a—with a—certain wish which his father had expressed."

Mr. O'Brien paused, his eyes moving back and forth sidewise in their sockets. In spite of the natural prejudice of the situation, he was considerably impressed with Jennie's pleasing appearance. He could see quite plainly why Lester might cling to her in the face of all opposition. He continued to study her furtively as he sat there waiting for her to speak.

"And what was that wish ? " she finally asked, her nerves becoming just a little tense under the strain of the silence.

"I am glad you were kind enough to ask me that," he went on. "The subject is a very difficult one for me to introduce—very difficult. I come as an emissary of the estate, I might say as one of the executors under the will of Mr. Kane's father. I know how keenly your—ah—how keenly Mr. Kane feels about it. I know how keenly you will probably feel about it. But it is one of those very difficult things which cannot be helped—which must be got over somehow. And while I hesitate very much to say so, I must tell you that Mr. Kane senior stipulated in his will that unless, unless "—again his eyes were moving sidewise to and fro—" he saw fit to separate from—ah—you "—he paused to get breath—" he could not inherit this or any other sum—or, at least, only a very minor income of ten thousand a year ; and that only on condition that he should marry you." He paused again. " I should add," he went on, " that under the will he was given three years in which to indicate his intentions. That time is now drawing to a close."

He paused, half expecting some outburst of feeling from Jennie, but she only looked at him fixedly, her eyes clouded with surprise, distress, unhappiness. Now she understood. Lester was sacrificing his fortune for her. His recent commercial venture was an effort to rehabilitate himself, to put himself in an independent position. The recent periods of preoccupation, of subtle unrest, and of dissatisfaction over which she had grieved were now explained. He was unhappy, he was brooding over this prospective loss, and he had never told her. So his father had really disinherited him !

Mr. O'Brien sat before her, troubled himself. He was very sorry for her, now that he saw the expression of her face. Still the truth had to come out. She ought to know.

" I'm sorry," he said, when he saw that she was not going to make any immediate reply, " that I have been the bearer of such unfortunate news. It is a very painful situation that I find myself in at this moment, I assure you. I bear you no ill will personally—of course you understand that. The family really bears you no ill will now—I hope you believe that. As I told your—ah—as I told Mr. Kane, at the time the will was read, I considered it most unfair, but, of course, as a mere executive under it and counsel for his father, I could do nothing. I really think it best that you should know how things stand, in order that you may help your—your husband "—he paused, significantly—" if possible, to some solution. It seems a pity to me, as it does to the various other members of his family, that he should lose all this money."

Jennie had turned her head away and was staring at the floor. She faced him now steadily. " He mustn't lose it," she said ; " it isn't fair that he should."

" I am most delighted to hear you say that, Mrs.—Mrs. Kane," he went on, using for the first time her improbable title as Lester's wife, without hesitation. " I may as well be very frank with you, and say that I feared you might take this information in quite another spirit. Of course you know to begin with that the Kane family is very clannish. Mrs. Kane, your—ah—your husband's mother, was a very proud and rather distant woman, and his sisters and brothers are rather set in their notions as to what constitute proper family connections. They look upon his relationship to you as irregular, and— pardon me if I appear to be a little cruel—as not generally satisfactory. As you know, there had been so much talk in the last few years that Mr. Kane senior did not believe that the situation could ever be nicely adjusted, so far as the family was concerned. He felt that his son had not gone about it right in the first place. One of the conditions of his will was that if your husband—pardon me—if his son did not accept the proposition in regard to separating from you and taking up his rightful share of the estate, then to inherit anything at all—the mere ten thousand a year I mentioned before—he must—ah—he must pardon me, I seem a little brutal, but not intentionally so—marry you."

Jennie winced. It was such a cruel thing to say this to her face. This whole attempt to live together illegally had proved disastrous at every step. There was only one solution to the unfortunate business—she could see that plainly. She must leave him, or he must leave her. There was no other alternative. Lester living on ten thousand dollars a year! It seemed silly.

Mr. O'Brien was watching her curiously. He was thinking that Lester both had and had not made a mistake. Why had he not married her in the first place? She was charming.

" There is just one other point which I wish to make in this connection, Mrs. Kane," he went on softly and easily. " I see now that it will not make any difference to you, but I am commissioned and in a way constrained to make it. I hope you will take it in the manner in which it is given. I don't know whether you are familiar with your husband's commercial interests or not ? "

" No," said Jennie simply.

" Well, in order to simplify matters, and to make it easier for you, should you decide to assist your husband to a solution of this very difficult situation—frankly, in case you might possibly decide to leave on your own account, and maintain a separate establishment of your own—I am delighted to say that—ah—any sum, say—ah——"

Jennie rose and walked dazedly to one of the windows, clasping her hands as she went. Mr. O'Brien rose also.

"Well, be that as it may. In the event of your deciding to end the connection it has been suggested that any reasonable sum you might name, fifty, seventy-five, a hundred thousand dollars "—Mr. O'Brien was feeling very generous toward her—" would be gladly set aside for your benefit—put in trust, as it were, so that you would have it whenever you needed it. You would never want for anything."

"Please don't," said Jennie, hurt beyond the power to express herself, unable mentally and physically to listen to another word. "Please don't say any more. Please go away. Let me alone now, please. I can go away. I will. It will be arranged. But please don't talk to me any more, will you ? "

"I understand how you feel, Mrs. Kane," went on Mr. O'Brien, coming to a keen realisation of her sufferings. "I know exactly, believe me. I have said all I intend to say. It has been very hard for me to do this—very hard. I regret the necessity. You have my card. Please note the name. I will come any time you suggest, or you can write me. I will not detain you any longer. I am sorry. I hope you will see fit to say nothing to your husband of my visit—it will be advisable that you should keep your own counsel in the matter. I value his friendship very highly, and I am sincerely sorry."

Jennie only stared at the floor.

Mr. O'Brien went out into the hall to get his coat. Jennie touched the electric button to summon the maid, and Jeannette came. Jennie went back into the library, and Mr. O'Brien paced briskly down the front walk. When she was really alone she put her doubled hands to her chin, and stared at the floor, the queer design of the silken Turkish rug resolving itself into some curious picture. She saw herself in a small cottage somewhere, alone with Vesta ; she saw Lester living in another world, and beside him Mrs. Gerald. She saw this house vacant, and then a long stretch of time, and then——

"Oh," she sighed, choking back a desire to cry. With

her hands she brushed away a hot tear from each eye. Then she got up.

"It must be," she said to herself in thought. "It must be. It should have been so long ago." And then—"Oh, thank God that papa is dead! Anyhow, he did not live to see this."

## CHAPTER LIII

THE explanation which Lester had concluded to be inevitable, whether it led to separation or legalisation of their hitherto banal condition, followed quickly upon the appearance of Mr. O'Brien. On the day Mr. O'Brien called he had gone on a journey to Hegewisch, a small manufacturing town in Wisconsin, where he had been invited to witness the trial of a new motor intended to operate elevators—with a view to possible investment. When he came out to the house, interested to tell Jennie something about it even in spite of the fact that he was thinking of leaving her, he felt a sense of depression everywhere, for Jennie, in spite of the serious and sensible conclusion she had reached, was not one who could conceal her feelings easily. She was brooding sadly over her proposed action, realising that it was best to leave but finding it hard to summon the courage which would let her talk to him about it. She could not go without telling him what she thought. He ought to want to leave her. She was absolutely convinced that this one course of action—separation—was necessary and advisable. She could not think of him as daring to make a sacrifice of such proportions for her sake even if he wanted to. It was impossible. It was astonishing to her that he had let things go along as dangerously and silently as he had.

When he came in Jennie did her best to greet him with her accustomed smile, but it was a pretty poor imitation.

"Everything all right ?" she asked, using her customary phrase of inquiry.

"Quite," he answered. "How are things with you ?"

"Oh, just the same." She walked with him to the library, and he poked at the open fire with a long-handled poker before turning around to survey the room generally. It was five o'clock of a January afternoon. Jennie had gone to one of the windows to lower the shade. As she came back he looked at her critically. "You're not quite your usual self, are you ?" he asked, sensing something out of the common in her attitude.

"Why, yes, I feel all right," she replied, but there was a peculiar uneven motion to the movement of her lips—a rippling tremor which was unmistakable to him.

"I think I know better than that," he said, still gazing at her steadily. "What's the trouble? Anything happened?"

She turned away from him a moment to get her breath and collect her senses. Then she faced him again. "There is something," she managed to say. "I have to tell you something."

"I know you have," he agreed, half smiling, but with a feeling that there was much of grave import back of this. "What is it?"

She was silent for a moment, biting her lips. She did not quite know how to begin. Finally she broke the spell with: "There was a man here yesterday—a Mr. O'Brien, of Cincinnati. Do you know him?"

"Yes, I know him. What did he want?"

"He came to talk to me about you and your father's will."

She paused, for his face clouded immediately. "Why the devil should he be talking to you about my father's will!" he exclaimed. "What did he have to say?"

"Please don't get angry, Lester," said Jennie calmly, for she realised that she must remain absolute mistress of herself if anything were to be accomplished toward the resolution of her problem. "He wanted to tell me what a sacrifice you are making," she went on. "He wished to show me that there was only a little time left before you would lose your inheritance. Don't you want to act pretty soon? Don't you want to leave me."

"Damn him!" said Lester fiercely. "What the devil does he mean by putting his nose in my private affairs? Can't they let me alone?" He shook himself angrily. "Damn them!" he exclaimed again. "This is some of Robert's work. Why should Knight, Keatley & O'Brien be meddling in my affairs? This whole business is getting to be a nuisance!" He was in a boiling rage in a moment, as was shown by his darkening skin and sulphurous eyes.

Jennie trembled before his anger. She did not know what to say.

He came to himself sufficiently after a time to add:

"Well. Just what did he tell you?"

" He said that if you married me you would only get ten thousand a year. That if you didn't and still lived with me you would get nothing at all. If you would leave me, or I would leave you, you would get all of a million and a half. Don't you think you had better leave me now ? "

She had not intended to propound this leading question so quickly, but it came out as a natural climax to the situation. She realised instantly that if he were really in love with her he would answer with an emphatic " no." If he didn't care, he would hesitate, he would delay, he would seek to put off the evil day of reckoning.

" I don't see that," he retorted irritably. " I don't see that there's any need for either interference or hasty action. What I object to is their coming here and mixing in my private affairs."

Jennie was cut to the quick by his indifference, his wrath instead of affection. To her the main point at issue was her leaving him or his leaving her. To him this recent interference was obviously the chief matter for discussion and consideration. The meddling of others before he was ready to act was the terrible thing. She had hoped, in spite of what she had seen, that possibly, because of the long time they had lived together and the things which (in a way) they had endured together, he might have come to care for her deeply—that she had stirred some emotion in him which would never brook real separation, though some seeming separation might be necessary. He had not married her, of course, but then there had been so many things against them. Now, in this final hour, anyhow, he might have shown that he cared deeply, even if he had deemed it necessary to let her go. She felt for the time being as if, for all that she had lived with him so long, she did not understand him, and yet, in spite of this feeling, she knew also that she did. He cared, in his way. He could not care for any one enthusiastically and demonstratively. He could care enough to seize her and take her to himself as he had, but he could not care enough to keep her if something more important appeared. He was debating her fate now. She was in a quandary, hurt, bleeding, but for once in her life, determined. Whether he wanted to or not, she must not let him make this sacrifice. She must leave him—if he would not leave her. It was not important enough that she should stay. There might be but one answer. But might he not show affection ?

" Don't you think you had better act soon ? " she continued, hoping that some word of feeling would come from him. " There is only a little time left, isn't there ? "

Jennie nervously pushed a book to and fro on the table, her fear that she would not be able to keep up appearances troubling her greatly. It was hard for her to know what to do or say. Lester was so terrible when he became angry. Still it ought not to be so hard for him to go, now that he had Mrs. Gerald, if he only wished to do so—and he ought to. His fortune was so much more important to him than anything she could be.

" Don't worry about that," he replied stubbornly, his wrath at his brother, and his family, and O'Brien still holding him. " There's time enough. I don't know what I want to do yet. I like the effrontery of these people ! But I won't talk any more about it ; isn't dinner nearly ready ? " He was so injured in his pride that he scarcely took the trouble to be civil. He was forgetting all about her and what she was feeling. He hated his brother Robert for this affront. He would have enjoyed wringing the necks of Messrs. Knight, Keatley & O'Brien, singly and collectively.

The question could not be dropped for good and all, and it came up again at dinner, after Jennie had done her best to collect her thoughts and quiet her nerves. They could not talk very freely because of Vesta and Jeannette, but she managed to get in a word or two.

" I could take a little cottage somewhere," she suggested softly, hoping to find him in a modified mood. " I would not want to stay here. I would not know what to do with a big house like this alone."

" I wish you wouldn't discuss this business any longer, Jennie," he persisted. " I'm in no mood for it. I don't know that I'm going to do anything of the sort. I don't know what I'm going to do." He was so sour and obstinate, because of O'Brien, that she finally gave it up. Vesta was astonished to see her stepfather, usually so courteous, in so grim a mood.

Jennie felt a curious sense that she might hold him if she would, for he was doubting ; but she knew also that she should not wish. It was not fair to him. It was not fair to herself, or kind, or decent.

"Oh yes, Lester, you must," she pleaded, at a later time. "I won't talk about it any more, but you must. I won't let you do anything else."

There were hours when it came up afterward—every day, in fact—in their boudoir, in the library, in the dining-room, at breakfast, but not always in words. Jennie was worried. She was looking the worry she felt. She was sure that he should be made to act. Since he was showing more kindly consideration for her, she was all the more certain that he should act soon. Just how to go about it she did not know, but she looked at him longingly, trying to help him make up his mind. She would be happy, she assured herself—she would be happy thinking that he was happy once she was away from him. He was a good man, most delightful in everything, perhaps, save his gift of love. He really did not love her—could not perhaps, after all that had happened, even though she loved him most earnestly. But his family had been most brutal in their opposition, and this had affected his attitude. She could understand that, too. She could see now how his big, strong brain might be working in a circle. He was too decent to be absolutely brutal about this thing and leave her, too really considerate to look sharply after his own interests as he should, or hers—but he ought to.

"You must decide, Lester," she kept saying to him, from time to time. "You must let me go. What difference does it make? I will be all right. Maybe, when this thing is all over you might want to come back to me. If you do, I will be there."

"I'm not ready to come to a decision," was his invariable reply. "I don't know that I want to leave you. This money is important, of course, but money isn't everything. I can live on ten thousand a year if necessary. I've done it in the past."

"Oh, but you're so much more placed in the world now, Lester," she argued. "You can't do it. Look how much it costs to run this house alone. And a million and a half of dollars—why, I wouldn't let you think of losing that. I'll go myself first."

"Where would you think of going if it came to that?" he asked curiously.

" Oh, I'd find some place. Do you remember that little town of Sandwood, this side of Kenosha ? I have often thought it would be a pleasant place to live."

" I don't like to think of this," he said finally in an outburst of frankness. " It doesn't seem fair. The conditions have all been against this union of ours. I suppose I should have married you in the first place. I'm sorry now that I didn't."

Jennie choked in her throat, but said nothing.

" Anyhow, this won't be the last of it, if I can help it," he concluded. He was thinking that the storm might blow over ; once he had the money, and then—but he hated compromises and subterfuges.

It came by degrees to be understood that, toward the end of February, she should look around at Sandwood and see what she could find. She was to have ample means, he told her, everything that she wanted. After a time he might come out and visit her occasionally. And he was determined in his heart that he would make some people pay for the trouble they had caused him. He decided to send for Mr. O'Brien shortly and talk things over. He wanted for his personal satisfaction to tell him what he thought of him.

At the same time, in the background of his mind, moved the shadowy figure of Mrs. Gerald—charming, sophisticated, well placed in every sense of the word. He did not want to give her the broad reality of full thought, but she was always there. He thought and thought. " Perhaps I'd better," he half concluded. When February came he was ready to act.

## CHAPTER LIV

THE little town of Sandwood, "this side of Kenosha," as Jennie had expressed it, was only a short distance from Chicago, an hour and fifteen minutes by the local train. It had a population of some three hundred families, dwelling in small cottages, which were scattered over a pleasant area of lake-shore property. They were not rich people. The houses were not worth more than from three to five thousand dollars each, but, in most cases, they were harmoniously constructed, and the surrounding trees, green for the entire year, gave them a pleasing summery appearance. Jennie, at the time they had passed by there—it was an outing taken behind a pair of fast horses—had admired the look of a little white church steeple, set down among the green trees, and the gentle rocking of the boats upon the summer water.

"I should like to live in a place like this some time," she had said to Lester, and he had made the comment that it was a little too peaceful for him. "I can imagine getting to the place where I might like this, but not now. It's too withdrawn."

Jennie thought of that expression afterward. It came to her when she thought that the world was trying. If she had to be alone ever and could afford it she would like to live in a place like Sandwood. There she would have a little garden, some chickens, perhaps, a tall pole with a pretty bird-house on it, and flowers and trees and green grass everywhere about. If she could have a little cottage in a place like this which commanded a view of the lake she could sit of a summer evening and sew. Vesta could play about or come home from school. She might have a few friends, or not any. She was beginning to think that she could do very well living alone if it were not for Vesta's social needs. Books were pleasant things —she was finding that out—books like Irving's *Sketch Book*, Lamb's *Elia*, and Hawthorne's *Twice Told Tales*. Vesta was coming to be quite a musician in her way, having a keen sense of the delicate and refined in musical composition. She had a natural sense of harmony and a love for those songs and instrumental compositions which reflect sentimental and passionate moods, and she could sing and play quite well. Her voice was, of course, quite untrained—she was only fourteen—but it was pleasant to listen to. She was beginning to show the combined traits of her mother and father—Jennie's gentle, speculative turn of mind, combined with Brander's vivacity of spirit and innate executive capacity. She could talk to her mother in a sensible way about things, nature, books, dress, love, and from her developing tendencies Jennie caught keen glimpses of the new worlds which Vesta was to explore. The nature of modern school life, its consideration of various divisions of knowledge, music, science, all came to Jennie watching her daughter take up new themes. Vesta was evidently going to be a woman of considerable ability—not irritably aggressive, but self-constructive. She would be able to take care of herself. All this pleased Jennie and gave her great hopes for Vesta's future.

The cottage which was finally secured at Sandwood was only a storey and a half in height, but it was raised upon red brick piers between which were set green lattices and about which ran a veranda. The house was long and narrow, its full length—some five rooms in a row—facing the lake. There was a dining-room with windows opening even with the floor, a large library with built-in shelves for books, and a parlour whose three large windows afforded air and sunshine at all times. The plot of ground in which this cottage stood was one hundred feet square and ornamented with a few trees. The former owner had laid out flower-beds, and arranged green hardwood tubs for the reception of various hardy plants and vines. The house was painted white, with green shutters and green shingles.

It had been Lester's idea, since this thing must be, that Jennie might keep the house in Hyde Park just as it was, but she did not want to do that. She could not think of living there alone. The place was too full of memories. At first, she did not think she would take anything much with her, but she finally saw that it was advisable to do as Lester suggested—to fit out the new place with a selection of silverware, hangings, and furniture from the Hyde Park house.

" You have no idea what you will or may want," he said. " Take everything. I certainly don't want any of it."

A lease of the cottage was taken for two years, together with an option for an additional five years, including the privilege of purchase. So long as he was letting her go, Lester wanted to be generous. He could not think of her as wanting for anything, and he did not propose that she should. His one troublesome thought was, what explanation was to be made to Vesta. He liked her very much and wanted her life kept free of complications.

" Why not send her off to a boarding-school until spring ? " he suggested once ; but owing to the lateness of the season this was abandoned as inadvisable. Later they agreed that business affairs made it necessary for him to travel and for Jennie to move. Later Vesta could be told that Jennie had left him for any reason she chose to give. It was a trying situation, all the more bitter to Jennie because she realised that in spite of the wisdom of it indifference to her was involved. He really did not care *enough*, as much as he cared.

The relationship of man and woman which we study so passionately in the hope of finding heaven knows what key to the mystery of existence holds no more difficult or trying situation than this of mutual compatibility broken or disrupted by untoward conditions which in themselves have so little to do with the real force and beauty of the relationship itself. These days of final dissolution in which this household, so charmingly arranged, the scene of so many pleasant activities, was literally going to pieces was a period of great trial to both Jennie and Lester. On her part it was one of intense suffering, for she was of that stable nature that rejoices to fix itself in a serviceable and harmonious relationship, and then stay so. For her life was made up of those mystic chords of sympathy and memory which bind up the transient elements of nature into a harmonious and enduring scene. One of those chords—this home was her home, united and made beautiful by her affection and consideration for each person and every object. Now the time had come when it must cease.

If she had ever had anything before in her life which had been like this it might have been easier to part with it now, though, as she had proved, Jennie's affections were not based in any way upon material considerations. Her love of life and of personality were free from the taint of selfishness. She went about among these various rooms selecting this rug, that set of furniture, this and that ornament, wishing all the time with all her heart and soul that it need not be. Just to think, in a little while Lester would not come any more of an evening! She would not need to get up first of a morning and see that coffee was made for her lord, that the table in the dining-room looked just so. It had been a habit of hers to arrange a bouquet for the table out of the richest blooming flowers of the conservatory, and she had always felt in doing it that it was particularly for him. Now it would not be necessary any more—not for him. When one is accustomed to wait for the sound of a certain carriage-wheel of an evening grating upon your carriage drive, when one is used to listen at eleven, twelve, and one, waking naturally and joyfully to the echo of a certain step on the stair, the separation, the ending of these things, is keen with pain. These were the thoughts that were running through Jennie's brain hour after hour and day after day.

Lester on his part was suffering in another fashion. His was not the sorrow of lacerated affection, of discarded and despised love, but of that painful sense of unfairness which comes to one who knows that he is making a sacrifice of the virtues—kindness, loyalty, affection—to policy. Policy was dictating a very splendid course of action from one point of view. Free of Jennie, providing for her admirably, he was free to go his way, taking to himself the mass of affairs which come naturally with great wealth. He could not help thinking of the thousand and one little things which Jennie had been accustomed to do for him, the hundred and one comfortable and pleasant and delightful things she meant to him. The virtues which she possessed were quite dear to his mind. He had gone over them time and again. Now he was compelled to go over them finally, to see that she was suffering without making a sign. Her manner and attitude toward him in these last days were quite the same as they had always been—no more, no less. She was not indulging in private hysterics, as another woman might have done; she was not pretending a fortitude in suffering she did not feel, showing him one face while wishing him to see another behind it. She was calm, gentle, considerate—thoughtful of him—where he would go and what he would do, without irritating him by her inquiries. He was struck quite favourably by her ability to take a large situation largely, and he admired her. There was something to this woman, let the world think what it might. It was a shame that her life was passed under such a troubled star. Still a great world was calling him. The sound of its voice was in his ears. It had on occasion shown him its bared teeth. Did he really dare to hesitate ?

The last hour came, when having made excuses to this and that neighbour, when having spread the information that they were going abroad, when Lester had engaged rooms at the Auditorium, and the mass of furniture which could not be used had gone to storage, that it was necessary to say farewell to this Hyde Park domicile. Jennie had visited Sandwood in company with Lester several times. He had carefully examined the character of the place. He was satisfied that it was nice but lonely. Spring was at hand, the flowers would be something. She was going to keep a gardener and man of all work. Vesta would be with her.

" Very well," he said, " only I want you to be comfortable."

In the meantime Lester had been arranging his personal affairs. He had notified Messrs. Knight, Keatley & O'Brien through his own attorney, Mr. Watson, that he would expect them to deliver his share of his father's securities on a given date. He had made up his mind that as long as he was compelled by circumstances to do this thing he would do a number of other things equally ruthless. He would probably marry Mrs. Gerald. He would sit as a director in the United Carriage Company—with his share of the stock it would be impossible to keep him out. If he had Mrs. Gerald's money he would become a controlling factor in the United Traction of Cincinnati, in which his brother was heavily interested, and in the Western Steel Works, of which his brother was now the leading adviser. What a different figure he would be now from that which he had been during the past few years !

Jennie was depressed to the point of despair. She was tremendously lonely. This home had meant so much to her. When she first came here and neighbours had begun to drop in she had imagined herself on the threshold of a great career, that some day, possibly, Lester would marry her. Now, blow after blow had been delivered, and the home and dream were a ruin. Gerhardt was gone. Jeannette, Harry Ward, and Mrs Frissell had been discharged, the furniture for a good part was in storage, and for her, practically, Lester was no more. She realised clearly that he would not come back. If he could do this thing now, even considerately, he could do much more when he was free and away later. Immersed in his great affairs, he would forget, of course. And why not ? She did not fit in. Had not everything—everything illustrated that to her ? Love was not enough in this world—that was so plain. One needed education, wealth, training, the ability to fight and scheme. She did not want to do that. She could not.

The day came when the house was finally closed and the old life was at an end. Lester travelled with Jennie to Sandwood. He spent some little while in the house trying to get her used to the idea of change—it was not so bad. He intimated that he would come again soon, but he went away, and all his words were as nothing against the fact of the actual and spiritual separation. When Jennie saw him going down the brick walk that afternoon, his solid, conservative figure clad in a new tweed suit, his overcoat on his arm, self-reliance and prosperity written all over him, she thought that she would die. She had kissed Lester good-bye and had wished him joy, prosperity, peace ; then she made an excuse to go to her bedroom. Vesta came after a time to seek her, but now her eyes were quite dry ; everything had subsided to a dull ache. The new life was actually begun for her—a life without Lester, without Gerhardt, without any one save Vesta.

" What curious things have happened to me ! " she thought, as she went into the kitchen, for she had determined to do at least some of her own work. She needed the distraction. She did not want to think. If it were not for Vesta she would have sought some regular outside employment. Anything to keep from brooding, for in that direction lay madness.

# CHAPTER LV

THE social and business worlds of Chicago, Cincinnati, Cleveland, and other cities saw, during the year or two which followed the breaking of his relationship with Jennie, a curious rejuvenation in the social and business spirit of Lester Kane. He had become rather distant and indifferent to certain personages and affairs while he was living with her, but now he suddenly appeared again, armed with authority from a number of sources, looking into this and that matter with the air of one who has the privilege of power, and showing himself to be quite a personage from the point of view of finance and commerce. He was older of course. It must be admitted that he was in some respects a mentally altered Lester. Up to the time he had met Jennie he was full of the assurance of the man who has never known defeat. To have been reared in luxury as he had been, to have seen only the pleasant side of society, which is so persistent and so deluding where money is concerned, to have been in the run of big affairs not because one has created them, but because one is a part of them and because they are one's birthright, like the air one breathes, could not help but create one of those illusions of solidarity which is apt to befog the clearest brain. It is so hard for us to know what we have not seen. It is so difficult for us to feel what we have not experienced. Like this world of ours, which seems so solid and persistent solely because we have no knowledge of the power which creates it, Lester's world seemed solid and persistent and real enough to him. It was only when the storms set in and the winds of adversity blew and he found himself facing the armed forces of convention that he realised he might be mistaken as to the value of his personality, that his private desires and opinions were as nothing in the face of a public conviction ; that he was wrong. The race spirit, or social avatar, the " Zeitgeist " as the Germans term it, manifested itself as something having a system in charge, and the organisation of society began to show itself to him as something based on possibly a spiritual, or, at least,

superhuman counterpart. He could not fly in the face of it.
He could not deliberately ignore its mandates. The people
of his time believed that some particular form of social arrangement was necessary, and unless he complied with that he could,
as he saw, readily become a social outcast. His own father
and mother had turned on him—his brother and sisters,
society, his friends. Dear heaven, what a to-do this action
of his had created ! Why, even the fates seemed adverse. His
real estate venture was one of the most fortuitously unlucky
things he had ever heard of. Why ? Were the gods battling
on the side of a to him unimportant social arrangement ?
Apparently. Anyhow, he had been compelled to quit, and
here he was, vigorous, determined, somewhat battered by the
experience, but still forceful and worth while.

And it was a part of the penalty that he had become measurably soured by what had occurred. He was feeling that he
had been compelled to do the first ugly, brutal thing of his
life. Jennie deserved better of him. It was a shame to forsake
her after all the devotion she had manifested. Truly she had
played a finer part than he. Worst of all, his deed could not
be excused on the grounds of necessity. He could have lived
on ten thousand a year ; he could have done without the
million and more which was now his. He could have done
without the society, the pleasures of which had always been a
lure. He could have, but he had not, and he had complicated
it all with the thought of another woman.

Was she as good as Jennie ? That was the question which
always rose before him. Was she as kindly ? Wasn't she
deliberately scheming under his very eyes to win him away
from the woman who was as good as his wife ? Was that
admirable ? Was it the thing a truly big woman would do ?
Was she good enough for him after all ? Ought he to marry her?
Ought he to marry any one seeing that he really owed a spiritual
if not a legal allegiance to Jennie ? Was it worth while for
any woman to marry him ? These things turned in his brain.
They haunted him. He could not shut out the fact that he
was doing a cruel and unlovely thing.

Material error in the first place was now being complicated
with spiritual error. He was attempting to right the first
by committing the second. Could it be done *to his own satisfaction?* Would it pay mentally and spiritually ? Would

it bring him peace of mind ?   He was thinking, thinking, all
the while he was readjusting his life to the old (or perhaps
better yet, new) conditions, and he was not feeling any happier.
As a matter of fact he was feeling worse—grim, revengeful.
If he married Letty he thought at times it would be to use
her fortune as a club to knock other enemies over the head,
and he hated to think he was marrying her for that.   He took
up his abode at the Auditorium, visited Cincinnati in a
distant and aggressive spirit, sat in council with the board of
directors, wishing that he was more at peace with himself,
more interested in life.   But he did not change his policy in
regard to Jennie.

Of course Mrs. Gerald had been vitally interested in Lester's
rehabilitation.   She waited tactfully some little time before
sending him any word ; finally she ventured to write to him at
the Hyde Park address (as if she did not know where he was),
asking, " Where are you ? "   By this time Lester had become
slightly accustomed to the change in his life.   He was saying
to himself that he needed sympathetic companionship, the
companionship of a woman, of course.   Social invitations had
begun to come to him now that he was alone and that his
financial connections were so obviously restored.   He had
made his appearance, accompanied only by a Japanese valet,
at several country houses, the best sign that he was once more
a single man.   No reference was made by any one to the past.

On receiving Mrs. Gerald's note he decided that he ought
to go and see her.   He had treated her rather shabbily.   For
months preceding his separation from Jennie he had not gone
near her.   Even now he waited until time brought a 'phoned
invitation to dinner.   This he accepted.

Mrs. Gerald was at her best as a hostess at her perfectly
appointed dinner-table.   Alboni, the pianist, was there on this
occasion, together with Adam Rascavage, the sculptor, a visiting
scientist from England, Sir Nelson Keyes, and, curiously
enough, Mr. and Mrs. Berry Dodge, whom Lester had not
met socially in several years.   Mrs. Gerald and Lester exchanged
the joyful greetings of those who understand each other
thoroughly and are happy in each other's company.   " Aren't
you ashamed of yourself, sir," she said to him when he made his
appearance, " to treat me so indifferently ?   You are going to
be punished for this."

" What's the damage ? " he smiled. " I've been extremely rushed. I suppose something like ninety stripes will serve me about right."

" Ninety stripes, indeed ! " she retorted. " You're letting yourself off easy. What is it they do to evildoers in Siam ? "

" Boil them in oil, I suppose."

" Well, anyhow, that's more like. I'm thinking of something terrible."

" Be sure and tell me when you decide," he laughed, and passed on to be presented to distinguished strangers by Mrs. De Lincum who aided Mrs. Gerald in receiving. The talk was stimulating. Lester was always at his ease intellectually, and this mental atmosphere revived him. Presently he turned to greet Berry Dodge, who was standing at his elbow.

Dodge was all cordiality. "Where are you now ? " he asked. " We haven't seen you in—oh, when ? Mrs. Dodge is waiting to have a word with you." Lester noticed the change in Dodge's attitude.

" Some time, that's sure," he replied easily. " I'm living at the Auditorium."

" I was asking after you the other day. You know Jackson Du Bois ? Of course you do. We were thinking of running up into Canada for some hunting. Why don't you join us ? "

" I can't," replied Lester. " Too many things on hand just now. Later, surely."

Dodge was anxious to continue. He had seen Lester's election as a director of the C. H. & D. Obviously he was coming back into the world. But dinner was announced and Lester sat at Mrs. Gerald's right hand.

" Aren't you coming to pay me a dinner call some afternoon after this ? " asked Mrs. Gerald confidentially when the conversation was brisk at the other end of the table.

" I am, indeed," he replied, " and shortly. Seriously, I've been wanting to look you up. You understand though how things are now ? "

" I do. I've heard a great deal. That's why I want you to come. We need to talk together."

Ten days later he did call. He felt as if he must talk with her ; he was feeling bored and lonely ; his long home life with Jennie had made hotel life objectionable. He felt as though he must find a sympathetic, intelligent ear, and where better than here ?  Letty was all ears for his troubles.  She would have pillowed his solid head upon her breast in a moment if that had been possible.

" Well," he said, when the usual fencing preliminaries were over, " what will you have me say in explanation ? "

" Have you burned your bridges behind you ? " she asked.

" I'm not so sure," he replied gravely.  " And I can't say that I'm feeling any too joyous about the matter as a whole."

" I thought as much," she replied.  " I knew how it would be with you.  I can see you wading through this mentally, Lester.  I have been watching you, every step of the way, wishing you peace of mind.  These things are always so difficult, but don't you know I am still sure it's for the best.  It never was right the other way.  It never could be.  You couldn't afford to sink back into a mere shell-fish life.  You are not organised temperamentally for that any more than I am. You may regret what you are doing now, but you would have regretted the other thing quite as much and more.  You couldn't work your life out that way—now, could you ? "

" I don't know about that, Letty.  Really, I don't.  I've wanted to come and see you for a long time, but I didn't think that I ought to.  The fight was outside—you know what I mean."

" Yes, indeed, I do," she said soothingly.

" It's still inside.  I haven't gotten over it.  I don't know whether this financial business binds me sufficiently or not. I'll be frank and tell you that I can't say I love her entirely ; but I'm sorry, and that's something."

" She's comfortably provided for, of course," she commented rather than inquired.

" Everything she wants.  Jennie is of a peculiar disposition. She doesn't want much.  She's retiring by nature and doesn't care for show.  I've taken a cottage for her at Sandwood, a little place north of here on the lake ; and there's plenty of money in trust, but, of course, she knows she can live anywhere she pleases."

" I understand exactly how she feels, Lester.  I know how you feel.  She is going to suffer very keenly for a while— we all do when we have to give up the thing we love.  But we can get over it, and we do.  At least, we can live.  She will.

It will go hard at first, but after a while she will see how it is, and she won't feel any the worse toward you."

" Jennie will never reproach me, I know that," he replied. " I'm the one who will do the reproaching. I'll be abusing myself for some time. The trouble is with my particular turn of mind. I can't tell, for the life of me, how much of this disturbing feeling of mine is habit—the condition that I'm accustomed to—and how much is sympathy. I sometimes think I'm the most pointless individual in the world. I think too much."

" Poor Lester ! " she said tenderly. " Well, I understand for one. You're lonely living where you are, aren't you ? "

" I am that," he replied.

" Why not come and spend a few days down at West Baden ? I'm going there."

" When ? " he inquired.

" Next Tuesday."

" Let me see," he replied. " I'm not sure that I can." He consulted his notebook. " I could come Thursday, for a few days."

" Why not do that ? You need company. We can walk and talk things out down there. Will you ? "

" Yes, I will," he replied.

She came toward him, trailing a lavender lounging robe. " You're such a solemn philosopher, sir," she observed comfortably, " working through all the ramifications of things. Why do you ? You were always like that."

" I can't help it," he replied. " It's my nature to think."

" Well, one thing I know——" and she tweaked his ear gently. " You're not going to make another mistake through sympathy if I can help it," she said daringly. " You're going to stay disentangled long enough to give yourself a chance to think out what you want to do. You must. And I wish for one thing you'd take over the management of my affairs. You could advise me so much better than my lawyer."

He arose and walked to the window, turning to look back at her solemnly. " I know what you want," he said doggedly.

" And why shouldn't I ? " she demanded, again approaching him. She looked at him pleadingly, defiantly. " Yes, why shouldn't I ? "

" You don't know what you're doing," he grumbled ; but

he kept on looking at her ; she stood there, attractive as a woman of her age could be, wise, considerate, full of friendship and affection.

"Letty," he said.  "You ought not to want to marry me. I'm not worth it.  Really I'm not.  I'm too cynical.  Too indifferent.  It won't be worth anything in the long run."

"It will be worth something to me," she insisted.  "I know what you are.  Anyhow, I don't care.  I want you ! "

He took her hands, then her arms.  Finally he drew her to him, and put his arms about her waist.  "Poor Letty ! " he said ; "I'm not worth it.  You'll be sorry."

"No, I'll not," she replied.  "I know what I'm doing. I don't care what you think you are worth."  She laid her cheek on his shoulder.  "I want you."

"If you keep on I venture to say you'll have me," he returned. He bent and kissed her.

"Oh," she exclaimed, and hid her hot face against his breast.

"This is bad business," he thought, even as he held her within the circle of his arms.  "It isn't what I ought to be doing."

Still he held her, and now when she offered her lips coaxingly he kissed her again and again.

## CHAPTER LVI

IT is difficult to say whether Lester might not have returned to Jennie after all but for certain influential factors. After a time, with his control of his portion of the estate firmly settled in his hands and the storm of original feeling forgotten, he was well aware that diplomacy—if he ignored his natural tendency to fulfil even implied obligations—could readily bring about an arrangement whereby he and Jennie could be together. But he was haunted by the sense of what might be called an important social opportunity in the form of Mrs. Gerald. He was compelled to set over against his natural tendency toward Jennie a consciousness of what he was ignoring in the personality and fortunes of her rival, who was one of the most significant and interesting figures on the social horizon. For think as he would, these two women were now persistently opposed in his consciousness. The one polished, sympathetic, philosophic—schooled in all the niceties of polite society, and with the means to gratify her every wish ; the other natural, sympathetic, emotional with no schooling in the ways of polite society, but with a feeling for the beauty of life and the lovely things in human relationship which made her beyond any question an exceptional woman. Mrs. Gerald saw it and admitted it. Her criticism of Lester's relationship with Jennie was not that she was not worth while, but that conditions made it impolitic. On the other hand, union with her was an ideal climax for his social aspirations. This would bring everything out right. He would be as happy with her as he would be with Jennie—almost—and he would have the satisfaction of knowing that this Western social and financial world held no more significant figure than himself. It was not wise to delay either this latter excellent solution of his material problems, and after thinking it over long and seriously he finally concluded that he would not. He had already done Jennie the irreparable wrong of leaving her. What difference did it make if he did this also ? She was possessed of everything she could possibly want outside of himself. She had herself deemed it advisable for him to leave. By such figments of the brain, in the face of unsettled and disturbing conditions, he was becoming used to the idea of a new alliance.

The thing which prevented an eventual resumption of relationship in some form with Jennie was the constant presence of Mrs. Gerald. Circumstances conspired to make her the logical solution of his mental quandary at this time. Alone he could do nothing save to make visits here and there, and he did not care to do that. He was too indifferent mentally to gather about him as a bachelor that atmosphere which he enjoyed and which a woman like Mrs. Gerald could so readily provide. United with her it was simple enough. Their home then, wherever it was, would be full of clever people. He would need to do little save to appear and enjoy it. She understood quite as well as any one how he liked to live. She enjoyed to meet the people he enjoyed meeting. There were so many things they could do together nicely. He visited West Baden at the same time she did, as she suggested. He gave himself over to her in Chicago for dinners, parties, drives. Her house was quite as much his own as hers—she made him feel so. She talked to him about her affairs, showing him exactly how they stood and why she wished him to intervene in this and that matter. She did not wish him to be much alone. She did not want him to think or regret. She came to represent to him comfort, forgetfulness, rest from care. With the others he visited at her house occasionally, and it gradually became rumoured about that he would marry her. Because of the fact that there had been so much discussion of his previous relationship, Letty decided that if ever this occurred it should be a quiet affair. She wanted a simple explanation in the papers of how it had come about, and then afterwards, when things were normal again and gossip had subsided, she would enter on a dazzling social display for his sake.

"Why not let us get married in April and go abroad for the summer?" she asked once, after they had reached a silent understanding that marriage would eventually follow. "Let's go to Japan. Then we can come back in the fall, and take a house on the Drive."

Lester had been away from Jennie so long now that the

first severe wave of self-reproach had passed. He was still doubtful, but he preferred to stifle his misgivings. "Very well," he replied, almost jokingly. "Only don't let there be any fuss about it."

"Do you really mean that, sweet ? " she exclaimed, looking over at him ; they had been spending the evening together quietly reading and chatting.

"I've thought about it a long while," he replied. "I don't see why not."

She came over to him and sat on his knee, putting her arms upon his shoulders.

"I can scarcely believe you said that," she said, looking at him curiously.

"Shall I take it back ? " he asked.

"No, no. It's agreed for April now. And we'll go to Japan. You can't change your mind. There won't be any fuss. But my, what a trousseau I will prepare ! "

He smiled a little constrainedly as she tousled his head ; there was a missing note somewhere in this gamut of happiness ; perhaps it was because he was getting old.

## CHAPTER LVII

IN the meantime Jennie was going her way, settling herself in the markedly different world in which henceforth she was to move. It seemed a terrible thing at first—this life without Lester. Despite her own strong individuality, her ways had become so involved with his that there seemed to be no possibility of disentangling them. Constantly she was with him in thought and action, just as though they had never separated. Where was he now ? What was he doing ? What was he saying ? How was he looking ? In the mornings when she woke it was with the sense that he must be beside her. At night as if she could not go to bed alone. He would come after a while surely—ah, no, of course he would not come. Dear heaven, think of that ! Never any more. And she wanted him so.

Again there were so many little trying things to adjust, for a change of this nature is too radical to be passed over lightly. The explanation she had to make to Vesta was of all the most important. This little girl, who was old enough now to see and think for herself, was not without her surmises and misgivings. Vesta recalled that her mother had been accused of not being married to her father when she was born. She had seen the article about Jennie and Lester in the Sunday paper at the time it had appeared—it had been shown to her at school—but she had had sense enough to say nothing about it, feeling somehow that Jennie would not like it. Lester's disappearance was a complete surprise ; but she had learned in the last two or three years that her mother was very sensitive, and that she could hurt her in unexpected ways. Jennie was finally compelled to tell Vesta that Lester's fortune had been dependent on his leaving her solely because she was not of his station. Vesta listened soberly and half suspected the truth. She felt terribly sorry for her mother, and, because of Jennie's obvious distress, she was trebly gay and courageous. She refused outright the suggestion of going to a boarding-school and kept as close to her mother as she could. She found interesting books to read with her, insisted that they go to see plays together, played to her on the piano, and asked for her mother's criticisms on her drawing and modelling. She found a few friends in the excellent Sandwood school, and brought them home of an evening to add lightness and gaiety to the cottage life. Jennie, through her growing appreciation of Vesta's fine character, became more and more drawn toward her. Lester was gone, but at least she had Vesta. That prop would probably sustain her in the face of a waning existence.

There was also her history to account for to the residents of Sandwood. In many cases where one is content to lead a secluded life it is not necessary to say much of one's past, but as a rule something must be said. People have the habit of inquiring—if they are no more than butchers and bakers. By degrees one must account for this and that fact, and it was so here. She could not say that her husband was dead. Lester might come back. She had to say that she had left him—to give the impression that it would be she, if any one, who would permit him to return. This put her in an interesting and sympathetic light in the neighbourhood. It was the most sensible thing to do. She then settled down to a quiet routine of existence, waiting what dénouement to her life she could not guess.

Sandwood life was not without its charms for a lover of nature, and this, with the devotion of Vesta, offered some slight solace. There was the beauty of the lake, which, with its passing boats, was a never-ending source of joy, and there were many charming drives in the surrounding country. Jenny had her own horse and carryall—one of the horses of the pair they had used in Hyde Park. Other household pets appeared in due course of time, including a collie, that Vesta named Rats; she had brought him from Chicago as a puppy, and he had grown to be a sterling watch-dog, sensible and affectionate. There was also a cat, Jimmy Woods, so called after a boy Vesta knew, and to whom she insisted the cat bore a marked resemblance. There was a singing thrush, guarded carefully against a roving desire for bird-food on the part of Jimmy Woods, and a jar of goldfish. So this little household drifted along quietly and dreamily indeed, but always with the undercurrent of feeling which ran so still because it was so deep.

There was no word from Lester for the first few weeks following his departure ; he was too busy following up the threads of his new commercial connections and too considerate to wish to keep Jennie in a state of mental turmoil over communications which, under the present circumstances, could mean nothing.  He preferred to let matters rest for the time being ; then a little later he would write her sanely and calmly of how things were going.  He did this after the silence of a month, saying that he had been pretty well pressed by commercial affairs, that he had been in and out of the city frequently (which was the truth), and that he would probably be away from Chicago a large part of the time in the future. He inquired after Vesta and the condition of affairs generally at Sandwood.  " I may get up there one of these days," he suggested, but he really did not mean to come, and Jennie knew that he did not.

Another month passed, and then there was a second letter from him, not so long as the first one.  Jennie had written him frankly and fully, telling him just how things stood with her.  She concealed entirely her own feelings in the matter, saying that she liked the life very much, and that she was glad to be at Sandwood.  She expressed the hope that now everything was coming out for the best for him, and tried to show him that she was really glad matters had been settled. " You mustn't think of me as being unhappy," she said in one place, " for I'm not.  I am sure it ought to be just as it is, and I wouldn't be happy if it were any other way.  Lay out your life so as to give yourself the greatest happiness, Lester," she added.  " You deserve it.  Whatever you do will be just right for me.  I won't mind."  She had Mrs. Gerald in mind, and he suspected as much, but he felt that her generosity must be tinged greatly with self-sacrifice and secret unhappiness.  It was the one thing which made him hesitate about taking that final step.

The written word and the hidden thought—how they conflict !  After six months the correspondence was more or less perfunctory on his part, and at eight it had ceased temporarily.

One morning, as she was glancing over the daily paper, she saw among the society notes the following item :

The engagement of Mrs. Malcolm Gerald of 4044 Drexel Boulevard, to Lester Kane, second son of the late Archibald Kane, of Cincinnati, was formally announced at a party given by the prospective bride on Tuesday to a circle of her immediate friends. The wedding will take place in April.

The paper fell from her hands. For a few minutes she sat perfectly still, looking straight ahead of her. Could this thing be so ? she asked herself. Had it really come at last ? She had known that it must come, and yet—and yet she had always hoped that it would not. Why had she hoped ? Had not she herself sent him away ? Had not she herself suggested this very thing in a roundabout way ? It had come now. What must she do ? Stay here as a pensioner ? The idea was objectionable to her. And yet he had set aside a goodly sum to be hers absolutely. In the hands of a trust company in La Salle Street were railway certificates aggregating seventy-five thousand dollars, which yielded four thousand five hundred annually, the income being paid to her direct. Could she refuse to receive this money ? There was Vesta to be considered.

Jennie felt hurt through and through by this dénouement, and yet as she sat there she realised that it was foolish to be angry. Life was always doing this sort of a thing to her. It would go on doing so. She was sure of it. If she went out in the world and earned her own living what difference would it make to him ? What difference would it make to Mrs. Gerald ? Here she was walled in this little place, leading an obscure existence, and there was he out in the great world enjoying life in its fullest and freest sense. It was too bad. But why cry ? Why ?

Her eyes indeed were dry, but her very soul seemed to be torn in pieces within her. She rose carefully, hid the newspaper at the bottom of a trunk, and turned the key upon it.

## CHAPTER LVIII

NOW that his engagement to Mrs. Gerald was an accomplished fact, Lester found no particular difficulty in reconciling himself to the new order of things ; undoubtedly it was all for the best. He was sorry for Jennie—very sorry. So was Mrs. Gerald ; but there was a practical unguent to her grief in the thought that it was best for both Lester and the girl. He would be happier—was so now. And Jennie would eventually realise that she had done a wise and kindly thing ; she would be glad in the consciousness that she had acted so unselfishly. As for Mrs. Gerald, because of her indifference to the late Malcolm Gerald, and because she was realising the dreams of her youth in getting Lester at last— even though a little late—she was intensely happy. She could think of nothing finer than this daily life with him—the places they would go, the things they would see. Her first season in Chicago as Mrs. Lester Kane the following winter was going to be something worth remembering. And as for Japan —that was almost too good to be true.

Lester wrote to Jennie of his coming marriage to Mrs. Gerald. He said that he had no explanation to make. It wouldn't be worth anything if he did make it. He thought he ought to marry Mrs. Gerald. He thought he ought to let her (Jennie) know. He hoped she was well. He wanted her always to feel that he had her real interests at heart. He would do anything in his power to make life as pleasant and agreeable for her as possible. He hoped she would forgive him. And would she remember him affectionately to Vesta ? She ought to be sent to a finishing school.

Jennie understood the situation perfectly. She knew that Lester had been drawn to Mrs. Gerald from the time he met her at the Carlton in London. She had been angling for him. Now she had him. It was all right. She hoped he would be happy. She was glad to write and tell him so, explaining that she had seen the announcement in the papers. Lester read her letter thoughtfully ; there was more between the lines than the written words conveyed. Her fortitude was a charm to him even in this hour. In spite of all he had done and what he was now going to do, he realised that he still cared for Jennie in a way. She was a noble and a charming woman. If everything else had been all right he would not be going to marry Mrs. Gerald at all. And yet he did marry her.

The ceremony was performed on April fifteenth, at the residence of Mrs. Gerald, a Roman Catholic priest officiating. Lester was a poor example of the faith he occasionally professed. He was an agnostic, but because he had been reared in the church he felt that he might as well be married in it. Some fifty guests, intimate friends, had been invited. The ceremony went off with perfect smoothness. There were jubilant congratulations and showers of rice and confetti. While the guests were still eating and drinking Lester and Letty managed to escape by a side entrance into a closed carriage, and were off. Fifteen minutes later there was pursuit pell-mell on the part of the guests to the Chicago, Rock Island and Pacific depôt ; but by that time the happy couple were in their private car, and the arrival of the rice throwers made no difference. More champagne was opened ; then the starting of the train ended all excitement, and the newly wedded pair were at last safely off.

"Well, now you have me," said Lester, cheerfully pulling Letty down beside him into a seat, "what of it ? "

"This of it," she exclaimed, and hugged him close, kissing him fervently. In four days they were in San Francisco, and two days later on board a fast steamship bound for the land of the Mikado.

In the meanwhile Jennie was left to brood. The original announcement in the newspapers had said that he was to be married in April, and she had kept close watch for additional information. Finally she learned that the wedding would take place on April fifteenth, at the residence of the prospective bride, the hour being high noon. In spite of her feeling of resignation, Jennie followed it all hopelessly, like a child, hungry and forlorn, looking into a lighted window at Christmas time.

On the day of the wedding she waited miserably for twelve o'clock to strike ; it seemed as though she were really present— and looking on. She could see in her mind's eye the handsome residence, the carriages, the guests, the feast, the merriment, the ceremony—all. Telepathically and psychologically she received impressions of the private car and of the joyous journey they were going to take. The papers had stated that they would spend their honeymoon in Japan. Their honeymoon! Her Lester! And Mrs. Gerald was so attractive. She could see her now—the new Mrs. Kane—the only *Mrs.* Kane that ever was, lying in his arms. He had held her so once. He had loved her. Yes, he had! There was a solid lump in her throat as she thought of this. Oh, dear! She sighed to herself, and clasped her hands forcefully; but it did no good. She was just as miserable as before.

When the day was over she was actually relieved; anyway, the deed was done and nothing could change it. Vesta was sympathetically aware of what was happening, but kept silent. She too had seen the report in the newspaper. When the first and second day after had passed Jennie was much calmer mentally, for now she was face to face with the inevitable. But it was weeks before the sharp pain dulled to the old familiar ache. Then there were months before they would be back again, though, of course, that made no difference now. Only Japan seemed so far off, and somehow she had liked the thought that Lester was near her—somewhere in the city.

The spring and summer passed, and now it was early in October. One chilly day Vesta came home from school complaining of a headache. When Jennie had given her hot milk—a favourite remedy of her mother's—and had advised a cold towel for the back of her head, Vesta went to her room and lay down. The following morning she had a slight fever. This lingered while the local physician, Dr. Emory, treated her tentatively, suspecting that it might be typhoid, of which there were several cases in the village. This doctor told Jennie that Vesta was probably strong enough constitutionally to shake it off, but it might be that she would have a severe siege. Mistrusting her own skill in so delicate a situation, Jennie sent to Chicago for a trained nurse, and then began a period of watchfulness which was a combination of fear, longing, hope, and courage.

Now there could be no doubt; the disease was typhoid. Jennie hesitated about communicating with Lester, who was supposed to be in New York; the papers had said that he intended to spend the winter there. But when the doctor, after watching the case for a week, pronounced it severe, she thought she ought to write anyhow, for no one could tell what would happen. Lester had been so fond of Vesta. He would probably want to know.

The letter sent to him did not reach him, for at the time it arrived he was on his way to the West Indies. Jennie was compelled to watch alone by Vesta's sick-bed, for although sympathetic neighbours, realising the pathos of the situation were attentive, they could not supply the spiritual consolation which only those who truly love us can give. There was a period when Vesta appeared to be rallying, and both the physician and the nurse were hopeful; but afterwards she became weaker. It was said by Dr. Emory that her heart and kidneys had become affected.

There came a time when the fact had to be faced that death was imminent. The doctor's face was grave, the nurse was non-committal in her opinion. Jennie hovered about, praying the only prayer that is prayer—the fervent desire of her heart concentrated on the one issue—that Vesta should get well. The child had come so close to her during the last few years! She understood her mother. She was beginning to realise clearly what her life had been. And Jennie, through her, had grown to a broad understanding of responsibility. She knew now what it meant to be a good mother and to have children. If Lester had not objected to it, and she had been truly married, she would have been glad to have others. Again, she had always felt that she owed Vesta so much— at least a long and happy life to make up to her for the ignominy of her birth and rearing. Jennie had been so happy during the past few years to see Vesta growing into beautiful, graceful, intelligent womanhood. And now she was dying. Dr. Emory finally sent to Chicago for a physician friend of his, who came to consider the case with him. He was an old man, grave, sympathetic, understanding. He shook his head. "The treatment has been correct," he said. "Her system does not appear to be strong enough to endure the strain. Some physiques are more susceptible to this malady than others." It was agreed that if within three days a change for the better did not come the end was close at hand.

No one can conceive the strain to which Jennie's spirit was subjected by this intelligence, for it was deemed best that she should know. She hovered about white-faced—feeling intensely, but scarcely thinking. She seemed to vibrate consciously with Vesta's altering states. If there was the least improvement she felt it physically. If there was a decline her barometric temperament registered the fact.

There was a Mrs. Davis, a fine, motherly soul of fifty, stout and sympathetic, who lived four doors from Jennie, and who understood quite well how she was feeling. She had co-operated with the nurse and doctor from the start to keep Jennie's mental state as nearly normal as possible.

" Now, you just go to your room and lie down, Mrs. Kane," she would say to Jennie when she found her watching helplessly at the bedside or wandering to and fro, wondering what to do. " I'll take charge of everything. I'll do just what you would do. Lord bless you, don't you think I know ? I've been the mother of seven and lost three. Don't you think I understand ? " Jennie put her head on her big, warm shoulder one day and cried. Mrs. Davis cried with her. " I understand," she said. " There, there, you poor dear. Now you come with me." And she led her to her sleeping-room.

Jennie could not be away long. She came back after a few minutes unrested and unrefreshed. Finally one midnight, when the nurse had persuaded her that all would be well until morning anyhow, there came a hurried stirring in the sickroom. Jennie was lying down for a few minutes on her bed in the adjoining room. She heard it and arose. Mrs. Davis had come in, and she and the nurse were conferring as to Vesta's condition—standing close beside her.

Jennie understood. She came up and looked at her daughter keenly. Vesta's pale, waxen face told the story. She was breathing faintly, her eyes closed. " She's very weak," whispered the nurse. Mrs. Davis took Jennie's hand.

The moments passed, and after a time the clock in the hall struck one. Miss Murfree, the nurse, moved to the medicine-table several times, wetting a soft piece of cotton cloth with alcohol and bathing Vesta's lips. At the striking of the half-hour there was a stir of the weak body—a profound sigh. Jennie bent forward eagerly, but Mrs. Davis drew her back. The nurse came and motioned them away. Respiration had ceased.

Mrs. Davis seized Jennie firmly. "There, there, you poor dear," she whispered when she began to shake. "It can't be helped. Don't cry."

Jennie sank on her knees beside the bed and caressed Vesta's still warm hand. "Oh no, Vesta," she pleaded. "Not you! Not you!"

"There, dear, come now," soothed the voice of Mrs. Davis. "Can't you leave it all in God's hands? Can't you believe that everything is for the best?"

Jennie felt as if the earth had fallen. All ties were broken. There was no light anywhere in the immense darkness of her existence.

## CHAPTER LIX

THIS added blow from inconsiderate fortune was quite enough to throw Jennie back into that state of hyper-melancholia from which she had been drawn with difficulty during the few years of comfort and affection which she had enjoyed with Lester in Hyde Park. It was really weeks before she could realise that Vesta was gone. The emaciated figure which she saw for a day or two after the end did not seem like Vesta. Where was the joy and lightness, the quickness of motion, the subtle radiance of health ? All gone. Only this pale, lily-hued shell—and silence. Jennie had no tears to shed ; only a deep, insistent pain to feel. If only some counsellor of eternal wisdom could have whispered to her that obvious and convincing truth—there are no dead.

Miss Murfree, Dr. Emory, Mrs. Davis, and some others among the neighbours were most sympathetic and considerate. Mrs. Davis sent a telegram to Lester saying that Vesta was dead, but, being absent, there was no response. The house was looked after with scrupulous care by others, for Jennie was incapable of attending to it herself. She walked about looking at things which Vesta had owned or liked—things which Lester or she had given her—sighing over the fact that Vesta would not need or use them any more. She gave instructions that the body should be taken to Chicago and buried in the Cemetery of the Redeemer, for Lester, at the time of Gerhardt's death, had purchased a small plot of ground there. She also expressed her wish that the minister of the little Lutheran church in Cottage Grove Avenue, where Gerhardt had attended, should be requested to say a few words at the grave. There were the usual preliminary services at the house. The local Methodist minister read a portion of the first epistle of Paul to the Thessalonians, and a body of Vesta's class-mates sang " Nearer My God to Thee." There were flowers, a white coffin, a world of sympathetic expressions, and then Vesta was taken away. The coffin was properly incased for transportation, put on the train, and finally delivered at the Lutheran cemetery in Chicago.

Jennie moved as one in a dream. She was dazed, almost to the point of insensibility. Five of her neighbourhood friends, at the solicitation of Mrs. Davis, were kind enough to accompany her. At the grave-side when the body was finally lowered, she looked at it, one might have thought indifferently, for she was numb from suffering. She returned to Sandwood after it was all over, saying that she would not stay long. She wanted to come back to Chicago, where she could be near Vesta and Gerhardt.

After the funeral Jennie tried to think of her future. She fixed her mind on the need of doing something, even though she did not need to. She thought that she might like to try nursing, and could start at once to obtain the training which was required. She also thought of William. He was unmarried, and perhaps he might be willing to come and live with her. Only she did not know where he was, and Bass was also in ignorance of his whereabouts. She finally concluded that she would try to get work in a store. Her disposition was against idleness. She could not live alone here, and she could not have her neighbours sympathetically worrying over what was to become of her. Miserable as she was, she would be less miserable stopping in a hotel in Chicago, and looking for something to do, or living in a cottage somewhere near the Cemetery of the Redeemer. It also occurred to her that she might adopt a homeless child. There were a number of orphan asylums in the city.

Some three weeks after Vesta's death Lester returned to Chicago with his wife, and discovered the first letter, the telegram, and an additional note telling him that Vesta was dead. He was truly grieved, for his affection for the girl had been real. He was very sorry for Jennie, and he told his wife that he would have to go out and see her. He was wondering what she would do. She could not live alone. Perhaps he could suggest something which would help her. He took the train to Sandwood, but Jennie had gone to the Hotel Tremont in Chicago. He went there, but Jennie had gone to her daughter's grave ; later he called again and found her in. When the boy presented his card she suffered an upwelling of feeling—a wave that was more intense than that with which she had received him in the olden days, for now her need of him was greater.

Lester, in spite of the glamour of his new affection and the restoration of his wealth, power, and dignities, had had time to think deeply of what he had done. His original feeling of doubt and dissatisfaction with himself had never wholly quieted. It did not ease him any to know that he had left Jennie comfortably fixed, for it was always so plain to him that money was not the point at issue with her. Affection was what she craved. Without it she was like a rudderless boat on an endless sea, and he knew it. She needed him, and he was ashamed to think that his charity had not outweighed his sense of self-preservation and his desire for material advantage. To-day as the elevator carried him up to her room he was really sorry, though he knew now that no act of his could make things right. He had been to blame from the very beginning, first for taking her, then for failing to stick by a bad bargain. Well, it could not be helped now. The best thing he could do was to be fair, to counsel with her, to give her the best of his sympathy and advice.

" Hello, Jennie," he said familiarly as she opened the door to him in her hotel room, his glance taking in the ravages which death and suffering had wrought. She was thinner, her face quite drawn and colourless, her eyes larger by contrast. " I'm awfully sorry about Vesta," he said a little awkwardly. " I never dreamed anything like that could happen."

It was the first word of comfort which had meant anything to her since Vesta died—since Lester had left her, in fact. It touched her that he had come to sympathise; for the moment she could not speak. Tears welled over her eyelids and down upon her cheeks.

" Don't cry, Jennie," he said, putting his arm around her and holding her head to his shoulder. " I'm sorry. I've been sorry for a good many things that can't be helped now. I'm intensely sorry for this. Where did you bury her ? "

" Beside papa," she said, sobbing.

" Too bad," he murmured, and held her in silence. She finally gained control of herself sufficiently to step away from him ; then wiping her eyes with her handkerchief, she asked him to sit down.

" I'm so sorry," he went on, " that this should have happened while I was away. I would have been with you if I had been here. I suppose you won't want to live out at Sandwood now ? "

" I can't, Lester," she replied. " I couldn't stand it."

" Where are you thinking of going ? "

" Oh, I don't know yet. I didn't want to be a bother to those people out there. I thought I'd get a little house somewhere and adopt a baby maybe, or get something to do. I don't like to be alone."

" That isn't a bad idea," he said, " that of adopting a baby. It would be a lot of company for you. You know how to go about getting one ? "

" You just ask at one of these asylums, don't you ? "

" I think there's something more than that," he replied thoughtfully. " There are some formalities—I don't know what they are. They try to keep control of the child in some way. You had better consult with Watson and get him to help you. Pick out your baby, and then let him do the rest. I'll speak to him about it."

Lester saw that she needed companionship badly. " Where is your brother George ? " he asked.

" He's in Rochester, but he couldn't come. Bass said he was married," she added.

" There isn't any other member of the family you could persuade to come and live with you ? "

" I might get William, but I don't know where he is."

" Why not try that new section west of Jackson Park," he suggested, " if you want a house here in Chicago ? I see some nice cottages out that way. You needn't buy. Just rent until you see how well you're satisfied."

Jennie thought this good advice because it came from Lester. It was good of him to take this much interest in her affairs. She wasn't entirely separated from him after all. He cared a little. She asked him how his wife was, whether he had had a pleasant trip, whether he was going to stay in Chicago. All the while he was thinking that he had treated her badly. He went to the window and looked down into Dearborn Street, the world of traffic below holding his attention. The great mass of trucks and vehicles, the counter streams of hurrying pedestrians, seemed like a puzzle. So shadows march

in a dream. It was growing dusk, and lights were springing up here and there.

"I want to tell you something, Jennie," said Lester, finally
rousing himself from his fit of abstraction. "I may seem
peculiar to you, after all that has happened, but I still care
for you—in my way. I've thought of you right along since
I left. I thought it good business to leave you—the way things
were. I thought I liked Letty well enough to marry her.
From one point of view it still seems best, but I'm not so much
happier. I was just as happy with you as I ever will be. It
isn't myself that's important in this transaction apparently;
the individual doesn't count much in the situation. I don't
know whether you see what I'm driving at, but all of us are
more or less pawns. We're moved about like chessmen by
circumstances over which we have no control."

"I understand, Lester," she answered. "I'm not complaining. I know it's for the best."

"After all, life is more or less of a farce," he went on a little
bitterly. "It's a silly show. The best we can do is to hold
our personality intact. It doesn't appear that integrity has
much to do with it."

Jennie did not quite grasp what he was talking about, but
she knew it meant that he was not entirely satisfied with himself
and was sorry for her.

"Don't worry over me, Lester," she consoled. "I'm all
right; I'll get along. It did seem terrible to me for a while—
getting used to being alone. I'll be all right now. I'll get
along."

"I want you to feel that my attitude hasn't changed," he
continued eagerly. "I'm interested in what concerns you.
Mrs.—Letty understands that. She knows just how I feel.
When you get settled I'll come in and see how you're fixed.
I'll come around here again in a few days. You understand
how I feel, don't you?"

"Yes, I do," she said.

He took her hand, turning it sympathetically in his own.
"Don't worry," he said. "I don't want you to do that.
I'll do the best I can. You're still Jennie to me, if you don't
mind. I'm pretty bad, but I'm not all bad."

"It's all right, Lester. I wanted you to do as you did.
It's for the best. You probably are happy since——"

"Now, Jennie," he interrupted; then he pressed affectionately her hand, her arm, her shoulder. "Want to kiss me for old times' sake?" he smiled.

She put her hands over his shoulders, looked long into his eyes, then kissed him. When their lips met she trembled. Lester also felt unsteady. Jennie saw his agitation, and tried hard to speak.

"You'd better go now," she said firmly. "It's getting dark."

He went away, and yet he knew that he wanted above all things to remain; she was still the one woman in the world for him. And Jennie felt comforted even though the separation still existed in all its finality. She did not endeavour to explain or adjust the moral and ethical entanglements of the situation. She was not, like so many, endeavouring to put the ocean into a tea-cup, or to tie up the shifting universe in a mess of strings called law. Lester still cared for her a little. He cared for Letty too. That was all right. She had hoped once that he might want her only. Since he did not, was his affection worth nothing? She could not think, she could not feel that. And neither could he.

## CHAPTER LX

THE drift of events for a period of five years carried Lester and Jennie still farther apart; they settled naturally into their respective spheres, without the renewal of the old time relationship which their several meetings at the Tremont at first seemed to foreshadow. Lester was in the thick of social and commercial affairs; he walked in paths to which Jennie's retiring soul had never aspired. Jennie's own existence was quiet and uneventful. There was a simple cottage in a very respectable but not showy neighbourhood near Jackson Park, on the South Side, where she lived in retirement with a little foster-child—a chestnut-haired girl taken from the Western Home for the Friendless—as her sole companion. Here she was known as Mrs. J. G. Stover, for she had deemed it best to abandon the name of Kane. Mr. and Mrs. Lester Kane when resident in Chicago were the occupants of a handsome mansion on the Lake Shore Drive, where parties, balls, receptions, dinners were given in rapid and at times almost pyrotechnic succession.

Lester, however, had become in his way a lover of a peaceful and well-entertained existence. He had cut from his list of acquaintances and associates a number of people who had been a little doubtful or overfamiliar or indifferent or talkative during a certain period which to him was a memory merely. He was a director, and in several cases the chairman of a board of directors, in nine of the most important financial and commercial organisations of the West—The United Traction Company of Cincinnati, The Western Crucible Company, The United Carriage Company, The Second National Bank of Chicago, the First National Bank of Cincinnati, and several others of equal importance. He was never a personal factor in the affairs of The United Carriage Company, preferring to be represented by counsel—Mr. Dwight L. Watson, but he took a keen interest in its affairs. He had not seen his brother Robert to speak to him in seven years. He had not seen Imogene, who lived in Chicago, in three. Louise, Amy, their husbands, and some of their closest acquaintances were practically strangers. The firm of Knight, Keatley & O'Brien had nothing whatever to do with his affairs.

The truth was that Lester, in addition to becoming a little phlegmatic, was becoming decidedly critical in his outlook on life. He could not make out what it was all about. In distant ages a queer thing had come to pass. There had started on its way in the form of evolution a minute cellular organism which had apparently reproduced itself by division, had early learned to combine itself with others, to organise itself into bodies, strange forms of fish, animals, and birds, and had finally learned to organise itself into man. Man, on his part, composed as he was of self-organising cells, was pushing himself forward into comfort and different aspects of existence by means of union and organisation with other men. Why ? Heaven only knew. Here he was endowed with a peculiar brain and a certain amount of talent, and he had inherited a certain amount of wealth which he now scarcely believed he deserved, only luck had favoured him. But he could not see that any one else might be said to deserve this wealth any more than himself, seeing that his use of it was as conservative and constructive and practical as the next one's. He might have been born poor, in which case he would have been as well satisfied as the next one—not more so. Why should he complain, why worry, why speculate ?—the world was going steadily forward of its own volition, whether he would or no. Truly it was. And was there any need for him to disturb himself about it ? There was not. He fancied at times that it might as well never have been started at all. " The one divine, far-off event " of the poet did not appeal to him as having any basis in fact. Mrs. Lester Kane was of very much the same opinion.

Jennie, living on the South Side with her adopted child, Rose Perpetua, was of no fixed conclusion as to the meaning of life. She had not the incisive reasoning capacity of either Mr. or Mrs. Lester Kane. She had seen a great deal, suffered a great deal, and had read some in a desultory way. Her mind had never grasped the nature and character of specialised knowledge. History, physics, chemistry, botany, geology, and sociology were not fixed departments in her brain as they were in Lester's and Letty's. Instead there was the feeling that the world moved in some strange, unstable way. Apparently no one knew clearly what it was all about. People were born and died. Some believed that the world had been made six thousand years before ; some that it was millions of years old. Was it all blind chance, or was there some guiding intelligence —a God ? Almost in spite of herself she felt there must be something—a higher power which produced all the beautiful things—the flowers, the stars, the trees, the grass. Nature was so beautiful ! If at times life seemed cruel, yet this beauty still persisted. The thought comforted her ; she fed upon it in her hours of secret loneliness.

It has been said that Jennie was naturally of an industrious turn. She liked to be employed, though she thought constantly as she worked. She was of matronly proportions in these days —not disagreeably large, but full-bodied, shapely, and smooth faced, in spite of her cares. Her eyes were grey and appealing. Her hair was still of a rich brown, but there were traces of grey in it. Her neighbours spoke of her as sweet-tempered, kindly, and hospitable. They knew nothing of her history, except that she had formerly resided in Sandwood, and before that in Cleveland. She was very reticent as to her past.

Jennie had fancied, because of her natural aptitude for taking care of sick people, that she might get to be a trained nurse. But she was obliged to abandon that idea, for she found that only young people were wanted. She also thought that some charitable organisation might employ her, but she did not understand the new theory of charity which was then coming into general acceptance and practice—namely, only to help others to help themselves. She believed in giving, and was not inclined to look too closely into the credentials of those who asked for help ; consequently her timid inquiry at one relief agency after another met with indifference, if not unqualified rebuke. She finally decided to adopt another child for Rose Perpetua's sake ; she succeeded in securing a boy, four years old, who was known as Henry—Henry Stover. Her support was assured, for her income was paid to her through a trust company. She had no desire for speculation or for the devious ways of trade. The care of flowers, the nature of children, the ordering of a home were more in her province.

One of the interesting things in connection with this separation once it had been firmly established related to Robert and Lester, for these two since the reading of the will a number of years before had never met. Robert had thought of his brother often. He had followed his success, since he had left Jennie, with interest. He read of his marriage to Mrs. Gerald with pleasure ; he had always considered her an ideal companion for his brother. He knew by many signs and tokens that his brother, since the unfortunate termination of their father's attitude and his own peculiar movements to gain control of the Kane Company, did not like him. Still they had never been so far apart mentally—certainly not in commercial judgment. Lester was prosperous now. He could afford to be generous. He could afford to make up. And after all, he had done his best to aid his brother to come to his senses—and with the best intentions. There were mutual interests they could share financially if they were friends. He wondered from time to time if Lester would not be friendly with him.

Time passed, and then once, when he was in Chicago, he made the friends with whom he was driving purposely turn into the North Shore in order to see the splendid mansion which the Kanes occupied. He knew its location from hearsay and description.

When he saw it a touch of the old Kane home atmosphere came back to him. Lester in revising the property after purchase had had a conservatory built on one side not unlike the one at home in Cincinnati. That same night he sat down and wrote Lester asking if he would not like to dine with him at the Union Club. He was only in town for a day or two, and he would like to see him again. There was some feeling, he knew, but there was a proposition he would like to talk to him about. Would he come, say, on Thursday ?

On the receipt of this letter Lester frowned and fell into a brown study. He had never really been healed of the wound that his father had given him. He had never been comfortable in his mind since Robert had deserted him so summarily. He realised now that the stakes his brother had been playing for were big. But, after all, he had been his brother, and if he had been in Robert's place at the time, he would not have done as he had done ; at least he hoped not. Now Robert wanted to see him.

He thought once of not answering at all. Then he thought he would write and say no. But a curious desire to see Robert again, to hear what he had to say, to listen to the proposition he had to offer, came over him ; he decided to write yes. It could do no harm. He knew it could do no good. They might agree to let bygones be bygones, but the damage had been done. Could a broken bowl be mended and called whole ? It might be *called* whole, but what of it ? Was it not broken and mended ? He wrote and intimated that he would come.

On the Thursday in question Robert called up from the Auditorium to remind him of the engagement. Lester listened curiously to the sound of his voice. " All right," he said, " I'll be with you." At noon he went downtown, and there, within the exclusive precincts of the Union Club, the two brothers met and looked at each other again. Robert was thinner than when Lester had seen him last, and a little greyer. His eyes were bright and steely, but there were crow's-feet on either side. His manner was quick, keen, dynamic. Lester was noticeably of another type—solid, brusque, and indifferent. Men spoke of Lester these days as a little hard. Robert's keen blue eyes did not disturb him in the least—did not affect him in any way. He saw his brother just as he was, for he had the larger philosophic and inter-pretative insight ; but Robert could not place Lester exactly. He could not fathom just what had happened to him in these years. Lester was stouter, not grey, for some reason, but sandy and ruddy, looking like a man who was fairly well satisfied to take life as he found it. Lester looked at his brother with a keen, steady eye. The latter shifted a little, for he was restless. He could see that there was no loss of that mental force and courage which had always been predominant characteristics in Lester's make-up.

" I thought I'd like to see you again, Lester," Robert remarked, after they had clasped hands in the customary grip. " It's been a long time now—nearly eight years, hasn't it ? "

" About that," replied Lester. " How are things with you ? "

" Oh, about the same. You've been fairly well, I see."

" Never sick," said Lester. " A little cold now and then. I don't often go to bed with anything. How's your wife ? "

" Oh, Margaret's fine."

" And the children ? "

" We don't see much of Ralph and Berenice since they married, but the others are around more or less. I suppose your wife is all right," he said hesitatingly. It was difficult ground for Robert.

Lester eyed him without a change of expression.

" Yes," he replied. " She enjoys pretty fair health. She's quite well at present."

They drifted mentally for a few moments, while Lester inquired after the business, and Amy, Louise, and Imogene. He admitted frankly that he neither saw nor heard from them nowadays. Robert told him what he could.

" The thing that I was thinking of in connection with you, Lester," said Robert finally, " is this matter of the Western Crucible Steel Company. You haven't been sitting there as a director in person I notice, but your attorney, Watson, has been acting for you. Clever man, that. The management isn't right—we all know that. We need a practical steel man at the head of it, if the thing is ever going to pay properly. I have voted my stock with yours right along because the propositions made by Watson have been right. He agrees with me that things ought to be changed. Now I have a chance to buy seventy shares held by Rossiter's widow. That with yours and mine would give us control of the company. I would like to have you take them, though it doesn't make a bit of difference so long as it's in the family. You can put any one you please in for president, and we'll make the thing come out right."

Lester smiled. It was a pleasant proposition. Watson had told him that Robert's interests were co-operating with him. Lester had long suspected that Robert would like to make up. This was the olive branch—the control of a property worth in the neighbourhood of a million and a half.

" That's very nice of you," said Lester solemnly. " It's a rather liberal thing to do. What makes you want to do it now ? "

" Well, to tell you the honest truth, Lester," replied Robert, " I never did feel right about that will business. I never did feel right about that secretary-treasurership and some other things that have happened. I don't want to rake up the past —you smile at that—but I can't help telling you how I feel.

I've been pretty ambitious in the past. I was pretty ambitious just about the time that father died to get this United Carriage scheme under way, and I was afraid you might not like it. I have thought since that I ought not to have done it, but I did. I suppose you're not anxious to hear any more about that old affair. This other thing though——"

"Might be handed out as a sort of compensation," put in Lester quietly.

"Not exactly that, Lester—though it may have something of that in it. I know these things don't matter very much to you now. I know that the time to do things was years ago—not now. Still I thought sincerely that you might be interested in this proposition. It might lead to other things. Frankly, I thought it might patch up matters between us. We're brothers after all."

"Yes," said Lester, "we're brothers."

He was thinking as he said this of the irony of the situation. How much had this sense of brotherhood been worth in the past ? Robert had practically forced him into his present relationship, and while Jennie had been really the only one to suffer, he could not help feeling angry. It was true that Robert had not cut him out of his one-fourth of his father's estate, but certainly he had not helped him to get it, and now Robert was thinking that this offer of his might mend things. It hurt him—Lester—a little. It irritated him. Life was strange.

"I can't see it, Robert," he said finally and determinedly. "I can appreciate the motive that prompts you to make this offer. But I can't see the wisdom of my taking it. Your opportunity is your opportunity. I don't want it. We can make all the changes you suggest if you take the stock. I'm rich enough anyhow. Bygones are bygones. I'm perfectly willing to talk with you from time to time. That's all you want. This other thing is simply a sop, with which to plaster an old wound. You want my friendship and so far as I'm concerned you have that. I don't hold any grudge against you. I won't."

Robert looked at him fixedly. He half smiled. He admired Lester in spite of all that he had done to him—in spite of all that Lester was doing to him now.

"I don't know but what you're right, Lester," he admitted

finally. " I didn't make this offer in any petty spirit though. I wanted to patch up this matter of feeling between us. I won't say anything more about it. You're not coming down to Cincinnati soon, are you ? "

" I don't expect to," replied Lester.

" If you do I'd like to have you come and stay with us. Bring your wife. We could talk over old times."

Lester smiled an enigmatic smile.

" I'll be glad to," he said, without emotion. But he remembered that in the days of Jennie it was different. They would never have receded from their position regarding her. " Well," he thought, " perhaps I can't blame them. Let it go."

They talked on about other things. Finally Lester remembered an appointment. " I'll have to leave you soon," he said, looking at his watch.

" I ought to go, too," said Robert. They rose. " Well, anyhow," he added, as they walked toward the cloakroom, " we won't be absolute strangers in the future, will we ? "

" Certainly not," said Lester. " I'll see you from time to time." They shook hands and separated amicably. There was a sense of unsatisfied obligation and some remorse in Robert's mind as he saw his brother walking briskly away. Lester was an able man. Why was it that there was so much feeling between them—had been even before Jennie had appeared ? Then he remembered his old thoughts about " snaky deeds." That was what his brother lacked, and that only. He was not crafty ; not darkly cruel, hence. " What a world ! " he thought.

On his part Lester went away feeling a slight sense of opposition to, but also of sympathy for, his brother. He was not so terribly bad—not different from other men. Why criticise ? What would he have done if he had been in Robert's place ? Robert was getting along. So was he. He could see now how it all came about—why he had been made the victim, why his brother had been made the keeper of the great fortune. " It's the way the world runs," he thought, " What difference does it make ? I have enough to live on. Why not let it go at that ? "

## CHAPTER LXI

THE days of man under the old dispensation, or, rather, according to that supposedly biblical formula, which persists, are threescore years and ten. It is so ingrained in the race-consciousness by mouth-to-mouth utterance that it seems the profoundest of truths. As a matter of fact, man, even under his mortal illusion, is organically built to live five times the period of his maturity, and would do so if he but knew that it is spirit which endures, that age is an illusion, and that there is no death. Yet the race-thought, gained from what dream of materialism we know not, persists, and the death of man under the mathematical formula so fearfully accepted is daily registered.

Lester was one of those who believed in this formula. He was nearing sixty. He thought he had, say, twenty years more at the utmost to live—perhaps not so long. Well, he had lived comfortably. He felt that he could not complain. If death was coming, let it come. He was ready at any time. No complaint or resistance would issue from him. Life, in most of its aspects, was a silly show anyhow.

He admitted that it was mostly illusion—easily proved to be so. That it might all be one he sometimes suspected. It was very much like a dream in its composition truly— sometimes like a very bad dream. All he had to sustain him in his acceptance of its reality from hour to hour and day to day was apparent contact with this material proposition and that—people, meetings of boards of directors, individuals and organisations planning to do this and that, his wife's social functions. Letty loved him as a fine, grizzled example of a philosopher. She admired, as Jennie had, his solid, determined, phlegmatic attitude in the face of troubled circumstance. All the winds of fortune or misfortune could not apparently excite or disturb Lester. He refused to be frightened. He refused to budge from his beliefs and feelings, and usually had to be pushed away from them, still believing, if he were gotten away at all. He refused to do anything

save as he always said, " Look the facts in the face " and fight.
He could be made to fight easily enough if imposed upon,
but only in a stubborn, resisting way. His plan was to resist
every effort to coerce him to the last ditch. If he had to let
go in the end he would when compelled, but his views as to
the value of not letting go were quite the same even when
he had let go under compulsion.

His views of living were still decidedly material, grounded
in creature comforts, and he had always insisted upon having
the best of everything. If the furnishings of his home became
the least dingy he was for having them torn out and sold and
the house done over. If he travelled, money must go ahead
of him and smooth the way. He did not want argument,
useless talk, or silly palaver as he called it. Every one must
discuss interesting topics with him or not talk at all. Letty
understood him thoroughly. She would chuck him under the
chin mornings, or shake his solid head between her hands,
telling him he was a brute, but a nice kind of brute. " Yes,
yes," he would growl. " I know. I'm an animal, I suppose.
You're a seraphic suggestion of attenuated thought."

" No ; you hush," she would reply, for at times he could
cut like a knife without really meaning to be unkind. Then
he would pet her a little, for, in spite of her vigorous conception
of life, he realised that she was more or less dependent upon
him. It was always so plain to her that he could get along without her. For reasons of kindliness he was trying to conceal
this, to pretend the necessity of her presence, but it was so
obvious that he really could dispense with her easily enough.
Now Letty did depend upon Lester. It was something, in
so shifty and uncertain a world, to be near so fixed and determined a quantity as this bear-man. It was like being close
to a warmly glowing lamp in the dark or a bright burning
fire in the cold. Lester was not afraid of anything. He felt
that he knew how to live and to die.

It was natural that a temperament of this kind should have
its solid, material manifestation at every point. Having his
financial affairs well in hand, most of his holding being shares
of big companies, where boards of solemn directors merely
approved the strenuous efforts of ambitious executives to
" make good," he had leisure for living. He and Letty were
fond of visiting the various American and European watering-

places. He gambled a little, for he found that there was considerable diversion in risking interesting sums on the spin of a wheel or the fortuitous roll of a ball; and he took more and more to drinking, not in the sense that a drunkard takes to it, but as a high liver, socially, and with all his friends. He was inclined to drink the rich drinks when he did not take straight whiskey—champagne, sparkling Burgundy, the expensive and effervescent white wines. When he drank he could drink a great deal, and he ate in proportion. Nothing must be served but the best—soup, fish, entrée, roast, game, dessert—everything that made up a showy dinner—and he had long since determined that only a high-priced chef was worth while. They had found an old *cordon bleu*, Louis Berdot, who had served in the house of one of the great dry goods princes, and this man he engaged. He cost Lester a hundred dollars a week, but his reply to any question was that he only had one life to live.

The trouble with this attitude was that it adjusted nothing, improved nothing, left everything to drift on toward an indefinite end. If Lester had married Jennie and accepted the comparatively meagre income of ten thousand a year he would have maintained the same attitude to the end. It would have led him to a stolid indifference to the social world of which now necessarily he was a part. He would have drifted on with a few mentally compatible cronies who would have accepted him for what he was—a good fellow—and Jennie in the end would not have been so much better off than she was now.

One of the changes which was interesting was that the Kanes transferred their residence to New York. Mrs. Kane had become very intimate with a group of clever women in the Eastern four hundred, or nine hundred, and had been advised and urged to transfer the scene of her activities to New York. She finally did so, leasing a house in Seventy-eighth Street, near Madison Avenue. She installed a novelty for her, a complete staff of liveried servants, after the English fashion, and had the rooms of her house done in correlative periods. Lester smiled at her vanity and love of show.

" You talk about your democracy," he grunted one day. " You have as much democracy as I have religion, and that's none at all."

" Why, how you talk ! " she denied. " I am democratic.

We all run in classes. You do. I'm merely accepting the logic of the situation."

"The logic of your grandmother! Do you call a butler and doorman in red velvet a part of the necessity of the occasion ? "

"I certainly do," she replied. "Maybe not the necessity exactly, but the spirit surely. Why should you quarrel ? You're the first one to insist on perfection—to quarrel if there is any flaw in the order of things."

"You never heard me quarrel."

"Oh, I don't mean that literally. But you demand perfection—the exact spirit of the occasion, and you know it."

"Maybe I do, but what has that to do with your democracy ? "

"I am democratic. I insist on it. I'm as democratic in spirit as any woman. Only I see things as they are, and conform as much as possible for comfort's sake, and so do you. Don't you throw rocks at my glass house, Mister Master. Yours is so transparent I can see every move you make inside."

"I'm democratic and you're not," he teased ; but he approved thoroughly of everything she did. She was, he sometimes fancied, a better executive in her world than he was in his.

Drifting in this fashion, wining, dining, drinking the waters of this curative spring and that, travelling in luxurious ease and taking no physical exercise, finally altered his body from a vigorous, quick-moving, well-balanced organism into one where plethora of substance was clogging every essential function. His liver, kidneys, spleen, pancreas—every organ, in fact—had been overtaxed for some time to keep up the process of digestion and elimination. In the past seven years he had become uncomfortably heavy. His kidneys were weak, and so were the arteries of his brain. By dieting, proper exercise, the right mental attitude, he might have lived to be eighty or ninety. As a matter of fact, he was allowing himself to drift into a physical state in which even a slight malady might prove dangerous. The result was inevitable, and it came.

It so happened that he and Letty had gone to the North Cape on a cruise with a party of friends. Lester, in order to attend to some important business, decided to return to Chicago late in November ; he arranged to have his wife meet him in New York just before the Christmas holidays. He

wrote Watson to expect him, and engaged rooms at the
Auditorium, for he had sold the Chicago residence some two
years before and was now living permanently in New York.

One late November day, after having attended to a number
of details and cleared up his affairs very materially, Lester was
seized with what the doctor who was called to attend him
described as a cold in the intestines—a disturbance usually
symptomatic of some other weakness, either of the blood or of
some organ. He suffered great pain, and the usual remedies
in that case were applied. There were bandages of red flannel
with a mustard dressing, and specifics were also administered.
He experienced some relief, but he was troubled with a sense
of impending disaster. He had Watson cable his wife—there
was nothing serious about it, but he was ill. A trained nurse
was in attendance and his valet stood guard at the door to
prevent annoyance of any kind. It was plain that Letty could
not reach Chicago under three weeks. He had the feeling
that he would not see her again.

Curiously enough, not only because he was in Chicago,
but because he had never been spiritually separated from
Jennie, he was thinking about her constantly at this time.
He had intended to go out and see her just as soon as he was
through with his business engagements and before he left the
city. He had asked Watson how she was getting along,
and had been informed that everything was well with her.
She was living quietly and looking in good health, so Watson
said. Lester wished he could see her.

This thought grew as the days passed and he grew no better.
He was suffering from time to time with severe attacks of
griping pains that seemed to tie his viscera into knots and left
him very weak. Several times the physician administered
cocaine with a needle in order to relieve him of useless pain.

After one of the severe attacks he called Watson to his side,
told him to send the nurse away, and then said : " Watson,
I'd like to have you do me a favour. Ask Mrs. Stover if she
won't come here to see me. You'd better go and get her.
Just send the nurse and Kozo (the valet) away for the afternoon,
or while she's here. If she comes at any other time I'd like
to have her admitted."

Watson understood. He liked this expression of sentiment.
He was sorry for Jennie. He was sorry for Lester. He

wondered what the world would think if it could know of this bit of romance in connection with so prominent a man. Lester was decent. He had made Watson prosperous. The latter was only too glad to serve him in any way.

He called a carriage and rode out to Jennie's residence. He found her watering some plants ; her face expressed her surprise at his unusual presence.

" I come on a rather troublesome errand, Mrs. Stover," he said, using her assumed name. " Your—that is, Mr. Kane is quite sick at the Auditorium. His wife is in Europe, and he wanted to know if I wouldn't come out here and ask you to come and see him. He wanted me to bring you, if possible. Could you come with me now ? "

" Why yes," said Jennie, her face a study. The children were in school. An old Swedish housekeeper was in the kitchen. She could go as well as not. But there was coming back to her in detail a dream she had had several nights before. It had seemed to her that she was out on a dark, mystic body of water over which was hanging something like a fog, or a pall of smoke. She heard the water ripple, or stir faintly, and then out of the surrounding darkness a boat appeared. It was a little boat, oarless, or not visibly propelled, and in it were her mother, and Vesta, and some one whom she could not make out. Her mother's face was pale and sad, very much as she had often seen it in life. She looked at Jennie solemnly, sympathetically, and then suddenly Jennie realised that the third occupant of the boat was Lester. He looked at her gloomily—an expression she had never seen on his face before— and then her mother remarked, " Well, we must go now." The boat began to move, a great sense of loss came over her, and she cried, " Oh, don't leave me, mamma ! "

But her mother only looked at her out of deep, sad, still eyes, and the boat was gone.

She woke with a start, half fancying that Lester was beside her. She stretched out her hand to touch his arm ; then she drew herself up in the dark and rubbed her eyes, realising that she was alone. A great sense of depression remained with her, and for two days it haunted her. Then, when it seemed as if it were nothing, Mr. Watson appeared with his ominous message.

She went to dress, and reappeared, looking as troubled as

were her thoughts. She was very pleasing in her appearance yet, a sweet, kindly woman, well dressed and shapely. She had never been separated mentally from Lester, just as he had never grown entirely away from her. She was always with him in thought, just as in the years when they were together. Her fondest memories were of the days when he first courted her in Cleveland—the days when he had carried her off, much as the cave-man seized his mate—by force. Now she longed to do what she could for him. For this call was as much a testimony as a shock. He loved her—he loved her, after all.

The carriage rolled briskly through the long streets into the smoky downtown district. It arrived at the Auditorium, and Jennie was escorted to Lester's room. Watson had been considerate. He had talked little, leaving her to her thoughts. In this great hotel she felt diffident after so long a period of complete retirement. As she entered the room she looked at Lester with large, grey, sympathetic eyes. He was lying propped up on two pillows, his solid head with its growth of once dark brown hair slightly greyed. He looked at her curiously out of his wise old eyes, a light of sympathy and affection shining in them—weary as they were. Jennie was greatly distressed. His pale face, slightly drawn from suffering, cut her like a knife. She took his hand, which was outside the coverlet, and pressed it. She leaned over and kissed his lips.

" I'm so sorry, Lester," she murmured. " I'm so sorry. You're not very sick though, are you ? You must get well, Lester—and soon ! " She patted his hand gently.

" Yes, Jennie, but I'm pretty bad," he said. " I don't feel right about this business. I don't seem able to shake it off. But tell me, how have you been ? "

" Oh, just the same, dear," she replied. " I'm all right. You mustn't talk like that, though. You're going to be all right very soon now."

He smiled grimly. " Do you think so ? " He shook his head, for he thought differently. " Sit down, dear," he went on, " I'm not worrying about that. I want to talk to you again. I want you near me." He sighed and shut his eyes for a minute.

She drew up a chair close beside the bed, her face toward his, and took his hand. It seemed such a beautiful thing that he should send for her. Her eyes showed the mingled sympathy, affection, and gratitude of her heart. At the same time fear gripped her ; how ill he looked !

" I can't tell what may happen," he went on. " Letty is in Europe. I've wanted to see you again for some time. I was coming out this trip. We are living in New York, you know. You're a little stouter, Jennie."

" Yes, I'm getting old, Lester," she smiled.

" Oh, that doesn't make any difference," he replied, looking at her fixedly. " Age doesn't count. We are all in that boat. It's how we feel about life."

He stopped and stared at the ceiling. A slight twinge of pain reminded him of the vigorous seizures he had been through. He couldn't stand many more paroxysms like the last one.

" I couldn't go, Jennie, without seeing you again," he observed, when the slight twinge ceased and he was free to think again. " I've always wanted to say to you, Jennie," he went on, " that I haven't been satisfied with the way we parted. It wasn't the right thing, after all. I haven't been any happier. I'm sorry. I wish now, for my own peace of mind, that I hadn't done it."

" Don't say that, Lester," she demurred, going over in her mind all that had been between them. This was such a testimony to their real union—their real spiritual compatibility. " It's all right. It doesn't make any difference. You've been very good to me. I wouldn't have been satisfied to have you lose your fortune. It couldn't be that way. I've been a lot better satisfied as it is. It's been hard, but, dear, everything is hard at times." She paused.

" No," he said. " It wasn't right. The thing wasn't worked out right from the start ; but that wasn't your fault. I'm sorry. I wanted to tell you that. I'm glad I'm here to do it."

" Don't talk that way, Lester—please don't," she pleaded. " It's all right. You needn't be sorry. There's nothing to be sorry for. You have always been so good to me. Why, when I think——" she stopped, for it was hard for her to speak. She was choking with affection and sympathy. She pressed his hands. She was recalling the house he took for her family in Cleveland, his generous treatment of Gerhardt, all the long ago tokens of love and kindness.

"Well, I've told you now, and I feel better. You're a good woman, Jennie, and you're kind to come to me this way." I loved you. I love you now. I want to tell you that. It seems strange, but you're the only woman I ever did love truly. We should never have parted.

Jennie caught her breath. It was the one thing she had waited for all these years—this testimony. It was the one thing that could make everything right—this confession of spiritual if not material union. Now she could live happily. Now die so. " Oh, Lester," she exclaimed with a sob, and pressed his hand. He returned the pressure. There was a little silence. Then he spoke again.

" How are the two orphans ? " he asked.

" Oh, they're lovely," she answered, entering upon a detailed description of her diminutive personalities. He listened comfortably, for her voice was soothing to him. Her whole personality was grateful to him. When it came time for her to go he seemed desirous of keeping her.

" Going, Jennie ? "

" I can stay just as well as not, Lester," she volunteered. " I'll take a room. I can send a note out to Mrs. Swenson. It will be all right."

" You needn't do that," he said, but she could see that he wanted her, that he did not want to be alone.

From that time on until the hour of his death she was not out of the hotel.

## CHAPTER LXII

THE end came after four days during which Jennie was by his bedside almost constantly. The nurse in charge welcomed her at first as a relief and company, but the physician was inclined to object. Lester, however, was stubborn. "This is my death," he said, with a touch of grim humour. "If I'm dying I ought to be allowed to die in my own way."

Watson smiled at the man's unfaltering courage. He had never seen anything like it before.

There were cards of sympathy, calls of inquiry, notices in the newspaper. Robert saw an item in the *Inquirer*, and decided to go to Chicago. Imogene called with her husband and they were admitted to Lester's room for a few minutes after Jennie had gone to hers. Lester had little to say. The nurse cautioned them that he was not to be talked to much. When they were gone Lester said to Jennie, "Imogene has changed a good deal." He made no other comment.

Mrs. Kane was on the Atlantic three days out from New York the afternoon Lester died. He had been meditating whether anything more could be done for Jennie, but he could not make up his mind about it. Certainly it was useless to leave her more money. She did not want it. He had been wondering where Letty was and how near her actual arrival might be when he was seized with a tremendous paroxysm of pain. Before relief could be administered in the shape of an anæsthetic he was dead. It developed afterward that it was not the intestinal trouble which killed him, but a lesion of a major blood-vessel in the brain.

Jennie, who had been strongly wrought up by watching and worrying, was beside herself with grief. He had been a part of her thought and feeling so long that it seemed now as though a part of herself had died. She had loved him as she had fancied she could never love any one, and he had always shown that he cared for her—at least in some degree. She could not feel the emotion that expresses itself in tears—only a dull ache, a numbness which seemed to make her insensible

to pain.  He looked so strong—her Lester—lying there still
in death.  His expression was unchanged—defiant, determined,
albeit peaceful.  Word had come from Mrs. Kane that she
would arrive on the Wednesday following.  It was decided to
hold the body.  Jennie learned from Mr. Watson that it was
to be transferred to Cincinnati, where the Paces had a vault.
Because of the arrival of various members of the family, Jennie
withdrew to her own home ; she could do nothing more.

The final ceremonies presented a peculiar commentary on
the anomalies of existence.  It was arranged with Mrs. Kane
by wire that the body should be transferred to Imogene's
residence, and the funeral held from there.  Robert, who
arrived the night Lester died ; Berry Dodge, Imogene's husband;
Mr. Midgely, and three other citizens of prominence were
selected as pall-bearers.  Louise and her husband came from
Buffalo ; Amy and her husband from Cincinnati.  The house
was full to overflowing with citizens who either sincerely
wished or felt it expedient to call.  Because of the fact that
Lester and his family were tentatively Catholic, a Catholic
priest was called in and the ritual of that Church was carried
out.  It was curious to see him lying in the parlour of this alien
residence, candles at his head and feet, burning sepulchrally,
a silver cross upon his breast, caressed by his waxen fingers.
He would have smiled if he could have seen himself, but the Kane
family was too conventional, too set in its convictions, to find
anything strange in this.  The Church made no objection,
of course.  The family was distinguished.  What more could
be desired ?

On Wednesday Mrs. Kane arrived.  She was greatly distraught, for her love, like Jennie's, was sincere.  She left her
room that night when all was silent and leaned over the coffin,
studying by the light of the burning candles Lester's beloved
features.  Tears trickled down her cheeks, for she had been
happy with him.  She caressed his cold cheeks and hands.
" Poor, dear Lester ! " she whispered.  " Poor, brave soul ! "
No one told her that he had sent for Jennie.  The Kane family
did not know.

Meanwhile in the house on South Park Avenue sat a woman
who was enduring alone the pain, the anguish of an irreparable
loss.  Through all these years the subtle hope had persisted,
in spite of every circumstance, that somehow life might bring

him back to her. He had come, it is true—he really had in death—but he had gone again. Where? Whither her mother, whither Gerhardt, whither Vesta had gone? She could not hope to see him again, for the papers had informed her of his removal to Mrs. Midgely's residence, and of the fact that he was to be taken from Chicago to Cincinnati for burial. The last ceremonies in Chicago were to be held in one of the wealthy Roman Catholic churches of the South Side, St. Michael's, of which the Midgely's were members.

Jennie felt deeply about this. She would have liked so much to have had him buried in Chicago, where she could go to the grave occasionally, but this was not to be. She was never a master of her fate. Others invariable controlled. She thought of him as being taken from her finally by the removal of the body to Cincinnati, as though distance made any difference. She decided at last to veil herself heavily and attend the funeral at the church. The paper had explained that the services would be at two in the afternoon. Then at four the body would be taken to the depôt, and transferred to the train; the members of the family would accompany it to Cincinnati. She thought of this as another opportunity. She might go to the depôt.

A little before the time for the funeral cortège to arrive at the church there appeared at one of its subsidiary entrances a woman in black, heavily veiled, who took a seat in an inconspicuous corner. She was a little nervous at first, for, seeing that the church was dark and empty, she feared lest she had mistaken the time and place; but after ten minutes of painful suspense a bell in the church tower began to toll solemnly. Shortly thereafter an acolyte in black gown and white surplice appeared and lighted groups of candles on either side of the altar. A hushed stirring of feet in the choir-loft indicated that the service was to be accompanied by music. Some loiterers, attracted by the bell, some idle strangers, a few acquaintances and citizens not directly invited appeared and took seats.

Jennie watched all this with wondering eyes. Never in her life had she been inside a Catholic church. The gloom, the beauty of the windows, the whiteness of the altar, the golden flames of the candles impressed her. She was suffused with a sense of sorrow, loss, beauty, and mystery. Life in all its vagueness and uncertainty seemed typified by this scene.

As the bell tolled there came from the sacristy a procession of altar-boys. The smallest, an angelic youth of eleven, came first, bearing aloft a magnificent silver cross. In the hands of each subsequent pair of servitors was held a tall, lighted candle. The priest, in black cloth and lace, attended by an acolyte on either hand, followed. The procession passed out the entrance into the vestibule of the church, and was not seen again until the choir began a mournful, responsive chant, the Latin supplication for mercy and peace.

Then, at this sound the solemn procession made its re-appearance. There came the silver cross, the candles, the dark-faced priest, reading dramatically to himself as he walked, and the body of Lester in a great black coffin, with silver handles, carried by the pall-bearers, who kept an even pace. Jennie stiffened perceptibly, her nerves responding as though to a shock from an electric current. She did not know any of these men. She did not know Robert. She had never seen Mr. Midgely. Of the long company of notables who followed two by two she recognised only three, whom Lester had pointed out to her in times past. Mrs. Kane she saw, of course, for she was directly behind the coffin, leaning on the arm of a stranger; behind her walked Mr. Watson, solemn, gracious. He gave a quick glance to either side, evidently expecting to see her somewhere; but not finding her, he turned his eyes gravely forward and walked on. Jennie looked with all her eyes, her heart gripped by pain. She seemed so much a part of this solemn ritual, and yet infinitely removed from it all.

The procession reached the altar rail, and the coffin was put down. A white shroud bearing the insignia of suffering, a black cross, was put over it, and the great candles were set beside it. There were the chanted invocations and responses, the sprinkling of the coffin with holy water, the lighting and swinging of the censer and then the mumbled responses of the auditors to the Lord's Prayer and to its Catholic addition, the invocation to the Blessed Virgin. Jennie was overawed and amazed, but no show of form colourful, impression imperial, could take away the sting of death, the sense of infinite loss. To Jennie the candles, the incense, the holy song were beautiful. They touched the deep chord of melancholy in her, and made it vibrate through the depths of her being.  She was as a house filled with mournful melody and the presence of death.  She cried and cried.  She could see, curiously, that Mrs. Kane was sobbing convulsively also.

When it was all over the carriages were entered and the body was borne to the station.  All the guests and strangers departed, and finally, when all was silent, she arose.  Now she would go to the depôt also, for she was hopeful of seeing his body put on the train.  They would have to bring it out on the platform, just as they did in Vesta's case.  She took a car, and a little later she entered the waiting-room of the depôt.  She lingered about, first in the concourse, where the great iron fence separated the passengers from the tracks, and then in the waiting-room, hoping to discover the order of proceedings.  She finally observed the group of immediate relatives waiting—Mrs. Kane, Robert, Mrs. Midgely, Louise, Amy, Imogene, and the others.  She actually succeeded in identifying most of them, though it was not knowledge in this case, but pure instinct and intuition.

No one had noticed it in the stress of excitement, but it was Thanksgiving Eve.  Throughout the great railroad station there was a hum of anticipation, that curious ebullition of fancy which springs from the thought of pleasures to come.  People were going away for the holiday.  Carriages were at the station entries.  Announcers were calling in stentorian voices the destination of each new train as the time of its departure drew near.  Jennie heard with a desperate ache the description of a route which she and Lester had taken more than once, slowly and melodiously emphasised.  " Detroit, Toledo, Cleveland, Buffalo, and New York." There were cries of trains for " Fort Wayne, Columbus, Pittsburg, Philadelphia, and points East," and then finally for " Indianapolis, Louisville, Columbus, Cincinnati, and points South."  The hour had struck.

Several times Jennie had gone to the concourse between the waiting-room and the tracks to see if through the iron grating which separated her from her beloved she could get one last look at the coffin, or the great wooden box which held it, before it was put on the train.  Now she saw it coming.  There was a baggage porter pushing a truck into position near the place where the baggage car would stop.  On it was Lester, that last shadow of his substance, incased in the honours of wood, and cloth, and silver. There was no thought on the part of the porter of the agony of loss which was represented here. He could not see how wealth and position in this hour were typified to her mind as a great fence, a wall, which divided her eternally from her beloved. Had it not always been so ? Was not her life a patchwork of conditions made and affected by these things which she saw—wealth and force—which had found her unfit ? She had evidently been born to yield, not seek.. This panoply of power had been paraded before her since childhood. What could she do now but stare vaguely after it as it marched triumphantly by ? Lester had been of it. Him it respected. Of her it knew nothing. She looked through the grating, and once more there came the cry of " Indianapolis, Louisville, Columbus, Cincinnati, and points South." A long red train, brilliantly lighted, composed of baggage cars, day coaches, a dining-car, set with white linen and silver, and a half dozen comfortable Pullmans, rolled in and stopped. A great black engine, puffing and glowing, had it all safely in tow.

As the baggage car drew near the waiting truck a train-hand in blue, looking out of the car, called to some one within.

" Hey, Jack ! Give us a hand here. There's a stiff outside ! "

Jennie could not hear.

All she could see was the great box that was so soon to disappear. All she could feel was that this train would start presently, and then it would all be over. The gates opened, the passengers poured out. There were Robert, and Amy, and Louise, and Midgely—all making for the Pullman cars in the rear. They had said their farewells to their friends. No need to repeat them. A trio of assistants " gave a hand " at getting the great wooden case into the car. Jennie saw it disappear with an acute physical wrench at her heart.

There were many trunks to be put aboard, and then the door of the baggage car half closed, but not before the warning bell of the engine sounded. There was the insistent calling of " all aboard " from this quarter and that ; then slowly the great locomotive began to move. Its bell was ringing, its steam hissing, its smoke-stack throwing aloft a great black plume of smoke that fell back over the cars like a pall. The fireman, conscious of the heavy load behind, flung open a flaming furnace door to throw in coal. Its light glowed like a golden eye.

Jennie stood rigid, staring into the wonder of this picture, her face white, her eyes wide, her hands unconsciously clasped, but one thought in her mind—they were taking his body away. A leaden November sky was ahead, almost dark. She looked, and looked until the last glimmer of the red lamp on the receding sleeper disappeared in the maze of smoke and haze overhanging the tracks of the far-stretching yard.

" Yes," said the voice of a passing stranger, gay with the anticipation of coming pleasures. "We're going to have a great time down there. Remember Annie? Uncle Jim is coming and Aunt Ella."

Jennie did not hear that or anything else of the chatter and bustle around her. Before her was stretching a vista of lonely years down which she was steadily gazing. Now what? She was not so old yet. There were those two orphan children to raise. They would marry and leave after a while, and then what? Days and days in endless reiteration, and then—— ?